Lean-Driven Innovation illustrates that the application of lean principles and practices entails more than simple cut-and-paste implementation of factory-floor practices to the complex knowledge work of engineering and innovation. Lean thinking applied to product and process development shares the basic principles of lean operations but goes about actualizing them in very different ways. In sharing the compelling story of applying lean principles to R&D processes in the large, global, complex enterprise that is Goodyear, Norbert Majerus offers a path for improving innovation processes that readers will find practical and applicable regardless of their business type or company size.

—John Shook, Chairman and CEO,
Lean Enterprise Institute

Lean-Driven Innovation provides a set of guiding principles for how to build an innovative organization that are based on science and hard-won experience. The principles are brought to life by great examples from Goodyear's impressive lean transformation in R&D. This is a must-read for innovation leaders. Although based on a transformation in R&D, the thinking applies equally well to software development and other project-based knowledge work.

—Peter T. Ward, Director, Center for Operational Excellence,
The Ohio State University

A candid and well-told story of the process by which a strong and innovative engineering culture incorporated the powerful principles of lean product development.

—Don Reinertsen, Author, *The Principles of Product Development Flow*

Norbert's work is a particularly impactful effort as it is not purely academic or theoretical, but rather based and vetted upon the years of hard-fought experiences and knowledge gained at Goodyear throughout its lean product development journey. Readers will undoubtedly gain insights into a number of promising continual improvement processes that may be applied at their companies for immediate and positive impact.

—Rich Gildersleeve, Chief Technology Officer, DJO LLC

In *Lean-Driven Innovation*, Norbert Majerus brings insight and understanding to how Goodyear successfully applied lean principles to its R&D processes, and he offers readers the know-how and encouragement to do the same. The book is especially effective at showing how Goodyear has been able to make its R&D capacity visible and manageable, repetitively surfacing and resolving constraint issues and regularly improving the innovation process. These principles will help nonmanufacturing processes far beyond R&D as well, such as administration, services, and healthcare.

—Peg Pennington, Executive Director, Center for Operational
Excellence, The Ohio State University

Norbert Majerus is a remarkable engineer and an extraordinary storyteller. This book tells the story of how he and his colleagues have taken their understanding of the basics of lean and applied it to the difficult task of product development. He is one of the few people I know who has so completely absorbed the concepts of the book, *Factory Physics*, that he has been able to apply them in a completely new environment—product innovation.

—Mark L. Spearman, Coauthor, *Factory Physics*,
and Former Department Head, Industrial and
Systems Engineering, Texas A&M University

When I first got to know Norbert Majerus at an LPPDE conference some years ago, I felt he was a remarkable man. He was sure of his deep knowledge, but he also was very interested in learning more, a lot more. This is a sign of a true lean practitioner. In *Lean-Driven Innovation*, Norbert shares some of his deep knowledge with us, and puts it in place with clear principles and real examples. He shows that focusing on true customer value—instead of the traditional focus on R&D cost—really pays off, and that building new value streams is the true objective for a product development organization. I love the last chapter "Lean Never Ends," showing that the journey has just begun!

—Peter Palmer, Senior Manager Process Support, Scania,
and Board Member of LPPDE

LEAN - DRIVEN INNOVATION

POWERING PRODUCT DEVELOPMENT AT THE GOODYEAR TIRE & RUBBER COMPANY

LEAN-DRIVEN INNOVATION

POWERING PRODUCT DEVELOPMENT AT THE GOODYEAR TIRE & RUBBER COMPANY

NORBERT MAJERUS

Foreword by James Morgan and Durward Sobek

CRC Press
Taylor & Francis Group
Boca Raton London New York

CRC Press is an imprint of the
Taylor & Francis Group, an **informa** business

A PRODUCTIVITY PRESS BOOK

CRC Press
Taylor & Francis Group
6000 Broken Sound Parkway NW, Suite 300
Boca Raton, FL 33487-2742

© 2016 by Taylor & Francis Group, LLC
CRC Press is an imprint of Taylor & Francis Group, an Informa business

No claim to original U.S. Government works

Printed on acid-free paper
Version Date: 20150616

International Standard Book Number-13: 978-1-4822-5968-1 (Paperback)

Visit the Taylor & Francis Web site at
http://www.taylorandfrancis.com

and the CRC Press Web site at
http://www.crcpress.com

Contents

Foreword

When we first began our research into product development more than two decades ago, we did not call it "lean." We were investigating what appeared to be a unique and transformative set of ideas and practices within the Japanese automotive industry. We recognized that while our observations were in a specific context—one industry (it happens to be a big one)—we felt that the fundamental challenges of design and development were the same regardless of where it happens. And we approached our work with the idea that while specific practices may be uniquely tuned to the context of a particular company or country, the underlying fundamentals should transcend industries and cultures because the act of creating something new, of generating new solutions to an identified problem or need, is fundamentally human. Consequently, we worked to extract the principles at work with the thought that, by understanding principles, we could apply those principles in myriad forms to suit the unique realities of any specific context. Over time, these principles have continued to evolve and coalesce, producing an emerging paradigm: lean product and process development.

We know the ideas are powerful. Compelling stories of successful product development system transformation have been filtering in from many industry sectors. Research in the United States and in Europe has further confirmed the efficacy of these ideas across dozens, if not hundreds, of companies. But just what does one of these transformations look like? Norbert Majerus tells us through the pages of the book you are about to read. In these pages, you will read about how the Goodyear team:

- Slashed tire development lead-time by more than 70%
- Increased on-time delivery from 30% to 98%
- Dramatically cut warranty costs
- Tripled the number of learning cycles or project iterations per year

All with no increase in budget. Now that is a compelling transformation!

By sharing in depth how Goodyear transformed the business of developing new tires, Norbert makes an important contribution to our understanding of how to go about a successful transformation. Success appears to hinge on at least a couple of key ideas. The first is taking the principles and applying them to a specific context, in this case, tire development. The second is deploying effective change management strategies along with a good dose of persistence. The third is enabling people to make change on their own through systematic training and followup coaching. Norbert shares how the team at Goodyear dovetailed these together to produce remarkable results. He also shares the many barriers and difficulties faced along the way. They had to deal with all the common barriers faced by companies trying to incorporate lean thinking and practice into their development organization (and perhaps a few unique to Goodyear).

Fortunately for us, with much persistence Goodyear was able to overcome those barriers and is willing to share them with us so that we all can learn and improve. We both walked the gemba at Goodyear Innovation Centers in Akron, Ohio, and Colmar-Berg, Luxembourg, and saw their challenges and successes firsthand. The story of the transformation of Goodyear's product development system should inspire product development teams in any industry that they can do it, too!

The Goodyear story is unique in another respect. Most of the transformation stories we hear about are from original equipment manufacturers, the companies that do the final production and assembly before delivering a product to the marketplace. But Goodyear is also a supplier. As a supplier, they must comply with performance, cost, safety, and delivery timing requirements from numerous customers in multiple industries (automotive, aerospace, heavy equipment) who all operate differently, in addition to the whims and demands of the aftermarket. This requires an extra level of capability not seen in other industries, making the transformation story doubly compelling.

But this book is more than a story. Part narrative, part textbook, part instruction manual, Norbert seamlessly integrates his experience with his own self-study of relevant literature to give us the theoretical underpinnings of the work he and the Goodyear team managed to accomplish. For example, he explains how WIP management and Little's Law manifest within product development, and how those insights led to training exercises, educational materials, specific countermeasures in practice, and ultimately a new way of working that far surpassed the conventional approach.

And he contributes a number of new concepts and insights, expanding our understanding of lean product development. Thus, he shares not only the "what" of the Goodyear story, but just as importantly he exposes many of the "whys," which are the critical insights needed if practitioners are to adapt the ideas to their own contexts.

The final result is a complete package! We get lean development principles combined with change management and people engagement and development. We get practice integrated with and supported by theory. We get comprehensive coverage of all aspects of a product development enterprise, from organizational structure to knowledge management, from the use of cutting-edge computing tools to simple, old-fashioned pencil-and-paper techniques, from stage-gate and conventional project management to investing in people. So get the highlighter out, and start your read. There is plenty to glean and learn from the experience and wisdom found in this volume.

Thank you, Norbert, for this wonderful contribution!

James Morgan
Traverse City, Michigan

Durward K. Sobek II
Bozeman, Montana

Acknowledgments

Writing and publishing a book is an innovation in its own right. Like developing a new product, it creates and reflects a value stream of activities and roles. Lean-driven innovation would not have been possible without the support and contributions of the many individuals in those roles.

I probably challenged Goodyear's leadership with the idea of publishing our lean product development story. I believed this transfer of knowledge was an important part of our lean evolution: sharing what we learned has become part of our new culture at Goodyear. The change described in this book is only a small part of the transformation that Chairman, CEO, and President Rich Kramer and his leadership team led the company through in the last 10 years. Goodyear is a better company and a better place to work today, as you may see when you read this book. I am especially grateful to Chairman Kramer for sharing his insights in *Chapter 7*.

Jean-Claude Kihn and later Joe Zekoski, our former and current chief technical officers (CTOs), respectively, are key players in this book, since they led the transformation to lean/operational excellence in Goodyear research and development. I am especially grateful to Jean-Claude Kihn for asking me to lead this important undertaking in the product development organization. Jean-Claude had the lean vision when few others would have believed in it and held to it through many challenges and setbacks. After Jean-Claude moved on to another challenge within the company, Joe took over without missing a beat. Jean-Claude and Joe also defined lean leadership and how to sponsor a lean initiative. I also want to thank Andy Weimer, my director during the writing of this book, for his leadership and for giving me all the support and the time needed to accomplish this big and unusual task.

In this book, I quote many Goodyear colleagues, leaders, coworkers, and friends. Our lean transformation would not have been possible without their contribution and support (Billy Taylor, Brad Heim, Brandy Moorhead, Chris Banweg, Chris Helsel, Dale Wells, Dave Hrusovsky, Dean Testa, Emmanuel Robinet, Guenter Wartusch, Jean Pierre Jeusette, Jeff McElfresh, Jeff Plauny, Jim Euchner, John Kullman, John Roman, Jon Bellissimo, Kelly King, Laurent Colantonio, Leyla Renner, Marc Nowacki, Matt List, Michael Rachita, Mike Wilps, Norm Anderson, Oliver Kim, Paul Dicello, Pawan Handa, Pete Yap, Phil Dunker, Rachel Graves, Ralf Mruk, Ralph Okonieski, Ricardo Gloria Olivera, Rick Laske, Rick Scavuzzo, Rob DeAnna, Romain Hansen, Stephanie Brown, Steve Rohweder, Surendra Chawla, Tim Lovell, Tom Laurich, and Tom Segatta). Some Goodyear associates helped me start the lean journey, and I am grateful for their coaching (Gene Miller, Karen Burke, Mark Whitmore, and Rick Laubacher).

Special thanks to Joe Zekoski, Dane Taylor, Bruce Hendricks, and Rob Whitehouse for "reading, correcting, and approving" the book content as it was developed.

Some former work colleagues deserve special mention: I worked with Sam Landers, a true "serial innovator," for many years in the trenches, inventing and commercializing innovative products. Since my expertise in innovation cannot measure up to that of Sam's, I asked him to challenge me in the chapter on innovation. Sam is the best in the field of innovation—and we had a great time debating how to make lean and innovation coexist. Cigdem Gurer, now CTO at Cyient-Insights, helped me to get started with lean product development. It was Cigdem who encouraged me to first learn lean principles, and then she helped me figure out how to correctly apply them.

I also have many friends outside Goodyear who are experts on lean product development and who taught me much over the years; they directly or indirectly contributed to this book. I start my sensei list with Jim Morgan. Jim learned lean product development at Toyota and Mazda and got a chance to apply the principles at Ford as director, Global Body Exterior, Safety and SBU Engineering. I also want to thank Durward Sobek, author of *Lean Product and Process Development, Second Edition*,[1] for the insights he has shared with me over several years now.

I want to thank the folks at the Lean Enterprise Institute, especially Jim Womack and John Shook, for teaching, coaching, and sharing valuable insights—Jim and John had lean innovation right many years ago although they never worked in product development. The advancement of lean, in general, and lean product development would not be where they are today without them! I worked for many years with Don Reinertsen, author of *The Principles of Product Development Flow*[2] and *Managing the Design Factory;*[3] Mark Spearman, author of *Factory Physics;*[4] Ed Pound, author of *Factory Physics for Managers;*[5] and many other experts and authors who have inspired and taught me.

There is a much longer list of friends and colleagues from other companies whom I have been fortunate to meet and from whom I learned a lot. I believe, though, that only a small portion of lean product development knowledge has been published—a lot of it is still in the heads of people like them: Josh Keriewski (Industrial Logic), Rich Gildersleeve (DJO Global), Joe Patula (FPC Food Plastics Pty. Ltd), Peter Palmer (Scania Group), Ovidiu Contras (Bombardier), Ken Bonenberger (PM Solutions), Will Lichtig (The Boldt Co.), Ron Marsiglio (Knowledge/PD), Peter Fritz (3M), Paul Zaffiro (P&G), and many others.

If you want to improve your operation, it is important to know what good looks like. I learned this by doing gemba walks and benchmarking the best companies that I could find locally or globally. This list includes Akron Children's Hospital, Autoliv, Delphi, Rockwell Automation, Cardinal Health, Nationwide, Menlo Innovations, Gojo Industries, CNH Industrial, and many others on the leading edge of the lean product development movement.

I also learned a lot about lean at universities and in consortia: The Ohio State University and its Center for Operational Excellence (Peter Ward and John Dix, codirectors, and Peg Pennington, executive director); the Savvy Consortium (Jim Jacobs, founder); the Society of Concurrent Product Development (Frank Hull, Peter Fritz, and Sarah Darmody); the AME Cleveland Lean Consortia (Richard Wiltse, chairman); the Northeast Ohio Lean Sigma Forum; and all the folks at the Association for Manufacturing Excellence (AME) and Lean Product and Process Development Exchange.

I also want to acknowledge the hundreds of individuals at Goodyear and other companies whom I had the privilege to teach, coach, and mentor. My students and mentees regularly provided great inspiration and feedback.

I am grateful to my publisher, Taylor & Francis, for giving me the confidence to write my first book. I thank Michael Sinocchi, executive editor at Productivity Press, for offering me this opportunity, and his colleagues Jessica Vakili, Tara Nieuwesteeg, and Mohamed Hameed.

An engineer-turned-writer needs help in pulling together a manuscript, especially if the engineer consistently received low grades for communications in annual performance assessments and wrote the worst essays in high school. It also did not help that I wrote this book in my fourth language: I grew up speaking Luxembourgish, learned German and French while in school, and eventually grasped English as my first "foreign" language. I was lucky that Goodyear's communications manager referred me to George Taninecz, who did a lot more than help me write a book; he became my coach and mentor. I did not supply "ready to edit" material to him, and I especially appreciate the patience he had in helping me turn my thoughts into a book. George also took my vision for graphics and made them a reality, working with the book's graphic designer Juan Quirarte. Goodyear design artist Jonathan Schondel provided book illustrations and proposals for the cover page. I am thankful for the work of Melissa Gould, who handled the tedious administrative chores necessary for publication.

I would also like to thank my family for putting up with those long hours of me traveling to learn all this stuff and for being holed away and writing.

Last but not least, I would never have started this book if I had not broken my leg in a severe skiing accident. I think the only reason I finished it was because I was not able to walk for eight months. Sometimes things happen for a reason.

Notes

1. Allen C. Ward and Durward K. Sobek, *Lean Product and Process Development, Second Edition*, Lean Enterprise Institute, Cambridge, MA, 2014.
2. Donald G. Reinertsen, *The Principles of Product Development Flow*, Celeritas Publishing, Redondo Beach, CA, 2012.
3. Donald G. Reinertsen, *Managing the Design Factory*, Free Press, New York, 1997.
4. Wallace J. Hopp and Mark L. Spearman, *Factory Physics*, Waveland Press, Long Grove, IL, 1996.
5. Ed Pound, *Factory Physics for Managers*, McGraw-Hill Education, New York, 2014.

Author

Beginning in 2005, Norbert Majerus has implemented a principles-based lean product development process at the three global innovation centers of The Goodyear Tire & Rubber Company, first in Akron, Ohio, and then in Colmar-Berg, Luxembourg, and Hanau, Germany. For nearly a decade, he has been Goodyear's lean champion in research and development.

Majerus, born and raised in Luxembourg, began his career there at Goodyear in 1979 with responsibility for materials development, aircraft tires, and competitor benchmarking. In 1983, he moved to Akron to start a "short assignment" in innovative products, which continues to this day. During that time, he was a recipient of discretionary funding for a revolutionary new product and manufacturing process, and he earned more than 60 patents and trade secrets (patentable ideas that the company chose not to patent).

Further assignments in Akron have included innovative processes; new tire development and project manager for North American, Asian, and European OEM customers; corporate benchmarking; design and test standards; activity-based R&D accounting; ISO/QS certification; and more. Majerus acquired a six sigma master black belt in 2003 and a lean master black belt in 2005. He holds a master's degree in chemistry from the Universitaet des Saarlandes, Saarbruecken, Germany.

Majerus would appreciate comments and feedback. He can be found on LinkedIn or reached at norbert.majerus@gmail.com or norbert.majerus@goodyear.com.

Introduction

Back in 2005, I would lay awake at night and review the day's events in my mind, mentally applying six sigma tools to address an issue or search for a breakthrough in our product-development processes at The Goodyear Tire & Rubber Company. Sometimes my sleepless nights yielded results, but just as often they did not.

Up to that point in my career, I had been asked to learn and deploy various improvement approaches, including six sigma. As an engineer by education (master's degree in chemistry), I appreciated the logic of the six sigma tools. I had heard of lean and read about its application in manufacturing, but had not grasped that it could have a place in research and development (R&D) or in my life at Goodyear. Even after reading many books on lean product development, I felt something was missing. The engineer in me wanted to know more. Why did companies adopt it? Why did or could it work? One day a colleague handed me a copy of *Factory Physics*.[1] I won't claim that I understood everything in the tome by Wallace Hopp and Mark Spearman—nor do I today—but it opened my eyes to the science of why lean could and does work in product development. I had just discovered the power of understanding the lean principles. And eventually lean worked at Goodyear in product development.

I was drawn into Goodyear's first lean product development initiative in 2005. Goodyear had just won its first JD Power award, to the surprise of everyone in the company, including the chairman, as a result of my first six sigma project. I was excited about applying the same six sigma approach to other projects and was about to do so when Jean-Claude Kihn, general director of Goodyear Innovation Center Akron (GIC*A), suggested that I experiment with some lean concepts. He had encountered lean while on assignment in Latin America, and immediately understood its potential for product development. I told Jean-Claude that I was not about to give up the fun I was having with six sigma, but he persisted. He suggested I try lean "on the side." I was never appointed to any position to implement lean, but my "side" work eventually overtook all other work for me at Goodyear, including six sigma projects. (Had we known about the A3 process at that time, I am sure Jean-Claude would have asked me to develop an A3 for starting lean in Goodyear product development.)

The years it took my colleagues and me at Goodyear to go from lean awareness to lean results were filled with fun, hard work, learning, and plenty of frustration. Much of what I had read was clearly never actually tried in an R&D setting. Other concepts were skewed to one type of organization or another or were purely theoretical. With *Lean-Driven Innovation: Powering Product Development at The Goodyear Tire & Rubber Company*, I hope to accelerate your fun and learning and minimize your frustration as you apply lean to the innovation processes of your company. I am confident that what worked within Goodyear can work anywhere, provided a few fundamental principles are understood and accepted.

Today, many types of organizations—manufacturing, finance, healthcare, construction, and so on—are adopting or considering lean thinking, and if you're reading this book, your organization is probably one of them. Ever since Jim Womack and John Krafcik coined the term "lean" in 1987 to describe the highly efficient processes of the Japanese auto industry, particularly those within Toyota,[2] "lean" has become a staple of the business lexicon.

A lot of what we understand today as lean came out of Toyota. Legendary Toyota executive Taiichi Ohno described his company's lean efforts as trying to minimize the time—from receipt of a customer order to when Toyota collects payment—by reducing all the waste in the process.[3] Lean thinking also has major contributions from Henry Ford (flow production), Alfred Sloan (mass customization), W. Edwards Deming (PDCA cycle), and countless others, including the U.S. military (Training Within Industry training and consulting concepts). All influenced how Toyota went about its business.

In describing what Toyota did and what lean is, Womack and colleague Daniel Jones clarified five principles of lean in their book *Lean Thinking*: identify value, identify the value stream, make it flow, as pulled by the customer, in pursuit of perfection. This description is as meaningful today as it was when first published more than 20 years ago,[4] and it is especially relevant to new product development.

In the decades since Womack and company shook up the business world, the term "lean" has spread in many ways. It has been grouped with six sigma principles to establish practices by which both methodologies coexist and from which a lot of current product development ideas are found (e.g., by Michael George).[5] Other significant lean-thinking contributions have come on the topics of knowledge management (e.g., by Michael Kennedy),[6] problem-solving and management culture (e.g., by John Shook),[7] and product development (e.g., by Jim Morgan and Jeff Liker,[8] and by Allen Ward and Durward Sobek[9]). Lean is currently in vogue as a way to create and nurture an entrepreneurial organization through experimentation and fast learning (e.g., by Eric Ries).[10] For some companies, though, it remains merely a corporate statement to convince stakeholders that improvements might be underway (e.g., you know who you are).

I initially thought that the term "lean" was nondescriptive, but over time I became convinced that it is capable of accommodating almost every type of process improvement imaginable, including those in product development. Evan Duncan and Ron Ritter described the collective ability of lean thinking as "... putting customers first by truly understanding what they need and then delivering it efficiently; enabling workers to contribute to their fullest potential; constantly searching for better ways of working; and giving meaning to work by connecting a company's strategy and goals in a clear, coherent way across the organization."[11]

Most companies begin their application of lean in manufacturing areas and use their successes there to enlist other functions. This makes sense because there is ample lean manufacturing knowledge and proof of concept; the Toyota Production System (TPS) is well established in industry and many adaptations and further developments have been validated. This also is a good starting point because lean in production involves work that is generally visible, allowing any return on lean initiatives to be seen relatively quickly.

But lean in product development is a different story:

■ Work is not visible, and processes are complicated and often fuzzy, locked in the minds of experts.
■ Engineers and designers can be challenging to train and prone to resist lean as a "creativity killer" and not applicable to a less repetitive work environment.
■ Quick-win opportunities in product development are not as obvious as in manufacturing (e.g., use of 5S, quick changeovers, inventory reductions), and so there is a misperception that it is not working.

■ Product development has some *good waste* in its value streams, related to exploring an innovation idea that does not initially bear fruit, which can still be a good use of time.

One enormous difference of lean in product development is that sufficient returns on lean initiatives may be apparent only after the development of a complete lean product development value stream—many will give up long before this moment is reached. Even short-term benefits of lean as seen in manufacturing do not necessarily appear in R&D: initial waste reduction in R&D may save a little money, but it is often not enough for businesses to notice, and it is difficult to track the savings to the bottom line, especially since a high percentage of R&D resources are distributed. What is more, R&D charges to the business are often small to begin with, but their indirect contributions can be an order of magnitude larger.

So, if you are looking for reasons *not to try* lean in product development, there are many. But there are far more reasons why you should do it. At Goodyear, we started lean in product development before applying it in manufacturing, and I think this helped. We learned to apply it to *our R&D processes*, rather than try to change our processes to look more like manufacturing. It was, nonetheless, not without many challenges, most of which were overcome. In *Chapter 1*, I share Goodyear's lean product development results: lean helped us dramatically improve revenue by having every new product available when the market needed it. It enabled us to take advantage of various cost-reduction opportunities in development processes. And the indirect contributions of lean R&D significantly improved our product development value streams, boosting Goodyear's bottom line.

When we started lean in product development, we noticed that we had a lot of good, foundational concepts already in place to support lean. We carefully left those in place, even though they were not exactly as the lean books at the time prescribed them. For example, we already had a solid knowledge base and great computer modeling tools. We also tried new lean things that had been validated and worked well in other companies, but we frequently did not find similar value from these efforts. I soon realized that just like the many products and manufacturing environments that exist, there are huge differences in R&D and product innovation among companies and across industries. Some industries focus on mature consumer products, where cost is a big deal. Others focus on high-tech commercial products where capability and service are important. Some rely on speed and efficiency. Others employ an army of creative PhDs, inventing and launching products over many years. Those lean concepts that help one industry may not be as beneficial to another industry and vice versa.

Even within Goodyear, there is R&D diversity. For example, we spend about 30% of our R&D resources researching new opportunities and 70% developing and releasing products. Lean applies quite differently to these two work streams.

What works for one company may not work for another, and what works in one work stream may need to be modified to fit another work stream in the same company. The application of lean will look different in each. For this reason and many others, there is a need to understand the *principles* behind lean product development, not just the tools, and how to apply them.

There are many good books on lean product development, many of which are mandatory reading for the lean training program for Goodyear's product development staff. These publications generally present six schools of product development, and they they comprise about 50% of the lean product development knowledge that is out there. I think many companies, like Goodyear, have developed knowledge far beyond what is published, but many of these companies have not shared their lean know-how.

- Knowledge-based approach
- Flow-based approach
- Concurrency approach
- Toyota school
- What works in manufacturing
- Lean/six sigma school
- Rebranding an old or failed method

I also have found that many published works present two fundamental methods of implementing lean product development: (1) plugging in the same lean system that works in manufacturing and (2) carbon-copying what worked in product development at another company (like at Toyota). As a lean prescription, neither of these works well.

When mimicking lean manufacturing, things like 5S and standardization only create resistance and angst. Don Reinertsen, author of *The Principles of Product Development Flow*,[12] tells the story of R&D standardization in which one engineer threatened to leave if he had to take a banana off his desk because it was not a standard work item. Hence, the standard was revised to allow an "active" banana to be on the desk of an engineer, with "active" being defined as "within a standard time of being consumed."

When copying another company's lean product development, the nature of a company's goals and objectives uniquely drive their approaches. For example, consumer product companies are trying to maintain mature product lines and they probably get the biggest benefits out of lean by looking at cost reduction, quick innovation, and fast consumer testing. A company that develops high-tech products for a small number of commercial customers or the government may get the biggest benefits out of a knowledge-management approach or a focus on problem solving. At Goodyear, we needed to cater to consumers *and* develop fundamental technology, and so a greater array of lean principles was applicable to our work.

Talking with R&D colleagues in my industry and others, I repeatedly hear that most learning that has taken place—books, conferences, training programs—leaves recipients short of what they need to actually *practice* lean in product development. I believe this contributes to why a lot of individuals and companies have difficulties with implementation and, if they do succeed initially, they have a hard time making the change sustainable. Roughly 10% of companies are venturing into a lean product innovation process.[13] Research in Sweden shows that of the companies that start a lean product development initiative, only 15% remain active 5 years after the initiative.[14] The two pieces of research combined indicate that just 1.5% of all companies have implemented and sustained a lean product development program (in reality, it is probably closer to 5%). Hence, there is a lot of lean knowledge yet to be developed, published, and leveraged.

Lean-Driven Innovation: Powering Product Development at The Goodyear Tire & Rubber Company validates some elements of the schools of lean product development, and it presents pieces of implementation methods that can and should be applied. It also describes new insights that we gained at Goodyear starting in 2005. I have come to understand what lean can accomplish—what will work and what will not work—and how to most effectively and efficiently apply lean to an organization's innovation processes. So, while there are libraries filled with books on lean and aisles of lean product development propositions, I felt that executives as well as engineers needed a book based on principles, grounded in reality, and proved over nearly a decade. From my learning and application of lean, I have distilled *ideas*, *practices*, *failures*, and *successes* into key principles for lean product development *practitioners*. (Lean R&D Principles appear throughout the book in shaded boxes; learning sidebars that drill down into a specific topic appear in bordered boxes.)

As of this writing, I have worked a total of 36 years within Goodyear, of which 10 have been directly involved in trying to develop, implement, and sustain lean in order to achieve the company's business objectives. I am not a consultant who applied lean to R&D, but an R&D engineer who pulled in lean. My experiences have convinced me that the best way to implement lean in product development—or any new process—is to learn the principles, teach the principles, and then let content experts and process experts figure out what change is needed and coach, mentor, and guide them through the improvement process.

At Goodyear, as we try to learn more about lean, we have had many "lean experts" come in. They have had a hard time selling their ideas. It is not that they did not know what they were talking about—most did—but that they had not actually done the work to which lean is being applied. Most of them never worked in product development. It took us a while to realize this, and we have since taken a path to teach lean to the engineers who work *in the process*, providing them training specific to what they need to know and when they need to know it (a four-phase training program that eventually results in a black belt–like designation). Most of our engineers have been very successful implementing their own ideas developed through this training.

I have met many successful lean R&D champions from many different companies. They have one thing in common—most are engineers who learned lean product development the same way we practice it at Goodyear: understand the principles, identify what is needed and where, and then do it.

Every day I learn something new about lean and our lean implementation, and there is so much more to learn. Nonetheless, I think that my experiences with lean, what Goodyear has accomplished, and the way in which we accomplished it is worth sharing. This book tells Goodyear's lean product development story, illustrates the application of lean principles and tools we used, and offers examples of what worked and why. This book is not based on observations of other companies, but what I did in my company for nearly a decade. This is an industrial novel, like those of Eli Goldratt[15] and Freddy and Michael Ballé,[16] but my story *is not fiction*. It is a true tale with real characters, one that should entertain, enlighten, and help the many companies I see struggling when applying lean in product development. (Many novels have a happy ending—my story of Goodyear does as well.)

My ultimate goal in writing *Lean-Driven Innovation: Powering Product Development at The Goodyear Tire & Rubber Company* is to provide a book that, when finished, you walk away with a good idea of how to start your own lean product development story, knowing where to begin and what to do, regardless of the industry or the process. And, most important, how to succeed.

Notes

1. Wallace J. Hopp and Mark L. Spearman, *Factory Physics*, Waveland Press, Long Grove, IL, 1996.
2. James P. Womack, Daniel T. Jones, and Daniel Roos, *The Machine that Changed the World*, Harper Perennial, New York, 1991.
3. Taiichi Ohno, *Toyota Production System: Beyond Large-Scale Production*, Productivity Press, Cambridge, MA, 1988.
4. James P. Womack and Daniel T. Jones, *Lean Thinking*, Free Press, New York, 1996.
5. Michael L. George, *Lean Six Sigma*, McGraw-Hill, New York, 2002.
6. Michael Kennedy and Kent Harmon, *Ready, Set, Dominate*, Oklea Press, Richmond, VA, 2008.
7. John Shook, *Managing to Learn*, Lean Enterprise Institute, Cambridge, MA, 2008.
8. James M. Morgan and Jeffrey K. Liker, *The Toyota Product Development System*, Productivity Press, New York, 2006.
9. Allen C. Ward and Durward Sobek, *Lean Product and Process Development, Second Edition*, Lean Enterprise Institute, Cambridge, MA, 2014.
10. Eric Ries, *The Lean Startup*, Crown Business, New York, 2011.
11. Edward Duncan and Ron Ritter, "Next Frontiers for Lean," *McKinsey Quarterly*, February 2014.
12. Donald G. Reinertsen, training class at Goodyear in Akron, OH, January 2013.
13. Dave Logozzo, Lean Enterprise Institute, presentation to Goodyear in Akron, OH, February 2012.
14. Håkan Ivarsson, *50 Nyanser av Lean*, Leadership Design Group Sweden AB, 2013.
15. Eliyahu Goldratt, *The Goal*, North River Press, Great Barrington, MA, 1984.
16. Freddy Ballé and Michael Ballé, *The Gold Mine*, Lean Enterprise Institute, Brookline, MA, 2005.

Chapter 1

Goodyear Today: Lean Product Development

In this chapter, I reveal the excellent business results that The Goodyear Tire & Rubber Company has achieved with lean product development through mid-2015 and touch the basics of how and why we got such results. What we have been able to accomplish at Goodyear should give you encouragement to begin, modify, or stay the course with your own lean product development work, regardless of the challenges.

Goodyear Results from Lean Product Development

Goodyear had pockets of lean activities in many of its functions, including a few initiatives in manufacturing, dating back to 2003. Some functions, such as manufacturing and supply chain, had pursued a lean project or two earlier. But Goodyear's first sustained, large-scale lean initiative started in product development in 2005. Several leading experts on lean, including Jim Womack, have since told us that they thought it was unusual to see a company start with lean in product development—but they all agreed that there really is no prescribed starting place in an organization.

One of the primary reasons that we could begin lean in product development was that we had begun to define and understand our value stream for the organization (even before actually mapping the stream as most lean consultants would advise us to do). Despite the hidden processes that existed in many R&D functions, I believe we had a better handle than most on what steps took us from idea to product (see *Goodyear Tire Development Value Stream*).

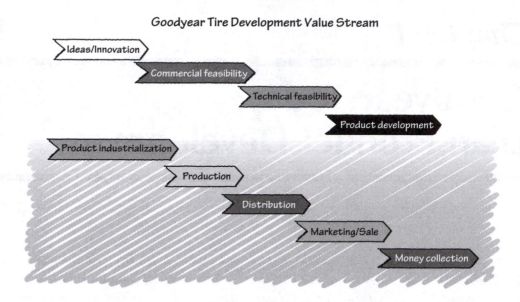

Goodyear Tire Development Value Stream

Ideas/Innovation

Commercial feasibility

Technical feasibility

Product development

Product industrialization

Production

Distribution

Marketing/Sale

Money collection

Within Goodyear, product ideas originate from many sources. The ideas are evaluated for commercial and technical feasibility, and a decision is then made to develop them into a commercial product. Product development—in collaboration with the customer, marketing, sales, manufacturing, and supply-chain functions—establishes targets for the product (e.g., performance, appearance, cost) and begins the task of creating the product.

There can be many disciplines involved in the tire-development effort, such as product design, materials development, and mold manufacturing. Drawings are generated and prototypes are built and tested. Eventually the product is released for production, manufactured, and distributed through the supply chain as original equipment for new cars or for aftermarket sales through the sales network.

During the development phase, many critical decisions are made to meet the targets that have been established by R&D—choice of materials, designs, features, complexity, manufacturability, and so on—and these decisions can have a profound effect on the product's profit equation: *profit = volume × (price − cost)*. For example, material choices affect the base cost of the product. Design and construction decisions affect the manufacturing process and the conversion cost. Performance and features affect the selling price of the product and the sales volumes.

One critical lean learning within Goodyear was to recognize that product development makes most of the choices regarding these critical decisions, and, therefore, has a huge influence on the profitability of the value streams for new products. What we do in product development reverberates throughout the organization long after our work is done. Ideally, all design decisions that affect the product's profitability are made in collaboration with business leaders and all other key functions and stakeholders (manufacturing, sales, supply chain, etc.).

It is now hard to imagine that once in Goodyear we used to think that R&D should design the best possible product and then "hand over" the product to manufacturing to develop the manufacturing process. Manufacturing eventually "handed" the product to sales and the supply chain to sell. And you know the rest of the story. Processes like this take forever because a downstream function sees a new challenge for the first time at the handoff. Many decisions that created these challenges were made upfront, long before a handoff by R&D, and they cannot be reversed—at least not at an affordable cost or in an acceptable time frame. Other decisions were changed downstream without involving those who made the initial decision, or the product came back to development for redesign long after the handoff. It is clear as to why this process used to exist within Goodyear and still exists in many companies today: R&D always looks good playing this game because the product, as designed and based on prototype tests, frequently worked quite well, and R&D did not feel responsible for downstream challenges and changes to the product.

Our approach to the product development value stream became more collaborative and concurrent when we implemented lean in R&D, but the fact remains that, even without lean, R&D still establishes the track for what happens downstream and is largely responsible for many decisions that determine product profitability. But rather than hand a product over, as we once did, R&D now stays involved, even with product launch and the advertising of the product through the first year of manufacturing.

One key principle that will come up repeatedly in this book is the need to "get the process right and the results will follow." This is true for all the processes in all the functions involved in a value stream. And, to be clear, the "results" are profits. You should be able to trace a profit back from every R&D project to the bottom line of the business or the company. Good R&D processes are not the only factors that drive profitability of a company, but they are also a major force.

In most North American manufacturing businesses, costs are driven by materials and manufacturing, with some costs contributed from carrying inventory, distribution of products, and sales and administration. R&D is typically a relatively small cost. At Goodyear it is about 2%, which is typical for manufacturing companies (see *Direct Cost to Business*). Applying lean thinking to manufacturing and supply-chain processes can have a quick impact on a company's bottom line, as wastes of time, rework, inventory, and so on are removed from these processes. For this reason, the pursuit of lean throughout industry has spread quickly through manufacturing and supply-chain functions. And as it spread, more knowledge (research, case studies, workbooks, guides) was made available to leaders, and, thus, more lean activities took place—a self-perpetuating improvement cycle of lean.

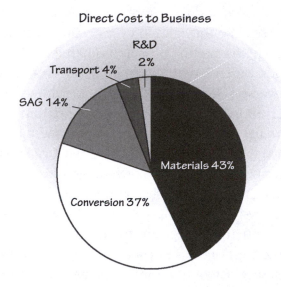

Seeing what occurs in manufacturing, many executives take the same tack in R&D. They look to remove wastes from the process, but they are trying to reduce the cost of their own function, not for improving the bottom line. This is an approach that rarely, if ever, makes anybody happy: 10% of 2% is not a big deal (<1%), and, what is more important, an unbridled focus on waste in R&D processes can negatively affect creativity and innovation. Can lean help to improve efficiencies and costs within R&D? Yes. Should that be the main objective of lean R&D? No.

This common cost-focused path with lean R&D at other companies has led to a history of challenging lean implementations. Few executives understand the potential they miss or see the negative effects on creativity and innovation (equating idea generation that does not produce a marketable idea as waste). What ultimately happens for many of these firms is that they find lean R&D hard to sustain because design staff feel suffocated and/or they do not see the impact to their bottom lines. Why continue?

So where did Goodyear—and where should you—focus your lean R&D efforts?

Remember that R&D has a huge influence on value streams and a big effect on profits (see *R&D Shadow*). Despite the relatively small cost base of R&D, it has an enormous influence on profits. Most understand what lean can do to reduce direct costs, such as in manufacturing, but few consider its application to influence profitability. This influence or shadow on profitability makes R&D an excellent target for investment and improvement. Lean can be used to leverage that shadow and lead to even greater profitability.

Like most, Goodyear focused lean on the R&D efficiency (direct cost), but we also recognized and improved its impact on the much more important R&D shadow. Rather than only impacting 2% of costs, we are impacting factors (performance gains, speed, agility) that influence a large part of our profitability. The application of lean principles to the product development process has had a multiplier effect on our shadows and we further improved our safety record and product quality.

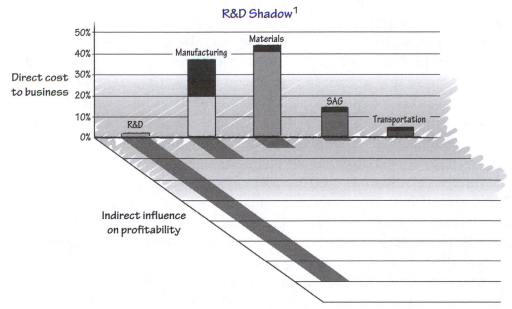

The dark area in the vertical bars is the direct effect that lean can have on the cost of those functions—it is barely visible for R&D.

R&D affects every part of the profit equation (*profit* = *volume* ×
(*price* − *cost*)). For example, R&D develops new materials that significantly
reduce the product cost. R&D improves product performance to a level superior to the competition, so a significant price increase can be achieved. R&D
can enhance development speed and agility, significantly affecting the availability and volume of new products. At many companies that have not had
success with lean R&D, these effects typically have been much smaller. If you
have a certain number of lean experts at your disposition, do you want to
use them to just reduce the cost of the R&D organization or do you use them
to further leverage the impact of R&D on the value stream and profitability?

> ***Can lean help to improve efficiencies and costs within R&D?***
> ***Yes. Should that be the main objective of lean R&D? No.***

As the shadows reveal, a cost-focused perspective of lean R&D misses
the crucial point about R&D/product development: *The purpose of R&D is to
help the company make money.* Joe Zekoski, Goodyear CTO, realizes this:
"My job as a CTO is to maximize the R&D investment." R&D is an investment and this investment must generate dividends and profit. The fact that
R&D often gets cut or reduced in a downturn shows the perception of many
executives that R&D is a cost. Such R&D cuts do not only waste talent and
knowledge that cost the company a lot of time and money to build up, but
they also prevent companies from having new products ready to sell when
market conditions improve.

Goodyear treats R&D as an investment, and the effect that R&D has had
on Goodyear profitability in its North American division—the one which has
profited the most and longest from redesign of product development—has
been dramatic. Even during the recent recession, Goodyear leadership kept
the product development process fully funded, which gave us a running
start when an economic rebound occurred. We aggressively were developing
new tires that would be *on the market* at the right time.

Goodyear Chairman Richard Kramer explained at one of our town hall
meetings in 2008: "We are in a challenging economic situation today, but I
am optimistic for the future! We keep investing for the time when the economy will recover, and we all know it will recover eventually. It takes a year
or more to develop a new tire line, and if we [wait to] fund the development
when the economy recovers, we will miss an important part of the market.
That is why we invest in the bad times for the better times to come."

Many factors beyond R&D affected Goodyear's revenue rise in 2010, but
it is clear that R&D provided great products when needed, without which

none of the other factors would have mattered (see *Goodyear North America Operating Income*).

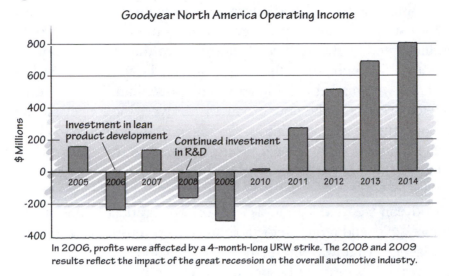

Goodyear North America Operating Income

In 2006, profits were affected by a 4-month-long URW strike. The 2008 and 2009 results reflect the impact of the great recession on the overall automotive industry.

By considering R&D as an investment that generates revenue, it forces us to further leverage product development with lean principles and look well beyond cost reductions and other common lean efficiencies. We need to focus first and foremost on the product performance and pricing benefits that lean improvements in R&D deliver, which overshadow the impact from other organizational components. R&D impacts profitability because it

1. Generates ideas, some of which will turn into successful products. These ideas do not come from marketing studies or boardroom strategies.
2. Develops products that outperform the competition and fetch a higher selling price.
3. Affects most functions throughout a company's end-to-end value streams (e.g., manufacturability, complexity, material cost).
4. Controls new product availability, which drives profit more than anything else—a delay in availability directly impairs revenue and the maximum profit-earning window for a new product.

The following chart (see *New Product Pricing Benefits*) gives one example of how the application of lean principles in R&D can improve product availability—at the right time—and, eventually, profitability. It also gives further direction of where to focus lean R&D: on the shadows.

The *dotted line* represents the typical price erosion of a new product in the marketplace. This erosion is due to the fact that as technology moves forward, competition reacts and advertising loses its effectiveness. As soon as this erosion starts, it is time for the organization to have a new product in the market (illustrated by the *top line*). Unfortunately, the optimum time window is not stable in time—it often moves forward, rarely backward. A new product enters the market at a higher selling price than the old product was able to fetch. The more the new product is delayed, the longer a company is forced to sell the old product, and a profit gap (the *vertical arrow*) appears. The longer it takes to get the new product to market, the wider the vertical arrow and the greater the losses. For Goodyear, this missed opportunity can be very significant.

At Goodyear, we used lean tools to make our product development process faster, more agile, and more predictable in order to ensure new product availability at launch windows, with highest quality standards, and at the right cost level, giving the business the best chance to make the highest profit.

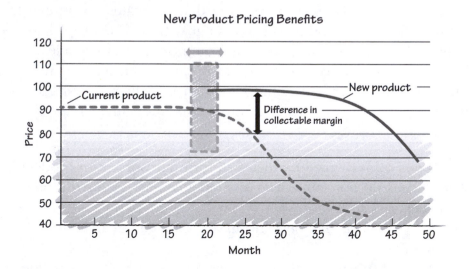

The next chart (*Optimum Time to Launch*) illustrates the relative differences between using lean to gain efficiency in R&D versus using lean R&D to create business opportunities:

- The optimum time to launch a new product is represented by the *0 on the time axis* (see arrow).
- The *tiny black bars* above 0 on the dollar axis represent the gain to the business from a 10% lean cost improvement in R&D, which accumulates month to month and, although quite small, still benefits the business.

- The *dark gray bar* represents the loss of profit to the business for failing to launch at the optimum time and having to sell the existing, lower-priced product. This is a modest example. We have seen missed opportunities in our company alone that have accounted for much higher losses.
- The *white bar* represents the loss of profits of a missed cost opportunity, such as not having a new material tested and released by R&D. It used to take us *years* to approve a new material given the exhaustive design work and testing that is needed. Today, we react quickly to such sourcing opportunities—and the cost savings and higher profit potential they might offer—and move prudently but rapidly through the design and testing because we recognize the costs associated with such delays.
- The *light gray bar* represents a case where a minor performance target was not achieved. With higher performance attributes in place, the product could have been sold at a higher price—without it, the product is sold at a slightly lower price and the full profit is not achieved. This creates a new set of decisions for R&D and the business: (1) sell the new product with some performance targets achieved at a slightly higher price now, or (2) continue to sell the older product at a much reduced profit and wait until the new product with all performance targets in place can be sold.

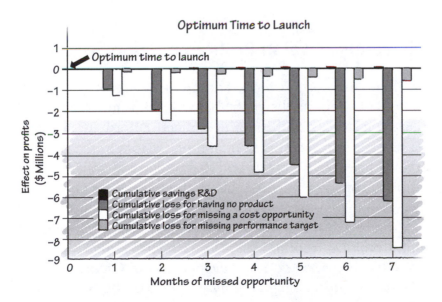

The comparison of the dark gray and light gray bars helps R&D make launch decisions. For example, the loss in profit of a new product with a slightly lower performance is often much less than the profit loss if no new product is available (i.e., if R&D decides to extend the development time to meet all the performance targets). This is where "agile" thinking kicked in at Goodyear. Some performance targets, like quality, are mandatory and never negotiable. But we used to meet *every* other conceivable performance target specified by marketing, such as wet traction, fuel economy, or noise, even if it meant delaying the launch by a year or more. Now we assess on a regular basis what is truly more important, launching when the product addresses the market opportunity with an acceptable product or waiting for a product that meets every conceivable performance target after another couple of development cycles.

This concept of making targets a variable and trading them for time is somewhat foreign to product development because engineers are used to getting targets thrust upon them, and they like the challenge of trying to meet them all. At Goodyear, we learned that the targets, the timing, and the cost of the product all have one common denominator—high-quality products at a good profit.

A concept and measure that helps R&D with these decisions is the idea of the cost of delay (COD). It has been described in detail by Don Reinertsen[2] and will be addressed more in *Chapter 6*. It is exceptionally helpful for organizations to prioritize projects or make investments in order to maximize profits.

Lean R&D Helps Develop Profitable Value Streams

Beyond the ability to impact revenue and profit based on new product launch timing, R&D impacts the profitability of the value stream in that it specifies design, materials, and so on that affect performance and cost. Here again, R&D has a significant effect on all three factors in the profit equation (profit = volume (price − cost)), and this underscores the real purpose of R&D, which is to consistently contribute to the creation of profitable value streams and, in doing so, create opportunities for many lean concepts and tools to be leveraged. But this role does pose a question for your product development group: *Do your engineers know how to design profitable value streams? Do all other contributors to the value stream know what they contribute and how they affect the profitability? And are all contributors aligned and collaborating in order to maximize customer value and profitability?*

Engineers are normally trained in the tools of the trade—good, solid, technical engineering skills. They know how their decisions affect the performance of the product. But they are not accountants or business strategists and often do not understand the marketing strategies, cost tradeoffs, manufacturing impacts, and cost complexities associated with their roles. This is where understanding of additional lean tools—such as customer value, knowledge management, collaboration, value-stream thinking—as well as basic understanding of the business, manufacturing costs, complexity, and distribution can have a positive effect on the value stream.

I think that most other functions also do not understand their role in influencing value streams and the shadows those functions cast, which may not be as large as that of R&D, but certainly impactful. Take, for example, purchasing. I recently presented lean training to a group from our purchasing organization. I had started writing a special version of Lean 101 (entry-level lean concepts) for the training session when I realized that their function contributes to the complete product value stream much like R&D. I really did not need a special training program, just a little different focus.

Of course, purchasing has its own functional objectives that they need to consider, but, just like R&D, applying lean in a manner that affects the complete value stream will always pay more dividends to the company than applying it to their own function and focused entirely on their own objectives. The key is that leaders and individuals in all functions understand the basic lean principles and then apply them correctly to the work they do for the benefit of the overall value stream.

During a recent stay in the hospital after breaking my leg in a skiing accident, I encountered a classic example that reminded me how small things or functions can have a huge impact on a value stream. I was aware that the hospital had started a lean journey and had hired some seasoned professionals with lean experience in healthcare. Overall, I was satisfied with the hospital and impressed with its lean practices, especially as they applied to safety and quality, but I was really annoyed by all the waiting for the internal transportation department. I waited when I was wheeled for tests, when I went to therapy, and when I was discharged. But the most striking case was when I waited to be taken to surgery.

My surgery had suddenly been moved up—probably due to a cancellation—but I was ready to go (doctors and hospitals always want a few patients readied just in case an opening occurs and the operating room can be optimized). As usual, I waited for at least half an hour for transportation to show up and take me to the operating room. Not only did I wait, but in the operating room waiting were the surgeon and a whole team of anesthesiologists, nurses, other doctors, and technicians. The operating room, a primary means for hospitals to earn revenue, was sitting idle. The money burned in that half an hour was significant. One seemingly unimportant function (inside transportation) created a huge cost of delay that certainly affected the profitability of the surgery value stream that day.

I discussed the transportation delays with the surgeon, who had eventually dispatched the operating room nurses to get me, as he told me he does frequently. I do not know the root cause of this transportation problem, but I have seen similar cases where across the board cost cutting or similar measures in one function can upset the balance of an entire value stream. Here is a great opportunity for the lean experts in the hospital: the effect of one seemingly insignificant function caused the hospital a substantial profit loss and is probably repeated frequently there.

At Goodyear through the years, principally before we applied lean, we encountered many instances where a function had cut its costs (i.e., reduced headcount) as required by corporate guidelines. These reductions were made as mandated without assessing the impact on the entire value stream: Goodyear once held a lavish press briefing for a new North American market winter tire in a resort in Switzerland. The tire generated a huge buzz, and tire experts raved about its performance and sales opportunities. The problem was that a function had recently closed a mold manufacturing plant, which temporarily reduced mold manufacturing capacity. On the surface, reasons for the closure may or may not have been sound, but, for certain, the effect of the decision on this tire's value stream was disastrous. Molds for the tire arrived after winter was over. Despite the glitzy launch, Goodyear never produced nor sold the tire, and several top executives felt the consequences of a major reorganization. Costs to design the product were eaten, profit was never realized, dealers were upset, and it was a huge embarrassment to Goodyear. In addition, the new management removed that winter tire line from plans for the following year, and the molds that had finally arrived were scrapped.

For R&D and any function within your organization, if the value-stream impact of a functional decision on resources and the impact to its shadow is calculated or understood, different decisions will almost always be made. For example, transportation in a hospital cannot be avoided and the cost of the function should be as low as possible. But the cost for bringing just one patient to surgery late would likely pay for an additional resource in transportation for many months. Of course, as processes are improved, resources might be applied elsewhere, to retain the needed balance and flow in the value stream.

At Goodyear, we take a hard look at the appropriate and balanced assignment of resources to our value streams to assure the right outcomes. We are not averse to overstaffing or buffering with capacity when we know a positive impact on the R&D shadow warrants it. In effect, it is not overstaffing—but "right" staffing.

This Lean "Stuff" Really Works

Most companies around the world are in business because they do many things right. Of course, they also need to improve those things that are not done well enough. But you do not have to be perfect, you only need to remain better than your competitors today and those that will emerge tomorrow.

Some companies think they must change everything when they pursue a lean business model, often encouraged by consultants who tell them, "It is the full Toyota system or nothing—you cannot implement pieces of the Toyota system." First, what the consultant calls the "Toyota system" works well at Toyota, which does not mean it will be a perfect fit for your company or your process. Second, you may have many sound solutions in place already for many of the aspects of your business. Do not dump the baby with the bathwater; look closely at what is needed, what is already in place, and implement *pieces* of the Toyota system or other lean principles that apply to your business model. It is not heresy, and even some of those who have studied the Toyota product development system endorse this approach.

Within Goodyear's product development function, we had many processes and tools that would fit under the lean umbrella before we heard about and implemented lean concepts (see *Goodyear's Brief History of Lean Product Development*). Our strengths were

- Computer modeling know-how developed in collaboration with Sandia National Laboratories and others and based on our technical knowledge
- Computer design systems that incorporated our design guidelines and codified our best practices through the years
- Vast, well-managed knowledge about our products and technology
- Design standards specific to every region of the world
- Release criteria, both for design release and product release
- Standard operating procedures
- Talent—great engineers and leadership

Goodyear's Brief History of Lean Product Development

Goodyear's foundation for lean product development, beginning in the 1990s and continuing through today as we incorporate new principles and tools, is tabulated as shown below.

1990–2000	Total quality control (TQC)
	Global product standards
	Supplier to most Japanese OEMs
	Standard operations manuals
	Global tire performance standards
	Computer modeling technology
2000–2003	ISO/QS certifications
	Six sigma in manufacturing
	Project teams
2003	Six sigma in R&D
	Staff adjustments and reorganization
	Stage gate
2004	Regaining stability
	Business reorganization
2005	Porsche Consulting
	First lean initiative
2006	Matrix organization
	USW strike, Herbie team
	Lean 101 training
	Elimination of priority lists
2007	Visual planning for development work at GIC*A
	Pull/kanbans
	Lean 201 training
2008	Operation management center GIC*L
2009	Direct ship Akron
2010	Lean product development implemented in GIC*L
	Abandon Herbie team
	Lean 401 training
	Lean sharing events
2011	Development speed contest
	Operations group formed

2012	"Pit crew" initiative
	Large-scale A3 implementation
	Lean tire flow
	Modular training (Lean 301)
2013	Lean leadership development initiative
2014	Zero loss concept in R&D
	Focus on sustainability
	New lean strategy going forward

Our strengths came through years of work and improvement—some long before I had heard of Goodyear—and kept the company on the forefront of innovation for more than a century:

- 1927—all-weather tread design tire
- 1934—studded mud and snow tires
- 1947—nylon tires
- 1970—tires on the moon (XLT tires on Apollo 14 transporter)
- 1977—all-season radial tires (Tiempo)
- 1991—new level of wet and dry performance (Aquatred)
- 1992—original equipment run-flat tires
- 1996—lifetime treadwear warranty tires (Infinitred)
- 2005—tire technology that repairs punctures when they occur (Duraseal)
- 2011—renewable biomass technology (Biosprene™)
- 2011—tire-pressure maintenance (Air Maintenance Technology)
- 2015—tire that recharges the battery of a car (BH03)
- 2015—tire that modifies inflation pressure based on need for stiffness or comfort (Triple Tube)

Yet despite this pretty remarkable innovation track record, many individuals—our internal improvement experts, consultants—often discounted some of the good processes and tools that we already had in the company in the name of lean and change. Most change agents had never developed a tire and did not really care to understand the designers and engineers who worked in the process. Only a few came to our "gemba." I personally had to fight an army of outsiders and insiders to keep the product development strengths we had in place and, going forward, to get them to understand where the lean changes would be applicable.

Goodyear had followed all management trends over the last 20 years, such as total quality control (TQC) and six sigma, as well as some created by Goodyear. From each of these initiatives, a little bit stuck. But before starting lean, Goodyear still was not serving its customers as it should. Less than 20% of all projects were delivered when the customer needed them. The few projects that were delivered on time were the projects that had a contract tied to them, such as deliveries to original equipment manufacturers (OEMs such as General Motors, Toyota, and Ford) and major commercial chains like Walmart or Sears.

It was during this time that Jean-Claude Kihn, who had been on assignment in Latin America, came back to Akron as the general director GIC*A (Goodyear Innovation Center, Akron). Most of our business leaders prior to then had grown accustomed to receiving good-quality and well-performing products from the R&D organization. But they also were used to getting the product when the R&D organization was done, not when they wanted or needed the product. Gradually, though, a new generation of leaders was joining the company from other companies. When these executives heard the complaints from customers and understood the negative impact on our business, they were far less willing to accept the R&D delivery performance, and they complained daily to Jean-Claude and the chairman about late projects and blamed the late projects for missed business goals.

Jean-Claude wanted to know what was going on. *All* the project leaders reported metrics that showed that *all* projects were on time—none of them indicated that there was a delivery problem. Eventually Jean-Claude went to the chairman and reported on the R&D projects. Instead of using our traditional metrics, he showed data I had developed that indicated a delivery rate of less than 20% to the date that the business wanted projects. To his surprise, the chairman said, "It certainly takes a lot of courage to show me this."

Jean-Claude and his team reflected on what he had at last seen (data), and they recognized the good news in the numbers because they had established a baseline from which it should be easy to improve. Our project leaders needed to recognize, just like Jean-Claude had, that we had a problem before we could begin to turn it around. They realized that there was a culture change needed and it had to start with all admitting we had a problem.

And we did have a delivery problem. There were weekly priority lists for every step of our R&D process. Sometimes more than 300 projects appeared on the list, of which only the first half dozen would be worked on. Project leaders and engineers spent a large part of their work day fighting to get their projects' priority moved up, usually reserved for projects with a contract and those with special management attention. Many projects died on the list. Every year, we deleted the projects that had not had any activity for more than *2 years*.

Goodyear was in a true downward spiral, similar to airplanes in distress and as described by Allan Ward.[3] When an "important" project fell behind, resources were moved at the last minute to help get the project back on track (and needed to appease the daily management updates). Of course, when resources were reapplied from other projects, those projects fell behind, and then they eventually would get additional resources—the downward spiral got stronger and stronger.

Ward points out that when an airplane goes into a downward spiral, the instinctive reaction of a pilot is to "pull up" on the controls—the wrong thing to do. The only way to get out of the spiral, he writes, is to push down to increase speed and restore flow and lift around the wings. Joe Zekoski, CTO, reflects: "The worst thing was that when we were in the downward spiral, we thought we were all doing the right thing." At Goodyear, we finally "pushed down," and rather than combat chaos with bureaucracy, implemented a very counterintuitive lean product development system and got out of the spiral.

As with every lean implementation, personal safety and quality should come first, and this is what happened at Goodyear. We had developed an industry-leading safety record before the start of our lean initiatives, and this trend continued. You cannot go wrong by first focusing your application of lean on safety. This shows the respect that the organization has for people, and improves trust, buy-in, and alignment of your organization. We, like many companies, are proud of our safety record and ongoing improvements; there is no shortage of safety-improvement ideas available to leaders who pursue better workplace safety.

Along with safety, quality is mandatory. Goodyear customers agreed that our product-development quality was good even prior to lean, that is, once we actually launched a product. Our leaders made it very clear that they would not subscribe to any initiative that would even come close to having an adverse effect on quality. One way that we measure product-development quality is by monitoring warranty costs as a percentage of sales (see *Warranty Costs*), which has continued to go down since the beginning of lean in product development at Goodyear.

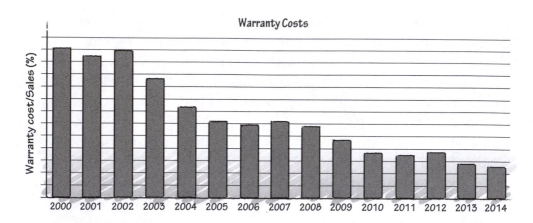

Once safety and quality objectives are met, reasonable minds will usually differ on what is next in importance: efficiency or service? It took me a long time to convince the organization that service should come before efficiency—if you do not have service (or delivery in this case), it does not matter how efficient you are. I also had an ally in Jean-Claude and our business leaders for pursuing improved on-time delivery (OTD), and so Goodyear focused its service measure on OTD to the business.

Our OTD goal was set originally at 100%, but we noticed that with such a goal, our project managers and engineers were reluctant to take innovation risks and try new ideas to make sure they were able to meet the delivery target. For that reason, the goal was lowered to 95% and then to 90%. If a product release is late, we can make up the time in the production-release phase because any delay, if it happens, is relatively short. Today, most delays are caused by technical reasons (as opposed to scheduling or process), such as underestimating the technical challenge. Even with the 10% buffer for on-time performance, our OTD recently has been higher than 90% (see *On-Time Delivery*).

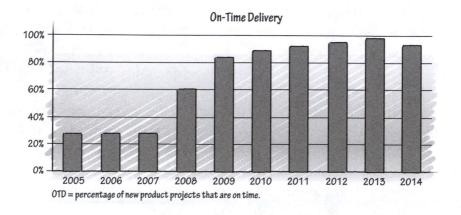

OTD = percentage of new product projects that are on time.

As we improved our service, we began to look at efficiency. We track "iterations per year" (or month) as a measure of efficiency. Our R&D budget had been relatively flat for many years, so an increasing number of iterations can be used as a good measure of efficiency.

When we began to monitor our efficiency, we validated a well-known experience with lean. Many authors have written about the "hidden factory," in which waste elimination frees up capacity so much so that there is a significant capital avoidance and, thus, it is like another factory emerges for free. We witnessed it in our product development. At Goodyear, we freed up capacity, which is now applied to more new products and development of fundamental technology and innovation (see *Goodyear R&D Project Iterations (Learning Cycles)*). The new capacity also was used to support the lean initiative and improve other processes in R&D. It would have been very tempting at this time, when the company had financial challenges, to reduce the cost of R&D. Since Goodyear considers R&D as an investment, the new capacity was reinvested in capability development.

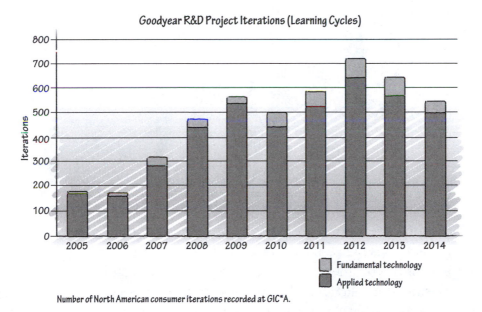

Number of North American consumer iterations recorded at GIC*A.

The above example shows the yearly increases in iterations or learning cycles for the North American consumer business unit, which were achieved without an increase in resources or budget. As you can see, we are now able to do fundamental development again, which had taken a setback when resources were needed for firefighting and launches. The increase plateaus due to fluctuations in the business, some degree of market saturation (i.e., we now supply *all* the new products that marketing and the OEM customers want), and because we manage our knowledge better and do not need as many learning cycles to launch new products. The R&D resources that are no longer needed for iterations now support new R&D opportunities.

The efficiencies we gained also worked hand in hand with lean efforts to increase product development speed. There is a clear business payback for investment in speed. At Goodyear, we noticed that when we focused on improving speed, we not only helped the business become more agile, but other efficiencies occurred simultaneously. For example, the most efficient way to increase speed is to eliminate waste from the process—such as over-processing or waiting—and removing this waste also saves money. Our focus on speed is illustrated by product development cycle time (see *Cycle Time*). Keep in mind that our impressive results for cycle time, like that for delivery, are due in some part because we had so much room for improvement.

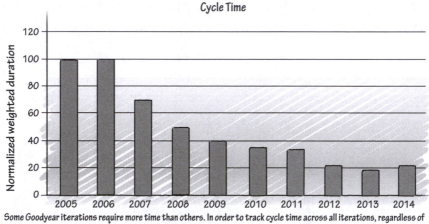

Some Goodyear iterations require more time than others. In order to track cycle time across all iterations, regardless of the varying time, Goodyear established a measure of normalized weighted duration, establishing a base of 100 in 2005.

Reflecting back on our lean initiative, there was nothing more important than to generate visible results, especially results that could be tracked to the bottom line of the business. Without those consistent results, I do not think that the business and R&D leadership would have endorsed all the change, and I do not think that R&D leadership would have kept supporting the effort. And without that support, we would not still be finding new ways to apply lean and improve R&D processes and even innovation.

Manufacturing operations have a "ticket" or a production schedule, and they mostly apply lean to meet that schedule as efficiently as possible. There is little creativity in *what* they do, although there can be a lot of creativity in *how* they do it. R&D is different in that it must also make decisions of *what* to work on, in some instances starting with a completely blank space for ideas. At the very least, R&D must always consider that *what* is sought today can rapidly change tomorrow.

In *Gemba Walks*, Womack writes, "I have long felt that a great weakness of the lean movement is that we tend to take customer value as a given, asking how we can provide more value as we currently define it, at lower cost with higher quality and more rapid response to changing demand. This is fine as far as it goes. But what if the customer wants something fundamentally different from what our organizations are now providing?"[4] Customers do not ask for disruptive innovation—that is normally an outcome of a good and innovative R&D process or good market research.

Making the right decisions on *what* to work on to ultimately create breakthrough products. Freeing engineers to pursue those ideas is a difficult task and one fraught with uncertainty. Good marketing research helps only so much with innovation decisions and can often lead to leaders drowning in data. With so many ideas usually available, these highly impactful decisions often are based on intuition and experience. The inability to make the right decision—especially what not to work on—can plug the product development pipeline with too many projects for months or years. When I meet with R&D associates from other companies, I usually ask them what their biggest problems are—*too much work* is always among the top three items mentioned, and I think I know why.

In discussions with engineering colleagues through the years, I have heard that lean will negatively affect innovation and creativity. This opinion has been shared by many, including Jack Welch and Steven Jobs. We saw a bit of this when we started lean within product development at Goodyear as well. It is true that lean and six sigma initiatives have resulted in a reduction of innovation and creativity in some companies. That is unfortunate, but it should not have happened and did not need to happen.

Lean principles can enhance innovation if applied correctly. Following the publication of *The Lean Startup*[5] by Eric Ries, many people began to view differently the potential of lean to coexist with innovation. Ries describes tools, such as minimum viable prototypes and quick consumer testing, which can be wielded by an organization or a product development group and are enhanced by lean thinking.

Your lean efforts should not only remove barriers that inhibit creativity among your product development staff, but also create more opportunities for innovation and make the idea-generation/innovation process more efficient. We addressed the concern very quickly at Goodyear by avoiding restrictive standards and creating a process that enables innovation by managing risk, variability, and uncertainty (rather than avoiding them). And to counter the perception among others in industry, I point to our list of innovation and product awards that we have achieved since we introduced lean, which are far more than we had been getting prior to lean. These included awards from *Consumer Reports, Car & Driver, Road & Track, R&D 100*, and many others.

I will not credit lean R&D for *all* the recent innovations and awards at Goodyear, but it certainly contributed to them. What I find to be most impressive about Goodyear's success with lean product development is that all the measures and achievements in the last decade have been accomplished without a significant increase in R&D funding. The cost of the lean initiative itself is a mere blip on the budget. What also should be encouraging to you is that lean R&D successes have not been limited to Goodyear and its processes for developing tires, but experienced by many other companies in many industries (e.g., Ford, Scania, Intel, Boeing, Bombardier, Steelcase, DJO Global, and on and on).

Lean Is a Lot of Work

Every change in an organization, especially one as large and globally dispersed as Goodyear, is difficult. Having worked on developing *new processes* for the better part of 10 years, I sometimes get jealous of colleagues who are focused on product design. They use their technical skills to develop a new product, travel to launch events and dealer conferences, and see the near-immediate appreciation for their work. But for those who work on new process capability, like myself, you will encounter much more resistance and frustration.

Remember that product development should be designing value streams, which means I am often trying to change processes over which I have no authority. I am trying to convince others over which I have no real power (e.g., authority, compensation) that they should embrace a different way of thinking and working. Over the years, I have run into some headstrong colleagues and lost a few battles. Occasionally, I lost a few friends who objected to my perseverance and who did not see lean as a way to improve R&D and Goodyear, as I did.

That was not the case with Guenter Wartusch, operations manager in the Goodyear Innovation Center in Hanau, Germany, and a lean change agent. Wartusch refers to himself as a gardener. He tells me about the work involved when gardening: the ground is prepared by spading, tilling, raking, and adding fertilizer. Then he carefully times the planting of seeds (too early and frost kills the young plant; too late and they will never bear fruit before the season-ending frost). Watering is regular and tedious. When the plants start to grow, he must pull the weeds—a messy job and you might pull out some plants with the weeds. Then he regularly cultivates and loosens the soil around the plants. It takes a lot of patience to nurture plants, and some die along the way. Plants that survive must be staked, pruned, monitored for pests, and so on, until eventually crops appear. After a lot of hard work, the gardener is rewarded. The gardener also deals with a lot of frustration; nothing is assured, regardless of the hard work that is invested.

Implementing change in a function or company requires similar skills to that of gardening, and it likewise is lot of hard work. Many people underestimate the time and effort that a lean transformation takes. But it is worth the effort—it will bear rich fruit if people are patient enough. Realistic expectations will help.

Many companies abandon lean product development too early. To avoid this problem, identify some low-hanging fruit to build interest and engagement and achieve early successes. This should also be something that can be implemented without too much resistance. As I noted, though, rapid results with lean in product development do not come as quickly as those in manufacturing, and there are not as many low-hanging fruits. But there are some. Look for the following in your organization:

- Obvious time-wasters—the later in the process they occur, the more they will affect the outcome.
- If you have a process where work is visible, like prototyping and testing, that is often a good place to start—those processes often have a big effect on the value stream, and, since the work is visible, the application of lean is a little easier.
- What is the biggest complaint of the customer? Even if you do not completely solve the problem, any improvement will go a long way.

Many lean product development projects are by nature large, and, therefore, it is important to set clear milestones and celebrate the milestones or at least communicate these intermediate successes. Many change experts recommend supporting lean and other business-improvement initiatives with an extensive, company-wide communications campaign. This can be good as long as there are good things to communicate, such as achieving targets and reminding people of the overall goal and progression of milestones to date. But keep in mind the story of the gardener—people can grow weary of reading about tilling and weeding; they want to eat the vegetables.

Just as the gardener often has to "go see" what is going on in the garden, change agents and leaders must go to the gemba regularly to see for themselves where the problems are and how the lean initiative progresses. Lean requires a different style of management than you and your staff are probably accustomed to—leaders and managers must coach and mentor rather than fix and firefight. Going to the gemba allows them to practice "respect for people," show their engagement with lean activities, offer help, and patiently spur improvements and overcome obstacles. Gemba walks are most efficient when the work and the results are visible in the work area and when clear expectations exist for milestones along the way. Of course, this is not always easy with invisible R&D work, but establishing visual mechanisms, such as flow and process-performance boards, help to illuminate problems and successes.

Gardens require manpower; lean implementations will require resources as well. Most organizations appoint change leaders to implement lean, who then run into functional leaders who are reluctant to appoint *their* resources to the cause. As lean as Toyota is today, it still appoints a large pool of employees (B-labor) to work on the improvement of their processes. For example, when functions or departments become overstaffed due to fluctuations in the business, Toyota will temporarily move key individuals from the function to improvement teams elsewhere, thus cross-training staff and giving the employee a reward for good performance.[6]

Many broken product development processes have no owner and/or have had no one interested in fixing them. The best lean projects span functions and even the company's end-to-end value chain. Many of the "horizontal" processes are organizational orphans, with few individuals willing to step up and try to change them. In many organizations, functions are owned and managed well, but projects that extend across functions or the value stream remain orphans and without management attention—your customer is the recipient of a value stream, not of the output of a single function.

As a change agent, you may have to step in to manage some orphans. After I created the new lean product development process at Goodyear, I found myself running and managing it as well. I was eventually given a technician to help, and it was a lot of fun. The fun stopped when our CTO removed me from direct involvement in the management of the process—as long as an organization could rely on me to manage the process, they would never dedicate individuals in their organization to be involved. The CTO was trying to facilitate functional and cross-functional engagement and application of resources to lean. This eventually led to the creation of the "lean operations" department.

The further you get on your lean journey, the more opportunities you see; it never ends. But not everyone will take that perspective. After our first year of lean product development, a lot of people, including some leaders, started to ask when we would start our next big initiative since we were done with lean. They wanted to know when this lean "stuff" would be finished so that we could try a different improvement flavor. Well, we have not started an initiative other than lean for 10 years now, and we still have a long way to go in improving the current one. Companies that genuinely embrace lean develop a culture with a heightened sense of waste and a sharper focus of what a successful process should look like. It is a relentless progression to better service to the customer, faster and more efficient processes, zero waste—costs, time, associate energy—and, ironically, the longer companies have been involved in lean, the more opportunities they find. It is this humble attitude that motivates people to keep improving and never be happy with only sustaining progress. The secret is to stick with what you have and keep improving it—not jumping on the next initiative that may only be new in name.

Lean Principles

Our lean journey in Goodyear product development offers guidance on how you can apply lean in your product development function to improve your value streams. The path we started on in 2005 is just one approach (a successful one), and some of it may not precisely apply to your company. I am, though, confident you will find many insights that will ease your startup of lean, help you improve your journey, or help you get your lean product development efforts back on track. Key to your success will be understanding lean principles.

Steven Spear wrote that if you read all the books and listen to all the consultants, you can only get as good as all the others—if you want to get better, then you have to develop beyond what is already known. That only happens based on an understanding of the principles of how and why lean works. It took me awhile before I realized that. Successful companies manage improvements based on principles, applying them throughout the organization (finance, mechanical engineering, production) over and over again to get better and better. According to Spear, "In most failed efforts, operational excellence or lean are defined as a vocational craft or the skilled application of tools onto problems—rather than as a principle-based profession."[7]

You cannot contribute much as an engineer if you do not know the key principles of math, physics, chemistry, and so on necessary for your engineering discipline. To lead a lean R&D initiative, you will need to know the *lean principles* that apply to product development before starting a transformation. This may sound trivial, but it is critical—most change agents learn tools, not principles.

I have seen several good lean product development transformations, and there is a common denominator: each company developed its own internal sensei or lean champion—leaders who know the company, the technology, the people—and teach the principles to everyone in the organization. Some companies started the effort with their own experts and some developed them over time, but all those able to sustain and grow the transformation seem to have them in place.

This book starts at the end—Goodyear's current success—and then shows in upcoming chapters how we navigated our way to this position, both our triumphs and our failures. Our lean journey has led me to identify the lean principles that drive the success of a lean product development initiative.

Knowing these principles—which Goodyear did not know a decade ago—will illuminate our story and show you how to begin your own success story (look for *Lean R&D Principle* sidebars throughout the book). Know this: lean principles are not intuitive. Some will seem trivial. And some you must first see in action before you believe they can ever work in your company. When I was asked to take a shot at developing a lean product development process at Goodyear, I started going to conferences, read books, did research on the internet, brought in consultants, and tried to find mentors. But the more I educated myself, the more confusing it became—actually a lot of what I had learned contradicted itself. Not until I read *Factory Physics*[8] did the pieces come together and make sense. *I began to understand lean principles.*

The lean principles for R&D that you will read about in subsequent chapters originated from many sources—we developed many within Goodyear, and others were found elsewhere (books, consultants, presentations, peers) and validated by Goodyear. Are there other lean principles? Absolutely. I learned and experimented with many others. But these are the ones that have been validated at Goodyear R&D, helped us achieve our current state, are sure to sustain us going forward, and are *universal—they can help any lean R&D initiative regardless of the work stream, company, culture, or business.*

Lean R&D Principle: Learn the universal lean principles and expertly apply them to your process.

Lean principles are universal. Although companies are different and processes are different within a company, the lean principles apply the same way that the principles of math and physics apply to a large variety of scientific and technical problems. Just like engineers must learn math, physics, and chemistry to develop new products, the people who are involved in a lean transformation must know the lean principles. Don't get scared; they are easy to understand and can be learned quickly. Eventually it helps if all involved in the lean transformation have a basic understanding of the principles.

Lean principles are not intuitive. Some will seem trivial. And some you must first see in action before you believe they can ever work in your company.

Knowing the principles will let lean practitioners see opportunities in their company, their work, and the world around them. A lot of people confuse tools with principles. They learn tools and "randomly" apply them, often to the wrong problems and wonder why they did not work.

Although the principles are universal, not all of them apply to every situation, just like not all that you learned in math applies to every single problem. Similarly, there are principles that apply in manufacturing, but they will have little effect on product development and vice versa.

At Goodyear: We started our lean product development transformation with a thorough understanding of the lean principles, especially those that apply to product development. The people involved in the change were trained in the principles. The team that was leading the transformation needed a deeper understanding than all the engineers in the organization, but everybody received the right education in the principles of lean product development.

Notes

1. The "shadow" graphic and concept was inspired by the work of Munro & Associates Inc.
2. Donald G. Reinertsen, *The Principles of Product Development Flow*, Celeritas Publishing, Redondo Beach, CA, 2009.

3. Allen C. Ward, *Lean Product and Process Development*, Lean Enterprise Institute, Cambridge, MA, 2007.
4. Jim Womack, *Gemba Walks*, Lean Enterprise Institute, Cambridge, MA, 2011.
5. Eric Ries, *The Lean Startup*, Crown Business, New York, 2011.
6. Jeffrey Liker and Gary Convis, *Toyota Way to Lean Leadership*, McGraw-Hill, New York, 2011.
7. Steven Spear, "Steve Spear: Why Lean Fails: Operational Excellence Treated as Tool Based Vocation, Not Principle Based Profession," *The Lean Edge*, April 3, 2011.
8. Wallace J. Hopp and Mark L. Spearman, *Factory Physics*, Waveland Press, Long Grove, IL, 1996.

Chapter 2

Success to Survival to a Foundation for Lean

*After reading this chapter, you will understand why The Goodyear Tire &
Rubber Company had to embark on its lean product development journey. As
a company, we had grown large and happy during "The Golden Age of Tire
Technology," but our industry did not necessarily challenge us to be faster or
more efficient. Fortunately, we had great tire technology and, although we
needed to be better, we had begun to piecemeal apply many elements that
would eventually support lean product development, for example, project
teams, knowledge management, stage gates, and so on, before even knowing
what lean was. Depending on your own organization's progress with lean,
you too may have some of these or similar concepts already embedded in your
R&D processes, which will accelerate your lean journey.*

The Golden Age of Tire Technology

Life was good in the 1970s and early 1980s. Goodyear was a great place to
work, money was being made in the tire business, and cash was invested in
R&D. The development process was simple: we developed tires for original
equipment—when they were produced, we supplied the OEMs, and the rest
of the tires went to the warehouse for the renewal market.

Goodyear's business in Latin America, Europe, and Asia was similar, and,
although it was difficult to get started, we eventually obtained approvals to
supply Japanese and other Asian car manufacturers. We realized we had the

technical capabilities for the Japanese OEMs, but it took us years to adjust to their processes and demands for consistency, delivery, service, and so on.

Research in those days was done for the purpose of advancing the science. Researchers decided what to work on. When a discovery looked good, it was taken to marketing or put on the shelf until somebody asked for it. I personally worked in a group called "Innovative Products." When our management or sales asked for a new product, we were supposed to give them a number of choices, and we typically had dozens of projects underway. They rarely asked, and few products and processes from this area quickly made it into the market, and some would not get noticed and commercialized for years or *decades*.

Some R&D money was spent on "discretionary funding," and the CTO managed that budget personally. I was the recipient of such funds. As an engineer and project manager, I had little supervision and was left alone to innovate. When a project got close to needing prototype equipment, money was allocated for the machines (almost $1 million), and we then made prototypes for customers to test. When the decision was made to go into production, the project was put into the capital plan, the funding mechanism changed, and we made the product. Life was good!

Before or since, this was definitely the best system I have seen to promote innovation. The use of discretionary funding, to which all other functions objected because it was not under their authority, was quite lean. Risk was controlled by metering funds on a just-in-time basis, with minimal bureaucracy in the process. Goodyear seed money generated many returns: several projects, in addition to mine, were funded in this way and added new, successful products to our line. In hindsight, the only thing that Goodyear could have done better was to recognize that "innovators" may have needed more skill in managing capital projects and, thus, offered training, coaching, or assigning an experienced project manager at least as a mentor. It is too bad that many companies forgot how to innovate in this manner, or never tried.

The golden age of tire technology was Goodyear's functional R&D organization at its best (see *R&D Organizational Structures*). Our functions included tire design (where my role was located), materials development, many disciplines of basic research, mold design, and prototype building, which occurred in a dedicated plant on site. Knowledge was developed in the functions, and it was maintained in the functions.

Excellent technology and knowledge was developed during those years, and our finite element analysis (FEA) computer modeling technology was second to none and on the cutting-edge for R&D organizations. Some of the other leading-edge technologies that we implemented included the following:

- CAD systems and other computer-drawing programs
- One of the first suspension parameter measurement machine (SPMM) car-testing rigs (many OEMs extensively used the rig to supplement their own capacity)
- Early versions of prototype molds made from cold metal spray and/or epoxy to reduce the tooling time and cost
- A laser-carving machine that carved sophisticated tire designs into smooth tires and a six-axis milling machine for mold tooling at our technical center in Luxembourg as early as the 1980s
- One of the first stereolithography machines (the first 3D printing concept on the market)

All the knowledge resided in the function, and the functions and engineers were trained by their senior colleagues. Other than this, the functions did not see a reason to share knowledge. Functions also excelled at developing talent, as they strived to develop the best possible skills in their specialty. In addition to the talent, functions were good at developing other capabilities, like knowledge, tools, and technology.

The downsides of Goodyear's functional R&D organization, though, were many:

- Slow lateral movement of projects across the functions and little cross-functional collaboration
- Personal advancement occurred mainly within a function, which created an inflation of layers and leaders fighting for promotions
- Typically only "functional" thinking was rewarded, and many project decisions were made for the benefit of the function, not the customer
- Projects were "thrown over the wall," function to function

The functional organization allowed the building of "empires." The knowledge and the capability of the functions gave the functions their power. Functions competed for funding, and so functional leaders used their positions and influence to increase their power and build larger organizations. At times, some powerful functions served their own interests more so than Goodyear in total.

Every function also had many balls in the air because it was important to always have "the right answer" quickly available when something was requested by management or marketing. Agility was achieved via a large inventory of all kinds of technical opportunities. Eventually, a sponsor—new manager, leader, or even the CEO—would come forward and pick one of those ideas, like the Aquatread or the run-on-flat concept, and sponsor a launch. Mind you, these were a small percentage of the *good* projects that were in the works. Most projects never were implemented.

Functional budgets were based on inflation adjustments of the previous-year budget or spending. Budget and spending, of course, were always identical. Managers often struggled to spend all the money, but did so because they feared it would not be allocated in the coming budget. (Does this sound familiar to you?)

Projects were managed only within the functions. Cross-functional projects were managed similar to functional projects, and the priorities conflicted. Functional leaders and managers spent most of their time managing priorities, which they received from marketing or sales, and this took an exorbitant amount of time because priorities changed constantly. Priorities often followed customer needs, and other times they were based on the power of the negotiators. To manage this seemingly uncontrollable river of projects and priorities, Goodyear gradually and organically developed a sophisticated traffic-control system. Functional leaders were managing process congestion rather than technologies, projects, people, or knowledge.

R&D Organizational Structures

There are at least four major organizational structures used within R&D organizations.

(A) FUNCTIONAL

This used to be the most typical R&D organization in the United States and in the Western industry. It is patterned after most corporate organizational structures, such as finance, operations, legal, HR, and purchasing, used in large corporations. The organization is based on competencies or skills. In Goodyear R&D, those competencies are materials development (chemistry), tire and mold/equipment design (mechanical), IT (computer programming), computer modeling (math, statistics), and testing (mechanical). Projects typically make their "stop" in a function, and when the function is done with the project, it moves over the wall to the next function. Many lean experts call the functions "silos" to depict their isolated nature.

Functions are good at developing knowledge and expertise. Young engineers can learn from the old engineers and ask them questions. Succession planning is relatively easy, as there is little lateral movement between functions. The amount and depth of knowledge held by functions can make them very powerful in an organization.

- *Advantages:* Clear responsibilities, continuity, good knowledge and talent management, and high technical specialization.
- *Disadvantages:* Focus on functional objectives can hurt the management of the projects across functions, cause a lack of collaboration with other functions, and generate high competition between functions.
- *Where to use:* Long-duration projects, highly technical products (e.g., medical devices, aerospace, basic research), and single-discipline projects.
- *Variant:* Temporary, multidisciplinary teams or projects managed by dominant function or dedicated leader.

(B) PROJECT

In a project organization, all disciplines that are needed are assigned permanently to one project for the duration of the project. All team members work for the same project leader. When the project is done, the team members are reassigned. If they cannot be reassigned (as on many military projects when the funding stops), the team members have to find different jobs or new employment.

- *Advantages:* Strong focus on the project, faster speed, often better quality, no handoffs, one boss, and better collaboration.
- *Disadvantages:* Limited knowledge sharing between projects and sometimes knowledge gets lost. Duplication. Often lack of responsibility for talent and capability development.
- *Where to use:* Large projects often with discretionary funding; many military projects done by private contractors or college projects with private or government funding are done using this structure.

(C) VALUE STREAM

In a value-stream organization, all the competencies and the resources are managed by a value-stream manager, who is responsible for the P&L of the value stream. In addition to marketing, finance, and manufacturing, R&D folks report to the value-stream manager.

- *Advantages:* Strong focus on the business, R&D is fully integrated with the business, no handoffs, one boss, and excellent collaboration.
- *Disadvantages:* Limited knowledge sharing between value streams and sometimes knowledge gets lost and inefficient sharing of resources. Talent and capability development limited to the needs of the value stream.
- *Where to use:* Mature or commercial businesses where R&D is more focused on maintaining and reinventing the products.

(D) MATRIX

The matrix organization tries to combine both the functional and the project/value-stream structures. Chief engineers (called "shusas" at Toyota) or project managers (at Goodyear) lead projects, and functional resources are allocated to the chief engineer on a temporary basis, full time or part time. The employees report to both the chief engineer/project manager and a functional leader. The project managers normally control the project budget, and the functional managers control the technology and manage the knowledge, the talent, and the capability development. Goodyear started using a matrix in 2006.

- *Advantages:* Best of both worlds—project focus and good knowledge, talent and capability management—and flexible use of resources.
- *Disadvantages:* Lack of "belonging" among engineers, and two or more reporting lines.
- *Where to use:* Products with a rather high multidisciplinary technical difficulty that also have well-defined marketing requirements requiring project management (e.g., cars, tires).

(E) BEYOND MATRIX

One new structure of R&D organization emerging is *dedicated multidisciplinary project teams*, based on their popularity in software development and in "agile" methodologies. The complete (colocated) and often self-directed team works on one project or one piece of a project (learning cycle) in a very small time frame (sprint) at one time. Although people may have been assigned initially according to their background (programmers, testers, architects), the team members are highly flexible in the execution of their work (i.e., almost anybody can do any job). Goodyear is experimenting with this concept in some areas.

- *Advantages:* Extremely quick execution, flexible expertise, continuity, and good communication and collaboration.
- *Disadvantages:* Lack of knowledge depth, and knowledge and talent management is more difficult.
- *Where to use:* Popular in IT and agile applications. Companies in various industries experiment with "rapid action teams." Can be used to execute traditional learning cycles in R&D organizations like Goodyear.

Another emerging structure is *pairing*, in which two people work together on the same contribution to a project: For example, two programmers write code together using one computer screen and two keyboards. Pairs rotate on a regular schedule. This should not be considered a separate organization since it can be used in any organizational structure.

- *Advantages:* High speed, better quality, fewer mistakes, good continuity, and effective onboarding.
- *Disadvantages:* Appears to require more resources, but companies that use pairing reject that argument.
- *Where to use:* Can be used in any structure.
- *Variant:* In many organizations, it is popular to pair people of different disciplines to encourage collaboration or continuity or to force a level of collaboration that did not exist before. That can be done on any level (e.g., pairing a design engineer with a marketing specialist, an engineer with a manufacturing expert, or a technical manager with an HR or purchasing specialist). Pairing people for training (new hires) and continuity (transfers) are well-established practices. Pairing project managers with functional managers of different functions also is becoming popular.

Early Building Blocks for Lean

Toyota did not invent all the elements that today are commonly thought of as lean tools, concepts, and techniques. They came from sources as diverse as Henry Ford and the U.S. military. And despite using many of these ideas for 50 years or more, not until recently did Toyota begin to define these ideas as a method or approach (Toyota Production System and The Toyota Way). Similarly, at Goodyear, we developed many good practices and benchmarked what other good organizations were doing, and we applied these ideas into product development well before we started with lean. I am certain that the following concepts helped us quickly gain traction with lean.

Early Project Management and Project Teams

In the 1980s, Goodyear created a project management group. High-potential associates with years of experience within the company were leading large projects that involved many functions and even divisions (e.g., tires, aerospace, energy, chemicals). Most of the projects from this group—such as composite car exterior parts and a high-speed polyester spinning process— were managed effectively because of three reasons:

1. They were led by a competent, experienced manager.
2. They had a powerful sponsor (often the CTO personally).
3. All functions and divisions were pulled together, even if they did not always collaborate.

Jon Bellissimo, general director of the Goodyear Innovation Center in Akron (GIC*A), worked in the project management department earlier in his career. Jon described the project managers as "super" chief engineers. They needed such attributes to obtain collaboration between the functional silos that would not talk to each other.

Eventually, a consulting group came to Goodyear, and the consultants concluded that a project management group added no value to the company. On the contrary, they said, this kind of organization hindered the company from finding the means and ways of managing projects through their functional organizations. The project management group was gone, but project management emerged in other initiatives, such as total quality management (TQM) and six sigma. Both promoted cross-functional teams and project leaders, which in turn focused on processes as well as products. The innovation center in Luxembourg had used what was called "committees" since the late-1970s. These temporary colocated teams were truly cross-functional, had a team leader, and reported to the general director. They were chartered to solve a difficult multidisciplinary problem. A team like that collaborated to develop the wire technology needed for high-performance tires in a truly concurrent fashion (chemical, processing, construction, etc.).

In the early 1990s, we created customer-specific teams at Goodyear, which looked like a matrix organization. Teams consisted primarily of individuals from within the design function, including the leader, and some loosely added members from other functions. The functional leaders actually started to manage projects, especially OEM projects. Due to the informal collaboration of staff from various functions, who recognized a common goal (OEM approval), these projects started to be relatively successful.

"Real" Project Teams

By the turn of the century, Goodyear had become an established supplier to Toyota. We never received any formal supplier "coaching" from Toyota in R&D, but we picked up many hints on how to develop product and create a project-team organization.

Goodyear was not quite ready to abandon its powerful functional organization; nonetheless, "real" project teams began to appear, inspired by feedback from Toyota: team members from different functions were colocated, and all team members huddled around a team leader, who reported to a function but was responsible for the delivery of the team's projects. Teams were assigned to different customers, internal or external. Every customer had specific requirements and, consequently, a different process was used for every customer. For this reason, the team members were not interchangeable between teams, and the teams were staffed for the worst case, that is, they were typically overstaffed, and rarely was everyone on every project team fully utilized (that would only occur when a major technical problem came up). The project teams were popular among the engineers: it felt good to belong to a team. Team leaders actually knew and appreciated what team members were doing and they managed the performance of the key members.

The teams allowed us to focus on customers. At Goodyear, we were struggling to become a better supplier to some Japanese customers, and the teams dealing with Japanese customers were given higher priorities and more attention in order to close this competency gap.

John Kullman, then chief engineer, used to head up the Toyota team. John noticed the increase in customer satisfaction by the service that his team was able to provide. But even with all the priorities offered to his team, it was still difficult to accomplish all the work related to the Toyota account, and other teams would not share engineers, even when they were in a lull.

Like John's team, most teams worked reasonably well and made a real difference in customer satisfaction, but the teams had a few inherent disadvantages.

Teams tended to develop projects by consensus, which made everyone happy *enough*, instead of by putting issues transparently on the table and creating "conflict" (as Toyota executives called it), which made for better products but left some engineers or functions unhappy. Conflict is often avoided by teams in the Western industrial culture, especially if team leaders are evaluated based on feedback from team members. The teams also competed against other teams: there was competition for resources and also among leaders for advancement and visibility. High-potential team leaders paid as much attention to internal competitors, as they did to our external competitors like Michelin or Bridgestone.

As the Goodyear organization became more project-oriented, we immediately realized that we needed an increased focus on knowledge management and sharing, which had been a strength of our functional organization.

Knowledge Management

The work of Orville and Wilbur Wright inspired the late Allan Ward[1] and Michael Kennedy[2] and helped them, me, and countless others to better understand the importance of knowledge management in R&D.

When the race was on to be first in the air, many pioneers of flight took the trial-and-error approach, which proved fatal for many. The Wright brothers, on the other hand, carefully developed the knowledge required by testing wings in small wind tunnels to understand lift and by flying kites to understand the aerodynamics of turning and banking. They recorded the wind tunnel knowledge in x–y plots that they could scale up to full-size planes. Eventually, they were able to use the knowledge to determine the size of the wings, the engine, and the controls, and could then design and build their first prototype, which needed only minor tuning prior to takeoff.

Most other pioneers, who did not live to tell their stories, designed and built their planes before they learned how they would perform. The Wright brothers developed the missing knowledge first and then they designed and built their prototypes.

This approach—"test before design"—was in use long before the term "lean" was coined and is still popular among scientists, developers, and companies (like Goodyear) to this day. I have used it many times since becoming an engineer.

One of my first big projects at Goodyear was to develop a large injection-molding machine with my team. We had absolutely no idea how to distribute the rubber so that a cavity as wide as a truck tire would fill in a short time without requiring too much pressure. Trial and error was no option for us because the cost of building a large prototype mold was prohibitive. We instead ran small-scale experiments on a laboratory extruder with a die consisting of drilled holes and also built a laboratory mold to make sure the rubber could fill the intricate tread pattern. Then we built a modular system that we could experiment with on a larger scale—we even rented an injection machine. We eventually had enough knowledge and courage to design the injection machine and the "runner system" that distributes the rubber to the mold—it was almost perfect. (Today, of course, we would simulate the flow of the material with a computer program.)

At that time, we just called "test before design" good scientific work. I have seen the technique used at other companies, too, and it is beneficial when

- Significant equipment investment is required
- Design is hard to figure out or there are too many options
- Many identical increments are required (like spokes on a wheel; test one spoke only)
- Scale up/scale down is possible
- Sufficient knowledge is not available

The concept of test before design ensures that, first, the lack of knowledge is identified and closed before the product or equipment is designed. It makes less sense, though, if the product is essentially already designed, and the experiments are run to fine-tune the product or perform certification testing, which often, like in Goodyear R&D, comprises more than 50% of a company's product development efforts.

A recent project at Goodyear used the test-before-design concept to design a new manufacturing system that used radically new technology. A complete tire plant costs more than $500 million, and a trial-and-error approach is clearly not possible. Even individual increments or work cells usually cannot be developed by trial and error. The project team broke down the technology into critical elements and developed bench-scale and full-scale equipment to foster the knowledge of the critical elements in place before they were combined with known elements to form the new manufacturing cell.

Akron Children's Hospital shared with us the process they used to learn how to design their new hospital tower. They set up full-scale mockups made from cardboard panels in a warehouse. They literally had full-scale sections of the new hospital and brought beds and operating tables in to simulate real scenarios, such as operating room procedures and patient transportation. Only when they were fully satisfied with the layout and the processes did they proceed with the design of the new facility. Now you may be thinking that all of this could have been done via computer simulations, and this is true, except for one critical difference: there are no real people in a computer simulation. The hospital's cardboard mockup allowed all the key people that would be involved in day-to-day activities—patients, surgeons, nurses, designers, crafts, and so on—the opportunity to see and contribute their knowledge and to participate in the eventual design.

Test before design and mockups are ways of developing knowledge before developing designs and they are two examples that exemplify a critical principle: *knowledge management.*

> *If you add up all the money your company has spent on R&D over the years, then you know how much your company spent on knowledge creation—probably billions of dollars.*

Besides designing profitable value streams, your R&D organization creates reusable knowledge. This knowledge represents a huge investment, and it needs to be managed well to assure the proper return for the investment.

Why Knowledge Management?

I remember a retirement celebration at Goodyear about 15 years ago where the VP of Tire Development GIC*A talked about the hundreds of years of experience who were walking out the door. Today, we make sure the knowledge does not walk out the door with the retirees. But that is only one of many knowledge-management initiatives.

A knowledge-based approach to lean product development is popular today in most companies because good knowledge management helps to

- Eliminate a lot of waste and cost in a development process by preventing reinvention
- Manage the risk in product development; managing risk is difficult everywhere, but it is especially difficult in a product development process
- Speed up the development, which often translates to profits

Since R&D is about developing reusable knowledge, most good companies have had a knowledge-management program for a long time, without putting it under the umbrella of lean, operational excellence, or continuous improvement. The same is true for Goodyear. As companies share their approaches to lean product development, more and more new insights become available, including use of knowledge management. There is a vast diversity of approaches that companies take to knowledge management due to differences in the business, the nature of their research and development, the maturity of the technology involved, and the lean development approach in use. I will share Goodyear's experiences with knowledge management because I think the underlying principles are universally acceptable.

Goodyear used to have a strong functional organization, and a functional organization normally does a good job managing knowledge. Even if the knowledge is not documented well, there are enough opportunities to collect it "in people's heads" within the function and to share it with the other employees in the function or make it available upon request by another function. With the move to project teams and/or a matrix organization, this functional approach to knowledge management has become more difficult. Engineers now report to two or more bosses, and the intimate contact of the members and their transfer of knowledge in the function can get lost. Also feeding concern over knowledge management today is the increased career mobility of engineers and the retirement of baby boomers, who could take a lot of knowledge with them in their heads when they leave the company.

There also is a big fear of documenting knowledge all in one place. This occurs in high-tech organizations as well as low-tech, with companies worried about losing their trade secrets. Computers can get hacked and companies have always been concerned that employees leaving the company "carry" trade secrets out and eventually share it with the competitors, suppliers, and consultants. At Goodyear, this concern was so great that certain "rubber formulas" were kept in a safe and were only shared on a need-to-know basis. This concern also led to a ban on modems when personal computers debuted because some leaders believed that hackers would use them to steal our secrets. While this attitude presents challenges, it also illustrates the high value that companies place on their knowledge.

Knowledge Assessment before Experiment

Many companies do a systematic knowledge-gap assessment before every project, and this assessment together with their understanding of the risks involved lets them develop the optimum development plan with the least amount of waste possible. This starts in the feasibility phase and is repeated in further phases as the development of the new product progresses and the risk is reduced. When the knowledge is available to close the gap, it should be reused, thus minimizing experiments; if not, then it needs to be developed. Tom Laurich, lead engineer, explains that you can normally predict 90% of tire performance based on existing knowledge, and the remaining 10% is where the skills of the engineers come in.

When Goodyear started its lean product development process, we obtained much better visibility for our experiments or iterations (learning cycles), which, in turn, allowed us to identify if and when knowledge was being sought and/or created. For example, one challenging project for a new truck-tire line was many months behind schedule, and the team had built over 80 different sets of test tires without making noticeable progress. When I talked to the project manager, it became obvious that he was frustrated with the technical issues. He talked to his team and realized that they had only taken a trial-and-error approach and repeatedly found no improvement. It was obvious that they did not have the knowledge they needed.

The lesson that I learned through this was that teams of technical experts are not likely to come forward and admit that they do not have the knowledge that is needed. Scientists and engineers are afraid that people confuse lack of knowledge with missing skills. We called a timeout on this project and assessed our knowledge base. We learned that virtually all the engineers who had developed the previous generation of this type of tire had retired, both in the innovation center and at the plant, and their knowledge was not retained. The project manager brought back a few available retirees as consultants and organized a workshop to document their knowledge. After this exercise, it took just a few iterations and the new tire met the development targets. Now the "missing" knowledge is documented for further generations of engineers.

What is often overlooked is that knowledge is extremely perishable. Sometimes it perishes fast, other times it perishes slowly. It is hard to predict, and there is no mold growing on it to indicate that it has gone bad. Even companies that do a good job of adding new knowledge do not always take the old knowledge out on a regular basis. Knowledge management requires purging of old and obsolete knowledge from the documentation. One reason for this is that it is hard for engineers to identify obsolete knowledge. This is especially important but hard to do with tools like computer modeling and predictive applications that are based on knowledge; they must be updated routinely because obsolete knowledge can lead to confusion and stale, uncompetitive products.

Knowledge is created all the time in an R&D organization—in test results, prototypes, processes, people's heads, discussions, and so on. It must be identified, captured, easily shared, and replaced when it becomes obsolete. This means that neither a database nor in an individual's mind is the best place to store it. In the end, knowledge has to find its way into standards (or the best way to do things) and design tools to assure that the knowledge is locked in, properly shared, and, above all, used.

Knowledge in a Usable Form—Modeling and Design Tools

When I was a young engineer, technical report writing was taught at Goodyear. Engineers' skills and work were assessed based on the quality of their technical reports. There was even staff to read and catalogue the reports in a hard copy and later electronic library. Unfortunately, my colleagues and I rarely found anything that we were looking for in those troves—we would have had to read through hundreds of pages.

The easier the knowledge is to find, understand, and use, the more engineers will benefit from it. Engineers are not likely to undertake a "data mining" effort before every design or experiment, and they often are reluctant to search a database. I believe that this is because engineers like to summarize knowledge in "efficient" engineering languages, like formulas or functions, and prefer graphical displays of knowledge, such as tradeoff curves that plot one dependent variable in function of an independent variable (see *Graphic Knowledge—Tradeoff Curve*).

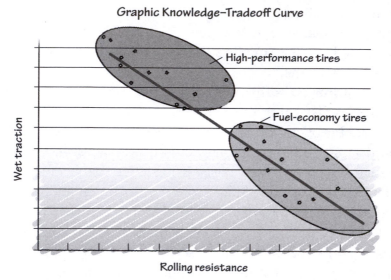

Graphic Knowledge–Tradeoff Curve

This tradeoff curve used at Goodyear documents the tradeoff between wet traction and rolling resistance of tread rubber. For a specified value of rolling resistance, we can determine whether we have the knowledge to deliver a wet traction product (traction specification falls within the bubble) or we must develop the knowledge (traction specification is outside the bubble).

Tradeoff curves are popular with many of the Japanese car manufacturers and have been described in many books about Toyota by Morgan/Liker, Sobek, and others. When I developed tires for Japanese car companies, I received constant requests for tradeoff curves: for example, tire weight versus fuel economy, or traction versus rolling resistance.

Many engineers at Goodyear used tradeoff curves on a regular basis and continue to do so. Tom Laurich, lead engineer, explains that tradeoff curves are more popular with young designers than seasoned designers, such as Tom, because he and other veterans have most of the relationships memorized and that they rarely need to look at the curves. Tom also explains that if the tire has been modeled on the computer, all possible curves and knowledge have already been applied by the computer and that the engineer usually only needs to fine-tune the product.

A disadvantage of tradeoff curves is that sometimes a large number of curves are needed to gain the knowledge an engineer needs. Authors who described the use of tradeoff curves at Toyota cite large folders full of tradeoff curves.[3] For example, the weight of the tire affects fuel consumption of a tire, and it also can affect the acceleration, steering, handling, and so on.

Due to the large number of curves, Ralf Okonieski, Goodyear senior associate, developed a multivariate computer system where he tried to describe most major tire performance attributes with three to five measurable parameters or tradeoff curves. Ralf says that generally at least 80% of every performance attribute can be described by three to five characteristics. For example, tire fuel economy can be explained by the tread rubber, the tire weight, and the width of the tire. Ralf also programmed the most important known interactions into the model. Ralf says that the engineers now have the possibility to just enter the design parameters into a spreadsheet and predict the tire performance based on all the known tradeoff curves and the interactions between them. This tells engineers whether the knowledge is available to meet the requirements or whether it needs to be developed.

Tradeoff curves are certainly one of the most user-friendly ways of making knowledge available to engineers. But like most knowledge management tools, tradeoff curves are only as good as the knowledge that is available and described in the curves or programmed in the computer. Nonetheless, the tool improves every day as new knowledge becomes available and incorporated. I believe the popularity of tradeoff curves will pick up, just as engineers initially had to get used to and embrace computer models. And at the heart of both trends is convincing engineers to trust existing knowledge.

Goodyear started investing into FEA computer models a long time ago and teamed up with Sandia National Laboratories on developing the computer code. Today at Goodyear most projects start with an elaborate FEA modeling effort. Set-based and designed experiments can be run efficiently, and the design space can be explored in detail at relatively high efficiency and with great speed. More than 50 years of Goodyear tire knowledge have been integrated into those models or the knowledge has been used to validate the models. In addition to the FEA models, custom-design tools based on CADAM or CATIA routines have been programmed based on the vast tire knowledge of the company.

Modeling has enabled a predictive approach to R&D, which is quite common today. For example, a few years ago, GM developed the Volt electric car—entirely new technology for the carmaker—first as a "virtual" prototype and experimented with that model before they made the first real prototype. GM gave Goodyear the virtual prototype, and the Goodyear engineers were able to develop a virtual tire for the virtual prototype. The Goodyear tires were fully developed before a prototype tire or a prototype vehicle was available. When GM had the first Volt prototype ready, we were able to supply real tires that needed only minor tuning, as the real vehicle prototype evolved.

A Little Knowledge Goes a Long Way

I used to coach high school students and they would participate in a balsa-wood bridge-building contest. The students assembled bridges from a kit provided by the organizer (balsa-wood sticks and glue). Bridges are assessed on strength (load at break) and weight. The load at break is divided by the weight, and the best "efficiency" wins.

My first year of coaching, I realized that no one in our school had any prior knowledge. But I found out that the organizer (University of Akron) had published the results from prior competitions on the web. Of course, there is high variability in the results because students are not very consistent in their craftsmanship and assembly. I presented the team with the graphic (see *Bridge-Building Contest Results*), and asked, "What bridge has the higher chance to win, a light bridge carrying less load or a heavier bridge carrying more load?" The students were quick to pick the lighter weight construction. I would never dare to show a graph like this to any of my engineering colleagues at Goodyear—they would reprimand me for the lack of a good correlation coefficient.

My team of high school students participated in this contest for 5 years in a row, and we swept prizes every time. Other schools copied our designs, but could never match the performance. To be fair, I should also mention that we experimented—another important factor in lean product development. Some students from other schools said their parents took our designs and optimized them by using FEA computer tools, but they never came close to achieving the results we did and wondered why.

Bridge-Building Contest Results

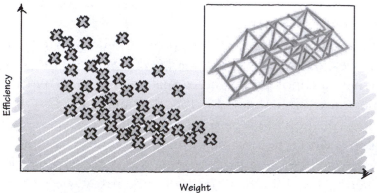

Efficiency = Load at break/weight

Our students also participated in a different balsa-wood contest, where we did not have any prior knowledge or data available. The students ranked in the bottom third the first time they competed, and it took them three contests to learn enough to move to the top third—but still far behind the winners, who had 15 years to develop knowledge.

Sharing/Not Sharing Knowledge

Regardless of the form in which knowledge is made available or where knowledge is stored, it is of no use unless people share it and use it. Sharing is not necessarily fostered in most companies. Engineers feel that they are more valuable to their company if they know more than their peers. In a system that ranks engineers against their peers for advancement and pay increases, their approach to sharing is not a surprise.

At a recent visit to a Toyota-inspired automotive supplier, I learned about the process of "yokoten," which we have not yet used at Goodyear. I understand this is a process that identifies any place in the company where new knowledge could apply. The process also assures that the new knowledge is effectively transferred to all the identified areas.

In our training programs, we like to run an activity where two teams perform the same exercise, but the one team gets to watch the other perform first. The team that performs the exercise second is always faster because they learned by watching the first team. We also run an exercise on quick learning cycles where, after each iteration, the teams share their findings and best practices. These exercises reinforce the fact that better solutions can be developed faster when knowledge is shared.

Sharing Speeds Progress

In *The High-Velocity Edge*,[4] Steven Spear explains that European cultures grew up close to each other and they learned from each other by copying the useful things they saw. Inventions like the wheel; war systems, including gunpowder; and agricultural know-how spread quickly through all the cultures. Isolated cultures, like the ones in Latin and South America or Australia, had no contact with each other and consequently they developed at a slower rate.

Knowledge versus Capability

Another one of our weaknesses in knowledge management, adds Steve Rohweder, director Consumer Tire Technology, North America, is an understanding of "capability" to complement knowledge. Steve says people sometimes confuse knowledge with capability: the two have to be considered together to make a good assessment of the development requirements and the project risk, timing, and resources.

Capability can mean many things: Do we have the means to produce a given product on our standard equipment, or do we need to purchase new equipment? Do we have a capable process? Do we have the right talent and specific skills that we need? Do we even have the resources, the funding, and cross-functional support to deliver on the project goals? Steve says that although we often assess the knowledge needed correctly for a new project, we sometimes misjudge the capabilities because they depend on other parallel projects where the visibility of interactions is not well known.

Capturing Knowledge Using Hansei

Often learning starts with a good reflection ("hansei" in Japanese means reflection and is an important piece of Toyota's success). Hansei is a way of identifying "what went well and what did not go so well," what new knowledge was generated, and how to apply the new knowledge gained going forward. This, too, is an area where our culture sometimes interferes with good knowledge management because as much can be learned from the failures as from the successes.

If we would take a survey at Goodyear or other Western companies today on lean practices, reflection would probably receive one of the lowest scores. Why?

- Reflection includes what went wrong and people do not like bad news, which can happen when you reflect on past projects or events, and individuals often associate the bad news with the person who reports it ("shoot the messenger").
- "Positive" thinking does not encourage people to write down what did not work so well.
- Reflection comes, obviously, at the end of a project or event, and everybody is eager to start the next assignment; some may already have been reassigned and have no time left to look back.

- When reflecting, people are prone to attribute mistakes to a "person" rather than a process or a product standard, and they assign blame (good people in bad processes look like bad people).
- There is a lot of competition between project managers and functional leaders for advancement, and so nobody wants to be associated with something that was not done perfectly.
- Leaders do not see the benefits of a reflection and they do not encourage attention to it.
- Reflection takes a lot of discipline, practice, coaching, and time.

A few years ago, Goodyear's top management had asked for a formal reflection on three recent new product launches. First, there was a lot of fighting about who would lead the reflection. Several months later, the agreed-upon leader of the reflection gave up in frustration. Our culture obviously was not ready at that time.

I believe in running a feedback or reflection event after every project milestone or a reflection on the launch and the first year of product performance. For hansei to work, there has to be a level of trust and there must not be negative consequences for surfacing problems (just as with people in the factory who pull an andon cord).

I also end every event, every kaizen event, workshop, and training class with a hansei event. I am still amazed by the improvement ideas I have been able to apply to the training classes based on feedback from students. I could never have come up with that stuff on my own. Here are a few lessons learned:

- Rather than asking for "plus" and "minus" items in the reflection, specifically ask, "What should we keep doing," and request "suggestions for improvement." This way you get suggestions that you can quickly act upon.
- "Interview" people individually to get more clarification; this also gives you an opportunity to show appreciation for their feedback.
- Thank people for pointing out problems and reassure them that it is OK to point out what they did not like.

Remember it is knowledge not emotions you seek. A Japanese elder once commented, "The first time you get angry is the last time you hear the truth." As proof of the cultural issue with the "bearer of bad news," many seasoned Goodyear engineers, like myself, can show the scars from years of trying to publicly reflect on mistakes that were made. Let us just say that positive reflection turned into painting bulls eyes on our backs. When this occurs, eventually people will be reluctant to ever be associated with a problem. Of course, this does not mean there are no problems. Meaningful reflection and knowledge capture become impossible when people associate problems with a witch-hunt rather than with an inadequate process or standard.

Goodyear is well ahead of the curve with knowledge management, but we have areas in need of improvement. Rick Scavuzzo, director Tire Engineering, notes two of these: our knowledge management does not capture enough of what does *not work* and what we *do not know.* Documenting "the good stuff" while rarely mentioning failures are characteristics of most companies' knowledge management, not just at Goodyear. John Dix, the codirector of the Center for Operational Excellence at The Ohio State University, told me about a successful leader in a big company who had his personal "good practice book," to which he attributed a lot of his success. John wondered why the leader also did not keep a "book of failures."

Rick says that another weakness of Goodyear's knowledge management is that even when people use the knowledge that we have, they often do not reflect back after an experiment and document where more knowledge was needed but not available. They may not need that knowledge for the current experiment, but the documentation may help identify areas where knowledge must be developed in the future.

Preserving Knowledge

Once knowledge has been developed, captured, and put in a usable form, it is important to think about how it is preserved and put to good use. At Goodyear, we have used the following means:

- Apply the product knowledge into standards, such as design standards, standard operating procedures, playbooks, or design rules. I believe this is the best approach for product knowledge.
- Summarize lots of knowledge in various forms, which make the knowledge relatively accessible and digestible by a large number of people.
- Incorporate knowledge into finite element computer models or the design tools. I believe that this, too, is an excellent way of preserving knowledge.
- Summarize knowledge in sets of tradeoff curves or multivariate systems that allow performance predictions.

■ Summarize process knowledge in playbooks, operations manuals, or similar repertoires.

Sometimes the best way of preserving, sharing, and reusing knowledge is the simplest and oldest: communicate person to person. Rick Scavuzzo comments, "My biggest problem with knowledge management is that people do not use it enough. It is not complicated, ask the person who sits next to you, run your ideas by the folks at the lunch table." All engineers should be encouraged to consult the senior or most experienced members of the organization, who have a wealth of technical knowledge and also know the company and its products well. Senior experts also should be consulted for all major technical decisions, like gate reviews, technical releases, or assessments of new ideas or opportunities. Companies should also make efforts to retain the senior experts as long as they can (e.g., as part-time employees or consultants) and make sure their knowledge is properly transferred when they retire. This will not be accomplished by an exit interview that is put in a file. People with the right education, background, and responsibilities should be learning from experienced staff on a regular basis.

Encouraging the Use of Knowledge

Not only can sharing knowledge be difficult, but I have seen engineers reticent to seek out existing knowledge. Young engineers, in particular, do not like to seek the advice of more experienced engineers. Here, again, they probably see it as a sign of weakness. And digging around for knowledge is about as popular as library searches were in college. It is more fun to build and test a new set of prototypes than to search for and analyze "old" data or knowledge.

What I tell young engineers is that their creativity should be used in creating new knowledge, not replicating existing knowledge. This aspect of knowledge management might be the biggest challenge at Goodyear and it is probably an equally large challenge at other companies. We have an excellent system of computer models and multivariate tradeoff curves, but we have a hard time convincing the engineers to use the system. Maybe there is a trust issue; maybe engineers need to *understand* what they use—they understand simple tradeoff curves, but they are suspicious of a computer system that looks like a "black box."

My experiences at Goodyear and those of others throughout industry indicate that generally only about one-third of all available knowledge is reused. That is unfortunate because the best knowledge is of no use unless people use it. We have seen many reasons why seeking out knowledge is not popular among engineers and where there is a lack of trust in the use of knowledge-based computer tools. There are a few good practices that can encourage the reuse of knowledge:

- Managers and leaders must ask for it and reassure themselves in gemba walks and design reviews that engineers took advantage of reusing existing knowledge.
- Knowledge search and reuse must be a formal part of project plans, playbooks, checklists, and so on.
- Engineers must be trained in the value of knowledge reuse. This training also should include the understanding and validation of the knowledge embedded in the design and modeling tools.
- Personal performance management should include knowledge creation and reuse management.

Lean R&D Principle: Learn to manage your knowledge well.

In addition to profitable value streams, R&D creates reusable knowledge. R&D organizations have invested a lot in the knowledge they created. Companies should make an effort to preserve and reuse the knowledge they have accumulated. Reusing existing knowledge saves money and makes the development process faster, more efficient, and more predictable, and it also reduces the risk.

Knowledge management starts with developing, identifying, and capturing new knowledge. The knowledge must be put into a usable form, so it can be easily retrieved and understood. The knowledge should be put into standards and design tools to assure it is reused and it is never lost. Ideally, R&D should only run experiments or undertake projects to generate new knowledge.

At Goodyear: By managing our knowledge well, Goodyear has saved a substantial amount of money and years of time by not duplicating knowledge that already exists. It also helped us design quality products and superior processes. At Goodyear, we lock the new knowledge in by updating our standards. The knowledge is also integrated into our design and modeling tools. Additionally, we are improving the knowledge-capture process. Experiments are only run when new knowledge is required, and it cannot be obtained by other means (i.e., purchasing it).

The Knowledge Management Process

My experiences in Goodyear have led me to conclude that there are eight fundamental steps that an R&D organization should follow in order to manage knowledge. A modest amount of success with all of the steps is required to become a "learning organization." When managing knowledge, Goodyear has relied heavily on computer modeling and FEA modeling, but you do not need to be using these tools to progress through the eight steps.

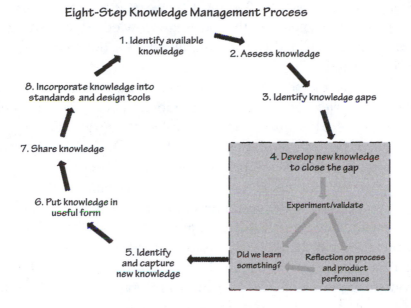

Eight-Step Knowledge Management Process

1. Identify available knowledge
2. Assess knowledge
3. Identify knowledge gaps
4. Develop new knowledge to close the gap
   - Experiment/validate
   - Did we learn something?
   - Reflection on process and product performance
5. Identify and capture new knowledge
6. Put knowledge in useful form
7. Share knowledge
8. Incorporate knowledge into standards and design tools

(1) Identify available knowledge

Start a research project or a learning cycle with a belief that you may not need to reinvent the wheel. What do you or someone somewhere already know? There are a lot of ways to find out:

■ Consult standards, tradeoff curves, or any other form of knowledge repertoire.

■ Talk to experts, senior engineers, and people who may have done this before.

■ Search the internet/literature for knowledge that other individuals and companies have shared.

- Benchmark other products and technologies.
- Talk to your suppliers, contractors, and customers.

You may have computer predictions, models, and design tools that will tell you what knowledge you have in your company. *All* existing knowledge is or should normally be integrated in those tools and models. The rapid growth of computing power has helped to increase accuracy and validity of the models.

(2) Assess knowledge

Whatever knowledge is available must be assessed. Can the targets of the new product be met with the existing knowledge? Can additional customer value be created beyond the targets? Or does new knowledge have to be created?

The simplest assessment comes from consulting with company experts, consultants, suppliers, and so on. Good tradeoff curves can also help with an assessment because for every X value, they show the range of Y values that can be achieved based on available knowledge. The same is true for computer models and predictions: Use the best standard product for the application and model for the specified conditions. The model will tell you if you can meet the customer requirements with current knowledge and where new knowledge is required. But remember that you cannot get better output than the data used to build the models and tradeoff curves. This includes error margins in the data that goes into the model.

Of course, experiments can be run or prototypes can be built to make a knowledge assessment. These experiments or prototypes should be simple and focus on the knowledge-assessment areas.

(3) Identify knowledge gaps

If you believe that all the knowledge needed is available, include it in the design of the product and proceed, if necessary, with the validation of the product. Use test results to update the knowledge and the validity of the models (i.e., the new data point must be added to the tradeoff curves).

If you feel that knowledge needed is not available—a knowledge gap—learning cycles or other means must be planned to develop or obtain the knowledge.

Knowledge gaps should not be confused with the capability gaps, manufacturing issues, or gaps in distribution, marketing, sales, and so on.

These gaps need to be addressed as well, but for the purposes of R&D, knowledge gaps are the critical pieces of technical information needed to move forward with a project.

Every knowledge gap should have a risk associated with it. For example, you can assess the risk by how far the prediction was away from the target or how far the points were away from the tradeoff curve. The FMEA approach works well here, too. To manage the risk, make sure the right amount of experiments are planned to assure that valid knowledge is created. The number and variety of experiments should correlate with the risk. Too often the number of experiments is determined by the amount of time or money available and then reduced by the interferences that occur.

(4) Develop new knowledge to close the gap

Scientific experiments, learning cycles, laboratory experiments, and so on can be performed to develop new knowledge and close the gap. For example, new materials can be evaluated in the laboratory or prototypes can be built and tested. Instead of experiments, computer models or predictions can sometimes be used to generate new knowledge, especially when interpolations between known relationships are all that is needed. Good experimental design and statistical evaluation makes experimentation efficient and accurate. Many models and experiments may be needed to close gaps.

When new knowledge is discovered, verification may be needed. Experiments may show that a technology is not ready, gaps cannot be closed in the required time frame, or the targets need to be renegotiated. Experiments that fail to generate new knowledge or meet the targets also generate knowledge.

Experiments can also be run to validate the computer prediction or run because new knowledge is required to improve the model. Regardless of why it is created, the new knowledge will eventually be incorporated into the product. More knowledge may become available later when the product is on the market and customer feedback becomes available.

New knowledge is not limited to product design. Experiments also can be run to develop a new capability or to improve processes. New knowledge does not only come from your own experiments. It may also be found in publications, books, and seminars or comes from reflections by the stakeholders. These reflections are especially popular when there is no good data available. Reflections should be held after every set of experiments, after major milestones, after the launch, and after the product has been on the market long enough to have meaningful feedback. The best knowledge comes from the many forms of customer feedback.

Some of the best knowledge can turn up unexpectedly—every experiment that yields a highly unexpected result should be further investigated.

In addition to creating new knowledge, you sometimes can buy it (i.e., hire a consultant or outsource for it) and/or work with a college or university to develop the knowledge.

(5) Identify and capture new knowledge

Before you can capture new knowledge, you must identify and validate it. At Goodyear, we like to use a peer validation process to identify and validate new knowledge, but there are many other good practices.

Knowledge is captured by the functions responsible for the knowledge, for example, tire design captures the knowledge about their discipline, and operations captures knowledge about cross-functional processes.

There are many events in a lean development process that may hint at new knowledge, such as design reviews, gemba walks, and huddles. Engineers, managers, and leaders must know that they are responsible for the knowledge capture in these situations, and take proper action.

Some companies employ "knowledge workers" to improve the odds that all knowledge gets captured. The knowledge workers also scan research publications, help with benchmarking, and attend conferences.

(6) Put knowledge in a useful form

If knowledge is scattered throughout the organization, it is of limited use. Knowledge must be summarized and put in a form that makes it easy to find and to use. Engineers like to use common engineering tools to describe knowledge, like formulas, curves, and plots. Engineers also like correlations, but they strive for *perfect* correlation factors. Remind them that a knowledge trend often is all that is needed.

Depending on the knowledge, popular useful forms include

- Tradeoff curves
- Models

- Manuals
- Drawings
- Graphs/spider charts
- Multivariate models

New knowledge may be nothing more than one point on a tradeoff curve or a few modified lines in a computer program. New knowledge may do nothing, but confirm a trend that was already captured in a tradeoff curve. Even in those cases, the knowledge can improve the correlation or the validation of the model.

Knowledge cannot be used if it is not also easy to find. It should be so obvious that people trip over it. That is important because using existing knowledge is not always popular with engineers, especially young engineers, and knowledge may need to hit them in face in order for them to use it instead of running fresh, unnecessary experiments. At Goodyear, a lot of effort is spent in helping people find knowledge by developing tools, training, and creating awareness.

(7) Share the knowledge

Sharing knowledge is not a common practice in many organizations. People feel they are of value to the organization for what they know, and if they share what they know, they diminish their value. On the other side of the knowledge-sharing relationship, engineers are often reluctant to accept and use new or existing knowledge. Both use and sharing should be encouraged by leaders, incorporated into personal performance management, and exhibited in formal knowledge-sharing events.

Japanese companies use a process called "yokoten." This process identifies any place in the company where new knowledge can be applied and then assures that the sharing effectively takes place.

(8) Incorporate knowledge into standards and design tools

The most efficient way of sharing knowledge and assuring it is properly reused is by making it part of the current best way—incorporating or "locking" knowledge into standards, computer models and design tools, playbooks, and so on.

When knowledge is within a standard, engineers apply it by adhering to the standard or taking on the responsibility of proving a better standard exists.

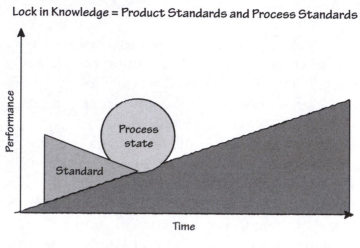

Use of Product Standards

Today's standardization, instead of being a barricade against improvement, is the necessary foundation on which tomorrow's improvement will be based. If you think of standardization as the best that you know today, but which is to be improved tomorrow, then you get somewhere. But if you think of standards as confining, then progress stops.

Henry Ford
Today and Tomorrow[5]

A good knowledge management system in R&D locks in the learning in a standard, either a product standard or a process standard like a playbook. Goodyear is certainly not unique in this approach. Many companies keep these standards in a safe or a safe place to make sure they never fall into the wrong hands.

The extreme secrecy of standards, though, is often unnecessary. Retirees who consult with competitors notice that the competitors have their own knowledge and standards, which, taken out of context (their systems), are often not meaningful. In addition, competitors rigorously benchmark our products, so they are well aware of a lot of our knowledge without fingering through our standards.

Every new design starts with the best knowledge from the standards. Designs that are outside the common standard require extra testing, and those that prove to be superior become the new standard and replace the previous standard. This methodical approach also limits the escalation of equivalent or similar designs in the lineup. If "similarly good" designs accumulate, they really add no value to the company—they just add cost due to complexity and force engineers to make unnecessary decisions.

John Roman, Goodyear RDE&Q global project manager, and responsible for the maintenance of our design standards, describes the process that we use to document the standards and to keep them current:

- *Usage:* Design standards are documented and communicated, as we develop or discover them to prevent everyone from relearning the same thing. Many have evolved over 50-plus years of tire design. Some standards are must-haves, some are specific to what we know works or what is compatible with our manufacturing processes, and many are best practices along with ranges or options that we know work based on experience.

    Except for the "must haves," designers can still go outside the rules, but they take on the responsibility to ensure whatever they design will work based on additional testing, processing trials, endorsement by peers, and higher approval escalation. This going outside the box requires extra effort on their part, but is encouraged and results in new discoveries and better standards once proven.
- *Maintenance:* Our design standards are constantly being updated by a process to include new but proven technology or construction (new materials, new manufacturing process, etc.). The updating process of "suggestion" and "peer validation" is very similar to the processes used by popular web encyclopedias like Wikipedia.

The other functions that participate in the Goodyear product development process (e.g., material science, mold engineering, testing) use a similar process to maintain and update their standards. A process similar to the design standards is used for the process and work standards (see *Chapter 5*).

Lean R&D Principle: Develop product standards and use them to lock in knowledge.

Product standards define the best known design of a product. Every new product design should start with that standard. Since the performance of the standard product is largely known, testing is often limited to government, regulatory, and validation tests. If a designer has a new idea that is outside the standard, for example, a new material, experiments must be run. Prototypes must be built and tested. If the tests prove that the new material is superior to the one specified in the standard, a process is kicked off that includes the new material in the standard.

Standards lock in knowledge, and continuous improvement is built upon standards—setting and consistently achieving one standard, and then developing a better, more advanced standard. Responsibility for the management of the standards must be established and standards must be updated on a regular basis.

Standards are an important part of lean product development, although you must be careful about where and to what extent standards are applied or you could inadvertently inhibit improvement and innovation. Standards should have rigid and flexible components, and there must be a process to allow innovation beyond standards.

At Goodyear: We have product standards based on our best knowledge, but the standards, nonetheless, allow us to push the envelope with new ideas and innovative concepts. The standards are updated with new knowledge and the changes are communicated. (In addition to the product standards, there are process and work standards at Goodyear, which will be discussed in Chapter 5.*) We use a suggest-and-validate system to update many of Goodyear's standards.*

Knowledge Management Office

Many companies, including Goodyear, have created knowledge management offices (KMO). Dean Testa, Testa, manager RDE&Q Knowledge Management Office, runs Goodyear's KMO. He sees his major role as leading the change from a "need to know" habit to a "need to share" culture. The strategy he has developed can be simply stated as "collect and connect"—collecting the right knowledge and connecting people via that knowledge.

Goodyear's KMO utilizes a balance between knowledge projects and outreach programs. Examples of knowledge projects that develop best practices and standards include Lessons Learned, Knowledge Network Mapping & Transfer, Intranet Portal, and "Findability." The KMO conducts numerous outreach programs to teach concepts, raise awareness, and gather feedback, including learning labs and global events.

Dean is trying to move Goodyear from an acting to a learning organization. The approach of using both projects and outreach is making a difference as documented by a maturity assessment that shows improvement year over year.

Stage Gates and the Product Creation Process

Goodyear got involved with the stage-gate® concept in 2004. Robert Cooper came to Goodyear to help implement the process and to train our people. Cooper had popularized the approach in the early years of the twenty-first century. The method has also been called a "phase-gate process" or "phase-gate model." All the terms, more or less, refer to techniques by which processes are separated into stages or phases, with a gate that leads to the next stage or phase. Based on information required when a gate is reached (viability, needs/business case, risks, resources, results, etc.), continuation of the process is decided.

Goodyear uses gated processes throughout R&D. We use the name "stages" for the product development process and "phases" for the technology development part.

Unfortunately, the use of stage gates was another change within Goodyear that did not stick, at least not right away. Most people at Goodyear agreed with the concept of gating, but support was far from unanimous. The folks in marketing were not comfortable with the concept because it required them to stop asking for *everything* and instead made them prioritize their needs earlier in the design cycle. The buy-in from the engineers was also not good because the system was advertised as a "project killer," and metrics were created to track how many projects were "killed." (Engineers are not likely to invest their time and energy into a project to see it killed, regardless of the reason.) Manufacturing folks were also uneasy with the idea because they had to "agree" to a concept early on, despite lacking sufficient information to really assess what they were getting into. All involved were uncomfortable with the fact that now everybody would "formally" know about a project, meaning it would be hard to plead ignorance later.

Despite the various objections, the process might have initially stuck had our rollout been better. Some meetings on minor projects were held with little participation, and projects were mostly rubber-stamped without the commitment of all stakeholders. People were simply overwhelmed with the bureaucracy that the system created, and the number of new meetings added to the schedule. Eventually, the concept died away. In hindsight, we were trying to avoid what the process brings to the table: collaboration of all stakeholders.

In 2005, Goodyear hired its first lean consultant (Porsche Consulting) to help develop a better product innovation process. The Porsche staff made a strong push once again for a good, collaborative, gating process. But the Porsche process, like that brought in by Cooper, was still bureaucratic and caused many delays: many meetings to get everybody together and reams of documents required to move through the gates.

Also in 2005, a new expert was hired by the business side to help Goodyear bring projects to the market faster and more successfully. Now the business and the whole value chain were involved in helping to build a better process, and the outcome was a well-defined gating process. This time around, though, marketing took ownership of the process, and slowly all other stakeholders joined in and they made it work. The process was much simpler and less bureaucratic than the processes proposed by either Cooper or Porsche. More efficient meetings were held on a regular cadence. Three things helped this third try at stages and gates succeed:

1. The strike in 2006 purged most projects out of the system—a case of force majeure that was accepted by the engineers, marketing, and manufacturing.
2. Product roadmaps were established and communicated clearly—what comes in and *what goes out*. What was going out was always a sticky point with everybody, especially marketing.
3. Marketing was eventually assigned to administrate the process, which assured their buy-in.

Our gating process for product development—eventually to be known as the "product creation process" (PCP)—is built around adding good value and avoiding traditional pitfalls. It currently is a six-gate process:

1. Stage—Initial ideas and basic feasibility
   Gate—The idea is viable
2. Stage—Market feasibility and basic technical feasibility
   Gate—Idea is feasible from a marketing and technical standpoint and we have a plan to develop the product (see *Success Assured*)
3. Stage—Technical development and marketing data

Gate—Technical release

4. Stage—Manufacturing/industrialization
   Gate—Release to production
5. Stage—Ramp up and launch
   Gate—Review initial sales and react if needed
6. Stage—Initial year of selling
   Gate—Sales and launch issues

A lot of lean scholars criticize the gating process as being wasteful, since it creates waiting time and sometimes overprocessing. They also point to the fact that there is no research that links a gating process with profitability. Despite criticisms from the lean experts, I see some form of gating at virtually every good company that I benchmark for lean process, although they may not refer to it as a "stage-gate process." Most companies use their own version of a gating process, like the one used by Scania and described by Allen Ward and Durward Sobek.[6] Through nearly a decade of usage, we have validated a number of advantages and disadvantages with the Goodyear gating process. And, like other companies, we have made the process work by keeping hold of its advantages and discarding or remedying the disadvantages:

Advantages	Disadvantages (based on original form)
• Achieves cross-functional collaboration, commitment, and alignment • Adds cadence to a process • Provides visibility for projects and their major milestones • Increases focus on value stream and profitability • Facilitates critical cross-functional decisions and risk management • Assures input from all parties involved, and nobody can claim not having known • Increases awareness of responsibilities and accountability	• Fairly bureaucratic • Requires all requirements complete and documented before moving to the gate • Batch process often with a lot of waiting • Overly controlling • Does not facilitate concurrent development • Requires a lot more discipline because meetings must be attended by the right people

Like many companies, Goodyear empowered the process users to make the modifications to remedy disadvantages/issues identified above. Improvements include

■ Late start, with decisions made as late as possible in the design cycle (see *Chapters 5 and 6*)

■ Simple and relevant information for decisions (80% of information is often enough)
■ Manage exceptions appropriately, especially at gate 2
■ Focus on adding value in short, focused meetings—focus on product and timing issues
■ Allow for concurrent work
■ Split R&D work into several processes, each with a different focus (e.g., products, technologies, innovation)
■ Regular/weekly gate meetings to allow decisions every week

Success Assured

An important milestone that must be understood and managed properly is the second gate of the PCP—the Success Assured gate. The term "Success Assured" was coined by Ron Marsiglio of Knowledge/PD, and I first heard it in 2013.[7] Success Assured for Goodyear means that we will have a product; we may not know all the properties, but we will have a launch at the agreed upon time.

This milestone splits the development process into a creative frontend and a backend that is all about execution. Steve Rohweder, director Consumer Tire Technology, North American Tire, and a gatekeeper, says, "My job is to create a profitable value stream from here on out in collaboration with the other stakeholders (marketing, sales, production), and I need the confidence at gate 2 that this is assured."

Success Assured means there will be delivery, the risk is known, there will be desirable return, and the project fits our strategy (customer, distribution, technology, manufacturing, value to customer, value to consumer, etc.). The gatekeepers may, however, balance product features with project timing or product cost.

Depending on the company, there is a different relative amount of work in the frontend versus the backend before or after Success Assured. Companies that produce or market mature consumer products spend a relatively lower amount of resources on the frontend. Goodyear, like most automotive companies, spends 20% to 30% on the frontend. High-tech commercial products with a small number of customers, such as medical and aerospace, spend a relatively high amount of resources on the frontend.

Key *cross-functional* decisions are made at specific gates, and the information needed for those decisions is provided at gate meetings. There is minimum bureaucracy and little extra work required of engineers—empowered technical project managers and enterprise project managers sit in the meetings together with the executives of all critical functions.

At Goodyear, work is normally not stopped waiting for the next gate meeting. The technical director can grant exceptions for spending money on a project ahead of a gate meeting. In this way, he takes a small risk, but the work can continue before a gate meeting that would authorize it to proceed; technical directors have a good idea what projects pass a gate, and which ones do not, especially if they communicate with other stakeholders.

All development work is on a "late start" schedule, which means that gate decisions happen as late as possible, with the best information possible, and at a point when changes have diminished and the decision is quite clear and easier to make. This often puts the gate meetings on the critical path, and all stakeholders respect the deadline for gate meetings. Due to regular huddle meetings between all stakeholders, there now is enough trust and spirit of collaboration to make the gate process efficient and value added.

Gatekeeper Steve describes the stage-gate approach as rigorous, cross-functional project management designed to achieve both timing and objectives of a new product development project. His role as a gatekeeper includes reviewing the proposal or project status, challenging the assumption and confidence levels, and ensuring risk management steps. He collaborates with his business partners to ensure a profitable value stream.

One common thread through all the companies and their customized stage-gate processes is that it brings cross-functional stakeholders to the table and creates alignment and at least some level of collaboration. But collaboration is not guaranteed or easy.

One initial common problem with gate processes is that stakeholders may show up regularly at meetings and say nothing until their commitment is required to proceed—and then they upset the apple cart. Everything changes at the moment when, for example, manufacturing needs to start producing the product. All stakeholders at Goodyear now understand that they have "skin in the game" from the first gate on and they are responsible to be engaged throughout the process and that commitment is not optional. For example, manufacturing now runs process trials much earlier to avoid surprises during the industrialization phase. This way the process also assures concurrent development.

Jeff McElfresh, former Goodyear Business Operations manager, helped develop and run our stage-gate process. He says it made a big difference when the business case was added to the process, which then meant that marketing had to justify the market viability of the product, study the impact on production, justify R&D funds, and look at cost to release, cost of supply, and so on. Other business criteria that are used and updated for all gates are net present value, portfolio view (strategically and by brand), need for capital, share of new products, and profitability index.

Like most who have managed gating processes, Jeff says the challenge is to minimize waiting. This is why most gate decisions at Goodyear can be made when 80% of the information is available, which prevents a slowdown. Projects can still be changed after the gate if the late information requires that decision. He also admits that stakeholders occasionally skip the reflective fifth and sixth gates (product launch and sales and launch issues). This occurs not necessarily because they are afraid of identifying what went wrong (although that does happen), but because they are too busy working on the next project. "The best information that we get out of the reflection gates is that we learn to make a better business case for future decisions and that is done regardless if we have a formal reflection or not."

For me, the "acid test" that validated our stage-gate process involved how it changed the dynamic between R&D, sales, and customers. Before gates, we accepted *every* request from *every* external customer. This was based on the principle that the customer is always right and that *the answer is "yes," regardless what the question was.*

The moment of truth came with a customer who sold tires to luxury car dealers, which would then switch out the higher-end tires for the OEM tires. This was a good niche market because the dealer was able to offer a tire different from the OEM tire, since the dealer was not bound by the government requirements for fuel economy. In one case, the Goodyear account executive *immediately* committed to a new project prior to the stage-gate process beginning. A few weeks later, the project was rejected at gate 2 for good business reasons. Despite the verbal commitment to the customer, the project remained "unapproved," and the account executive had to call the customer and apologize—there would be no product.

Today our account executives know better and make sure the project is approved (this includes making sure that resources and capacity are available) before making a commitment to a customer. As important, the internal process is quick enough so that no sales opportunities are missed. The process has not hurt sales, and it certainly has not hurt profitability.

Prior to the gating process, when sales were not as expected, Goodyear nearly always dropped the price, says Jeff. We changed the process, and now try to find out why sales are low. In many cases, it is because customers are simply not ready to take the product due to excess inventory; it is not that the product does not perform as expected. This illustrates the importance of making gate 5 decisions at 3 months into the sales cycle, when there is still an opportunity to quickly adjust the sales or marketing strategy or the annual operating plan (AOP). Jeff says that before the gating process, complete business cases were not done for new products and many of them ended up being unprofitable. We did not have a good process to weed out the unprofitable ones and we continued to take on business based on momentum. Today, the process is much more complete and transparent, and we have nearly 100% profitable new projects.

Based on the success of the gating process with product development (PCP), Goodyear extended the concept in 2008 to its technology creation process (TCP), which is complemented by our innovation creation processes (ICPs) and business model innovation (BMI) activities. All processes are global, except for the PCP, which is a regional process.

Technology Creation Process

Before Goodyear had a TCP, any engineer was able to start a project as long as the engineer was able to get a manager's signature on a mold or a test order. Our system was stuffed with good and bad projects, and we missed out on opportunities because we had no resources to quickly jump on potential good ones. Deciding what to work on is an important and difficult task specific to R&D (and covered in more detail in *Chapter 6*).

Although there must be a certain generosity to let engineers tinker with new ideas, there is a time when a decision has to be made to determine whether the project is worth continuing. If the project continues past the explorative stage, it must turn into a managed process. The TCP is not designed with the same profit-focused criteria that apply to the PCP. It is designed to pursue the right ideas and opportunities for effective technology development.

The first criterion in the TCP is "Is it relevant? Does the idea have a sound technical basis?" The second criterion is customer value

(Is it reasonable?); the third and fourth criteria are company fit (Is it real?) and viable path forward (Is it ready?). They should be considered in that order—from the criteria that is least controllable to the one that is most controllable.

When the TCP was started, there were hundreds of projects in progress at Goodyear, and the process to sort them out was trying, to say the least. Many highly unpopular decisions had to be made, and managers and directors almost had to shut all projects down and start over.

When we were getting TCP underway, Chris Helsel, at the time Goodyear director Global Technology Projects, said the best way to make all the technology projects visible was to create a simple gate process where all the projects had to be reviewed on a cadence and money was allocated in small chunks, based on the progress that was made.

Projects can enter TCP from many sources—from ICP/BMI or from an individual idea an engineer may have explored or an idea that came from open innovation (e.g., contributions from customers, suppliers, outside organizations). In order for an idea to enter the phase gate from the discovery phase, it is judged by two criteria:

1. *Project must fit into targeted market segments.* There must be a focus on where Goodyear chooses to compete.
2. *Knowledge gaps must be identified.* We like to use the A3 process to identify the knowledge gaps and come up with countermeasures to close those gaps.

When a project enters TCP, a project manager is appointed who owns the project charter. The project manager works closely with the inventor or the source of the idea, but the project from then on out is managed according to the Goodyear project management playbook or standards.

One challenge that Goodyear had with new ideas and new technology was to get the stakeholders on board and committed before the R&D money was spent. Stakeholders could be from marketing, manufacturing, the business unit, or R&D itself. Stakeholders took the approach, "Keep developing … when you are done we will tell you if we like it." Similarly, production would say, "We will see if we can manufacture it when it is fully developed." Too many projects were not "picked up" at the given time by the stakeholders for many reasons, and a lot of money was wasted. Today, stakeholders are gradually brought on board during phase

1 and no project moves through phase 2 without a solid commitment of the stakeholders—if the commitment cannot be achieved, the project will not get funded any further.

ICP and BMI

The ICP and BMI are not gated processes. They link the customers and the markets to the technology.

The ICP collects ideas and concepts from many sources, including the regional businesses and puts them into the appropriate category.

- *Step* innovation is largely incremental innovation. It deals with known technology and existing customers. Examples of this by Goodyear would be a major breakthrough in fuel economy or the traction of tires. Other industry examples would be four-razor blade shavers or a car that parks itself.
- *Jump* innovation is product innovation that still relies on existing business models (customer-centric innovation), but uses new technology. Goodyear examples would be run-flat tires or sealants. Other industry examples would be flat screen TVs and the Dyson vacuum cleaner.
- *Leap* innovation is disruptive innovation that requires new technology and a completely new business model. A Goodyear example would be a nonpneumatic tire that only is sold online. Other industry examples would be Amazon (especially drone delivery of products) and smartphones.

The ICP also decides how much money to allocate and spend based on a process that prioritizes ideas within each of the three buckets. It is very important to have a well-balanced portfolio of all three categories. Although leap innovation may be the most attractive from a business standpoint, it is the most risky as well as the most resource- and time-consuming category. Jump and step innovation are required to create regular revenue and to at least to keep up with the competition.

Romain Hansen, director Global Technology Projects, explains that the ICP originally tried to come up with lots of new ideas to feed the TCP. But as with every unfocused idea-generation process, it ended up with too many ideas and not a lot of value.

Today the ICP uses a more focused approach to collect global input. The regions do their homework and then a core group meets in every region, visits customers, meets with consumers, and talks to people in the plants. They come up with a focused and prioritized list of innovation opportunities for the region. Once a year, a smaller team with representation from all the regions meets at headquarters and combines all the regional requirements. They develop a short list of needs, problems, and opportunities. In 2014, the list had eight areas of innovation, such as run-flat mobility systems and tire electronics.

BMI studies disruptive innovation and focuses on new customers, sometimes new technology, and sometimes a new business approach. The innovation can be developed organically (i.e., with company resources and knowledge). It may require a business integration (from inside or outside) or it may require acquisitions or outside resources.

Neither the ICP nor the BMI process may have the knowledge or data needed to develop a disruptive innovation concept. In that case, small projects are assigned to the TCP to determine feasibility or even develop rough prototypes or run small experiments.

Examples of recent output from ICP/BMI and interaction with TCP include

- Air maintenance: automatic air maintenance in the tire for convenience and fuel economy
- Biomaterials: bio-isoprene, soybean oil, and silica from rice husk ash
- Intelligent tire: tire with a computer chip
- Spring tire: tire without air

To some people, all these processes may appear to be "processomania" or overprocessing. This definition of processes, however, is critical in a lean environment. If everybody does work their own way, it is inefficient and little can be learned. A process establishes a baseline based on the best current knowledge and it can be improved and standardized from there. The processes described above have been improved many times since they were established, and I would be the first to admit that there is a lot of improvement yet to come. Together with the process, clear ownership and responsibilities must be defined.

Lean R&D Principle: Define your processes and responsibilities, so you can improve them as you learn.

Process capability development starts by establishing and documenting a process. It really does not matter too much how good the process is when you start, just that you do have a process. Once the process is stable and the ownership and responsibilities are established, it must be developed and improved and the gains locked in with new standards. This should happen on every level of the organization, functionally and cross-functionally. There must be standard processes for leaders, too, because leaders need to learn and improve too.

Without a stable process, it is very hard to find a current state and the root cause of a problem because there is too much variability. It is not hard to get started: pick the best process you have at the time, document and validate it, and then you are ready to improve it.

At Goodyear: We first defined our processes, such as PCP and TCP, and then we created a cross-functional team that was responsible for establishing and documenting our processes and the standards. The innovation processes looked very confusing when they were first explained to the associates. They have changed a lot since their creation 6 years ago, and they keep improving. Today the Goodyear PMO documents the cross-functional processes for product development in the PMO playbooks.

R&D Processes at Goodyear

Goodyear uses standard R&D processes, from the idea to the launch of a product. Two of these involve gating processes and two do not:

Product creation process

The purpose of PCP is to develop and industrialize profitable products and launch them on the market.

New ideas enter the PCP in stage 1 (basic feasibility). New technology comes in at gate 2 (Success Assured).

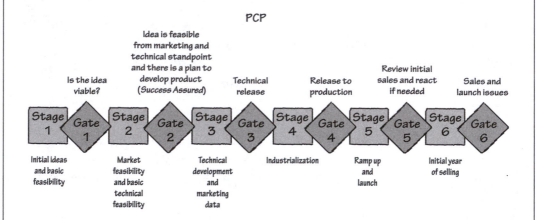

Technology creation process

The TCP develops new technology to feed into the PCP. TCP also aligns all the stakeholders from the beginning, so we do not develop technology that nobody accepts when it is done. Projects enter TCP after a "free" exploration or discovery phase, or the projects come from the ICP/BMI process or other sources.

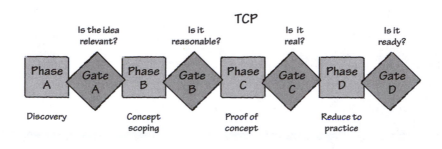

Innovation creation process

The purpose of ICP is to collect and organize the input to TCP. It also tries to align the customer with the technology in all regions of the world. The process manages a portfolio of business opportunities that are established with the businesses in the different regions (market-back innovation).

The phases and gates of ICP, TCP, and PCP also interact: The ICP feeds the discovery phase of the TCP. If new technology from the TCP is ready to get integrated into a new product, the project enters the PCP at gate 2 (Success Assured).

Business model innovation

BMI is a cross-functional *business* process that looks at disruptive innovation that requires new technology and/or new customers and a new business model. Concepts developed by the BMI can be developed organically or obtained through acquisition.

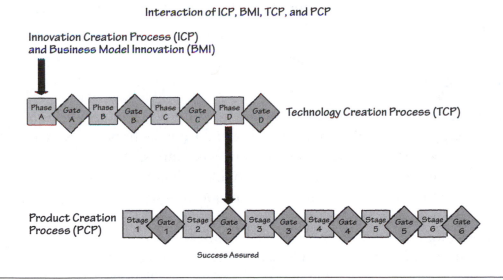

New Business Objectives

Goodyear was a very diversified company in the 1980s. In addition to our tire division, we had business lines that included an engineered products division, an oil business, an aerospace unit, and a wheel-manufacturing division. During this time, the golden age for Goodyear ended with a corporate takeover attempt in 1986. In fighting off the acquisition by corporate raider Sir James Goldsmith, Goodyear sold off several of its divisions for cash.

Focus was placed on making tires, selling tires, and invoicing for tires, as our chairman mandated at the time. Due to the financial situation of the company, the innovative products group was disbanded. And like every other cost, product development costs came under scrutiny. Many programs were stopped and activity-based cost tracking was introduced to help people stay within budget. Investment and projects needed to be justified—R&D changed to more of a short-term product focus, scaling back the long-term vision. Fortunately, due to the insight of our leadership at the time, R&D efforts were continued on tire modeling, predictive tools, and other key technologies and capabilities. These and other concepts would intertwine with our lean efforts and they continue to reward us today.

Tire Modeling

Goodyear had a lot of functional knowledge on tire design and materials technology, but our main competitors had the same technology. New competitors, especially from newly industrialized countries, started to emerge because some of the basic radial tire technology had become common knowledge through benchmarking. The major tire industry players, like Goodyear, needed to invest in new technology to create a new kaikaku (Japanese for "radical change").

To gain ground on technology, one of the investments that Goodyear chose was computer modeling and performance predictions. Computer technology had advanced to the point that a complicated structure like a tire—with viscous material properties—could be modeled with finite element tools. Also, advanced modeling technology became available from Sandia National Laboratories. The U.S. government had invested heavily into modeling and predictive tools for strategic reasons, and that technology was shared to some extent with American companies, including Goodyear. Goodyear also felt that this investment would be ideal to leverage our knowledge.

Computer FEA modeling has several great advantages, in that it

- Is more efficient than prototype building and testing.
- Is faster, provided you have access to the right computers. A leading world expert in FEA technology considered tires the most complicated "objects" that he had seen in his career, which begins to describe how large and power-hungry the models are.
- Allows a designer to explore a much larger design space than prototype building. For example, the designer can explore designs that we may not know how to build or materials that do not yet exist.
- Offers a means to aggregate and leverage company knowledge in the models.

However, modeling requires unique talent to develop and maintain the models. And models are only as good as the knowledge that is available. The models should be built with state-of-the-art knowledge and updated with every new knowledge that becomes available. Of course, this means that the models have to be validated on a regular basis; since most projects are scheduled for prototype builds at some point (i.e., release testing), these can be used to validate the models. In fact, our computer models were not so efficient when we started with them, but through the relentless use of PDCA (plan, do, check, adjust) over many years, they are industry-leading today.

I would certainly encourage a modeling approach for any company in any industry that seeks to implement a faster, better, and more efficient product development process. The predictions do not have to be with a finite element program. As we have shown with sets of tradeoff curves, a simple spreadsheet can do the job. Just keep in mind that the tools must be validated from time to time and they must be updated with every new knowledge that becomes available.

Joe Zekoski, CTO, gives high marks to his predecessors, one of whom made the decision to invest in computer modeling technology. "He certainly could not have imagined at the time the decision was made how important those tools would become with lean product development—where development speed and agility became dominant factors and where knowledge management is critical."

Renewed Focus on Customer

Many new players entered the tire market in the 1990s, many from low-cost countries. Our industry also consolidated rapidly with Michelin buying Goodrich and Uniroyal, Bridgestone buying Firestone, and Continental buying General Tire. In addition, automotive fuel-economy standards made it necessary to split the OEM and the renewal business, creating an opening for anybody in the renewal market. This trend raised the competiveness of the business to a new level, and that level had to be met with increased focus on the customer. Suddenly it was not enough to do what the OEMs wanted. We now had to understand and service customers and consumers.

Understanding the specifications of an OEM customer—even many new Asian OEMs we had begun to serve—is relatively straightforward. That was not the case when we began to look harder at dealers and end users. There is a lot more diversity and variability. It took us quite some time to figure out how to serve this more diverse customer base with a much more diverse and complex product line. This, too, helped set the stage for where we are today with lean because *every* lean initiative must start with the customer and focus on the value for the customer (e.g., "Would the customer be willing to pay for this?").

TQC

While we were awakening to the need to understand our end users, we also joined the TQC movement in the late 1990s. Since Goodyear produced the first tire there has been an acute awareness that product quality is a key element to the success of the company. Tires are an important part of vehicle safety and require the highest possible quality standards. The company would not have stayed in business for more than 100 years without the ultimate concern for safety and product quality.

None of the product safety and quality standards were questioned in the quality movement. Although many people questioned the effectiveness of the movement, some principles that we would consider lean today stuck from this initiative. Among other things, the TQC "storyboard" resembles an A3.

One of the new things the TQC movement brought to Goodyear was a focus on the *internal* customer. Many R&D projects suffer from handoffs. In the construction industry, there is a popular saying that "buildings leak at the intersections of the contracts." TQC taught us not to throw projects over the wall, but to instead try to serve the internal customer just as we would serve an external customer. When I had first started to work for Goodyear, we were taught to "let them figure it out"—"them" being the function after us in the value stream. With the quality movement and lean, we heard and read how hard the folks in Japan worked to make absolutely sure the function downstream had exactly what they needed, and how they went out of their way to have no exceptions to that rule.

A friend of mine summed it up the best. He was working in IT, and he asked me what the concept of the internal customer was all about. I tried to explain, since I was on a core TQC team. He said the concept would never work in IT. "Customers ask us for the wrong stuff. We in IT know best what the customer should have and that is what we give them." No further comment needed.

Something else that sticks in my memory is the fact that we started multidisciplinary teams not only to solve technical problems, but to solve administrative problems or problems that stretched over several different functions. The protocol that came with the TQC teaching was useful, and it still reminds me of the kaizen events that we use today.

In Goodyear, we also introduced the short and focused weekly cross-functional "business operational" meetings at that time, where the functional leaders (just between directors) would develop solutions to short-term, non-technical problems related to the launch of new products. These meetings, of course, today have been replaced with a standup daily huddle involving all associates.

Of course, our knowledge-management practices also served Goodyear well during this time of focus on product quality: our design standards assured a high level of product quality and robustness.

The effectiveness of Goodyear's design quality system (design standards) was proved in 2000. Some of our competitors had problems with their products, which caught the attention of the National Highway Transportation Safety Association. National consumer organizations and the press went on high alert, and eventually the issue made it to a Congressional hearing and new legislation: Transportation Recall Enhancement, Accountability and Documentations Act (TREAD Act). Goodyear's well-established quality processes and standards reassured us through this time that would redefine the tire industry. We already knew our standards included all the lessons we learned in the past, but now we found out that we had enough buffer to handle new and thus-far-unknown challenges for our products.

ISO

Along with our TQC efforts came ISO. The OEMs demanded ISO certification or, better yet, QS 9000 certification (specific to the auto industry) for the design organization, and Goodyear obtained its first product development certification in 2002. Most companies like Goodyear still maintain their certifications today, although the benefits of the system have been questioned many times and there has not been much published research that shows a rise in product quality due to companies achieving the certification.

Nonetheless, the ISO certification again taught us a lot about lean. At Goodyear, ISO required that we document our processes—we already had documented our products, but not much of our processes. And we had to do this documentation under the watchful eye of an auditor.

Six Sigma and Design for Six Sigma

Six sigma is intended to eliminate variability in an operation and it relies on the process of DMAIC (define, measure, analyze, implement, and control). General Electric and Motorola published a lot about their early successes with six sigma. Goodyear jumped on the six sigma bandwagon, too. (Due to the general nature of this section, I do not distinguish here between six sigma and design for six sigma (DFSS).)

At Goodyear, six sigma taught us how to bring the following to a development process:

- A cross-functional project approach is used to solve problems.
- The focus is on the problem regardless of who owns the problem, who caused it, or who has to implement it.
- A focus is on data and measurement. First the "accuracy" of the measurement system must be established and appropriate statistical tools are used to analyze the data and identify significant and statistically relevant gaps.
- Designed experiments and other models are used to assure the feasibility and effectiveness of the solutions.
- After a solution is implemented, six sigma closes the loop in good PDCA fashion to assure that the problem is fixed or that the process has been improved.
- A control plan makes sure that the solution that was implemented remains implemented and that it is sustained.

■ Six sigma also is a tool to eliminate wasteful variability, like unrepeatable test results.

At Goodyear, six sigma was more successful in manufacturing; applying six sigma within Goodyear product development yielded very few successes. There were reasons for that:

■ Most of the problems in product development were process-related, and it was sometimes awkward to force them into the prescribed DMAIC process.
■ Although a lot of people were trained, only a few actually had the time to work on the six sigma projects because these projects were extremely time-consuming.
■ Contrary to manufacturing, it was hard to quantify financial benefits of the projects in R&D.
■ Six sigma uses a relatively rigid framework—a lot of R&D problems, especially the ones that require a creative approach, are hard to force into that mold.

There were additional concerns that six sigma kills creativity because it can eliminate good variability with bad variability. I believe that if people understand six sigma principles and apply them correctly where they are needed—just as with lean principles—they will know what can work and give their organization yet another beneficial toolset/methodology. You should by now begin to see the pattern: the ability to stifle innovation is not inherent to six sigma or lean, and, if this happens, the program has not been implemented or focused correctly.

New leadership at Goodyear R&D in 2006—Jean-Claude Kihn, general director GIC*A at the time—was convinced that lean would be a better fit for product development. But after TQC, six sigma, project management, computer solutions, and a few other homegrown global initiatives, it was really hard to convince associates that we really needed *another* initiative.

Notes

1. Allen C. Ward, *Lean Product and Process Development*, Lean Enterprise Institute, Cambridge, MA, 2007.
2. Michael L. George, *Lean Six Sigma*, McGraw-Hill, New York, 2002.

3. James M. Morgan and Jeffrey K. Liker, *The Toyota Product Development System*, Productivity Press, New York, 2006.
4. Steven Spear, *The High-Velocity Edge*, McGraw-Hill, New York, 2010.
5. Henry Ford, *Today and Tomorrow*, Doubleday, Page & Co., Garden City, NY, 1926.
6. Allen C. Ward and Durward K. Sobek II, *Lean Product and Process Development, Second Edition*, Lean Enterprise Institute, Cambridge, MA, 2014.
7. Ron Marsiglio, *Knowledge-Driven Product Development*, LPPDE Europe 2013, Amsterdam, June 2013.

Chapter 3

The Beginning of a Lean Process

Nearly every organization that embraces lean has a burning platform, inflection point, or whatever you want to call it—that moment that forces radical change (kaikaku) from long-held behaviors. Goodyear too had such a moment in early 2000 (and others since). Business conditions at that time helped push the R&D organization toward an awareness of what today we would call "lean" and learning about and pursuing lean practices. The start of our lean initiative was helped by reasonably sound change-management and project-management systems that were already in place, the key characteristics of which are described in this chapter. But even more important than understanding the systems that helped Goodyear facilitate change are the lessons that we learned when we truly started with lean, when we began to see our processes through a lean lens (i.e., value-stream mapping) and apply lean changes. We ran into many obstacles that probably exist in your company and every organization—functional optimization, outdated processes, and a flat-out refusal by some to participate. We overcame it all.

The First Kaikaku—Eroding Profits at Goodyear

In 2000, Goodyear formed a joint venture with Sumitomo Rubber Industries Ltd. and took on its Dunlop tire brand and a large loan to finance the deal. The move left us trying to generate cash for several years, unfortunately during a time when Goodyear products in the marketplace needed an overhaul and few new products were debuted. Compounding our difficulties, low-cost tires from overseas were beginning to erode the margin of Goodyear's custom tire brands and left us with excess capacity.

These events led Goodyear to suffer massive financial losses in 2001–2003 and to teeter on the brink of bankruptcy, necessitating a large-scale restructuring and right-sizing. The restructuring meant major changes for Goodyear product development as well. This event signaled the start of a 10-year period of change in Goodyear R&D, resulting in more changes than had been experienced in the previous 100 years in the history of the company. And, in hindsight, it started at the right time—*before* we began our lean journey.

Jim Womack and Dan Jones write that personnel issues must be handled before the start of a lean initiative.[1] Staff reductions, they argue, should never be the result of a continuous-improvement event—employees should not be asked to improve themselves out of a job. One of the main objectives of lean is to increase efficiency through the elimination of waste. Often the improved processes require fewer resources, including less staff than the old processes. Thus, the movement of staff to other areas of need can and should be expected with lean.

In a perfect world, an improved organization is creating more demand and growing, and so staff merely move *around* where they are needed but *not out* of the company. Some of these lateral moves may be a temporary assignment in the company's continuous-improvement office. If lean initiatives and waste elimination lead to regular staff elimination, individuals will not be motivated to contribute to the improvement initiative. Without their involvement, improvement stops, and leadership eventually will seek out another initiative.

Staff eliminations could have sunk our lean efforts before they ever really got underway. In 2009, Goodyear was planning to eliminate a large warehouse for prototype tires that would no longer be needed as a result of process improvements. Only after R&D engineers saw that all the staff working in the warehouse (hourly and salaried workers) had been reassigned were they willing to discuss process improvements needed as a result of the elimination of the warehouse. This case went a long way to increasing the trust and the confidence among the engineers in our lean initiative. The warehouse workers also were motivated and worked hard to facilitate the phasing out of the warehouse, and the big task of the closure went relatively smoothly.

Womack and Jones do not necessarily prescribe that companies reorganize ahead of lean initiatives, as we unknowingly did at Goodyear, but in our case it resolved some issues that helped pave the way for the large-scale lean transformation.

Kaikaku and Kaizen

Kaikaku (Japanese for "radical change") is about making fundamental and revolutionary changes to a system or process. It also can mean "innovation," as in a disruptive innovation or disruptive event that leads to radical change. The objective of kaizen (Japanese for "change for the better") is continuous, incremental improvement of an entire value stream or an individual process. I noticed that engineers search for kaikaku breakthroughs in the products they develop, but they resent kaikaku changes in the way they do their work. Both types of change need to be applied during your lean journey.

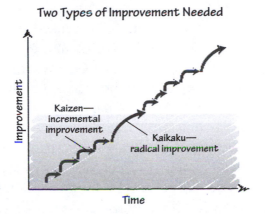

Two Types of Improvement Needed

A good example for kaikaku and kaizen comes from track and field. For the high jump competition, in which athletes leap to clear a bar, a scissors-like move was an early approach when making the jump. The high-jump record gradually rose through the years. Russian Valeriy Brumel introduced a straddled approach in the early 1960s, shattering the world record (kaikaku) and winning the Olympic gold medal in 1964. Other athletes soon learned the technique and made changes in small increments to nudge the world record higher (kaizen). Then in the late-1960s, Dick Fosbury began working on the "Fosbury flop," by which he jumped over the bar backward. The world record was shattered at the 1968 Olympics (kaikaku) and jumpers have since been in an era of small, incremental improvements (kaizen).[2]

The Goodyear financial situation in 2003 required massive restructuring and led to job losses throughout the company, even within R&D, something no one had ever experienced at Goodyear. I cannot imagine trying to lead our lean R&D initiative in such an environment. Was the restructuring needed? Probably, as investors and industry analysts clamored for it at the time, and it probably kept Goodyear solvent. Although we did not know it then, it was our signal for kaikaku (Japanese for "radical change").

Change Management

Many companies are used to constant reorganizations and a new improvement "flavor" every month. Usually, these are caused by new leadership or management's kneejerk reaction to a problem, and, often, not understanding or caring what happens after the change. At Goodyear, change was needed to appease shareholders, the media, the board, and higher management.

A lot of companies redraw organizational charts, not understanding the impact of change on the associates. There are frequent changes in leadership, and new leaders are especially likely to reorganize or to start new initiatives. Poorly managed change eventually leads to lower work output and productivity and a waste of resources, thus, necessitating another round of misguided change. From a lean and operational standpoint, a lot of these random changes unbalance value streams and can lead to significant delivery or performance issues.

But change, when done correctly and as typically occurs within Goodyear now, can be a powerful competitive weapon. Even when done correctly, change is difficult, because most people associate change with something negative and believe they are bound to lose something due to the change.

I often conduct an exercise I learned from Josh Kerievsky, the CEO of Industrial Logic.[3] During the exercise, which you can find various versions of in change-management literature, people are paired face-to-face and told to memorize the appearance of the other. Then they turn around, change their appearances (they take off their shoes, ties, you name it), face each other again, and must identify the changes in the other. This cycle continues until people object, fearing they'll do something to embarrass themselves. I ask them why they are focused on taking stuff off. The room is full of stuff that they could have *added* (hats, tape, markers, tags), but I've never seen a person add something. Most people, especially those in my company, associate change with giving up or losing something. This may be based on personal experiences and memories of previous restructurings and some of the uncertain conditions that resulted.

We have always given up something in every "change" that we went through in the last 20 years at Goodyear, so I cannot blame people for subtraction thinking. I use the Kerievsky exercise for our Lean 401 class in which I prepare folks to *lead* lean change. Although I am convinced that all the change that those folks will be leading is mostly positive, I want to make them aware of the mindsets of those with whom they will work.

Lean implementation and the events involved constitute drastic change to an organization and it is important to understand a few facts about change at the onset:

- People normally do not like change—they like the comfort of security and prefer a stable marginal process to the disruption of an improvement. Psychologists say that change is actually causing physical pain or discomfort. Peter Senge wrote, "People don't resist change. They resist being changed."[4]
- People are afraid of change. The more fear is prevalent in an organization, the more resistance there will be. The more people trust management, the easier they buy into the change.
- If change is needed (e.g., to remain competitive), it is better to make that change when things are stable and going well.
- If things go well, people must be convinced that the change is needed.
- Associates are the most likely to buy into the change after a kaikaku event, like a layoff or a game-changing event in the business.
- In a typical business culture, people associate change with something negative—often based on natural instincts or past experiences.
- Change deals with people—changing the process or the organization may be easy, but changing the people part is more challenging and takes more time. The more people are engaged in the change, the easier it will be to make the change and to sustain it.
- Change often results in temporary chaos or instability that can be minimized with a well-managed change process. There can also be a drop in motivation and productivity as a result of the temporary chaos.
- Middle management has the most leverage to get everyone engaged in the change, but that also seems to be the hardest group to get on board with changes.

■ Most engineers or change leaders are not psychologists—it is important for them to understand the mindset of the people involved in the change.

Many companies pride themselves on their long-held traditions, which often are associated with a strong culture—"It's the way we have always done things around here." The culture that may have served the company well in the past can be a big obstacle and block the needed change. Taiichi Ohno says that organizations are self-protecting like the human body: the culture is like antibodies that protect it against all the changes. When the foreign element enters the system, the antibodies not only become more active, but they also multiply more rapidly.[5]

Good change management can be taught, and it can be learned. It is an essential part in any transformation, especially in one that is as difficult as the implementation of lean. A lean product development implementation requires individuals who are adept at their technical skills (their work in the process) and open to changing a process (work on the process), even when there is no obvious reason to change.

We teach and offer our change leaders at Goodyear a range of change-management tools, and there are plenty to choose from. Chris Banweg, Goodyear change agent, says that change-management approaches "are all very similar—pick one, but follow it." Looking back at how we have approached change management at Goodyear, I believe, in hindsight, we followed a method similar to that described in *Our Iceberg Is Melting* by John Kotter.[6] It certainly is one of the more colorful and illustrative descriptions of change management, and the book is easy to read and understand.

Our change-management approach at Goodyear usually consists of the following 11 key steps.

1. Do Your Homework

Get a realistic perspective of what you are getting into and what is possible: understand the conditions within your organization as well as what is being accomplished beyond your four walls. Benchmark, do a survey, perform a good gap analysis, gather facts, go, and see. Data and facts will be easier to sell to engineers than opinions.

Write down what you will try to accomplish, often done in the form of a project charter (described later in this chapter). Define the scope and the goals, which should have a line of sight to corporate goals or objectives. Do not forget to document a baseline or starting point; that will allow you to track progress later.

One invaluable homework exercise is to survey the battlefield—who are the allies, and who and where are the opponents that are likely to offer resistance. It is also important to have a clear idea who are the power holders, and whether the change is consistent with their strategies or preferences. Not that you should not go against power holders, but you should be aware of what you are up against.

You should assume that 5% of the population will support the change, and 5% will visually or covertly oppose it. The other 90% will wait and see and need to be convinced.

While data are helpful, people are necessary: a good change agent analyzes his or her relationships in the company and finds some "crusaders"—those individuals willing to go to battle with the change agent and help convince the rest of the organization of the need for change.

2. Get Leverage

At Goodyear R&D, we started the lean transformation during a 4-month strike by the United Steelworkers of America. The strike put a big dent into our development work, and most tire-development programs slowed down or stopped. This was a great time for change. At the time our CTO Jean Claude Kihn said, "The strike presents an opportunity for change, not an obstacle." Jim Morgan says, "Never underestimate the power of a good crisis."[7]

Womack and Jones stress the importance of "kaikaku" or disruptive events in change. In fact, they say if you do not have such an event, then you may want to think about creating one. People are more likely to embrace change after a business disaster, when something disruptive occurs in a company (a disappointing financial performance that demands action), or if there is some other sense of urgency. When things are OK, few leaders are anxious to undertake change, and few employees are motivated to join in. That is precisely the time, though, that more change (improvements) should be sought.

We had the opportunity to use a disrupting event of the strike to facilitate the lean change in our innovation center in the United States. Our innovation center in Luxembourg (GIC*L) did not have such an event, and, therefore, it took several attempts to copy what we already had accomplished in Akron, Ohio.

3. Engage the Right People to Lead the Change

The change leader should be picked carefully—knowing how to lead people through a change is more important than knowing the details of the new process. I have seen internal and external advisers who call themselves "change agents," many of whom acquired that title because they managed projects in a large organization, like the implementation of a new software system. These change agents are often experts in the process or the tool, but may or may not have experience in dealing with resistance and often lack the means of digging into cultural and personnel issues that a large change like lean implementation requires.

A technically difficult change like the implementation of a lean process may also require a "sensei," a teacher and experienced person who can advise the change leader.

In addition to the right change leader, there should be a team representing the "people" engaged in the change. This group should consist of individuals who have an open mind about the change and the motivation to make it work. They will be influential both up and down in the organization, so they should be respected members of the organization and be intimately familiar with the process. This puts the focus on middle management, which I found is the most reluctant group to accept change; unfortunately, those also are the folks that must be counted on to influence up as well as obtain the engagement of all the associates.

Jean-Pierre Jeusette, general director GIC*L, says, "The key to the implementation was the small coalition of open-minded people who embraced the change, who found the low-hanging fruit to convince the rest."

Team members are crusaders because they fight the battle with or for the change agent. It also is a good idea to invite one or two people on the team who you believe will actively oppose the change. This will lead to a much better discussion in the team: (1) lead to an understanding of other viewpoints that will help the crusaders better prepare for battle and (2) potentially surface a counter position that was not considered by the change agent.

4. Develop a Vision and Make Plans

To develop a vision, imagine coming to work after the change has been implemented: how will things look? Plans should include all aspects of the change process, incorporate the timing of events that will lead to change, and include contingency plans. Change is best implemented quickly, not in a long, drawn-out initiative. When establishing timing, ensure no other significant changes are underway at the same time, which could lengthen the time required.

Plans should incorporate training for team members and the organization—for a lean implementation, all involved have to be trained well in the principles of lean—and an approach to communicate the change, specifically addressing various constituents (opponents, management, employees). It is important to understand that this cannot be a "one size fits all" approach. Everyone views change through their own personal lens, and so you want to consider the various perspectives when you roll out your plan and enlist their support in designing the right strategy. Good change leaders also know that plans cannot stop with the implementation, but that they must also cover the sustaining of the change.

5. Get Support

One of the first questions that people ask me when I talk about lean outside Goodyear is, "Did you get support?" Fortunately I can answer, "Yes." Top-down initiatives are not always a good idea because associate buy-in is hard to get, but most "grassroot" initiatives will fail to take off until at least some support comes from leadership. The right sponsor will help make the grassroot effort successful. The sponsor can be formal or informal, visible, or invisible (in the background).

Even with a sponsor, other management and leadership play key roles in a transformation, and the change should engage them in the process early and often. They must, at a minimum, allow change to happen. If product development associates witness engagement and vision at the top of their organization, they are more likely to support—and continue to support—the lean effort and the changes that result, even when the bar is set high.

Joe Zekoski, Goodyear CTO, gives his predecessor Jean-Claude Kihn, our sponsor, credit for sticking with the lean initiative and staying the course through many challenges and setbacks: "You need the right leaders in key positions—the ones that not only tolerate the change, but the ones who embrace it." Joe adds that if we had to do it over again, he would pay a lot more attention to preparing the organization ahead of time and anticipate more challenges and potential obstacles.

For most change agents, a coach can add a lot of value. Besides giving advice, the coach can help with motivation and encouragement to keep things on track (like a diet coach does).

6. You Cannot Overcommunicate or Overtrain

Open and honest communication is important to build trust, obtain buy-in, and deal with obstacles and resistance. I personally prefer the communication that Richard Sheridan, owner Menlo Innovations, calls "high-speed human voice."[8] That is, people should be communicated to by their leadership, and it *must* be two-way communication. Weekly company news, posters, and slogans are much less effective. Town hall meetings with questions and leadership blogs, which take on a conversational tone, can work well.

The GIC*L organization worked hard on its lean transformation. Jean-Pierre says, "Our biggest mistake was that we did not communicate enough; we assumed everybody knew."

Communication must be *honest* and humble, not the typical PR announcements with "spins" that make the worst story look positive. It also should be messaging that adds insights each time, not a daily publication that rehashes the same subject over and over. That type of overcommunication can have adverse effects—people will get tired of it. Communication should focus on benefits—less so on the means or tools—and positive results should be shown whenever possible. It also helps to acknowledge that change is not necessarily easy on the associates, but that their effort is needed and appreciated. Training can be included in the communication strategy or it can be done by other means, including web-based education. The need for training can vary with the nature of the change. The lean initiative in Goodyear required an exceptionally large amount of training because engineers needed to understand why we were implementing a lean process. We actually had to train three times during the implementation, and we engaged the R&D leaders as teachers.

7. Deal with Resistance

Some people in your function and company will see lean as something foreign and disruptive and try to throw up obstacles. A lot of established companies and engineers are risk-averse and not willing to experiment or leave their comfort zone. I occasionally ran into elements at Goodyear that met that description. Some were only small pockets of resistance ("this too shall pass"), but others created real obstacles.

When we started our lean changes, I had underestimated the obstacles and I overestimated the "power" of our sponsor. The problem with resistance is that often the resistance is invisible. Years after the implementation I found out about an effort by a leader of the organization to derail the change effort. I had no idea. I was not prepared for a significant covert resistance from my peers either. This is why you want to identify resistance as early as possible. People may have been afraid to try something new, but they were not afraid to try to prove me and the sponsor wrong.

I have seen some companies plot a "resistance" map before their implementation, which enables them to keep a pulse on their friends and enemies—something I learned the hard way. The resistance map is not only for an understanding of the political situation in your company, but it is also instrumental for what the Japanese call "nemawashi" (preparing the ground for planting). Sometimes the ground takes a lot of work, as my gardener friend Guenter tells us. Sometimes you may even postpone the initiative and wait for a little rain or other changes before you decide that it is the right time to start.

Do not expect a lot of help dealing with obstacles. That is not necessarily a bad thing. Interferences of people with authority—even when they think they are helping—can kill the engagement of the associates.

8. Engage the Employees

At the end of the day, you will work with mostly the same product development people after the transformation that you did before the transformation. Get everyone involved in the transformation as much as possible. People affected by the change must feel they are part of the effort. The more the people affected by the change help shape the change, provide their input, and express their opinions and feelings, the easier it is implement and to sustain lean. What is important is to give people a chance to voice their opinions and concerns, and for them to see that they have been heard. You may not be able to act on everything that you hear.

Oliver Kim, HR manager at GIC*L, likes to say that there are only two types of change-management strategies: the effective one with those involved and the ineffective one without those involved. Lao Tzu, founder of Daoism, said, "Go to the people. Live with them. Learn from them. Build with what they have. But with the best leaders, when the work is done, the task accomplished, the people will say, 'We have done this ourselves.'"

Rachel Graves and Tom Laurich, development engineers, remember how chaotic it was when we implemented the first step of our new lean product development process. They remember learning about the lean principles first and then learning about the new process. Nonetheless, they felt engaged by the way the change was rolled out by their leaders—this was not something that was forced upon them. They understood why it was done and the expected benefits, and they were invited to provide their feedback and input. Of course, it took a little while to see the benefits.

Brandy Moorhead, at the time chief engineer Tire Engineering, was a member of the first lean team (Herbie team), and she helped design the new process. When she introduced one particular change to her staff, she presented the problem to a small subset of her team members—a few early adopters and key influencers on the team—expecting they would help drive the changes. She encouraged the team members to experiment in short time periods to evaluate potential lean solutions. Through regular reflections, coaching, and discussions, the first adopters engaged the rest of the staff and made significant improvements to a process they owned.

9. Do Good Things and Talk about Them (German Proverb)

One reference that I like to use is by Virginia Satir, a psychologist who worked in the middle of the last century and specialized in helping families who went through traumatic change. Her model for change suggests that there is a resistance to change, followed by a chaotic situation after a change occurs. There are ups and downs in this phase, and Satir suggests to catch the "ups" and build on the positives during this phase to move the curve up and eventually end up at a higher level of performance.[9] Of course, people who do not like the change will do the opposite—talk about the low points.

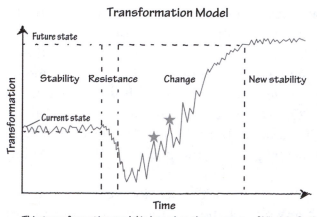

This transformation model is based on the concepts of Virginia Satir and inspired by a Steven M. Smith illustration.[9,10]

We had a few quick wins during the Goodyear lean transformation that we shared with the organization. The biggest one came when our project-priority lists were abolished. Everybody hated the priority lists and was happy to see them go. We had used them for so long that nobody believed that they could ever be replaced, and I am sure some people thought, "They will be back soon." The fact that this major step happened smoothly and was led by the least likely function (manufacturing) gave the members of the Herbie team a lot of confidence.

A smaller win occurred during a meeting with our CTO, when an influential senior member of the R&D organization stood up and said, "I have seen too many of these initiatives to get excited any longer. But the way this one took off and what I have seen so far, I think you have a chance to make this one stick."

10. Remember PDCA (Plan/Do/Check/Adjust)

We will talk about the PDCA cycle throughout this book. Virtually every lean consultant or expert visitor to Goodyear innovation centers pointed out that at Goodyear we were good at planning and executing, but dropped the ball when it came to checking and adjusting. That is a universal problem with companies. After the implementation, the team disbands and people move on. The need for organizational adjustments to sustain the change will soon be forgotten.

Any plan to implement change must include plans to go back and verify that the change process accomplished the goals—if not, adjustments must be made. The check also presents an opportunity to learn what worked well and what did not to improve the success rate next time.

At Goodyear, many years after the change was initiated, we are still working on it. We made many adjustments early and we are not done today.

11. Sustain the Change

Change must be sustained and eventually anchored. Do not underestimate the work to make sure the change sticks and remains stuck. There are rarely initiatives that are so good that they sustain themselves. The more people affected by the change are involved in the change, the easier it is to sustain it. You still want to plan early on for the activities to sustain the change.

A change consultant told me that most inmates who break out of jail get caught within 10 miles of the institution. He says that inmates are so focused on the plan and the execution of the breakout that they rarely plan what to do when they get outside. (Or maybe they did not believe that their "change" was going to be successful.) Similarly, change agents are so focused on the plan and the change process that sometimes they forget to make and implement plans to sustain the change.

One common mistake in the sustain phase is that the change agent is pulled off too early. That is where the plan helps most—good change agents appropriately plan for and pick the right time for their exit. Another mistake is failure to allocate resources after the change. Often the change agent is the only person managing the new process. Strong functions are not likely to give up resources, even if the initiative has taken work off their plate—they measure their power and influence by the size of their staff—and they likely will reassign the resources "internally," leaving the new lean process unstaffed. It is a good idea to get the stakeholder commitment upfront, so the staff reallocation to the new process happens when needed.

At Goodyear, we often had to restart initiatives. The reasons for this are often poor timing; absence of a good kaikaku event; the lack of understanding of the resistance; the lack of engagement by those involved in the change; and the lack of a good sustainability plan. I find that it helps to put anchors in place wherever possible and in whatever form to help sustain improvements to make the change permanent. These anchors could be a change in procedures, standards, or the organization (i.e., permanent staff allocations). Sometimes a control plan may be required: verify metrics, conduct audits, and "go see" from time to time.

Many publications on the topic of change end the change process with a celebration. Although I like celebrations and rewards as much as the next guy, I am careful with celebrations because people think that the project or the change is *complete* after the celebration; they declare victory and move on.

> ### Lean R&D Principle: Carefully manage change to make change easier and more effective.
>
> The implementation of lean in a product development organization is a major cultural change. The chances for the implementation to be successful are much higher if the change process itself is understood and carefully managed. And even when change is successful, sustaining the change can be difficult.

Your company's change leaders should have a basic understanding of good change management. Your organization should know how to select and train change agents, identify those who support/champion change, communicate change to functions and individuals, and planfully execute change.

The 11 steps we follow at Goodyear R&D are a good roadmap for managing a change process:

1. Do the homework on the current situation, the people, and the organization.
2. Get leverage—time the start correctly—and use a kaikaku event if possible.
3. Involve the right people to lead the change.
4. Develop a vision and make plans.
5. Get support on all levels—find a sponsor.
6. You cannot overcommunicate or overtrain.
7. Deal with resistance.
8. Engage the employees.
9. Advertise the small successes.
10. Remember PDCA.
11. Sustain and anchor the change.

At Goodyear: Having influential people leading the change and engaging the rest of the organization was crucial in the Goodyear R&D lean transformation. For Goodyear, the timing of the change was very important—we leveraged the right events to initiate the change. The "Herbie" team developed the strategy and helped with the communications, the training, and the implementation. As the change progressed, leadership anchored the initiative by making the required organizational changes.

We now teach change management in Lean 401 training, our most advanced lean class, because change has to be managed on every level. One part of change management that many ignore, but which we cover in our training, is "stakeholder" analysis. I saw stakeholder analysis represented in one company with a sort of topological map of "who influences whom" and a software program that allowed "what happens if" games. That could certainly have helped avoid some surprises with the resistance at Goodyear.

Changes for the Worse

The application of computer systems to business processes was a reflex decision in the 1980s and 1990s when more affordable and powerful computer systems became available. These delivered huge gains in manufacturing, administration, finance, and procurement (e.g., materials requirement planning and enterprise resource planning systems). Computer systems also revolutionized the design process (e.g., CAD and drawing tools, modeling tools like FEA, and analytical tools). PCs also became an indispensable tool for engineers, including the engineer's best friends: Excel and PowerPoint.

But not all computer systems benefit the organization—especially a lean organization—equally. For example, master plant scheduling systems, such as materials requirement planning (MRP), often rely on a push process and can have a hard time coexisting with a much more effective pull system.

In 2001, Goodyear realized its weakness in bringing large projects to market when the market needed them. One big issue was to get the mold manufacturing resources aligned between experimental and production molds. We also needed to coordinate the prototype manufacturing resources that were shared with production in the factories.

Many attempts were made to manage complete projects or the complete value stream (although we were not calling it that then), but functional considerations and functional rules always prevailed, leading to daily changes. For example, when production capacity was needed to meet production tickets, development builds were postponed. Similarly, production runs were very long, even for low-volume product, so short development runs could not be squeezed in. Functions kept suboptimizing their own process, which caused long delays in the cross-functional new product development projects.

At this time, there was a powerful project management software emerging on the market. Since large, enterprise-wide global software programs had been successfully used at Goodyear (e.g., SAP), some computer wizards were convinced that good project management was just "selecting the right software" for the task. They sold Goodyear leadership on implementing global project management software to assure efficient execution and on-time delivery (OTD) of projects. I was privileged (or punished) to oversee the implementation of the software.

First, we trained the whole organization (one more time) in project management and the use of the new software. The project was rolled out according to good principles of change management (although we skipped a few steps). Then we got into the normal politics—some functions came on board, others did not, some developed their own software, some bought other software, and there was a lot of fighting about the ownership of the new system (since it was also supposed to track cost, finance tried to take on a dominant role).

We eventually succeeded in running a pilot. "Monster" project plans were created to minute detail, and each individual plan looked reasonably good. Dependencies between tasks were created, and the tasks within *individual* projects aligned well. But in Goodyear R&D, all the projects used the same resources and interfered with each other. These interferences were handled through "rollups," where you could see when interferences occurred and a function was getting overloaded. When that happened, the overload or the interference had to be reconciled or corrected and dozens of other schedules changed. In order for the system to work, it required *daily* updates to deal with these reconciliations and to update projects that fell behind. Daily setbacks and changes to the priority lists also complicated the process. These updates took a lot of time, and many phone calls were needed to get the information—as a result, project teams took shortcuts or fell behind. An update that was made at 8:00 am was obsolete by 9:00 am because there were new interferences with other projects that had just been updated.

Before we knew it, significant investment had been made in this software, training, customizations, and the consulting fees needed to implement the program. One of our directors finally had the courage to say the "emperor wears no clothes"—he concluded that this management approach (although technically sound) would only work if the system is current all the time. Due to the immense variability and uncertainty of development work, updates were needed at least once per day. This director subsequently submitted a budget for a dozen resources, which were deemed necessary in his center alone to maintain and update the system. Not surprisingly, this budget was rejected, and the project died. *If you computerize a bad process, you end up with an expensive bad process.*

Fortunately, I remembered this lesson when we implemented a lean method to schedule our projects: a much more simple and flexible project management tool was needed for an unpredictable and variable product development process. The lean method does not depend on a computer system (we use a highly visible board and notecards), and the variability is managed by the appropriate use of lean principles (see *Chapter 5*).

Lean R&D Principle: Be cautious with computers—computerizing a bad process creates an expensive bad process.

The power of computers can be used to create powerful tools. Some of those tools in R&D are FEA modeling tools, statistical analyses tools, and computer-aided design (CAD) tools. There are nonengineering computer tools that engineers cannot do without any more—internet, e-mail, social media, spreadsheets—that also affect how we do work.

Some lean concepts do not need computer tools—visual management, management of variability, kanban systems, A3, and so on—although lean practitioners have figured out ways to apply digital tools to some of these as well. But there also are processes used in a good lean product development where computerization can be an obstacle—conflict visibility and resolution, problem solving, and visual planning are good examples. Jim Morgan and Jeffrey Liker describe a principle in *The Toyota Product Development System*,[11] instructing readers to "adapt the technology to fit your people and your processes"—not the other way around.

Wherever you decide to computerize a process, make sure the process is well developed, defined, and focused on internal or external customer needs; that computerization adds value; and that you do not become a victim of the program and limit your options and capabilities. Lastly, and by all means, apply and test computer applications to the process in small batches with small learning cycles—identify where technology nicely fits a good process, possibly improves the process, or constrains or weakens the process. Funding software in small batches avoids scope creep and projects that last for years, cost a fortune, and deliver little value at the end.

At Goodyear: In R&D, we have embraced information technology where it supports our needs, such as the use of FEA analysis and in simulation tools. We also have learned that computers and software are not solving every problem. This is especially true if there is not a good process, as was the case with our failed attempt at project management software. We also learned to manage process computerization in small batches, so we can change direction quickly and even stop the initiative, thus saving time and money. We also are glad we never tried to computerize our lean project management process, and we are especially careful computerizing a process that thrives on regular human interaction.

CTO Joe Zekoski claims, "Not computerizing lean product development was one of the most effective decisions we have ever made in IT." Both he and I believe that you can easily become a victim of a computer system. Sometimes ignoring the system is not an option, but many engineers find themselves losing valuable options. Flexibility can be compromised, and computer output is only as good as the assumptions and the input. Beware.

Policemen, Ambulances, and the Downward Spiral

In Goodyear R&D, we had no criteria for accepting new work. A project could start as a result of a meeting with marketing, a request for new raw-material approval by a supplier, or a function deciding to develop new technology. Virtually everything was accepted and a project began. It was culturally unacceptable to say "No" to a request from another function, a customer, or a stakeholder. We always had a lot more projects than the capacity to complete them.

In Goodyear R&D, as with many other companies, projects rely on shared resources. Since we did not have unlimited resources to attend to the huge amount of work prior to our lean initiative, we used a "sophisticated" priority system, in which priority spots were awarded based on need, arguments, and power. This priority process for product development (priority list) existed in all functions: mold manufacturing, development/ building of test tires in the plant, and for every single test. Since functions decided between functional and cross-functional projects, priorities were often assigned based on what was in the best interest of the function. For example, the plants understood they needed new product from time to time, but too much development work lowered their performance indicators. They ignored the fact that their short-term production targets always allocated an anemic capacity for prototype tires.

A priority list would have between 200 and 300 projects, and only the first few on the list actually got done. Unless your project was at or near the top of the list, you had no idea when you would get your work done. Every function had its own priority meetings, and project managers spent a lot of time in those meetings or on the phone fighting for their projects.

Goodyear's priority process also was extremely unpredictable. Decisions made in a meeting about which project to pursue were obsolete 5 min after the meeting following a hallway discussion. The only predictable priority was for OEM projects—the more important the customer, the higher the priority—and, unfortunately, the importance in the ranking of the customer also changed from time to time. Sometimes several projects were identified as "the highest priority," and there had to be high-level arbitration to sort them out. The priority process was eventually "institutionalized," and crept into departments beyond R&D. Marketing figured out that they could only have *one* big project of high priority, so they wrestled for months selecting a project, only to change the decision a few days later. I am not sure who learned from whom, but similar priority queues existed in other functions as well, such as purchasing and HR.

Sometimes there was an important project that had to be done quickly, such as to fill a gap in the portfolio or an important customer needed to be placated. In these instances, a "special" project manager was assigned with all the privileges needed, and the project was delivered as expected. Unfortunately, the special project managers could not repeat the stellar performance on their next project when they had to share resources with all other projects.

At Goodyear, we called the absolute top-priority projects "ambulances." As an ambulance moved through the development process, it consumed all resources and all other work stopped. This is what happens when an ambulance rushes down the road: it makes a lot of noise, and everybody else must stop and figure how to merge back into the traffic when the ambulance has passed. At one time, the business started to designate so many ambulances that the ambulances got in each other's way. Imagine three ambulances showing up at the intersection at the same time or coming to the same hospital at the same time.

Innovation Traffic Jam

Goodyear's priority system turned managers and leaders into "policemen," trying to manage a traffic jam of projects and keep "ambulances"—highest priority projects— from getting stuck in product-development gridlock.

To make matters worse, when high-priority projects fell behind (and this always happened), management would get intimately involved and ask for daily updates. These updates, of course, took a lot of time and resources and caused projects to fall further behind. Eventually resources would be added to the high-priority projects, which rarely proved effective as predicted by Brooke's Law. (Brooke's law states that adding resources at the 11th hour is not effective because they rarely can contribute.)[12] With our focus on ambulances and doing anything to clear the road for them, all other projects were delayed and missed their deliveries, and another cycle of delays started, just much worse than the previous mayhem (i.e., the downward spiral described by Allen Ward).[13]

Instead of managing people and technology, Goodyear managers and leaders at the time felt more like policemen trying to manage traffic (see *Innovation Traffic Jam*). We eventually came out of the spiral when we discovered lean—and began to implement all those counterintuitive principles that come with lean.

It is not surprising that project managers and engineers became more creative at figuring out how to get something done than they were at inventing new tires. They say that if you reward firefighting, you create a team of arsonists. Many people in Goodyear learned how to create a "panic" to get attention for their project. Asking for forgiveness later was more popular than asking for permission in the first place.

Outside Help Does Not Help Out Enough

In 2005, Goodyear hired Porsche Consulting to help us bring products out on time. Porsche Consulting was formed by the Porsche car manufacturer after they learned enough about lean in manufacturing and R&D to make a business out of sharing their knowledge. Womack and Jones describe in *Lean Thinking*[1] how Porsche almost went bankrupt (despite having *the best* product on the market). After Porsche had implemented lean in manufacturing, they extended it to product development, resulting in the release of a new car model every couple of years, which they could not do prior to lean.

I was part of the team that traveled with the consultant through our innovation centers and plants and walked them through our process. After seeing the Goodyear product development process, the Porsche consultants would not commit to any improvement target, declaring that they could only help us improve a process *if we had a process*. They concluded that every engineer had their own process and that process knowledge was managed similar to the way ancient tribes managed their wisdom—by word of mouth. The consultant also identified the Goodyear priority system as a major issue, but Goodyear was not willing to mess with that process in the absence of a suitable replacement.

Although Porsche Consulting did not give us solutions, they taught us some tools during the gemba walks, brought us to their academy to teach us lean principles, and offered to coach us if we needed that service. To their credit, they did not sell us fish, they tried to teach us how to fish—a philosophy that I still maintain for internal lean implementations.

A number of our CIS experts and six sigma black belts were trained by Porsche during that tenure. When the six sigma activities slowed down at Goodyear, we had many full-time CIS experts without a CIS role. After word got out that we were starting lean in product development, they wanted to jump on board. The problem, from my perspective, was that some of these CIS experts, although trained well by Porsche Consulting in lean thinking, knew little about R&D or product development.

Several CIS experts were assigned to the product teams to "inspire" the teams and coach them to move toward a lean process. This did not work very well. Although many of the CIS experts had the right ideas and good suggestions, there was almost no acceptance by the teams. Some of the CIS experts picked a small process (normally a subprocess) and did good work redesigning the process, but the improvements to the subprocess did not have an impact on the overall process, and all the implemented improvement fizzled out quickly.

This illustrates a major problem with internal and external consultants when working on a lean initiative or any kind of initiative: they approach the work as an outsider (even when they are an internal CIS expert), rather than one inside and living and doing the work. They know what they know and want to advise on what they know, not necessarily what is needed and what is accepted by the people who work the processes. Another problem was that the lean improvement attempts were applied randomly and often to subprocesses.

When training, I give our participants a little homework to teach them about consultants and the diversity of thinking in the improvement marketplace. I ask them to research famous names in the lean world and then report for a few minutes on a couple of facts about these individuals and what they promote. The research is easy, since there is an abundance of information on the web. Then I ask the class to reflect on what they just learned.

Their first answer is always that no one guru has all the answers, and participants are always surprised by the volume of lean wisdom and tools that exist. Or, put another way, if we hired consultants, we would have to hire a lot of them. The same is true with most books and publications—they often promote only some of the principles that apply to a process, which eventually leave the most impactful problems unsolved.

I also have noticed that a lot of the consultants have a problem understanding a company's culture. The reason for that is that it takes more time than the consultants can afford to spend in a company (or that the company can afford to spend on the consultant), and so they rely on reports and interviews rather than firsthand observation (go and see). It is, however, the culture that must change in a lean transformation, and it helps to know the baseline.

With culture I mean all the behaviors, ways, habits, and means that worked well over the years as well as what makes people feel safe and comfortable in their roles. Unless there is a kaikaku, where things get shaken up, associates like to stay with their habits and ways of doing things. Few consultants are able to work through the cultural challenges of a large company—I have seen some terribly "culturally challenged" consultants in my company and other companies. On the other hand, I have seen successful consultants who focused on educating the associates and let the associates lead the change.

Matrix and Project Management

Goodyear's second kaikaku came in May of 2006 when we switched to a matrix organization within R&D. Our functions were already very flat and on their way to becoming globally oriented (e.g., global tire engineering, global material science, global testing). The big change was the creation of a matrix organization and the institution of project managers to manage projects horizontally across the functions. The business had already created EPLs—enterprise project leaders—and R&D alignment was needed.

Before the reorganization to a matrix, projects were managed in R&D by the functional chief engineers (we always called our functional managers "chief engineers" at Goodyear and retained that title through the reorganization)—they managed staff, technology, and projects. The engineering chief engineers were the default project managers because they made the biggest contributions to the projects, but they were not trained in project management skills. Instead, they learned by making mistakes, there were no standards for managing projects, and they typically managed projects within their function and then handed it off to manufacturing.

R&D leadership did their homework on the reorganization: an all-day workshop was organized in the Goodyear Theater—the attendees were all leaders, managers, and chief engineers that would be affected by the change. The workshop was chaired by our CTO at that time and the general director GIC*A, Jean-Claude Kihn. The new structure was explained and input was solicited and discussed. A few days later, the complete R&D organization was assembled in the same theater, and Jean-Claude explained to them why the organization had to be changed, and then the technical directors presented the newly appointed project leaders—the equivalents of the Toyota chief engineer or shusa. Then the functional directors presented the new functional organizations and their leaders. Goodyear was becoming a very flat, matrix organization.

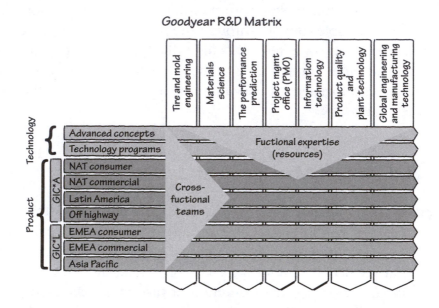

Goodyear R&D Matrix

Jean-Claude explained that project management itself would become a new function. Just as all engineers report to a functional boss and a project manager, the project managers would report to the regional technical directors and have a secondary reporting line to the leader of the project management function. I do not believe that there was a "lean" master plan at the time yet—the matrix reorganization came with the arrival of a new leader (Jean-Claude) and seemed to be the right thing to do—but it certainly turned out to be a prerequisite for the changes to follow, and I am glad it was done ahead of and not as a result of the lean initiative.

New Approach to R&D Project Management

The matrix organization brought to R&D a new approach to project management. Project management is often misunderstood as making project plans with software programs and Gantt charts and then communicating those plans and executing accordingly—giving everyone deadlines and then checking on progress. Project management in lean initiatives is so much more, and crucial in a lean process environment.

At Goodyear, we created a project management office (PMO), which is in charge of the project management standards and, of course, project management training and coaching. Jeff McElfresh, manager R&D PMO and a certified project management professional, heads up the PMO function. Jeff worked in many functions, learned how to bring projects to market, and learned project management by doing it. Today Jeff reports to Andy Weimer, director of Global Operations. Andy explains that every R&D project must be managed according to our project management standard work (reflected in our PMO Playbook) and that those project management standards integrate industry best practices with our specific internal processes and standards, including our lean standards. As our project standards evolve, the standards are communicated to the project managers with specific training as required.

Toyota often described their chief engineers as "supermen" because they are responsible for every aspect of a new car—Toyota refers to the new car as the "chief engineer's car." Although at Goodyear the project managers do similar things that the chief engineers do at Toyota, the Goodyear project managers have not reached the "supermen" stage yet, nor do I think that is the goal. What is part of the goal is that we learn to manage projects to assure maximum customer value and profitability of our value streams and that we get better at it all the time.

Every part of a project needs to be managed, even the "fuzzy" innovative and creative stages. Many companies leave this task up to the innovator or the inventor. This may work for some time if the inventor happens to have good project management skills, but there certainly comes a time when the innovator gets overwhelmed with the sheer amount of work, and many great ideas die in this phase.

Project management does not only include the roles of the project managers, but it also includes the roles of the sponsors, the engineers, management, and leadership in an effective R&D organization. Project managers also manage the project risk, which is the likelihood of achieving goals for a particular project (e.g., achieve technical performance or cost or financial targets).

Brandy Moorhead, once a Goodyear project manager, was managing an important lean project for our then-VP of Tire Development (Joe Zekoski). She like many other project managers relied on the PMO coach: "My PMO coach held me accountable to the PMO Playbook and standards every step of the way. This support was important as I was a new project manager."

Lean R&D Principle: Develop project management standards and competencies.

Generating knowledge and value across disciplines and managing the creation of new and profitable value streams are critical activities that require specific skills. Project management is a competency or discipline like engineering or material development and must be treated, trained, learned, and managed just like any other discipline. Every project in R&D must be managed according to solid project-management standards—and that includes projects related to the "fuzzy" frontend that deal with creativity and innovation.

Project management standards must be created and maintained. As new knowledge becomes available, it must be captured and the standards must be updated to lock in the new knowledge and make it available to all the managers. As you can see, one responsibility of project management is to generate knowledge, as projects move across functions. This role is similar to the functions that develop knowledge (vertically) in their function.

An R&D organization must define responsibility to manage the project management knowledge—one possible method to do that is to create a PMO or a project management function.

At Goodyear: Toyota uses chief engineers (called "shusas") for project management; at Goodyear, we simply call these individuals project managers. Project managers represent the customer and manage the creation of customer value across functions. Our use of well-trained project managers and sound project-management techniques has enabled us to advance projects in a meaningful manner and helped to deliver projects on time, on performance, and on budget. The project management organization also has contributed a lot to making virtually all new products profitable today. The PMO is a global function integrated in the development operations that maintains the project management standards and drives continuous improvement.

A lot of the Goodyear PMO standards are reflected in the many books and publications that were written about project management, including PMBOK® standards.[14] I would like to limit the discussion here to four aspects of project management that I found very important in the lean product development organization: project sponsor, project charter, project goals, and risk management.

Sponsor

The project sponsor is a person who demonstrates an interest in the outcome of the project and who is responsible for securing spending authority for the project. The sponsor should be a vocal and visible advocate, who legitimizes the project's goals and objectives, stays informed on major project activities, and supports the project decisions. The sponsor also is needed because most projects are cross-functional in nature, which often require functions to change the way they work and could affect the ability of the functions to meet their functional goals or metrics.

The Goodyear R&D sponsor of the year in 2013, Jean-Pierre Jeusette, general director GIC*L, defines a sponsor as someone being able to listen to, help, and coach the manager and the team as needed and visibly respect the project management principles, for example, not allow scope creep. (We had a hard time getting management to accept their roles as sponsors, so in 2013 we created the "sponsor of the year" award.)

At Goodyear, many sponsors considered their role "representative" or "ceremonial." Some sponsors did not even implement the project recommendation in their own function or realm of influence, and project managers would question why they accepted the sponsor role in the first place. Although sponsors should be visible, some leaders prefer it when project managers use their own influence to gain functional support for their projects and only use the sponsor for mentoring and consulting—unless project success is put into question. Of course, every sponsor must get involved when problems escalate to their level or if resource decisions require their involvement. At Goodyear, we had to organize sponsor training to make sure current and potential sponsors understand their role and responsibility.

Project Charter

The charter, approved by a sponsor, authorizes a project to be undertaken and resources to be expended. The charter is a broad definition of the project—broad enough that it does not need to change as the project progresses and specific plans are altered.

The charter defines accountability, the deliverables, the timing, and the responsibility of all functions involved, including that of the project team. It also aligns all functions involved. Brandy said that through a difficult change process the charter was "True North"—the compass that empowered the team to drive the changes required to reach the project goal. For her particular project, the functional leaders were uncomfortable that a team was "messing around" with the way the functional processes were operated. The charter and the authority it provided helped her assure alignment, stakeholder buy-in, and a focus on clear measurable deliverables.

Project Goals

The goals for a project should be SMART (specific, measurable, attainable, realistic, and time-bound). Although traditional project management advocates attainable goals, lean goals are often called "aspirational." They are normally three to five times higher than attainable goals. Jean-Claude explained it like this: "If I ask for 10%, I will get 10% and the goal is met. If I ask for 50% and get 30%, I am 20% ahead. These aspirational goals require that people sometimes must think outside the box."

Joe Zekoski, CTO says, "A goal of 10% just makes people pedal faster. With a goal of 50%, they must change the way they do business."

Attainable goals are often negotiated to the bitter end, especially if there are consequences if the goals are not met (i.e., you are expected to achieve them, or else), and there often is no incentive for going above the goal. Aspirational goals have the disadvantage that they are considered almost impossible, but the project normally delivers the best possible result. If aspirational goals are used, it must be clear what the expectation is and that it is aligned with the performance management system. With either SMART or aspirational goals, all stakeholders should be involved in setting the goals and empowered to meet the goals.

Often it is difficult to set a good goal at the beginning of a project; I believe initial goals should reflect an understanding about the "best possible" outcome of the project based on information available at that time. Then, as more information becomes available, goals can be changed to become more realistic. In every case, there has to be a measurement to assure progress is made. This method of adjusting goals is popular with quick learning cycles—where goals are set by the team members with the customer for each short cycle, and they are reset in the reflection at the end of the cycle.

Risk Management

The PMBOK® definition of risk as it relates to project management is, "An uncertain event or condition that, if it occurs, has a positive or a negative effect on a project objective."[15] (It is important to recognize that project risks can sometimes be positive.) A project risk has three defining elements, which are also the basis of FMEA tools:

1. It is an identifiable event.
2. It has a probability of occurring.
3. It has an impact (or consequences) to the project if it does occur.

A lot of waste in today's R&D processes is linked to inadequate risk management. Risk management is the systematic, iterative process of identifying, analyzing, and responding to project risk. Its goal is to maximize the probability and impact of any positive risk factors and to minimize the probability and impact of any negative factors. The project manager has ultimate responsibility for risk management in the project and is responsible for initiating and leading the risk management process.

Initially at Goodyear, we noticed that as more capacity was created through the implementation of lean principles, most of that freed up capacity was used to indiscriminately reduce the project risk, that is, new capacity was used for additional iterations and testing. This is a natural reaction by engineers and project managers in the absence of good risk-management standards. Engineers are perfectionists, and in the absence of good risk-management standards, they like to err on the safe side. Currently, at Goodyear, a team sponsored by the directors of design engineering and product evaluation is defining risk-management standards. Tools like FMEA are used for the assessment and the mitigation specifies an array of computer modeling and tests that must be run.

Laurent Colantonio, director Global Tire Performance Prediction, says that project risk is assessed at the beginning of a project, after every new iteration, and at the end of the project based on the current knowledge and the performance target. A DFMEA is maintained by a team of experts and the stakeholders, and the results of the DFMEA specify if the technical risk is acceptable, if another iteration is needed, and the modeling or testing that is required. Laurent explains that all the performance parameters affect each other and that without the scrutiny of this process the interaction can potentially be overlooked. No process is perfect, he notes, but when applied rigorously, we continuously improve as we learn with every cycle.

Lean R&D Principle: Combine risk management with project management.

A lot of waste in a product development process is due to the lack of good risk-management standards. Standards for risk management are probably some of the most important standards in a product development process because random or "one size fits all" risk management can have undesirable consequences.

It is fortunate and common that engineers are perfectionists who like to err on the side of overengineering or too much testing. Risk-management standards should establish a prudent and conservative baseline and get improved as more is learned.

Project risk depends on many different things: the technology, the phase of the project (beginning or end), the ease of detection, the potential exposure and consequences, the manufacturing processes, and so on. Until better tools are invented, FMEAs, DFMEAs, PFMEAs, and the like are still appropriate tools to use for risk management.

At Goodyear: When we began removing waste from product development, it created additional capacity. This newfound capacity was then used by engineers and project managers for more iterations and more testing. At Goodyear, engineers and project managers took the "belt and suspenders" approach with a couple of spare suspenders in the back pocket. Today, they have better suspenders, and the suspenders are customized based on the conditions. A cross-functional team has recently established a set of conservative risk-management standards that may or may not need improvement as more is learned.

Lean Firsts at Goodyear

With many building blocks for lean in place and others gradually being established, Goodyear's R&D department was about to begin its lean initiative for real in 2006. We were about to make many, many changes and some mistakes along the way, but we would learn from our mistakes and radically change the way we worked.

Crusaders, a White Knight, and a Map

After I received my charge to start trying some lean "stuff," I pulled together an informal team of open-minded R&D experts. I did not look to our CIS experts to be the members on this team, instead following what I had learned about Toyota. At Toyota, the best people to improve the assembly line process are the people who assemble the cars every day, not the industrial engineers who use scientific principles to design assembly lines. I am convinced the same is true for product development: the best people to improve the R&D process are the engineers, technicians, project managers, directors, scientists—those who operate in the process every day.

All team members I gathered were volunteers. They also were "crusaders," willing to go to battle for a better way to develop new products. We named our team "Herbie" after the Boy Scout character in Eli Goldratt's book, *The Goal*.[16] (Those of you who have read the *Goal* will ask, "Wasn't Herbie the kid who caused a bottleneck?" Please be patient until we get to *Chapter 5*.)

The Herbie team consisted of several project managers, enterprise team leaders, functional leaders, and engineers representing many disciplines; they had experience in product development and were held in high regard by their peers. We also had marketing and manufacturing representation (adjacent functions), and there were a few CIS experts as well who wanted to be part of the team. The CIS experts, by the way, disappeared soon—they could not relate to the mostly technical conversations of the Herbie team.

> *The best people to improve the R&D process are the engineers, technicians, project managers, directors, scientists—those who operate in the process every day.*

None of the team members had authority to make changes across the value stream, but they all had the capability or the influence to make change happen, often beyond their area of responsibility. They also had the credibility to influence upward. Later in the implementation, the Herbie team members frequently discussed our undertaking at functional meetings, and they participated as trainers in the lean training.

Early on, we also had a few team members who were not at all convinced that we were doing the right thing—those folks, without knowing it, provided valuable input on what the arguments and the obstacles would be out there. They also added to the credibility of the team's recommendations and prepared us for questions to come. Unfortunately at that time, I did not know the tools that could have been used to exploit the antagonistic team makeup. Jean-Claude personally quizzed the team members about their commitment to collaborate and make this happen (sort of like the "oath of a crusader" pledging allegiance to the cause).

Although we were on a lean journey, almost all discussions by the Herbie team early on were of a technical nature, talking about what was done in the design process, why it was done, and where we had strengths and weaknesses. Only after the team was aligned on *what* had to be done did we start the discussion on *how* to do it, leading into the process discussions. We, of course, had a few false starts and meanderings. This eventually led the team to conclude that we needed a *charter* and a few goals, beyond "implement lean."

> ### Lean R&D Principle: Improve processes from the inside out.
>
> Those who know a process and the work are the best suited to improve it. This approach to process improvement assures that the people trying to improve the process know the process in detail. It also assures sustainability, since those individuals making changes will be the ones working with and benefitting from those changes (i.e., rarely if ever is a changed process more challenging for an individual—different, yes, but challenging, no).
>
> Teaching people in the process the lean principles and engaging them in improving the process is an efficient and successful method to make meaningful improvement. This approach mimics Toyota teaching and practice, whereby the people who work on the assembly line are the ones making the improvements.
>
> It is normally easier to teach and coach those who know a process the lean tools than to take "universal" improvement experts or consultants and teach them enough about the skills of the trade and the product development process. Training should begin early in your implementation, and it may need repeated. It also needs to occur throughout the value stream; if R&D is participating in designing value streams, then those individuals manning adjacent processes throughout the value stream need to get on board as well.
>
> The difficulty when taking this approach is freeing resources available for training and improvement events. You will encounter those

who believe that process improvement is the job of the continuous improvement organization. You will be faced with the challenge of freeing up time for individuals from "their real work" to be trained and find the time to work on process improvements.

At Goodyear: We have learned that the people best suited to improve a process are the people who work in the process. Similarly, cross-functional collaboration between all value-stream members is the best way to improve a value stream. This approach proved to take more time and effort than recruiting a few CIS experts or consultants. We invested a lot of time and resources on lean training, but we got sustainable improvements as a return.

One of the hardest parts was to get functions to understand that they had to assign their resources to cross-functional process *development, just as they assigned them to cross-functional* product *development. They had to learn their responsibility in developing products and capability.*

Goodyear engineers have always had a problem when some other function or service "messed" with their processes and tools. "Help" was rarely appreciated, and engineers were reluctant to use tools, like models and predictive tools, that were developed by another function. Chris Helsel, former director Global Technology Projects, says, "At Goodyear we have always had problems when functions build capability for other functions to follow. Those who do the work must develop the process, not the process-building experts."

Our First Value-Stream Map

The early discussions of the Herbie team were all technical, but the team soon got into discussion on how designers do their work. These *process* discussions are very difficult because you cannot see the work and, consequently, you have a hard time to see the process—if you cannot see it, it is hard to improve it. This is when you need a flowchart, process map, or a value-stream map.

One of the first value-stream maps that I ever saw was in one of our plants. The person responsible for the map took us into this large room and proudly showed us a map that wrapped around the room. Pointing out the myriad steps and processes on the map, she admitted that she and the team eventually sort of gave up trying to use it—it was too complicated.

At one time at the Goodyear Innovation Center in Akron (GIC*A), we had what looked like "value-stream maps" in every conference room. Many of these were not really value-stream maps, but process depictions drawn on sticky notes and glued to brown paper and pasted on walls—we had a very large roll of brown paper. The people who used the conference rooms wondered how and by whom the maps were used.

Jim Womack visited Goodyear in 2011 and met with Goodyear R&D leadership. Among other things, he said most companies that he visited had walls full of value-stream maps (VSMs), but they had little involvement or action by anyone with the maps. Our leaders really picked up on that, and we had to prove that some maps actually led to results. Unfortunately, we also did not understand the tool well enough, and we wasted a lot of time making value-stream maps for problems that did not need a map.

Paul Dicello, project manager, who participated in several value-stream maps early on at GIC*A, remembers that developing the maps was a lot of fun. Even the engineers who did the work for many years had no idea where a lot of the work went when they finished their part. Paul was amused to see so many "black holes" in the process. For example, nobody in the room seemed to know how money got allocated; all they knew is that somebody typed a request in a computer system. Engineers understood their piece of the process, but few understood the contributions of others. Some convoluted, undocumented processes were the remnants of functional power struggles many years ago. Paul says that even if our early maps were not yet used to drive process change, they began to open our eyes to process handoffs and other significant process issues.

When the Herbie team made its first value-stream map, it became obvious that our product development process was too cumbersome and far too complicated. Some products were delivered when they were needed, and others were not. And if they were delivered late, it was because of individuals who had the final word on setting the preference lists (mostly production)—at least we found whom was to blame!

In the absence of something better to do, the team decided to brainstorm solutions to the problem. We came up with ideas, and the team ranked the solutions and voted. The idea that got the most votes was to improve the process step of preparing samples for prototype analysis. As the team started to work on this idea, everyone realized that this could not be what we were supposed to do!

To help us through this confusion, I brought in a colleague, Cigdem Gurer, who at the time was in charge of implementing an engineering outsourcing program in R&D. Cigdem, who has gone on to become chief technology officer at Cyient-Insights, had lean experience from manufacturing, knew the development process, and was a good thinker. She first convinced me that I knew nothing about lean and that my team knew nothing either (she is the one who told me to study *Factory Physics*[17]). In addition to reading *Factory Physics*, I started attending workshops on lean product development and took the time to read more books on lean product development. I gradually began to understand some of the problems with our development process, and, as important, the principles and tools that we could use to correct them. And I was able to begin teaching my teammates what I was learning.

From those early Herbie team days, we eventually learned how to correctly develop a value-stream map that led to improvements (see *Value-Stream Mapping 101*).

Brad Heim, manager New Product Industrialization, led an initiative in 2011 that used value-stream mapping the way it is intended, and Brad's team achieved meaningful process improvements:

> As the plants were challenged to reduce the cycle time for the prototype development, we put a team together that traveled to all the plants in North and Latin America to study the process. The team trained the plant staff in the basic lean principles. Then the team went to the gemba and walked the complete development process back to front, talking to machine operators, fork truck drivers, schedulers, engineers, etc. Eventually the teams documented the process from each plant in a value-stream map and assigned responsibilities to address quick fixes and low hanging fruit.
>
> Next plant representatives from all the plants were brought together, and all the processes were shared. The plant representatives put together a map of the best process that can be done today with the combined knowledge they all had. Based on this ideal case, a gap analysis was done for each plant and a list of action items was established to close those gaps. The plant representatives went back to their plants and started implementing the improvements.
>
> As a result of the improvements, plant iteration times were reduced by 60%, which was key to success with the single-piece-flow initiative that followed. In addition to driving cycle time down drastically, OTD continued to be increased to levels above 95%. We also proved to our leaders that value-stream mapping is a very powerful tool in the lean practitioner's toolbox when used correctly: i.e., these value-stream maps do not decorate an office wall.

Value-Stream Mapping 101

Today we teach value-stream mapping in several of our lean classes, and we teach our people when to use the tool and how to get the most out of a value-stream map (VSM).

Before you make a VSM, you need to understand what a value stream is. According to Jim Womack and Dan Jones, "A value stream is the connected activities that create value."[1] John Shook and Mike Rother describe in *Learning to See*[18] that you need a value-stream map to make a process visible that you cannot yet see.

Since Shook and Rother's work, many books have been written on the subject, and value-stream mapping has become one of the most popular lean tools; actually, it is so popular that it became the default tool for many lean projects, even if it was not necessarily the right tool.

So when should you create maps in product development, and how do you create them so that they lead to measurable results? Let us start with what a VSM is supposed to do: a map makes the flow of value visible, so that you can better understand it, so that the process can be improved. What a lot of lean practitioners do not understand is that the map does not solve a problem or improve a process. It is only a tool to make a process visible, so that problems can be made visible and identified by people—the problems then are fixed by people with various lean or other tools. *For many people the first value-stream map is their first attempt at finding out if there is even a process, and they sometimes realize how little process there is. That is OK—there does not have to be a lot at the start, as long as there is a basis for improvement.*

There are many standard symbols, conventions, and best practices that make drawing a map easier and make it possible to communicate VSMs throughout an organization. Ideally, it becomes another language, a kind of shorthand that everyone in your company recognizes and speaks. There are computer programs for creating maps, but I rarely use them. I prefer to draw the map on the wall with the team.

To understand the power of VSMs, begin by imagining a process that you want to understand better—it does not have to be a process from work. Pick a process at home or one that has bothered you at a place that you often visit. Keep this process in mind as you continue reading.

Value-stream maps require a

- *Purpose*—Make a VSM because you believe a problem (quality, delivery) can be surfaced via the map, not because it is a popular lean tool or because a manager likes value-stream maps.
- *Viewpoint*—A map from the perspective of the patient going to the doctor and waiting in the waiting room will look different than the view from within the doctor's office that examines the efficiency of their process to see patients. Both maps are meaningful but different.
- *Process*—Maps must visually describe a process. I have seen many failed attempts to use maps to illustrate a technical product problem, a policy or behavioral issue, or a job-satisfaction concern.
- *Action*—Each map should be accompanied by the motivation to do something about the problem once it has been identified on the map. This is what fails most of the time, and that is why all those lonely maps hang in offices. Value-stream maps make many problems visible, but it takes resources to fix those problems. Those resources often must come from the process owners.

If these requirements exist for your map, resist the temptation to jump in and begin putting sticky notes on your large brown paper. First find a sponsor—not a sponsor of the value-stream map, but a sponsor who will help you obtain resources to work on the problems that the map will uncover. That often will need to be an individual with some authority or influence over various process owners.

With requirements identified and the backing of a sponsor, conduct a few gemba walks. Go out there and see for yourself what is going on. Walk the process, talk to the people, collect data, and gather some facts. Meet the people who know the process—the individuals you need to bring into the meeting room to help draw the process. Then it is important to train those involved in the exercise in some lean principles and the VSM tool.

Once you begin drawing the map, it may be helpful to use a facilitator, who can help to settle arguments that may come up during the mapping process. You will be surprised by the varied perspectives of an identical process, even when there is alignment. Many people see the complete process for the first time in this exercise and they may not know who they interface with and why.

You also will encounter disagreement about what should be represented on the map. You cannot show everything. Your map should, though, incorporate the following:

- *Concise, high-level view on one page*—Shook and Rother recommend that maps should only be *one page* with a small number of blocks that depict process steps. That is excellent advice, and I always limit the space. It helps people focus, and it forces everybody to draw the map at the highest level, without losing themselves in details. You may eventually have to draw another map of subprocesses to better see those details, but start high level.
- *Focus on flow*—Start with the main process steps and lay out the flow of the value and the information. Add the relation between the steps (push, pull, concurrent) and the key inputs that are needed for each step. Most R&D VSMs have iterations, loopbacks, and corrections. It is important to depict those on the map too.
- *Pertinent data and facts*—Include data that relate to the problem that you are trying to solve. The maps that decorate conference rooms rarely have enough data or facts. Often just adding data to the current-state map alone shows you where the problems are. Typical data used for VSMs are cycle times, delivery, accuracy, loopbacks, and so on.
- *The objective*—Remember that at the end of the exercise, you should implement an improvement. Always keep that in mind.
- *Constant reality check*—The map must represent what is going on, so keep questioning the experts to make sure your map represents reality.
- *80/20 rule*—80% is always, and 20% is rarely or never. Processes have many tangents, special cases, and unique customers. Your map cannot address all of these perspectives in the first pass. But if you find that all the problems you are trying to solve are related to a special case, then draw the map for the special case.

If you have a hard time creating a good current-state value-stream map, it may be that there is no process or you are trying to map too many different processes in one map.

Mapping experts often advise that you draw a current-state map (what the process looks like now), and then you draw a future-state map (what the improved process should look like). This can be a good approach, but keep your future state to something that is achievable within a short timeframe. Do not, however, draw a future-state map without a good understanding of the current state and the real needs and shortcomings of the process.

When analyzing the current state and the data, facts, and opinions you have gathered, look for insights related to your *purpose*—the problem(s). Often you will find waste (time, effort, movement, etc.) or a lack of flow (waiting, inventory piling up, and/or poor handoffs from step to step). Your map should surface causes to your problem. Once you identify causes, you and your mapping team must then identify the root causes and develop solutions and propose changes.

A lot of people identify "issues" after they finished the current-state VSM. Issues are typically represented by a starburst on the map. Teams then try to find solutions to the problems or issues and develop countermeasures. They will then incorporate these countermeasures into a future-state map. Resist the temptation to draw the future state before a solid understanding of the current state and before supporting the current-state map with the data needed for a good analysis. Based on my experience, future-state maps are not always needed and can lead to fewer improvements because too much time is spent mapping rather than solving problems. Continue to use observations, data, facts, and root-cause analysis rather than simply brainstorming.

Here is the method that I teach:

■ If after creating your current-state map, and especially after adding some data to it, the issues or problems stare you in the face, then just move on that. Pick the low-hanging fruit and get results. Find the root causes before you fix problems.

■ After the low-hanging fruit has been picked or you conclude that there is none to pick, identify key remaining issues. Rather than brainstorm solutions, I recommend to focus on those issues that are tied to the reason why you made the map in the first place and get enough data and facts related to those issues. Then prioritize them by potential effect and ease of implementation.

■ If more visibility is needed to understand where you want to go, then draw the map for a short-term future state. This future state can be inspired by a long-term "dream" state (i.e., the ideal process), but it has to be able to be implemented in the near term. Then examine and quantify the gaps between the future state and the current state. What must happen to get to the future state?

■ If you have identified problems or gaps that must be addressed, I suggest you move on to developing one or more A3 projects: get a sponsor for the specific problem-solving A3 efforts, and then assign the A3s to qualified and motivated people (*for more on A3, see Chapter 7*). The creation of an A3 is one method to assure the problem is understood and a root cause has been identified. The individual assigned to the A3 will identify the countermeasures to close gaps and show how the work will get done.

■ Gaps and the work to close them are sometimes overwhelming. It is a good idea to break that work down into small steps. The steps should have a specific goal, and the time to close the gap should be limited; without this focus, the work can drag on for a long time because the people who work on the problems also have func-tional responsibilities as well.

Lean 101 Training

The Herbie team consisted of R&D technical experts trying to implement lean—not lean experts trying to apply the methodology to R&D. Members understood our slow process, but had little or no knowledge of lean and how to use lean to improve the process. Together with some of our teaching experts and a few in-house lean experts from other parts of the organiza-tion, we developed a simulation that mimicked our product development process. People had fun with the exercise, and they were amazed how real-istic the simulation was.

We had participants draw the simulation process out in a value-stream map, then we taught them some simple lean principles, such as waste, flow, and pull. This exercise highlighted some of our largest issues—the focus on functional efficiency at the expense of project speed, the waiting time, the lack of standard work, and the wastes. The feedback from that simula-tion was good, and associates agreed, "This was like us working every day."

They could finally see the process we were using, the issues, and what we could do about them.

We then broke the group into small teams and let them redesign the process based on the principles they had just learned. Each small team made huge improvements by identifying where and how to eliminate wastes like motion, overprocessing, waiting, and rework, and the simulation was a positive experience.

We got the message across that the basic lean principles, when applied correctly to the product development process, could make a big difference—more important was the fact that the engineers themselves were applying the principles and redesigning a process. I believe the fact that we made the redesign process a competition made it fun and interesting.

We presented our Lean 101 training to our leaders as well, who then made it mandatory for every associate. Lean 101 is now part of the core training for all new employees. Tom Laurich, lead engineer, says, "The Lean 101 training is priceless. It is simple, clear, and tells the engineers why we do certain things. We used to just be told what to do."

Now we had a Herbie team with members who understood the development process and the technical aspects and technology (which they already knew), *and* they had experienced the effect of applying lean principles. They had the lean knowledge they needed at that moment of our journey (see *Hands-on, Just-in-Time Training*). We now had an influential team of experts, not quite empowered yet but almost ready to make changes.

Now I understand why W. Edwards Deming wrote, "Everyone doing his best is not the answer. Everyone is doing his best. It is necessary that people understand the reason for the changes that are necessary. Moreover, there must be consistency of understanding and effort."[19]

Lean R&D Principle: Train, train, train—and then train again.

Since successful lean product development relies on the process experts and leadership to learn and apply lean principles, training plays a crucial role and should begin early in the transformation. Of course, "early" training may need repeated because people may forget parts of what they learned before they apply the principles. More advanced lean training must be phased in as the process changes and lean is taken to a new level.

As an engineer, I could only understand lean principles when I could understand the background and math or science behind them. Others will want to see the concepts in action or need to apply them to understand them. For this reason, both an explanation of the principles and hands-on training and subsequent practice are core components of lean training. Remember that it is difficult to explain counterintuitive concepts, and so a well-structured training regimen should be planned for your implementation, one that addresses the many ways individuals learn and that ties their learning to their transformation needs. Training also should be delivered on a "just-in-time" basis.

Your lean training also should be targeted at *all* those involved in the process, and that includes management and leadership. A lean transformation and new processes require different behaviors for managers and leaders, which also must be taught through formal education and practice.

Leaders should teach part of the classes. This sends a powerful message to all the associates that leaders understood this stuff and want all the associates to learn it too.

All training must be checked for effectiveness, including knowledge checks and feedback. Gemba walks and feedback will assess if people use what they learned in their regular work.

At Goodyear: We have four levels of lean training, from mandatory Lean 101 and Lean 201 courses to an optional Lean 300 series and Lean 401 certification (the equivalent of a six sigma black belt). Features common in all of our lean training are

- *Learn by doing*
- *Engage the class in interactive training*
- *Simulations and experiments*
- *Go and see what good looks like*
- *Coaching and mentoring*
- *Check on effectiveness of the training*
- *Fun*

Hands-on, Just-In-Time Training

It is important to teach people who work on the process the lean principles, and this will not happen without training. As with any developmental program, good training principles must be followed: set objectives, verify the learning and knowledge, and follow up with a good PDCA. As we learned in change management, the idea is to lead with education and communication. Musicians who learn a new piece often practice one little piece at a time—the same is true for lean training. The training also must be delivered just in time, so people can practice and use right away what they learned.

Since everybody who works in the process will be counted on for helping with the lean improvement, your whole organization should be trained in lean basics. Regardless of how you approach the training, it is important to teach people the lean *principles*, not just the tools. Lean principles are counterintuitive and they must be explained with a lot of examples from work and everyday life. Traditional Toyota-type training, mentoring, and learning on the job from managers and coaches may work for some organizations and transformations, but at Goodyear we needed to move quickly and went a different route. We found that hands-on activities (e.g., mapping) and simulations worked well, were fun, and helped the training to stick. I packed our Lean 101 Training with exercises, games, and activities.

Many people learn by doing. There has to be coaching after the training to help people apply what they learned to their jobs and help them practice and get better.

Gemba walks help to show training attendees what good looks like and are an effective aspect of lean training, especially is you can go to a different company, walk their process, and then discuss what you have seen. *Seeing* is an effective lean-training tool—videotape processes and review them together. You also can purchase videos depicting lean process changes.

During our lean initiative, we learned that one-time training was never enough. People often forgot what they learned before they were able to make use of what they learned. CTO Joe Zekoski remembers how we had to train several times: first to teach the principles to get individuals engaged in changing the process (Lean 101), then training them on the new process, and then one or two follow-ups as the process evolved (Lean 201). Today, new employees learn the lean product development processes when they go through onboarding—lean is now the way we do work, and we do not specially call it out as "lean" any more.

Jean-Claude Kihn, our initial lean sponsor, listened to many criticisms and concerns during our lean start and would often ask me if I was sure that the training was effective. Eventually, I understood that it takes repeated training sessions, and my answer to Jean-Claude eventually became, "Looks like we need to train again."

This training and learning process eventually led us to time our lean training and topics to what was needed and when it was needed—just-in-time training—so that attendees could apply the information soon after their training. This approach became the foundation for our four-phase training program: Lean 101 and 201 (mandatory) and 301 and 401 (optional).

Goodyear Global Lean Curriculum

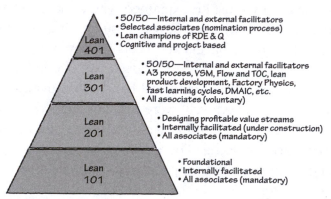

Lean 401
- 50/50—Internal and external facilitators
- Selected associates (nomination process)
- Lean champions of RDE & Q
- Cognitive and project based

Lean 301
- 50/50—Internal and external facilitators
- A3 process, VSM, Flow and TOC, lean product development, Factory Physics, fast learning cycles, DMAIC, etc.
- All associates (voluntary)

Lean 201
- Designing profitable value streams
- Internally facilitated (under construction)
- All associates (mandatory)

Lean 101
- Foundational
- Internally facilitated
- All associates (mandatory)

We believe the Goodyear Lean 401 training is unique in the industry. It is patterned after six sigma black belt training and consists of 3 weeks of classroom training, three books to read (and discuss), two A3 projects to complete, and a test. The content of the 401 training includes

- Principles of lean product development
- Knowledge management
- Some common lean tools like value-stream mapping and root-cause analysis
- Change management
- Influence management (how to lead without authority)
- A3 (managing to learn)

- Integrated lean project delivery
- Quick learning, scrum, and lean startups
- Basic DMAIC
- Lean management principles
- Gemba walks (to see what good looks like)

Participants in the 401 class are handpicked based on potential and need for practitioners. The class is taught by Goodyear associates and by outside teachers and consultants. We try at least one new subject or consultant for every 401 class. After every class, we interview the participants and ask for suggestions for improvement. Based on the feedback, we decide what good content should be continued and what should be replaced or improved. This also evolves the content as the company learns more. Sometimes we include participants from other companies, including Goodyear customers and suppliers, to broaden the content and get more diverse feedback and interaction. Joe wants all future managers and leaders to be certified in lean product development.

The results of this program are slowly becoming obvious. With this class we are now starting lean initiatives everywhere, and the initiatives are started and led by the people who work in the process, not by a consultant or a CIS expert. The best news is that these initiatives produce sustainable results. The lean 401 graduates (Joe calls them "apostles") also become teachers and coaches. We also now have the first 401 graduates in management positions.

Goodyear does not have a lean "green-belt" program in R&D, at least not yet, but we have an excellent six sigma black-belt program. The popular lean/six sigma green-belt program in other companies is a mini-version of the six sigma/DMAIC process and incorporates some lean tools. We use our A3/problem-solving process as a substitute for a green-belt program now, but we may create a more formal green-belt program in the future, probably adding lean and DMAIC training beyond A3/problem solving. We will focus the green-belt program on both functional and cross-functional problems. We also will make sure that the program is aligned (not random), does not duplicate other training efforts, focuses on the essentials, achieves results, and improves as we learn.

Jon Bellissimo, general director GIC*A, says that our training was the most important part of our lean transformation. He notes that some associates had real skepticism going into the initiative for R&D, viewing lean as just for manufacturing. Others thought they were the process experts and wanted to continue working the same way they always had. It was not until individuals were trained in lean and our overall metrics started to improve did we see acceptance to change.

Jeff Plauny was the director of Tire Engineering at the time, and he reflects back on the training: "It was very hard to get all leadership to support the lean initiative. It was pushed with training. Senior leaders were supposed to give a piece of the training. If you have to do that you will become a disciple very fast."

Herbie Gets Help

After our initial work with value-stream maps, the Herbie team continued to examine our process. We eventually came to an understanding that the speed and delivery of our process was terrible. The team collectively gathered data to support this hypothesis.

It was during this time that the Herbie team met regularly with Jean-Claude, general director GIC*A. We noticed that he was becoming increasingly engaged in the work that the team was doing and he gradually became our official sponsor. We met with him for 30–45 min every other week. This was a standup meeting in front of our value-stream map, which morphed into an improvement board, and issues were visualized and countermeasures were explained.

Adding a formal sponsor was an important and necessary evolution of our team and our lean progress, especially as he drew in functional leaders with whom we needed to cooperate for changes. With more functional observation during our Herbie meetings—if not actual involvement—the gatherings increasingly became defensive and finger-pointing events.

I recall one manager who refused to come into the meeting room—he decided to "listen in" from the adjacent room, and he occasionally peaked over the partition. Eventually, a confrontation happened between this manager and another manager who was in the room, and they came face to face across the partition. I learned that during a change process as big as this one, things get personal very quickly. Functional leaders were extremely defensive and took problems with their process personally, but since we had made the process highly visible, they eventually had a hard time coming up with excuses, instead asking, "Why are we defending a bad and broken process that we did not even create?"

Lean R&D Principle: Find a sponsor to support the change.

A *sponsor*—an individual in your organization who can "help make things happen"—is as important for a successful transformation as those actually making changes. The sponsor must have a relatively good background in lean processes, but does not necessarily have to be involved with (or have the time for) all the project details, problems, solutions, experiments, and so on. The sponsor supports and promotes the lean initiative, bringing awareness of lean achievements to others in the organization, and he or she has the authority or influence to allocate resources, make organizational changes, and help remove obstacles that might arise.

At the end of an initiative, the sponsor is responsible to help institutionalize the new process, which could mean changing policy, making organizational adjustments, updating standards, or allocating permanent resources. Most lean grassroot initiatives will need or use a sponsor eventually to grow and sustain the initiative.

At Goodyear: When we implemented the lean product development process at Goodyear, we had an excellent sponsor in Jean-Claude Kihn. It helped that our sponsor was the general director GIC*A, who eventually became the CTO during the initiative. We discussed new plans, and when he agreed with the plan, Jean-Claude fully supported the actions. He always encouraged me to use my own influence rather than counting on his authority, but I could always rely on his help, advice, and coaching. I eventually gained the authority needed to drive the change on my own. Jean-Claude led by example: he showed up at every team meeting, asked questions, motivated the team members, and helped with the training. He visually supported and defended the initiative when questions or obstacles came up. He knew the lean principles well and repeated the same arguments given by other promoters. When Jean-Claude left the innovation center in Akron for another assignment, we did not lose a beat because his successor, Joe Zekoski, and several other leaders stepped up to fill the role.

The First Lean Process

As the Herbie team took gemba walks, we learned that many parts in the organization each had their own product development process. One reason was that two development centers (Goodyear in Akron, and Kelly in Cumberland, MD) had been merged in the 1990s, but the engineers from those centers worked as they had learned when they joined the company at their disparate centers. In addition, many also had figured out shortcuts, further customizing the different processes. It also appeared to those of us on the team that different tire lines (like passenger cars and truck tires) did their work differently from one another. Even the team that developed passenger car tires for Ford seemed to have a different process than the team who developed tires for GM.

Only when we looked deeper at the details did we find pockets of consistent work—common blocks and problems in each process. I started to understand what the Porsche consultant had told us—we did not have *one* process, but as many processes as we had products and customers. *If we had to individually remedy all the processes it would take forever, and we were only looking at the first of three Goodyear innovation centers.*

One of our earlier efforts, which lasted about 6 months, was to try to improve one of those individual processes, the one that used to develop "private brand" tires (product that Goodyear makes for independent chains that have their own tire brand). We did great work to eliminate waste and gain speed in the process by applying lean principles and by using new computer design and drafting capabilities. But the results of our improvements could never be validated. Our improved process merged back into the slow overall mainstream and all our improvements were "absorbed." So even though most work from the private-brand development process was delivered early to the main process (mold-making, testing, etc.), this meant it only waited somewhere else. Our low-level efforts were having no impact on the overall process.

I once heard of a similar situation from a design manager of a furniture company. The design team of this company had done a marvelous job reducing the design time from 10 weeks to 10 days with standard work, modular designs, and new CAD design systems. The designers there were quite frustrated, though, because their reductions in design time (more than 85%) did not make any difference to the total time needed to launch a new product.

I knew how the furniture designers felt. No improvements had been made to the tire-development processes that came before, after, or interfaced with our private-brand design process. It still took a very long time for marketing to set goals for the product and as long to name the product. When the design was finished, it still took industrialization and testing the same amount of time as it always had. In fact, it turned out the adjacent functions had soon used up all the time gained in the design process. And, of course, the launch was not any faster either. This approach could not work.

But we plowed forward. We made value-stream maps for all individual consumer tire lines (high performance, OEM, broad market, SUV) and added design processes for aircraft tires, earthmover tires, and truck tires. The maps initially took up substantial room, but we gradually focused on limiting the space for the maps, and because of this they began to look more and more alike as we cut out detail and forced them to a higher, more general level. We saw that every team or function seemed to do some kind of modeling and design work—they all made molds, built prototype tires, and tested them. They would then repeat that process until they met their targets and proceeded with the industrialization of the product.

Through our mapping, we realized that there really was *one process after all*, and it seemed to be a very simple process. Today we are still working on and improving that same high-level process, but every improvement is leveled across many design teams and the three global innovation centers.

The Herbie team realized that if we could fix the issues on the highest level, where all the processes were the same, we only had to fix them once. If we could find a best way, we could make it a global standard, and everybody gets to take advantage of the learning. If process improvements are made on a lower level, they should be worked "up" to the highest level where they can be leveraged and examined to see how many other processes are covered at the same time.

It also became immediately clear to us that if we wanted to avoid what happened to the furniture company, we had to stay aligned with the other functions in the value stream, especially the adjacent functions—if not, the improvements in the design process would not be realized in the complete value stream. Fortunately, representatives from the adjacent function in the value stream (marketing and manufacturing) were represented on the Herbie team. Over time, we maintained alignment and we also improved their processes based on what we learned in product development. We also aligned the remaining functions (sales and distribution). To be quite honest, before this exercise I never really understood what it meant when I read about random kaizen and system kaizen. I also finally understood what Womack and Jones were describing in their book *Seeing the Whole Value Stream*.[20]

Lean R&D Principle: Make process improvements on the highest level and align functions end to end for highest benefits.

Processes should be improved or optimized on the highest level, so that all subprocesses can take advantage of the improvement. If at all possible, this should be done globally. Standards should be set on the same level, so best practices are shared and implemented everywhere in the most efficient manner.

The improvement in one process of a cross-functional value stream can best be leveraged if the adjacent processes remain aligned. As the alignment is maintained, all cross-functional processes in the value stream can be "leaned out" for maximum leverage of the improvements. This approach also assures the maximum benefit of a lean initiative, providing the kind of benefits that get the attention of leaders and associates alike, building their support.

At Goodyear: We develop many products, including tires for racecars, airplanes, SUVs, light cars, earthmovers, and trucks. We develop winter tires, summer tires, and tires for most OEMs. All those developing these varied products claimed to use a different process, but when we rolled it all up to the highest level, we recognized one consistent process, which consisted of computer modeling, engineering, materials development, tooling, prototyping, and testing. We standardized that process and used it for the baseline, so improvements made are realized by all global functions. We maintained the alignment of the design process with the adjacent functions in the value stream (marketing and manufacturing) through collaboration with all the stakeholders of the value stream. The alignment and the further improvement of all functions in the value stream yielded the largest improvements for the company.

All of this looked great on the value-stream maps, but how could we get the R&D functions on board, or more important, how could we get the value-stream stakeholders engaged?

The Herbie team consulted our sponsor about development of a high-level, value-stream map and our idea to standardize processes at that level. Of course, that was heresy in an organization that prided itself on its complex and diversified products and where managers had suboptimized their share of the process at the cost of the other processes and the expense of the end-to-end value stream. A meeting was arranged with all the functional leaders and project leaders, and Jean-Claude asked the question: "Can anybody not live with this high-level process?" There was a long pause in the room, but the faces of attendees gave away their thoughts: "Please don't do this to us!"

Then the least likely individual in the room—a director who led the most "special" process—said, "We can live with that," and, furthermore, suggested that there was no reason why others could not live with it as well.

After that meeting, we had *one* process, and we could start talking about meaningful improvement and standard work. Every improvement that we would do would benefit everybody. We also will leverage learning and be able to move resources between design disciplines, which we had never been able to do before.

This seismic change did not mean that everything was going to be put on the lowest common denominator: aircraft tires will be designed to work on an aircraft, Ford and Toyota will still get the tire they need because we have the automotive engineers (engineers in direct contact with customers) on every development team. It did mean, though, that modeling tools are deployed globally and molds are designed to the same standards globally and with the same design tools. It also opened the door for global engineering standards, prototypes standards, test standards, and so on. Most importantly, we would be using the same lean product development process in all our innovation centers. Tools, knowledge, and training also would be aligned, and resources exchanged, which would drastically improve the flexibility of the organization. We could even align standard working hours on three different continents to collaborate on the same drawing.

Today in Goodyear we still have some "individualism" going on—and that is OK. It does no damage, and it helps people feel good about their work. And nothing is cast in stone. Anything can be changed if justified and, especially, if we find a way to improve it.

> ### *Technical products are complicated; the processes to design them do not have to be.*

I listened many times to lean champions from other companies about their frustrations to leverage best practices through several technical organizations, usually the result of corporate acquisitions. They would talk about spending all their energy on futile efforts to share lean improvements across the "independent" processes. One company, a fraction of the size of Goodyear, operates 14 technical centers in seven countries—no two approach their work in the same way. In a situation like that, a lot of resources must be spent on individual improvements, and the results will not add up and they will wonder why lean is not giving them visible results.

The Herbie team continued to do most of its work in and on the consumer-tire workstream because that is the largest in Goodyear, but we did so with the confidence that our work would be applied at the broader, higher level and that other workstreams would eventually benefit. Then we realized: so now that we have only *one* process, what do we do to *improve* it?

Lean R&D Principle: Make things simple (again!).

The law of entropy says that everything in the universe strives to an order of more and more chaos. The same is true in large companies and the government—despite all the gains in efficiency and other improvements, things seem to always get more complicated over time. This is especially true for R&D organizations, where diversified products, complicated technology, and computer systems compound the complexity exponentially with each passing day.

"Simplicity is the ultimate sophistication," said Leonardo Da Vinci. Any lean implementation must attempt to restore simplicity to processes, and lean offers many great tools to restore simplicity.

Making things simple does not only apply to high-level processes; it is sound thinking for all levels, including day-to-day work. Most complications in work processes are "self-inflicted" and can be the result of an accumulation of rules and standards over time, which often turn obsolete. Questioning the way we work is a good first step toward making things simple again. Since the complication is self-inflicted, *we* (individual, function, organization) hold the key to reducing it. Technical products are complicated; the processes to design them do not have to be.

At Goodyear: Value-stream mapping was used to identify and simplify our processes that stretched across many disciplines and across several global development centers. Other lean tools to restore simplicity that we have used are standard work, waste-reduction techniques, and applications of common-sense approaches, such as go and see. Work is managed today on a visual planning board and short, standup meetings have replaced long status update meetings.

Face to Face with Functional Optimization

At Goodyear, functions used to be very strong and powerful. People had to demonstrate capability in the function to advance. Advancement was through the function—the step after the functional leadership role was leading more than one function—and the best functional leader would be picked for that job. Functions had their own metrics, and functional leaders would do anything to achieve their functional metrics, even when those metrics were counter to achieving benefits for the value stream.

For example, manufacturing had cost metrics, such as percentage of cost reduction per year. One manufacturing director limited the number of tire-development iterations, knowing the more iterations they did for R&D in the plant, the more new products with which the plant had to deal. Of course, new products can cause additional complexity and differentiation. New products also needed a ramp-up, which often requires the plants to spend time and effort to certify the tire. All of this could affect the performance indicators of the plant.

Another example of functional optimization was with testing. The most important functional metric in testing used to be machine utilization: 100% machine utilization is hard to achieve because of the variability in test times. Transporting tires from a plant to testing typically took a long time and was unpredictable as well. For that reason, the testing function liked to buffer with inventory (at least 1,400 tires per center) and keep an excessive number of tires queued up for every test, which, of course, increased the waiting time for test results.

In the face of such functional optimization, the Herbie team looked to our sponsor for guidance and support on how to improve the high-level, value-stream results and not the functional performance. We had weekly meetings in a little war room, usually with managers, directors, and project managers attending. One day, Jean-Claude explained to all of us that he noticed that the business units that complained the least about not getting new product were the most profitable. We all realized that our sponsor was nudging us toward a focus on *delivery*.

R&D Lean Principle: Focus on the baton, not the runner.

In a relay race, it is important that all the runners run fast, but it is more important that they collaborate to efficiently pass the baton and get it to the finish line, ideally before the batons of competitors. Imagine the runners are in different functions and the baton is a project—all that matters is that they perform well as a team and not lose the baton along the way in a bad handoff. All runners move in the same direction, each supports the other, and all agree that they are using one baton. They are ready and up to speed when the handoff occurs. It is absurd to think that they would carry many batons, participate in more than one race at the same time, or put the baton down while in the race because they have to compete in a different event, or wait because the other runner is not ready yet. They only focus on the one race.

Another major factor in a relay race are the handoffs of the baton. Just look at the recent performance of the American relay teams (Olympic Games and World Championships) where the best individual runners did not win because they dropped the baton. Similarly, poor handoffs can derail excellent projects. Handoffs do not just happen; they must be prepared on both sides and require a lot of good collaboration.

In a relay race you can see the baton. In a factory you may not be able to see the complete process, but you can attach a tag to one piece and track it through the process. In a project development process, the project is the baton, but it is hard to see. Eventually the baton should emerge from the process, and with minimal delay as smooth handoffs occur from function to function and each function runs with the baton with the same level of purpose and desire.

At Goodyear: It took us a long time to move from recognizing great individual runners to bringing the baton to the finish line first and winning races. Interestingly enough, the change was not accomplished with incentives, like rewarding the best runners or individual performances. Instead, we got everybody to understand their role in the overall value stream and gave them a project manager who cared about the value stream, like a coach of the relay team who strives to get faster times for the relay team. We also focused on team results (like profits or losses), not just results of individual performances.

We started with more education on the process and became convinced that OTD was a bigger opportunity than gains in R&D efficiency. (Attention to safety and quality was a given.) The team also discovered the concept of cost of delay (COD) (see *Chapter 6* for more on COD).

Knowing what we needed to improve was one thing; setting targets and figuring out how to measure them was a lot more difficult. People often want to set a target as low as possible so that it is easy to achieve. Jean-Claude believed that if you set a target of 10% improvement, you will probably get 10%. If you set an outrageous target of 100%, you could get as much as a 50% improvement.

Our target would enable us to define a gap, or the amount of improvement required. But to set the gap we also needed to agree on the *current* OTD—this was another big hurdle for Herbie. Nobody could say for sure what the current delivery was, so we agreed to treat all projects for which we had a contract as on time, and recorded all others as not on time. This established the current OTD at approximately 18%, but, in reality, trying to get to this degree of granularity was an exercise in futility. Six months after the process was changed, we had already reached more than 50% OTD—it made no difference if we started from 18% or 21%.

At this time, about a third of the Herbie members had left the team—several of the CIS experts had found themselves other jobs. One member, who had joined the team for possibly dubious reasons, realized that she could not derail the team, and she gave up (no kidding). All new members were experts in product development who we trained in lean principles.

In our efforts to establish targets and apply measures to our mapping, the Herbie team learned that it was difficult to get data. First of all there was not a lot of it. The Herbie team generated decent data, but management would always raise doubts about its accuracy—they called it lack of "fidelity." The team learned that every function had their own data about their performance, but that there was simply no data on the high-level process that was accepted by everybody. And nobody seemed to be responsible for the overall process—project managers were responsible for their products, but nobody owned the overall process.

Despite these challenges, the Herbie team finally had a focus, some decent goals, and the opportunity to track the high-level process with a measurement. Now it was time to rethink our charter and develop some measurable goals. The regrouped team, all members of which understood the business quite well, realized what was needed:

- Give the business what the business needs when the business needs it. All businesses have to get their products on time, not just the OEM customers.
- Deliver perfect quality without rework.
- Complete development before we launch the product (no going back to rework designs after release).
- Be fast and agile to accommodate any new technology and market changes.
- Leverage our knowledge as best as we can.
- Increase the efficiency and reduce the cost of R&D.
- Increase employee satisfaction.
- Become more innovative.

And, of course, we also needed to do all of this in the safest environment possible. We had our work cut out for us.

Notes

1. James P. Womack and Daniel T. Jones, *Lean Thinking*, Free Press, New York, 2003.
2. Vijay Govindarajan, *Thinking Inside the Boxes*, Tuck School of Business, Dartmouth.
3. Joshua Kerievsky, *Sufficient Design*, Lean Software and Systems Conference, Long Beach, CA, 2011.
4. Peter M. Senge, *The Fifth Discipline*, Doubleday/Currency, New York, 1990.
5. Taiichi Ohno, *Toyota Production System: Beyond Large-Scale Production*, Productivity Press, Cambridge, MA, 1988.
6. John Kotter, Holger Rathgeber, and illustrator Peter Mueller, *Our Iceberg Is Melting*, St. Martin's Press, New York, 2006.
7. James M. Morgan, presentation at Goodyear Innovation Center, Luxembourg, June 2014.
8. Richard Sheridan, *The Business Value of Joy*, AME Innovation Summit, Irvine, CA, March 2014.
9. Virginia Satir, John Banmen, Maria Gomori, and Jane Gerber, *The Satir Model: Family Therapy and Beyond*, Science and Behavior Books, Palo Alto, CA, 1991.
10. Steven M. Smith, "The Satir Change Model," *Accelerating Team Productivity*.
11. James M. Morgan and Jeffrey K. Liker, *The Toyota Product Development System*, Productivity Press, New York, 2006.
12. Frederick P. Brooks Jr., "Adding Manpower to a Late Software Project Makes It Later," *The Mythical Man Month*, Addison-Wesley, Reading, MA, 1995.
13. Allen C. Ward and Durward K. Sobek II, *Lean Product and Process Development*, Second Edition, Lean Enterprise Institute, Cambridge, MA, 2014.

14. Guide and standards developed by the Project Management Institute, a leading not-for-profit professional membership association for the project, program, and portfolio management profession.
15. Project Management Institute.
16. Eliyahu Goldratt, *The Goal*, North River Press, Great Barrington, MA, 1984.
17. Wallace J. Hopp and Mark L. Spearman, *Factory Physics*, Waveland Press, Long Grove, IL, 1996.
18. John Shook and Mike Rother, *Learning to See*, Lean Enterprise Institute Brookline, MA, 1999.
19. W. Edwards Deming, *Drastic Changes for Western Management*, The W. Edwards Deming Institute, July 1986.
20. James P. Womack and Daniel T. Jones, *Seeing the Whole Value Stream*, Lean Enterprise Institute, Brookline, MA, 2002.

Chapter 4

Finding and Removing Waste from Product Development

We all have become accustomed to waste in our lives, both at work, and away from work. As our lean Herbie team got rolling—literally by using the "Womack Wheel"—identification of customer value and removal of waste in our R&D processes were our initial objectives. But to do that, we needed to determine what was waste and what was value. For the latter, we looked to our customers, both internal and external, for the answer. As you move forward with lean in your product-development processes, ask, "What do our customers value? Will our customers be willing to pay for this?" If you are like us at Goodyear early in our lean initiative, you will be surprised at what you learn and amazed at the amount of waste that gets in the way of delivering value.

Focus on the Customer

An enterprise project leader (EPL) was invited to join the Herbie team to represent the business and the customer, so we asked him what the business needed. His answer was short and clear—"Everything!" That sounded like our sponsor, who asked, "What will it take to give the business everything the business wants when the business wants it?"

As our lean team got rolling, nothing was terribly easy or clear. We were all used to the "business" asking for twice as much as they needed because they usually got half of what they requested. In R&D, we just never worried about it.

The Herbie team had gained some authority to change and improve Goodyear's high-level R&D processes, but, truth be told, we did not have a path or a roadmap, as to how to go about it. The books we were reading at the time seemed to fall short on a practical way to get started with lean product development. We had mapped our high-level process in a rough value-stream map, and we had identified the main problems. But there were as many opinions about the approach we should take to improvement as there were Herbie team members—until we discovered the "Womack Wheel."

We had taught in our lean training the five steps of lean thinking postulated by Jim Womack and Dan Jones,[1] so why not go at our problem using those same five, with minor changes. We made the five steps a circle, focused it around Goodyear R&D objectives, and called it our "Womack Wheel" (see *Getting Traction with the Womack Wheel*).

The critical first step on the Womack Wheel is to define value—what does the customer really want? That is easy—everything! Marketing (our internal customer) wanted all its programs launched—OEM, renewal, cost-downs, government, technology development, and so on. But we asked a few more questions to get more detail from our customer:

- Everything had to meet quality and safety targets that were as good or better than we had been delivering (this also was demanded by our R&D management).
- Everything had to meet performance goals that were agreed upon by the value-stream stakeholders or external customers.
- Everything had to be delivered on time so that launches would go off without a hitch.
- When product starts selling, there would be no complaints or adjustments from dealers, stores, or end users.
- All the requirements applied to all types of customers.

We knew we had external customers (e.g., OEMs, retail chains, consumers, fleets), but we also realized that since the business pays for this work—they pick up the R&D charges—the business was our customer, too. We had not always considered them as such, but now we had to define value for that customer as well. It was a start.

Getting Traction with the Womack Wheel

Without a road map, it took Goodyear and the Herbie team a long time to figure out how to get going. You may wonder why we did not just make an A3 at the time to figure out a way—we tried. Maybe it did not work because *Managing to Learn*[2] had not been written yet, and we had not yet learned the A3 process sufficiently. Possibly our problem was still too broad and it needed to be broken down into smaller A3s.

This "spinning" led us to the "Womack Wheel." When I told Jim Womack that we were using the "Womack Wheel" as our roadmap to implementing lean, Jim said, "I did not know that I had wheels."

Five Steps to Get Lean[1]

Specify value for the customer while providing opportunity for growth

Focus on value stream
Go see—grasp the situation...
End-to-end

Start over

- Safety
- Quality
- Delivery
- Cost/efficiency = Speed

Work to perfection
Kaizen/CIS

Create flow and speed
Build confidence

Implement pull
Standardize
Build organization

(Adapted from a five-step concept by James Womack and Daniel Jones to start a lean initiative.)

I would recommend this simple path to everybody who starts a lean initiative. It may not be perfect, but it perfectly fits the 80/20 rule—it will work about 80% of the time to get a lean initiative started. The one variation we made from the five steps prescribed by Womack and Jones was to put the five steps into a recurring loop—you do not want to stay on the fifth step for too long. In fact, as soon as you see enough of the implementation working, move on—run through the entire loop again (with a different objective or target, of course). I needed one of our lean experts in manufacturing to explain the need for the loop to me.

At Goodyear, we have gone through this loop many times, once to find improvements to delivery, and several times for speed and other improvements. I certainly plan many more loops in the future.

Here is my approach to the five steps of the wheel:

1. *Specify value:* Figure out what the customer wants, and start defining "value" for the customer. The customer could be an external customer who pays directly for the service or product that you or your team provides. The customer may be a part of your company. The key is that you treat the internal customer the same as an external customer. Remember that you can always create more customer value by reducing the price of your product or your service. For that reason, I try to teach people to give the customer the best value as long as you are consistent with the goals of your company or your organization (Jim Womack taught me that). If the goal of your company is to make a profit, which I hope it is (at least long term), then you should focus on customer value and making a profit. The same thought applies for serving an internal customer with whom you may collaborate for that company goal, and for an internal goal of your own organization.

2. *Focus on the value stream:* Look at the entire value stream, not the individual functions that create the value. You must first understand the value stream in total and how R&D and other contributors and stakeholders fit in. Look at the *complete* value stream and the steps by which value is created—that is usually your R&D project. In order to do that you need to know how your R&D decisions create the value and affect other functions in the value stream (e.g., can the product be manufactured efficiently?). You may draw a value-stream map to visualize the value stream.

3. *Create flow:* This is difficult because most organizations were not set up with flow in mind. In the Toyota Production System, *everything* flows through the value stream all of the time. And flow occurs in every step (manufacturing, administration, etc.) of the value stream. As the first action to create flow, it is a good idea to eliminate waste from the process. You may have identified waste in step 1 when defining customer value, but after the value stream is better defined, the waste may be more obvious. In order to create flow, many lean principles and tools are available. Designing a new

process with flow in mind is much easier than creating flow in an existing process. As Womack points out in his book *Gemba Walks*,[3] it is important to be patient during this step, and give your work a little time to stabilize—which means go see, observe, and change, as needed. Move on when you see the stability.

4. *Implement pull:* Pull is effective in an environment of high variability, such as R&D, but it can be subtle. There are many ways to design a pull process—some experimentation may be required. Also in step 4 it is important to have everybody on board and aligned, including adjacent functions. People should know the lean principles, many of which relate to pull, and be truly engaged at this time. This also is the time to standardize the process, and put an organization in place to sustain the change.

5. *Work to perfection:* The next step (there is never a final step) is the application of PDCA or whatever method you use to drive ongoing continuous improvement. This also is the time at which we brought in the A3 process. Remember that there is a "C" in PDCA—it is the orphan of the process. People are often satisfied with "do," but the check and adjust are crucial steps, too. Of course, you can spend an eternity trying to reach perfection—not a good idea either. Move on earlier than later. Where to? To where the customer's needs for value point you. Create more value for the customer by going through the loop again.

In our case at Goodyear, the customer wanted what they needed delivered on time and to the agreed-upon targets. We had mapped the value stream. The responsibilities were clear enough, and we had the capability and the knowledge to deliver to specification. But there was no flow—projects were pushed from function to function where they waited a long time before they were picked up. We developed a better process by removing waste, improving flow, and managing variability. All people involved in the process were engaged, trained, and aligned, and we eventually implemented a pull process. We put an organization in place that owns and improves the process using tools like A3 and PDCA. We improved the process, but not to perfection; only to a state where it was acceptable—then we moved to the next highest customer priority (speed), and went through the cycle again.

What Do Customers Value?

Womack says, "The customer is the sole judge of value."[4] But it is often difficult to figure out what the customer values. Another approach is to ask, "Would the customer pay for this?"

Let us assume you just bought a set of new tires—Goodyear, I hope. You did your homework, bought the tires that you like, and are sure you got the best price. Then you are asked if you want the tires mounted and balanced. Well, you probably cannot do that at home, and you agree to pay for mounting and balancing. Then you are asked if you want a roadside warranty, which would cover you in case you get a flat tire (somebody will come out and install a new tire for you at no charge); this additional service is (only) $11 per tire, for as long as you own the tires. You do the math, assess the risk, quickly compare the price to other roadside assistance programs, and you decline the offer because it does not add enough value for you. By the way, they also charge you for the disposal of your old tires. And because of environmental requirements, there could be a tax for the disposal service, and you cannot decline that payment. Most customers grudgingly accept the presentation of these surcharges, and probably recognize some value in them.

Now imagine that when you get the bill, you also see charges for transportation and carrying the inventory of the tires. The sales clerk explains that the tires were made 1,000 miles from the store, and then they were moved to a warehouse that was 1,000 miles in the opposite direction. "Somebody must pay for the warehousing, transportation, and the shipment to the store," the clerk reasons. Are you willing to pay for this? Certainly not. While the mounting and balancing of the tires added value for you, (although you would have preferred to get that for free) and you have no choice on disposal fee and tax, transportation and inventory clearly adds no value to you or any other customer.

Let us take this situation a little further with a more scientific explanation in the way of the Kano model (see *Kano Model*).[5] The Kano model categorizes customer preferences, and describes three kinds of value:

■ *Expected features:* Those are the features that everybody expects in a product. You do not get extra satisfaction if they are present, but you quickly lose a lot of satisfaction when they are missing. For example, your tires should hold air, support the vehicle, give you steering ability, and so on, and, you would be upset if these qualities were missing.

- *What you pay is what you get:* This type of value is called "satisfiers" in the Kano model, and satisfaction is a linear function of the price. You can buy a base tire or you can buy a more expensive tire, and as you pay more, you expect more from your tire—better ride comfort, less noise, higher mileage, and so on.
- *Delighters:* These are the unexpected and exciting features that you get without paying extra for them. For example, free mounting and balancing of tires, and a free service to bring you a new tire when one goes flat, would be delighters.

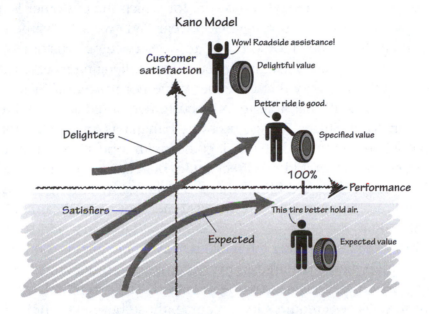

Value is what the customer is willing to pay for. This sounds very simple, but how do you really know what the customer values? The best way to find out is to *ask,* and then *listen.* For established products, you probably can also rely on a lot of company knowledge.

Many companies have slogans such as, "We meet or exceed customer requirements." Exceeding requirements only adds value if it delights the customer.

A powerful example of the importance of customer value is described by Jeffrey Liker and Gary Convis in *The Toyota Way to Lean Leadership.* Convis, a Toyota-trained leader, joined Dana Corp. later in his career to help the company out of bankruptcy. Dana had closed some plants and laid-off workers when its bankruptcy coincided with the great recession. Convis had built a position of trust with the union leaders and workers, especially by working alongside them during 5S, and cleanup events at the plants.

As soon as the economy began to improve, the union leaders asked Convis to hire back some of the workers who were laid off. Convis said, "That is not my decision." The union leaders were surprised and asked, "Well, whose decision is it then?" Convis replied, "That is entirely the decision of the customers. When they buy our products again, we need to manufacture them, and then we will need to bring workers back." He explained that the key to getting the customers back was to produce value for the customer, the best product at the lowest cost—nothing else.

Value is the opposite of waste, which is anything that takes up time, resources, space, costs, money, and so on, for which the customer is not willing to pay. In a broader sense, at Goodyear R&D we ask, "Is there a return for this? Do we need to do this? Can we service our customer just as well without this?" Often, waste is obvious, but challenging to eradicate.

There is a third category that is neither value nor waste: business required. There is stuff that, if asked, the customer would say they are not willing to pay for it. Shigeo Shingo used the banana as an analogy for this, saying that when you buy a banana, it comes with a peel. In our industry actions are required that add no direct value, but cannot be eliminated.[6] We need to do a lot of tests and filings that are required by law—granted they may add indirect value and cost to the customer, but we still cannot charge the cost directly to the customer. There are certain industry standards that we may follow without getting a billable return. There also is a minimum of administration that is required in every company—orders must be filled, bills must be paid, salaries need to be managed. This "stuff" adds no direct value, but the business requires it. Of course, those business-required tasks should be executed as efficiently and free of waste, as possible.

Womack advises to give the customer the value desired, but not at the expense of sacrificing what is important to your own company (i.e., make money on the product sold to *external* customers). This is particularly important to R&D, because R&D has a substantial influence on the profitability of the value stream.

External Customers

External customers are those individuals or companies, not belonging to your company, who purchase or use your products or services. So what constitutes value for these customers? You can ask your marketing and sales department, and conduct or read marketing surveys and studies to find out. But I am convinced that the best approach is from direct observation and listening. Most lean experts agree that the best method to figure out what the customer really wants is to "go see" what they want. Many good companies send engineers out with their sales, marketing, and service personnel to give the engineers an opportunity to learn customer value.

Professor Shoji Shiba, a TQM expert and Deming Prize winner, called this "swimming in the fish tank."[7] Richard Sheridan of Menlo Industries calls the "go see" approach industrial anthropology—the science of studying customers in their natural environment.[8] There are many examples of Toyota illustrating how the Toyota chief engineers studied customers for a year before they wrote the requirements for a new car.

When I developed tires for aircraft, I could not test them on Goodyear test planes (we did not have test planes). The most common sizes also fitted cargo planes, and I had to fully test the tires in the lab and get FAA approval before I could give them to a customer. We made a deal with a freight airline, and they put the tires on their planes. I went to the airport every week. I inspected the tires; took measurements; talked to the engineers, tire maintenance staff, and pilots; and examined all the tires that had worn out and been removed. I eventually started to understand many things. For example, I learned a lot about how pilots land and taxi 747s, and how tires wear—faster on the left side of the aircraft than on the right side, among other traits—and this led to improving the number of landings per tire, which delighted the customer.

Dale Wells, lead engineer, develops earthmover tires for Goodyear. Dale likes to go to the mines where the tires are used to observe and talk to the drivers and maintenance crews of the large dump trucks. There he learns about the tires, how they are used, and how they perform. In order to understand why tires were overheating in an Australian mine, Dale watched the drivers there for some time. He eventually found out that the drivers did a "hot seat switch" when they needed a break, which means the driver rested but the vehicle did not. This did not give the tires a chance to cool off, so Dale created customer value by redesigning the tires to accommodate this operating pattern.

Goodyear race-tire engineers develop all the tires in conjunction with the racing teams and their drivers. They are in the race pit during the race, working with the mechanics, and they talk to the drivers at the end of the race. Sometimes, after the race, they go back to Akron and develop a new tire during the week prior to the next weekend's race. In the off-season, the engineers work with the teams and drivers to develop more competitive race tires. They take the tires out to tracks where the teams train in the winter, let the racers try the tires, and then they make the improvements based on the feedback from the drivers.

Another great example of direct observation is the participation of engineers in the testing of OEM submissions. Some OEM test drivers (who also approve the tires for use on the vehicle), take the engineers in the car and demonstrate to them what they like about the tire, and what they do not like. There is no report that can replace this experience.

A good example of creating customer value by go see occurs at 3M. Steve Heinecke tells the story of how the company had developed transparent wound coverings, but, according to the marketing department, had received negative feedback from customers, when surveyed. Heinecke, an engineer, was not happy about that, and asked to go to a hospital with the marketing staff to see for himself. After the engineer observed how the nurses covered IVs with tape and cotton balls, he showed the nurses a prototype of the transparent covering—the nurses instantly loved the product. It was easier to apply, and they could see when a problem developed underneath without having to remove the covering. Then 3M further developed the product, getting nurse input, and by watching how they used it.[9]

The 3M approach also shows the power of having prototypes to show to customers. Using minimum feasible prototypes to gauge customer interest is getting increasingly popular, and I encourage engineers to think that way. I am not saying to start doing the job of the marketing organization, but generate safe, minimum acceptable or feasible prototypes *and* participate in the customer evaluation of those prototypes—go see for yourself.

Sometimes it takes a little experimentation to find out what the customer perceives as value. According to Jim Jacobs, chairman and founder of the Savvy Consortium, staff at General Mills debated for years if it would be a good idea to coat Cheerios with honey and nuts (and, of course, other flavors). Finally, somebody got the idea to do it and see what customers thought. You know the rest of that story.[10]

This approach should not be limited to external customers and products. Internal customers should be served the same way, and the same thinking applies to processes as well as products. I recently saw Goodyear's R&D HR staff observe an award presentation and a peer review they had designed in order to learn firsthand how the recipients reacted.

Engineers are not trained marketing experts, and dealing with a customer may not be part of their skillset. That should not be surprising: engineers like to get a specification, and then be left alone for several months or even years. They deal in technical language and want details that can translate customer value into numbers or engineering terms. Add go see to their repertoire of skills.

In order to teach customer value creation to engineers, I run the following exercise in our lean training classes. This exercise is adopted from the work of Joshua Kerievsky, CEO of Industrial Logic. After minimum instructions, I ask teams to develop a set of glasses for me made out of pipe cleaners. I tell the teams to look at the complete value stream, because eventually, the glasses must be manufactured and supplied. Some teams leave the room and come back 30 minutes later with piles of glasses, none of which will fit. Some teams actually work with me, the customer. They build one set and see how it fits. They show me several styles and colors. Eventually I find a pair that I like, and I place my order.[11]

In the exercise—in which you can ask the class to build anything (e.g., jewelry, hats, and decorations)—I try to teach students the following:

- Always work in short learning cycles with the customer. Make something, show it, change it, and show it again. Look at what the other teams are doing as well, and learn from them.
- Go see and ask, ask, ask.
- Practice good listening skills. Repeat back what you hear to assure proper understanding.
- Clarify customer priorities, and rank them from the most important to the least important.
- Be positive, but recognize that the customer may ask for the impossible. Discuss it, but do not commit to it.
- Assess customer value versus what is important to you—explain that and negotiate, if needed and appropriate.
- Make commitments only when you are sure you can deliver the value desired.
- If the job is too big and complex, break it down into manageable pieces.
- Be prepared to educate the customer as needed—that is what sales people do in the stores.
- Provide honest and professional advice to the customer if you notice that the customer needs an education.

There are many ways to create value for customers:

- Reduce the cost to compete with other suppliers of the product, especially suppliers from countries with lower labor costs (least desirable option).

- Innovate and always offer the customer more value than the competition and, possibly, collect a higher price.
- Offer products that customers do not even know they want (iPad).
- Offer new solutions to known problems.

Great companies have such a clear idea of what customers want that they can describe it in just a few sentences. For example, Jeff Bezos, chairman and founder of Amazon, defined what his company knows about what customers want:

- Low price
- Vast selection
- Fast, convenient, reliable delivery[12]

It really can be as simple as that.

Internal Customers

Internal customers are the functions downstream in the value stream that rely on your contribution to the value stream, in order to provide their contribution to the value stream. For example, in product development, we design a product that manufacturing must produce and that sales must sell. IT, HR, and procurement needs to support the effort of all the functions in the value stream.

I heard for the first time about the internal customer when I got involved in total quality control in the early-1990s. At Goodyear at that time, there were constant internal communications about the famous internal customer, but many people still did not understand the concept. Most functions looked out for themselves.

If you are dealing with an internal customer, remember, somebody eventually pays the bill for R&D and all the valuable new products that R&D creates. So imagine you will send them a detailed bill this month for all costs incurred by R&D—would you get questions? You would probably be asked, "Why so many R&D hours? Did we need all those prototypes? Why is R&D transportation cost so high? Why do we ship so many prototype tires with expedited carriers?"

Most of the time the internal customer represents an outside customer, and then things get a bit more complicated. This is especially true when the people who represent the external customer (business) also are responsible for the P&L. When there is an internal representative of the external customer, two rules *must* be clear:

- Outside customer value must be understood by everybody.
- All contributors are aligned to create a profitable value stream, and tradeoffs are made accordingly.

These rules help to address circumstances, such as when an internal customer sets higher priorities or different requirements for the internal function goals than the actual customer would request. The rules also help to resolve conflicts for when an internal customer promises so much that it negates profitability or exceeds resources or capabilities. Such problems are deeply rooted in culture and company history. Conflicts between contributors to the development and stakeholders should be solved by bringing everything back to the two previously mentioned rules.

When I was developing tires for an OEM, I frequently had to attend meetings with functional leaders where the OEM engineers were "accused" of promising too much to a customer and, thus, jeopardizing the functional efficiency. For example, a customer engineer (the Goodyear engineer who calls on the customer, and in some cases is located at the customer) agreed to run a test for an OEM customer that was time-consuming and required specialized resources. In those days the functional power sometimes prevailed. Today, this rarely happens because we now focus on a common interest, and we all collaborate to make a profitable value stream. Also, the customer engineers understand the value streams, have the information they need to make informed decisions, and are empowered to make the right commitments to the customer.

As pointed out earlier, you can always increase customer value by reducing the selling price. Womack addresses the point in *Gemba Walks*, citing the automotive industry leading up to the great recession.[3] OEMs tried to cut their costs aggressively and renegotiated existing contracts with their suppliers. The aggressive cost cutting drove many automotive suppliers into bankruptcy. I understand that some OEMs had project rooms set up where they tried to triage the industry problem, deciding which supplier needed cash at what time to slow down the default process, but many suppliers could not survive.

The key is to understand how to deliver great value to the customer *and* make money on your products. Some lean scholars only talk about creating value as if that was the *only* thing that counts for a business to be successful. While I agree that creating customer value is important, making a profit and meeting other company objectives also are important. Selling a product that adds value for the customer is a necessary condition, but it is not sufficient. We have seen products on the market that added great customer value that were hard to sustain because the companies could not make a profit.

Creating R&D Value

For many years the product development expense has been considered "cost of doing business"—it has been seen as an overhead, distributed back to the business, where leaders would only complain when the distribution was deemed unfair. It was very hard for business leaders to assess the efficiency of the organization, and scientists were thought to be the most innovative when left alone, anyway. This is a situation similar to the health-care industry, where the process has historically been left to doctors, nurses, and other providers to design—although these providers are professionals and experts at their tasks, a lot of waste has been identified in the process of administering those services. Today we consider R&D an investment, and the R&D cost is part of the business case for a new product.

As startling as it seems, most manufacturing operations spend as little as 5% (or less) of process time creating value. That means you start the clock when you put a tag on the first raw material that enters the process and stop the clock when the tagged product is finished. You add up all the time when the product actually undergoes work, and you take that as a percentage of the overall process time.

I remember a study in our testing organization, where they determined that the average value-added time was 1.3%. Everybody was surprised by this low number, which is quite typical, and not only for R&D organizations. But this also shows what an opportunity we have, given the importance of speed in product development! This, of course, means that more than 98% of that process is waste (mostly waiting), which we can attack. When we similarly examined our product development process prior to lean, it was difficult to establish the value percentage: it is hard to put a tag on the work that engineers are doing, and we did not have good data either. Even today, the numbers are not obvious. Engineers do not like to be timed—which is like artists who will not reveal how long they worked on a painting. But when we look at engineering work we must understand that engineering work does not automatically create value.

In his book *Product Development for the Lean Enterprise*, Michael Kennedy states that at Toyota, engineers spend 80% of their time on engineering—and he suggests that in Western companies it may be the opposite (20% of their time on engineering tasks).[13] This topic spurred a lot of questions at Goodyear, and I understand it did in other companies, too. The challenge in trying to make sense of the 80/20 numbers is that we should not confuse engineering work with value-added work. Engineers could be busy all day doing engineering work on a product that never gets launched (thus, little or no value other than lessons learned that can be applied to another product).

The concept of 80% engineering work intrigued me, and it puzzled Phil Dunker, Goodyear development engineer and a graduate of our Lean 401 program (lean product development certification). As part of Phil's certification, he examined value-added work of Goodyear engineers. We also thought that we had to settle the "engineering work" question first—"How much engineering really took place?"—before digging in to see how much of the engineer work was value-added work.

Phil got an idea from the book *Fast Innovation*,[14] to create a sheet with bar codes for engineering work, interruptions, nonproject related meetings, training, and so on. He gave three engineers scanners to scan the bar codes. Every time the engineers started a new task, they scanned the corresponding bar code. The data was automatically entered into a spreadsheet where the times and durations were recorded. By the way, Phil's study was done relatively early in the implementation of our lean development process.

Phil determined that tire design engineers at Goodyear spent about 75% of their time on engineering tasks (e.g., designing tires, writing specifications, analyzing test results, developing new materials, documenting knowledge, supporting production or marketing, helping HR). About 14% of the engineers' time was spent on tasks that could be considered "straight waste," which were due to interruptions, changes, cancellations, rework, and so on. The remaining 11% of the engineers' time was spent reading nonproject related e-mails, sick time, training, vacation, and so on, which added no value but could not be avoided (business required). Phil ran the experiment for enough time to ensure that his data was statistically valid.

We were a little surprised at the high level of true engineering work (75%), and how little straight waste there was (14%). We also were surprised by the low level of nonproject-related work (11%)—all of which seemed to contrast with Kennedy's numbers. But we also knew that there was still much "hidden" waste in the 75%, which we decided to find and eliminate. At the time of those tests we had not begun to delve into engineering work and identify wastes within the engineering work, but I was convinced that half of the work was waste.

Now that lean is fully implemented (although, we continue to improve the processes), I think that engineering work is closer to 80%, and the amount of hidden waste in that work has been significantly reduced. Our metrics show that our engineers get about three times as much value-added work done during their engineering time than they did prior to the lean initiative.

Value and Waste

We try to find waste because it costs money that cannot be recovered and consumes resources, both of which could be better applied elsewhere.

Remove Waste, Free Up Resources

Increasing workload, without waste reduction:

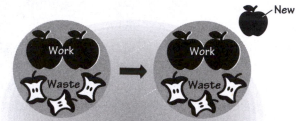

Reducing waste to free space for value-adding work in the process:

Take waste out   Replace with a value-adding task

Engineers always have a full plate of work. When new work comes in, it normally gets piled on top of the full plate. Of course, what normally happens is that other work gets removed from the plate, or the engineers learn to deal with the overload. You need to take something off the plate—waste—to free-up capacity for value-added work. Common sense, right? You don't need lean to understand that, but it is not as easy as it sounds.

Tom Segatta, chief engineer Material Science, tried to make the work of his staff visible to better understand why all his engineers were so overloaded. Tom asked his engineers what would be the maximum number of projects they could handle at a given time, and they agreed that four projects was the maximum. Engineers working for Tom can have several active projects because they switch projects or tasks when they wait for lab data, test results, and prototypes.

Tom asked every engineer to make a small card for every project or activity that took more than four hours to complete. Most engineers filled out between eight and 12 cards. Then, Tom asked his engineers to pin the cards on a whiteboard—every engineer had only four slots. The remaining projects went into a "Parked" slot, and Tom also created slots for projects that were "waiting" on something, such as test results (see *Making Work Visible*).

Making Work Visible

Tom notified the stakeholders of projects in the Parked position that their projects were parked until further notice. As new projects came in, they were assessed versus the active projects. If the incoming project was deemed important, then it went into an active slot, and an active project now considered to be less important was removed from that engineer's slot and went into a Parked position. If the project was not important enough to displace an active project, the new project was Parked right away, and the stakeholders were informed.

After 2 months, Tom had collected quite a pile of Parked cards. Jean-Claude Kihn, CTO, was on a gemba walk and noticed the Parked projects. He asked how long they had been parked and if any of the stakeholders had complained. Tom replied, "I was thinking about that myself. As a matter of fact, nobody complained!" The Parked cards then ended up right where waste belongs—in the wastebasket.

This is not a highly scientific method to control and distribute incoming work, but it certainly worked. I recommend Tom's approach of dealing with incoming work as a first step in a lean initiative:

- Cap the work per engineer.
- Evaluate every new piece of work versus work in progress.
- Consider a rule that active projects rarely get interrupted; new work waits for a slot to open.

Removing waste through this technique captured low-hanging fruit at Goodyear and at many other places as well. And while it was low fruit, it also was quite big and valuable (either removing costs or having a big impact on our value stream), and it was easy to pick. I have always been convinced that the best way to avoid overloaded engineers and an accumulation of waste is to assess value and place some controls on the volume of incoming work (more on that to come in *Chapter 6*).

Lean R&D Principle: Take waste out of your operation and replace it with value-added work.

Since every R&D organization has a limited budget and resources, it is not unusual that all the work that you would like to do cannot be done. Of course, you can limit incoming work across the board, and sometimes that is the right thing to do. The first thing that should be done, though, to free up resources for value-added work is to eliminate or reduce nonvalue added work.

There are times that complete R&D projects are waste, since they never come to completion or if they are complete, fail to deliver any value to customers. Occasionally tasks within a project are waste and can be eliminated. Most often, though, waste is hidden inside projects and tasks, and is hard to find.

Waste can be eliminated to create capacity for value-added work. Removing waste also is the first thing that should be done to create flow and speed. Waste can even affect quality. Waste costs money and if for no other reason, waste should be reduced to reduce cost and improve efficiency.

At Goodyear: The first initiative we did at Goodyear was to stop all work that nobody seemed to be interested in. We changed a lot of default requests (like send all lab samples back to the engineer after tests were completed, because most samples ended up in the recycle bin without being looked at), and we eliminated requests for information that was known or not needed. We learned to say "no" to work we knew would not add value. A little later we stopped all projects that did not get approved at the entry gate of our PCP process. You may say, "Why would anybody with a gate process work on something outside of the process?" Well, we did—just in case.

The elimination of waste created a lot of extra capacity, which Goodyear reinvested. Waste elimination also helped improve flow, which led to gains in speed and on-time delivery—collateral benefits.

The waste identified by Tom at Goodyear was easy to find, but after picking the low-hanging waste, it gets progressively more difficult to find and eliminate additional waste. Waste can be hidden and disguised:

- "There is surely nothing quite as useless as doing with great efficiency what should not be done at all," said Peter Drucker.[15]
- "The hard part for developing eyes for waste is that most waste is caused by doing things right, within the conventional system," said Allen Ward.[16]
- Shigeo Shingo said, "We must always keep in mind that the greatest waste is waste we don't see."[6]

In most work settings these days, people are busy. But we often do not distinguish between being busy and adding value. In fact, people are often so busy that they do not question what they are doing. It is hard to examine your practices when you are overloaded—you just want to jump to the next task or project. I developed a simple exercise to illuminate this type of hidden waste.

In our training simulation, one person in the value stream is assigned to a cluttered desk and told to draw as many shapes as possible to keep up with the demand of the simulation. They are given a ruler and a compass. They begin using the ruler and compass, not noticing what sits in front of them: a folder with stencils. Few people in the simulation ever lift their head from the task in front of them and notice that folder. They are told to draw shapes, so they draw as many as needed as fast as they can using what they believe is the best approach—wrong.

> *It is a common approach in industry to throw more at something that, in reality, should receive less or nothing at all.*

Similarly, at Goodyear we eliminated a warehouse for experimental tires—a significant annual saving and an improvement in the speed of our process. The warehouse was our ruler and compass: it was run relatively efficiently given what it was charged to do, but it added no value, contributed a lot of cycle time and mistakes, and caused delays.

At the start of the elimination of the warehouse, members of the implementation team suggested that we instead *double* the warehouse staff and do more improvement kaizens. Their plan was to do more efficiently what did not need done in the first place—they really thought this was a viable alternative. I see this kind of thinking all of the time. It is a common approach in industry to throw more at something that, in reality, should receive less or nothing at all. Today our engineers agree that we are much better off without a warehouse. We always think we will lose something when we eliminate waste, but most of the time we are better off.

So why did Goodyear have so much waste in our system? Why do we still have waste in our system? A strong functional organization and functional rules that historically served the functions well did not focus on the work that moves across functions and creates customer value.

It is this history that created another source of waste: outdated rules, policies, and operating procedures. A lot of our policies or rules (mostly functional) were created when something went wrong years ago. A rule was created to prevent it from happening again, and the rule was never changed, although it was never needed again. This includes a lot of work that engineers do. For example, we once had expedited the building of tires in a plant, but the mold did not show up on time, causing the plant to scrap the uncured tires. A rule was created by which the plants will not start building tires before the mold is physically in the plant. This rule was still in effect 20 years later, even though our mold delivery time had improved to virtually 100%. Yet, it still took *3 years* to change the rule once these facts were brought to light.

Much waste is created by trying to please everybody and, thus, avoiding conflict. It is not in the American industrial culture to put conflict on the table and resolve it as a team or group. We instead opt to accommodate everyone as best possible. This often leads to a "one size fits all" solution that causes at least a little waste for everybody and, usually, a lot of complexity for everybody. Over time all those little wastes and complexities add up.

Other wastes in Goodyear R&D are caused by poor processes (waiting in a priority system), inadequate risk management, lack of planning, turf issues, poor knowledge management (reinventing things), inadequate facility layout, poor talent management, and on and on. We did not design these wastes into our processes and policies, they just organically accumulated. Jean-Claude referred to them as geological layers, embedded and buried by a new layer of management over and over again. The challenge for us—and you—is to bring them to the surface.

It is surprising how quickly new companies build up wasteful sediments. I heard a presentation recently by a lean champion from a major "young" company in the high-tech industry. I was surprised to hear that this company, which started almost 100 years later than Goodyear, had already developed many of the same issues that we just eliminated: poor control of incoming work, too much WIP, variation, firefighting culture.

I was encouraged that the same lean principles are used at this company to improve the process as we have been using at Goodyear.

Waste Not, Want Not

Many years ago, Shigeo Shingo and Taiichi Ohno talked about and grouped seven wastes, and, eventually, an eighth waste (knowledge and talent utilization) was added to their original list. All these wastes can be found in an R&D organization, but some are more common than others. The most common of the eight Shingo/Ohno wastes that I find in an R&D organization are waiting and project inventory (see *Eight Shingo/Ohno Wastes*).

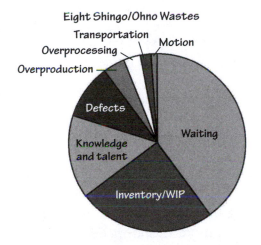

I also find that forcing all R&D wastes into these eight categories is somewhat artificial and can inhibit your ability to locate the wastes. So I have added a few waste categories (call them subcategories of the eight or a combination of categories, if it makes you feel better). I also prioritized them by their impact on creating profitable value streams. In every case, the greatest returns are obtained by eliminating the waste that has the most detrimental effect on the value stream.

You may decide that the order of wastes for your company is different, but I encourage you to examine, prioritize, and attack them. Use the following order (see *Norbert's Order of Waste*) unless you come up with a better one. The R&D wastes are identified in this chapter, and more details about our approach to eradicating them will be shown in upcoming chapters.

Norbert's Order of Waste

1. Not taking advantage of what lean product development can do for you
2. Believing you already did lean or that lean did not work
3. Designing a product that nobody wants
4. Favoring functional optimization over value-stream profitability
5. Random versus value-stream improvements
6. Waiting
7. Inventory or WIP
8. Knowledge and talent
9. Design errors
10. Overproduction
11. Overprocessing or poor processing
12. Transportation
13. Motion

---

1. Not Taking Advantage of What Lean Product Development Can Do for You

The first waste—not doing lean—applies to every company, and all parts of every company. I did not come up with this idea of waste on my own: "The biggest waste is thinking that you cannot do it," writes Womack in *Gemba Walks*.[3] This waste is even more pronounced in product development, where many companies cannot see the opportunity for it to work, and don't even try. Dave Logozzo of the Lean Enterprise Institute (LEI) estimates that 90% of companies have not tried or seriously tried lean in product development.[17] Not doing lean within R&D leaves a huge amount of money on the table!

A CTO from another company once visited us at Goodyear, and we showed him our process and the improvements that we were able to achieve. The executive replied, "This seems to work well for Goodyear, but it would not work for us because we are a slow company." They were quite comfortable meeting the pace of innovation demanded in their industry, and he saw no reason to put forth the effort to introduce lean. I hear this from many executives and hear about it frequently at lean product development conferences.

Some companies are not compelled to change unless they see no other way to reduce costs or extinguish a burning platform. Maybe they have not had a burning platform as did Goodyear and other companies. When things go well in a company, who would think of changing. That would be like a coach making changes to a winning team. One day, these leaders will recognize competitors quickly bringing innovations to market that the customers find appealing—then it will be a whole new ball game.

2. Believing You Already Did Lean or That Lean Did Not Work

This waste is similar to the first, but probably a bit harder to admit to. You are convinced that you tried lean, and that it did not work. Really? There are so many different aspects to lean that it is hard to imagine some piece of it not making a company better. I still scratch my head when I hear this, and I once heard it at Goodyear.

In fact, "Didn't we do this years ago?" and "We tried this a long time ago, and it did not work—why are we trying it again?" were the most popular arguments when we rolled out lean in R&D. While few start lean in R&D, even fewer keep it alive: Of the 10% of companies that try lean in R&D, only 15% of those efforts remain active 5 years into the initiative[18]—and that is certainly before reaching their true potential. I would not be surprised to find evidence that Goodyear started something like lean somewhere at some time, since lean looks like and incorporates a lot of various tools and techniques. But, I can assure you, it was not the lean that we are applying religiously today.

Not sustaining a lean initiative wastes the effort already invested and, much worse, the untapped opportunities. Sadly, most people think a lean initiative is over when you get recognition or win an award. Striving for such recognitions take a lot of energy, like a sprint after which everyone is exhausted and the adrenaline disappears. Recognitions are not bad, but you should use them to drive momentum and more improvements.

After a lean initiative has been abandoned, it will be hard to restart it because people are not motivated to support an initiative that they believe has failed once or twice before. Some people call this effect "poisoned wells." Many companies will give the initiative a new name (like "Operational Excellence") when new management starts the initiative again, thinking that alone can help rejuvenate interest.

It takes many years for a successful lean initiative to take hold in R&D—it will actually take longer than *one* management cycle! Companies like Toyota are still improving their processes.

3. Designing a Product That Nobody Wants

So what does this have to do with lean or wastes? Well, it touches many, many different wastes.

Eric Ries, author of *The Lean Startup,* has promoted a lot of lean tools for quick experiments to improve the chances of a successful startup. He recalls one R&D project in which he was involved. "I had committed the biggest waste of all: building a product that customers refused to use. That was really depressing!"[19]

R&D has one big challenge that most other functions in a corporation do not have: R&D has to decide what to work on. And while that is challenging, it is also the thrill of the field. There are many studies that show that most big inventions of our times originated in R&D. A scientist or an engineer saw a problem or an opportunity and connected a technology to it—for example, disposable diapers, sticky notes, iPhones.

The decision what to work on (or *not* work on) is an important subject for R&D and affects all lean development processes (see *Chapter 6*). Clearly completing and launching the wrong product is a waste, but just working on the wrong project is a lot of waste, too. Often you need to try something to see if it works and has potential—experimenting is OK and builds knowledge, which is not waste—but the key is knowing when to stop. When does knowledge cease to emerge and the potential for a viable project disappear? Working too long on bad projects prevents the good ones from coming in, because there is no capacity to accommodate them. Remember, you must take waste out to create the capacity to work on value.

Based on my experience, few companies have a good process to manage the many sources of incoming work, and they do not learn how to get good at it. Even harder than assessing incoming work is dealing with work in progress. It is very difficult to stop projects in which engineers have invested a lot of time and effort, even when it becomes clear the projects are likely to go nowhere. There are human factors that influence those decisions, but there also is the fact that we do not like to just write off the investment and move on. Leaders often procrastinate and leave the decision to their successor.

Not all the work of engineers in an R&D organization leads to new products. There is work that leads to developing capabilities, there are services requested by other parts of the organization, and many other categories of work that may never be used or lead to little or no improvement. Richard Sheridan estimates that $75 billion worth of software is developed every year but not used.[20]

It also is a waste to *not develop* a product that the company knows customers need—you are not applying resources to where they are needed. That is clearly a missed opportunity, even though no resources are invested, but this is more an issue about innovation and where to innovate, than waste (see *Chapter 6* on lean and innovation).

4. Favoring Functional Optimization Over Value-Stream Profitability

Optimizing a function or a local organization at the expense of the complete value stream or the profitability of the company is a huge waste.

A good example of function/local optimization are decisions that help individual functions meet their function goals but have a negative effect on customer value and value-stream profits.

A few generations ago, one of our manufacturing directors put a limit on the number of new products that he was allowing into Goodyear plants. Unfortunately at the time, functions had a lot of power in the company, and he succeeded and enforced the limit. From a function standpoint, his argument was pretty good: new products take a lot of effort and resources to ramp up in manufacturing, introduce new complexity (new materials, components), often initially lead to higher scrap losses, and are more costly to manufacturing. The plant saved money, but eventually, they would have nothing to run because the market demands new products.

The savings of one function also can lead to increased work for other functions and/or wasted effort. We visited an automotive supplier that performed a high volume of R&D work and had implemented lean in its accounting department. The accountants made new rules for expense reports to make *their* work more efficient. They asked all the engineers (and the rest of the company) to glue all receipts on special forms in a certain sequence and according to a defined pattern. The new process saved the accountants more than an hour a day processing the expense reports. Then, the engineering manager asked the engineers how long it took them to glue and sequence receipts—many additional hours per day, and, thus, a significant net loss to the company.

I would also like to put in this functional-savings category cases where employee satisfaction is ranked higher than customer satisfaction. The simplest example is seen at stores where store employees get the best parking slots because they come in early. Store employees who value customers park in the back and leave the convenient parking slots for the customers. Even in R&D, I have seen where compromises are made to customer value, service, or the profitability of a value stream, simply to accommodate the desire of functions or team members. Sometimes, team leaders or managers prefer happy employees over happy customers.

Many companies make their regions or business units responsible for their P&L, and the business leaders do what they can to achieve a good profit. Would a region or a business give up some capacity and profit to help another business or region, if that means higher profit for the company? They will if they rank the profitability of the company higher than their individual P&L. And if they do not, that is waste.

5. Random versus Value-Stream Improvements

This waste is about well-executed lean initiatives that cost time and money and may improve or change a process or piece of a process, but they have no effect on the complete value stream. We found this out at Goodyear when we improved subprocesses, but still saw no visible results to the overall R&D process. This is called "point kaizen" or "random kaizen," in contrast to the preferred system improvements ("system kaizen").

Improving a subprocess sometimes fails to achieve visible results at the value-stream level—the savings or improvements get eaten up by other functions—or worse, many performance measures (speed, delivery, costs) could even get worse.

You may wonder why I put this waste high on my list. This waste may not seem so large if you only consider the lean investment, but it can have large consequences because it produces no visible results. Many companies start their lean initiatives with great intentions, but these random activities bear no meaningful fruit, and eventually, they give up for lack of results.

One of the first lean initiatives that the Herbie team started was to improve the cycle time of the tire-cutting operation. The engineers like to look at tire sections to see if the tire was built according to the specifications or to understand failure modes, after a test. After many meetings with the innovation center manufacturing organization, which provides the tire-cutting service, their staff agreed to a maximum turnaround time of 1 week. We tracked their performance meticulously, and found the initiative had only improved the time for the nonpriority projects—and even for these projects, the saved time was quickly wasted away in another queue. Only after *all* the adjacent processes were shortened and aligned years later, in a higher-level improvement, did we see the results of the cutting improvements (and eventually a cycle time of 1 day).

Before we aligned everybody behind one process in R&D, we had many initiatives aimed at improving subprocesses that yielded no visible results. One such initiative was sponsored by Jean-Claude when he was general director GIC*A. This particular project was executed well, but Jean-Claude kept asking for results. We could show him none. It turned out that the improvements to the subprocess immediately hit another bottleneck in an adjacent function. This absence of results was used by many leaders to question the potential of lean to improve R&D.

Many scholars promote the idea that kaizens must happen alternatively on a local or subprocess and on a system level. That is a good suggestion because some initiatives start as grassroots efforts, and some of these initiatives will prove promising and should be elevated whenever possible to the system level. In order to avoid waste, though, you must understand the value stream well and focus on those initiatives that show the greatest promise for a high-level effect. Of course, if your lean work occurs at higher level processes and encompasses the complete value stream, chances for visible results and sustainability are greater than when working on subprocesses. Once lean improvements are made at the highest level, you can then cascade those improvements down to all subprocesses.

In Goodyear R&D we only saw the improvements after the adjacent marketing and the manufacturing functions came to the table, and we aligned everything for customer value and the profitability of the complete value stream. This is why Joe Zekoski identified patience during a change process as one of the biggest challenges a company will encounter.

6. Waiting

Waiting is the most prominent of the traditional Shingo/Ohno eight wastes in R&D. Engineers and R&D scientists surely understand this waste. They have grown long beards while they practiced patience and waited. Years ago at Goodyear, it seemed that waiting is all we did—we spent most of the day trying to find out where our projects were and influencing the priority lists to get them moving again.

Why is waiting so prevalent in R&D? One reason is because resources are often scarce and work is unpredictable and abundant. Project managers have to buffer their projects because of the poor predictability. At Goodyear, they never knew what priority they would be getting, so project managers would pad their projects with time. The reason they could do that at Goodyear and other companies is because we put a cost on resources, but did not put a cost on time or on waiting lines. This can quickly lead to a vicious circle or downward spiral: The buffer time is added to the process, a later delivery date is established, and the functions then shoot for the buffered (later) date. So deliveries are still missed because other projects interfere, and the next time the project manager adds even more buffer time. The cycle only stops when the business steps in and gives a project priority status.

The other reason for excessive waiting in R&D is its functional focus. Like a doctor's office where the patient always seems to wait, in R&D the project is the patient. In both situations, there is a high specialization of resources, people, and equipment, all of which are expensive and scarce, so their utilization is the first priority (not the interests of the patient/project).

If you cannot figure out the exact cost of waiting time, put a rough dollar estimate on it. A large dollar amount will always get more attention than talking about a big chunk of time. When Steve Rohweder, now regional technical director, was heading up global testing, he quantified the total time of all the tires that were between being finished at a plant and the end of testing. He calculated an astronomical number, and Steve considered it his job to get that number as low as possible, as fast as possible.

At Goodyear, we implemented *cost of delay* (COD) as a powerful measure to translate waiting time to dollars. This is one way to quantify the effect of time on the profitability of projects. It helps set priorities, but, more importantly, it lets project managers and leaders make economic decisions. For example, at Goodyear we use COD to assess whether it is worth working overtime in the plants that make molds or tires or if we need to create extra capacity in testing (more about COD in *Chapter 6*).

Maybe waiting also is a psychological or cultural issue. Even outside of work we spend a lot of time waiting—on the expressway, at the restaurant, in the airport, on the phone—and we are just used to it or numb to it. So let us get impatient. Get upset over every waiting time that costs money, and eliminate it with a passion. The effort will pay off.

7. Inventory or WIP

Inventory wastes exist in R&D as in manufacturing, and it can be found in both finished-goods and work-in-process inventory. It is a lot harder to see in R&D, and you do not get a bill from the warehouse to remind you that it is there.

Finished-goods inventory in R&D is less frequent than in manufacturing, but is a big issue because it is perishable. You've invested a lot in finished designs, and they do not produce returns when they sit on a shelf. In an environment that is already overloaded, finished designs that go nowhere were probably created at the expense of something that is needed but now late—a double whammy.

Some lean scholars argue that lean is about creating knowledge and that it is OK to create knowledge and put it on the shelf. That sounds good in theory, but, in reality, I have not seen many people do that in an industrial R&D environment. Most knowledge that I have seen on shelves is there because it was not needed at the time it was created.

The waste of work-in-progress inventory (WIP) dwarfs that of finished goods in a typical R&D environment and has a devastating effect on flow, speed, and waiting. Just like finished-design inventory, WIP has a lot invested in it, and it cannot get a return until it is further developed into a design and a product. High WIP used to be—and still is, to some extent—a big problem at Goodyear, and most companies list high volumes of WIP (too much on our plate) as one of the top issues of product development.

WIP waste also is harmful because it becomes more difficult to detect mistakes: Imagine a new engineer makes a mistake on a drawing. The drawing goes into a queue at mold-making, and the engineer continues to develop drawings that incorporate the same mistake. Eventually the mold-making process discovers the mistake and there is a flurry of activity to find and fix all the faulty drawings. This is one reason that engineers should be frustrated when they do not quickly see results of their work.

WIP also has a lot of costly effects on

- Cycle time
- Learning
- Design perishability
- Inefficiencies due to stop and go

Some amount of WIP always exists in R&D—engineers are working at something for some amount of time. It often is good to have something to work on when one activity gets blocked or if an engineer needs to wait for something. There is an optimum amount of WIP, but there are key reasons why WIP volumes go far beyond the optimum:

- Inadequate control of incoming work
- Lack of resources or timely availability of resources
- High specialization and cost of resources
- Slow execution

- Insufficient work leveling
- Inefficient processes
- Early start, hoping for an early finish

There are many ways to reduce WIP or at least to manage it appropriately. I will address those in *Chapters 5 and 6* when I show you how to improve flow and speed and how to control incoming work.

8. Knowledge and Talent

The waste of knowledge and talent can be difficult to understand or even assess, and this waste category often turns into a catchall bucket for everything that we cannot put into the other waste categories. In manufacturing, waste of knowledge and talent is often associated with command-and-control environments where shopfloor associates are not asked to contribute ideas on how to improve their own jobs/work. In product development, that, too, can happen, but knowledge waste is even more problematic because of the many ways it occurs and because *knowledge* is not always recognized as an intended outcome of R&D.

Knowledge can be wasted when

- People retire and take with them all the undocumented stuff they learned in their years with the company.
- Young engineers do not seek out the knowledge and experience that is available to them. Based on my experience, this problem is bigger than the capturing and the documenting of knowledge.
- A basic knowledge management process is not in place, so 1) knowledge is not captured or documented and everything needs to be reinvented and 2) knowledge created in one part of the company is not shared with other functions.

At Goodyear, we had our share of knowledge wastes, but there are many efforts now underway to manage knowledge more efficiently. One of the most promising is a pilot initiative in the innovation center in Luxembourg where key experienced engineers are paired with new engineers for a period of time. Since the pairings rotate on a cadence, the new engineers receive good training while the knowledge and the experience of the senior engineers are passed on in an appropriate fashion. The pairing is hands-on learning in the right context with the possibility to ask questions and to clarify. Engineers close to retirement should be paired in a similar fashion with possible successors; the pairing beats the documenting of what a retiree knew in the hope that somebody else can put it to good use before it becomes obsolete.

You say this seems like just a lot of common sense. I agree. But to unendingly incorporate hands-on learning and on-the-job training as Toyota has done, both in manufacturing and product development, is no small feat, and runs into a lot of obstacles. For example, I blame the many cost-reduction efforts at Goodyear through the years for wasting a lot of knowledge. With all the hiring freezes in the last 20 years, on-the-job training and proper knowledge transfer was not always possible.

The other aspect of this waste is not effectively managing talent. Too often the effort is invested in getting approval for key positions—engineers, scientists—and not in properly filling, onboarding, and managing that position. Positions are frequently filled with a person who is qualified for the most difficult demand of the job (technical expertise). Yet, it is assumed that other tasks, which require fewer qualifications or less education (e.g., clerical work, administrative tasks, lower level technical work), also will be handled by the individual. This "other" work increases over time, and the scientists get frustrated. Engineering work like measuring samples, observing experiments, and clerical tasks could be done by assistants and technicians (but these are often the first roles cut during downsizing).

Hospitals and healthcare providers seem to be good at balancing their talent. I rarely see a doctor or a professional, such as a therapist, do the work that an administrator or a technician could do, and doctors are often assisted by several roles: nurse, technician, receptionist/registrar, office support. Each role's talent is applied and layered, according to the skillset. In order to leverage those resources, doctors like to work in groups. Imagine the wasted talent if a doctor had to schedule patients, perform billing, deal with insurers, and so on. Growing healthcare requirements for documentation are probably driving more of this distribution of work than is ideal, but the model is, nonetheless, a good example of stratified teamwork that can apply to engineering work. Unfortunately, this model is not yet popular in R&D organizations.

At Goodyear, we have made progress with the addition of technicians whose services are shared by a certain number of engineers. Goodyear also has outsourced a lot of routine, frequent, standardized tasks to an off-site organization. We have found that good R&D organizations have administrative talent shared by a group of engineers. And it is "talent." The administrative assistant and travel counselors who fill out my expense reports and arrange my trips perform their roles in a fraction of the time it would take me, and do so with better results. The time this would take me and other engineers and managers in Goodyear would add up quickly.

Some companies are getting quite creative these days in minimizing their waste of talent by

- Keeping key talent available as long as possible by extending retirement age and/or offering consulting contracts
- Pairing people with complementary skills to create a better combined role
- Establishing knowledge management offices to reduce the waste of talent and knowledge
- Incorporating technology to take over routine tasks (e.g., automated design and engineering systems)

Products and technologies are becoming increasingly complicated, and more and more specialists and experts are needed to achieve innovation. Although, many companies do a good job identifying and promoting management or leadership talent, the technical talent often plays a secondary role. At Goodyear and other companies, the focus has recently increased on managing the "dual ladder"—a career path for valuable technical talent. Some companies even evaluate their engineers on "value" and contribution. Some companies even evaluate talented associates based on the value for their company, and other companies. At Goodyear, there is succession planning for managers and leaders, as well as for the most common top technical talent.

Although technical talent receives attention now in many companies, other talent is still unrecognized, and not managed. This includes innovators, change agents, process experts, and the various services in R&D that do not fit the core engineering competencies, like finance, IT, or HR.

Waste of knowledge and talent is more subtle than the other wastes, and it can be harder to find and quantify. Lean training is, of course, a remedy. It also helps to bring your HR organization into your company's lean initiatives, and let them see how the principles and tools can be applied in their roles and help them with talent management.

9. Design Errors

Design errors are easy to understand as a form of waste; if detected early, they are generally easy to correct. But it is even better to avoid making errors. The problem with certain design errors is that if undetected they can multiply, and have a significant impact or consequences on many products, not just one in which the error occurs. R&D is about exploring new ground and discovering new things. This is not an excuse to make more mistakes. Even in discovery, standards should be followed. If a mistake occurs, efforts must be made so that it only occurs once.

Placing design errors ninth on my list does not infer that error prevention is not important at Goodyear. We always have had a rigorous quality system, without which we would not have survived in our industry designing and making tires. But Goodyear, like many other companies, used to bank on sophisticated systems and inspections to catch mistakes before they affected a finished product. Since our processes used so many layers, we had plenty of opportunities to catch design mistakes before they affected a product. Inspection is not an effective method to avoid mistakes, because if people know there is inspection of their work they often rely on the inspection process rather than taking responsibility for their own quality.

Today, in our lean process, we use tools and processes like poka-yoke, jidoka, in-process inspection, and checklists to isolate R&D mistakes *as they occur or even before they occur.* This is because avoiding mistakes is a lot more efficient than catching mistakes.

Poka-yoke (mistake proofing) is an especially effective tool in product design because it can be built into many computer design tools. For example, in our computer design system there is a feature that requires different design features for tires used on cars that drive on the left side of the road. "Jidoka" is a Japanese word to describe a process where robots can detect abnormalities like humans—autonomation or, as Ohno described it, "automation with a human touch."[21] Jidoka methods apply to modeling tools, prototype building, and testing.

In a lean design system everybody is responsible for their own work—that is, do not pass mistakes. Engineers use checklists to check their own work.

Product launches can be a dreadful event for many companies, often because projects are over budget and late. And in some industries, such as software, companies will launch the product "ready or not," knowing that "patches" or "version 2.0" will follow. In such industries, the worst part is that some problems are known to engineers, but there is not enough time to fix them prior to launch. We all have purchased such products.

Consider the number of quality recalls in the automotive industry, and the enormous wastes this causes the OEMs, their dealer networks, and their customers (they may rate this waste higher). Many of those problems are design-related, and solving design problems after a product is sold is extremely costly and has disastrous consequences for product loyalty. Ideally, all problems that could possibly occur after the sale should be identified and resolved before the launch. Sometimes not everything is known about the users and the conditions of use, but in talking with executives from other industries, they still point to the time crunch as the culprit. A former Toyota leader taught me a good method: ask your team to come up with at least 100 things that could be missed before a launch. Then, ask them to rank the likelihood of occurrence and mistake-proof them, starting at the top of the list.

This is similar to other preventive tools, like DFMEAs (design failure mode effect analysis), to fix problems on existing projects. Many companies designed their own DFMA or PFMA (process FMEA) tools and use them extensively. At Goodyear they are becoming more popular, especially because we now have time to effectively use the tools. These kinds of preventive tools, combined with the risk management, can have a huge impact on further reducing design mistakes in your company.

The easiest way to deal with wastes of defects in design and R&D is to make more time available before the launch to identify and resolve potential problems. Lean is ideal for this: it eliminates time-consuming wastes, frees up time to do things right before the launch, and even offers time if last-minute issues pop up. And as will be discussed in *Chapter 6*, launch crunch time can be reduced by assigning resources early in the development cycle rather than at launch time—another counterintuitive lean principle. Reducing the WIP and giving engineers the opportunity to focus on one project or task at a time also help.

10. Overproduction

Ohno used to consider overproduction the mother of all wastes because it encompasses many other wastes (e.g., inventory, motion, and transportation). I do not want to go that far for R&D, but I consider overproduction a close cousin of inventory, and I discuss it separately to be consistent with and respect Ohno's popular list of wastes.

You're thinking, "We cannot even produce what is expected of us and we are late most of the time, so how can we overproduce?" Overproduction in R&D is everything that is designed that does not get used—or at least, not used right away. Designs that stay on the shelf collecting dust until they are obsolete or molds that have been produced at great expense and are waiting to be used are examples of overproduction. I have occasionally seen designs still being worked on even though marketing had given up on the product, but did not tell R&D. Finished-design overproduction is usually easy to see, but overproduction also occurs with WIP in the form of partial designs being worked upon, although the overall design plan has changed; this occurs much more frequently than finished-design overproduction.

In R&D, overproduction most frequently occurs in the form of early delivery. In a process that has a lot of late deliveries, there are normally a lot of early deliveries as well, which run the risk of needing, changed. Early delivery is a waste because

- The activity took the "space" of another project that now may be late.
- Significant investment has been applied to the work, especially if tooling is involved.
- Necessary changes or advances in technology that may have occurred in the correctly timed cycle cannot be accommodated in an earlier cycle.
- There is a high chance for rework when changes are made by the customer or other stakeholders.

Another form of overproduction that is common in R&D is starting something and not finishing it. Often the reason for that is something more important came up, in which case documenting the learning from the stalled effort also does not occur. Other times, projects are started because they seemed like a good idea and are abandoned after a lot of time and resources have been exhausted.

Countermeasures for overproduction include managing incoming work, good work standards, late start, good project risk management, and flow principles, which we will cover in *Chapter 5* as we progress farther around the Womack Wheel.

11. Overprocessing

Overprocessing is doing more processing than is needed, but it can also mean using bad processes. Examples of overprocessing in R&D include

- Too much testing
- "One size fits all" processes

- Excessive detail on drawings
- Too many prototypes
- Too many experiments

At Goodyear, a former testing director liked simple procedures and used a one-size-fits-all approach, but unfortunately, it was the largest size. Every time a test was run, it was run to all conditions and customer specifications. This was stopped in one of the first lean initiatives in the testing organization.

Overprocessing and project risk management often go hand in hand in a product-development environment. As I have noted, the first new capacity that became available at Goodyear through waste elimination was used for additional testing and more iterations. Safety and quality always come first. But there still comes a point where "good was lost in the pursuit of perfection."

Standards are a necessary component of risk management, with process requirements linked to the standards, and they also set boundaries of project manager or engineer decision-making. The right amount of design, testing, and processing is established, which helps prevent project managers from coming up with their own methods. (Like any standard, it can and should be improved over time and replaced.) The lack of a standard leaves all risk decisions to the project manager or engineer, and such decisions are inconsistent and, generally, unnecessarily conservative. At a recent AME conference in Irvine, Calif., Richard Sheridan, owner of Menlo Innovations, described how his software development engineers used an informal "done-done" standard, which compelled Sheridan to ask what was wrong with "done."[20]

The challenge in creating the standard is that all project managers and engineers must contribute and collaborate to get to that point. A great tool that helped us at Goodyear with this process is the use of reflection after every learning cycle. This process is managed with an A3 where the effectiveness of the iteration—including all the testing, modeling, etc.—is assessed and documented. Lessons learned and countermeasures are spelled out and implemented using the PDCA cycle. This way, we are learning and we can improve this complicated process and standard. And since all are involved and the decisions are transparent, the likelihood that all will come to a consensus is greater.

Other popular forms of overprocessing are meetings, status reports, updates, and so on. I remember the times when I wrote weekly status reports that probably nobody ever read—no more of that at Goodyear. I used to spend countless hours in staff meetings, project update meetings, emergency or panic meetings, follow-up meetings—very few of those are still around at Goodyear, and today we only schedule meetings for the time truly needed (not an hour by default). A lean product development process needs new and better management tools than these!

At Goodyear, projects are reviewed in regular, brief, standup meetings or huddles, and only problems are discussed. There are formal meetings, but only if a real problem arises that needs a meeting to get resolved. Managers and leaders are encouraged to keep a pulse on the organization by doing regular gemba walks—rather than forcing information to be submitted to them—which gives engineers and project managers more time to create value. Today, reports are written to document knowledge; knowledge briefs have replaced long research reports that resembled college dissertations. Writing fewer reports was easy to implement, but we are still working on identifying the *right* reports to write. With the communication tools available to us today, meetings should not be needed as much to communicate and "pass down" information. But also, do not substitute brief meetings or huddles for cryptic emails and expanding email trails.

As I noted at the beginning of this section, unsuitable, complicated, or otherwise poor processes also contribute to overprocessing. A good example of that is a process with a lot of stop-and-go. Another poor process that had been used a lot at Goodyear was our former product development process that relied on a priority system for every step.

12. Transportation

If you have tools, hard-copy drawings, prototypes, and samples, then you have transportation. At Goodyear, transportation and warehousing of prototype tires was a heavy waste for many years. The elimination of that waste in warehousing (a monument to waste that is difficult for all but the simplest of business models to get rid of) was one of our first lean projects. That effort resulted in a large reduction of transportation cost as well.

At Goodyear in R&D, expedited shipping of test tires (FedEx, DHL) had become the standard. It allowed us to make up some time that we wasted in poor processes, but we got so bad that expedited became the standard, and schedules were based on expedited delivery times. Fortunately, we had poor visibility and nobody noticed the large annual charge. But transportation also takes time, and most companies, like Goodyear, do not know the cost of time (or cost of delay) very well. Let us assume you operate in the United States or Europe and you purchase a mold in China because purchasing tracks mold costs and the price plus freight is lower than a local vendor. Did purchasing or the project manager calculate the cost of time for the transport, and the effect the increased time can have on projects? Today at Goodyear we have minimized transportation, and we make the best decision looking at all the cost effects, including time. Many good companies today evaluate business options on total delivered cost, not only manufacturing cost, and some leading-edge companies have started to also include the cost of time.

13. Motion

It is ergonomically good for engineers and others to get up from their desk occasionally, and move their limbs as well as their eyes away from the screen. But I often find excessive motion occurs in the placement of individuals and functions, forcing people to spend time finding their colleagues. Similarly, printers and shared office resources are usually placed where an architect decides they are convenient or where the plug is, not where the engineers need them.

R&D processes also include laboratories and prototype-manufacturing facilities, where motion waste is a bigger issue, and quite comparable to motion waste in manufacturing. A popular tool to visualize this kind of waste is a spaghetti diagram, which is a map with all paths taken by an individual to accomplish a task drawn out in detail. As you draw, it eventually looks like spaghetti on a plate. Knowing the motion (the path) is the first step toward eliminating the waste of motion.

It can be quite amazing when you make the motion of a person visible. We have used motion mapping in our labs and prototype shops. As we plan to relocate a lab in one of our innovation centers, avoiding motion will play a key role in the planning and layout of the lab. I have seen many companies lay out labs in full size in an empty warehouse by gluing tape on a floor. Then they build furniture props out of cardboard, and play through the main scenarios to maximize flow and reduce motion.

In one Goodyear lab, a new "showpiece" equipment was installed by the entry door because the VP of the division was planning to have company executives tour the lab. He wanted to show off the equipment, without subjecting the group to a full tour of the lab. Unfortunately, the samples to be tested on that equipment were made in the opposite corner of the lab. Twenty years later, that equipment still sat in the same location. In those 20 years, many thousands of miles were walked by lab technicians using or servicing the equipment, which cost the company money and risk of injury.

This is my list of wastes, brought to you by years of fighting them and, prior to lean, even more years of frustration by not understanding them or by accepting them as a way of doing business. Other fine lean minds have come up with their own and different lists of wastes, including the following two examples:

Mary and Tom Poppendieck identified seven classifications of wastes specific to the software-development industry that also apply to product development:[22]

1. Partially done work (overproduction)
2. Extra features (overdesigning or overprocessing)
3. Relearning (overprocessing)
4. Handoffs (motion)
5. Delays (waiting)
6. Task switching (overprocessing)
7. Defects

Allen Ward and Durward Sobek came up with the following R&D wastes:[23]

■ *Scatter:* disruptions to knowledge flow
  - Add more people to get project back on schedule
  - Stop work to go and report on the status
■ *Handoffs:* disconnected knowledge, responsibility, action, and feedback
  - One person defines project plan, another person executes
  - Holding manufacturing plants responsible to meet a specification developed by somebody else
  - Reassigning team members in the middle of a project
■ *Wishful thinking:* decisions without data
  - Overselling a project
  - Setting specifications at the beginning of a project
  - Testing to specification (rather than test to failure)
■ *Useless information*
  - Reports nobody reads
■ *Discard or lose knowledge*
  - Disband the team
  - Fix a problem and move on (without documenting learning)

You might find other lists of R&D wastes or develop your own. I found vast amounts of waste just using the traditional Shingo/Ohno list, and still find plenty, many years later.

Note that I defined waste in the context of customer value—that for which the customer would not be willing to pay. Taiichi Ohno described Toyota's lean efforts as trying to minimize the time—from receipt of a customer order to when Toyota collects payment—by reducing all the waste in the process.[21] Many take that definition to equate waste with process costs, and, thus, lean cost-reduction initiatives. That is a myopic view of lean and one that can harm creativity in product development. And it is unfortunate, given that the correct application of lean principles in R&D, including waste elimination, can lead to large benefits in speed, efficiency, and value-stream profitability.

Lean R&D Principle: Never stop eliminating waste.

Removing waste from processes may still be the most effective and efficient way to achieve results with a lean initiative. Those results can be gains in quality, delivery, efficiency, and speed, some of which will lead to improved customer value and profitability.

Many people think that if you removed a lot of waste already, there is not much left, and they move to another facet of the implementation. But people who have practiced lean for some time agree that the more waste you remove, the more you seem to find. This is largely due to education and observation skills, and experience. But it is also due to the fact that new waste creeps in constantly, and due to the fact that as more adjacent processes align and remove waste, the more waste becomes apparent.

I rarely cite a side effect with a lean principle, but I will here: Waste elimination has lost a lot of popularity. Some companies found that focusing a lean initiative exclusively on removing waste and cost from their processes negatively affected innovation. This negative effect can be avoided by doing everything in moderation and by a good understanding and correct application of lean principles.

At Goodyear: We removed lots of waste from our R&D processes, including waiting and overprocessing, but we first focused on customer value rather than R&D cost. The main reason to eliminate this waste was to create flow and speed. We have avoided the negative effects on innovation and reinvested the gains from the waste elimination into value-stream and capability improvements. Today, we focus on the "zero-loss" approach, which consists in defining the theoretical and practical bottom line. That establishes the gap, and also the opportunity. It also provides direction and helps determine where the largest results can be obtained. But, here too, the zero-loss approach should be introduced and managed with great caution in an R&D environment.

When I go to conferences on lean and talk with experts and consultants about lean product development, I sense that "waste" ideas are not "selling" like they once did—too many new and exciting aspects of lean continually surface, such as the topics of lean startups and rapid improvement teams. Do not be fooled! When you start a lean initiative, removing waste from your R&D process will likely deliver better results than most other tools. I don't know your processes like you do, but my 80/20 rule tells me that they are probably like most processes, and will benefit like most (see *Norbert's 80/20 Rule*).

Norbert's 80/20 Rule

I have always contended that 80% of all companies face similar problems in R&D. I estimate that only 20% of companies are unique and face unique R&D issues. So given that, you should first use the lean principles that have been proven to work at companies, like Goodyear. When you truly think that your R&D is unique, then experiment with other methods and principles.

Muda, Muri, and Mura

The Japanese word for "waste" is "muda." Two Japanese words closely related to muda are "muri" and "mura." These are related wastes and refer to overloading and bad distribution of a load, respectively, and they are especially prominent and damaging in a product development process (see *Muri and Mura*). Overloading and lack of balance in R&D is often caused by high specialization, fluctuation, and unpredictable nature of incoming work, into product development.

Muri and Mura

The overloaded highway on the right represents muri (overburden).
The two highways together illustrate mura (imbalance).

It can be easy to see overburdening in a manufacturing organization—workers overreaching to apply parts, maintenance staff struggling to lift a die—but you may only see the consequences of overburdening in an R&D organization. Sometimes there is high specialization and expertise needed to accomplish a project, but you lack sufficient talent in those disciplines. The consequence is that you wait for the few experts to complete their tasks, and they have work pile up in front of them, which adds stress to their jobs and long cycle times to the process. Some specialists like to be overloaded, feel important when overloaded, may equate overload to job security or importance, and point to their overload to promote themselves. Do not overburden them, and do not let them embrace it.

High workload correlates with stress. Stress management is the subject of much industrial and healthcare literature, but why not *stress avoidance*. These techniques can help to avoid stress and avoid overloading:

- Waste elimination
- Late start or other methods to reduce WIP
- No multitasking
- Visual planning
- Increased flexibility
- Outsourcing noncritical work

Similar to overburdening in an R&D environment is uneven work distribution. This is due primarily to highly cyclical or seasonal nature of most R&D businesses. The seasonal effect at Goodyear used to get compounded by real or created panics and fires that needed immediate attention by a lot of resources. Before Goodyear moved toward a matrix organization, teams were staffed to meet maximum demand levels because the workload fluctuated greatly, and teams rarely would share resources. There were certain customer demands, such as OEM requirements, that were governed by a contract, and occasionally required this level of capacity. As you can guess, while the teams addressed high demand fairly well, they were often severely underutilized.

A matrix organization was a powerful force in improving the balance of work in Goodyear's product-development organization. There are many nuances to organizing in a matrix, but it really helps with the distribution of work. Give it a try—you can do a little bit of matrix (people are still to some extent assigned to projects based on their skills and experience) or a lot of matrix (everybody can do any job).

Even within a matrix organization, specialists and special equipment present barriers to eliminating wastes related to workload balance, and flow principles will be needed to help your organization break through (*see Chapter 5*).

A lot of lean experts recommend that you deal with overloading and workload balance before attacking wastes. I find that they are all connected and intertwined with the flow of work. There is, however, one overall suggestion I make regarding distribution of work: balance the work at the highest level, just as you would standardize all processes at the highest level possible. Start on the highest level of the value streams and stagger the launches as best as you can, and work your way down to assure optimum use of all your talent and resources. All these decisions must be sound business decisions that balance profitability of the complete project portfolio with the availability of scarce resources.

This will require cross-functional operations teams to have the visibility, the authority, and the tools (item takt, flexibility) to make those decisions, and execute on them. Similarly, avoid pushing down work-leveling decisions into every function, which leads to reestablishing priorities and large queues.

Zero Loss

The zero-loss concept is popular in manufacturing, although, sometimes I think it is just another name for lean and an aggressive waste-removal or cost-reduction initiative. The idea, when correctly applied, is to define the theoretical minimum (resources, costs, time, inventory) that a task or a job takes, and use that to *guide* where to improve (you are unlikely to ever get to zero). The gap between the current and the theoretical best represents the opportunity for ultimate efficiency. In an LPPDE presentation, Jim Womack defined lean as "creating progressively more value with less resource until you reach perfect value with zero resource."[4] It is important to note that Jim leads in with creating more value, not with zero resources. Unfortunately, Jim did not tell us how knowledge is created with zero resources.

Due to the high influence on the value stream, in R&D the zero-loss concept can be applied to both, the product and the process. Some companies have set minimum weight targets for their products, and some are even able to calculate a minimum cost target, and they define everything above those targets as loss. The concept also applies well for areas where everybody agrees that "zero" really is the goal, as for safety incidents, mistakes, or customer complaints. Zero experiments or a reduced number of experiments is not the way to go in R&D because no knowledge would be generated. But zero wasted experiments, however, is a good target.

Besides zero waste in the design of the product, the concept allows organizations to dream of the perfect state—look at what happened in the imaging industry and entertainment industry with distribution of music and videos. The zero-waste concept is a powerful directional tool that helps companies identify wastes and resources, and then incrementally attack those targets. Some areas will be difficult to get to zero, but companies can move toward that end, just as we have been pursuing perfection in the earlier lean models.

Zero loss can quickly turn into a zero-cost initiative, and those initiatives are known to hurt innovation, creativity, and R&D productivity. It's also important to figure out how learning and capability development are affected by zero-loss goals, because you don't want a zero-learning environment. Zero-loss calculations in R&D should not be made based on zero cost but on zero value added.

The biggest problem I see with zero-loss approaches is that they are often used randomly, sometimes to reduce cost in one function. As we have seen many times already, those initiatives can have drastic effects on other functions and the profitability of the value stream. Every zero-loss initiative must be assessed by its effect on the value stream, and not the function that starts it. In manufacturing, a lot of successful zero-loss initiatives are run by finance experts. If you try a zero-loss initiative in R&D, it may be a good idea to make sure the following is understood by the zero-loss experts:

- Good variability and experiments cannot become zero.
- R&D has large shadows—it is hard to quantify R&D's influence on the profitability of the value streams.
- It is especially difficult to put a dollar value on knowledge, talent, capability, and experience.

Waste Removal Gets Underway at Goodyear

The Herbie team realized that if we ever want to serve the customer better, we needed to remove a lot of the waste from our value stream—we needed to first create the capacity for value-added work. It wasn't rocket science either that we realized that if we spend so much time waiting we would never be able to deliver on time.

We had already learned how difficult it was to engage the functional leaders in our lean ideas. But we also recognized that data, which would help us when assessing waste, could be an ally when we had to sell functional leaders on our countermeasures.

Based on good lean teachings, we first looked at the muri and mura (overloading and the load balance). Overloading was manifesting itself as long waiting lines—engineers were used to having dozens of projects on their plate, and they handled them in the order of priority. The engineers never really felt the "overloading" effect because they focused on the priority of the day; they were numb to the "complaining" routine. The same was true for the other functions—manufacturing, testing, prototyping.

Work balance was quite a different story. If we looked at the recently completed projects in the value stream we found an interesting distribution (see *Distribution of Work within R&D*).

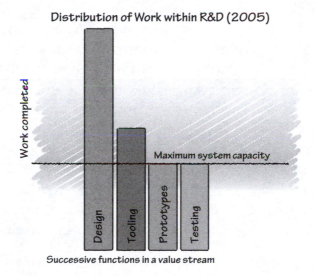

At a glance it looked like we were "stuffing" the front of the development pipeline. Design started every possible project as soon as possible in hopes to finish them earlier, but all they did was put them in a waiting line earlier in the downstream function. The design functions—the first in the process—were staffed for the worst situation and had capacity to accept all work as soon as it came in, but obviously their capacity was not aligned with the capacity of the pipeline. Some of the projects started early by product development were rejected in the stage-gate process later or abandoned for other reasons. Most of the engineering work, however, was completed, and then waited in some queue for priority.

We realized that the product development value stream cannot produce more than its bottleneck (we were, after all, named "Herbie"), and that we had to address the bottleneck before we could address the work leveling! This is typical for problems that arise in a lean initiative—there rarely is a single, simple solution. Things always seem intertwined, and most of the time it takes more than one countermeasure to resolve a problem.

Lean R&D Principle: Expect most lean product development problems to need multiple countermeasures.

Rarely is there a lean silver bullet when improving R&D processes. You may find purely technical problems that can be fixed with one solution, but, based on my experience, process problems rarely can be addressed with only one solution. Usually, many lean principles need to be pulled together to address a problem, and many functions need to collaborate.

We have seen several times that waste of waiting time cannot be eliminated simply by focusing on waste. We need additional countermeasures, such as applying flow principles to the process. That is why in the lean language we do not like to use the term "solutions," implying fixed and done. In lean vocabulary, we prefer "countermeasures" (plural), and we also imply that countermeasures must be implemented with a good PDCA cycle.

There also are times when a single countermeasure can cause unintended consequences, and it should have been applied with other countermeasures. This is why it's always good to evaluate a set of countermeasures—you might find that the collective sum of their impact may be greater than the sum of the individual countermeasures.

At Goodyear: Our materials development lab had to drastically reduce its cycle times to keep up with the faster pace of the other contributors to the value stream. They quickly determined that the lab mixer was their bottleneck. They initially thought that long downtimes were the root cause of their problem, but when they dug a little deeper (and made a fishbone diagram), they found that there were three additional root causes that needed different countermeasures. In the end, they implemented a quick-repair program and a preventative maintenance program; installed a camera to record the condition of the rubber coming out of the mixer so that it could be seen by an engineer; implemented a pull system for raw material weighing; and changed the mixing rules.

Since we had the data now, we could calculate where the projects waited the longest. We figured out quickly that about 50% of all waiting time was spent in the queue of prototype manufacturing. Why were we not surprised? We knew that Goodyear plants had arbitrarily limited the capacity to maximize the plant efficiency. It became obvious to the Herbie team that there was no reason to start more projects than the plant would process—design just created a lot of waste by starting projects that went nowhere but into a queue in manufacturing. No more.

As you may have noticed by now, we attack all problems according to the Pareto principle, and we always start with the highest contributor. (Waiting is the most common waste in R&D, and manufacturing has the longest waiting time in the product development process.)

While we had good data to show what the problem was, it also pointed a finger at where the problem was, which in Goodyear was interpreted as *who* the problem was. Functions did not like it when other people identified them as a problem, and it did not matter to their leadership if you had data or not. Often the data was contested and functions became extremely defensive. But some of them took the same approach that Jean-Claude had taken with the chairman—just admit that you have a problem, and be happy that the low baseline makes it easy to show improvement.

In the end, even with data and aware of how carefully we needed to proceed, we had a terrible time getting people to agree with the countermeasures. It is hard to get people to change—it is even harder to get them to change for the benefit of others, and if they are not convinced that the change will improve things.

After we found the bottleneck, we counted more than 400 projects queued in front of our plants alone, waiting for prototype tires. What was absurd was that we also found more than 100,000 prototype tires sitting in a central warehouse, a plant, or a test lab. The prototype tires that were built in our U.S. and Canada plants were trucked to one warehouse from which they were dispatched to customers (submission for an OEM program) or a test site. We quickly determined that more than half of the tires would never be used because the projects were never authorized or they were abandoned. Another reason was that the engineers, who sometimes waited 6 months or more to get their tires built, frequently made multiples because they knew they would never make it through the queue again if more tires were needed.

While we were developing the countermeasures to address overloading (muri) and imbalance (mura)—and the waiting time and high WIP associated with them—we also attacked the waste in the product development process (muda) by picking some of the low-hanging fruit. For example, we reduced transportation waste by shipping tires direct from the plant where they are made to the final destination (for testing or to customers). We also eliminated a lot of motion when we moved the return tire-inspection station from the warehouse back to the campus. We even eliminated the storage space in the area where they cut the tested tires for analysis. We found out the workers only cut tires when they ran out of space, and since they had a lot of space, they let tires accumulate. Now with no more space to store the tires, they have to cut a small batch every day, which of course, cuts down the cycle time.

Another waste that we were able to address right away was the use of technicians to help the engineers, just like staff in a doctor's office is available to help the doctor with nonclinical tasks. In addition, many routine tasks with lower technical content were outsourced. There were many other large and small wastes that the team identified that could be eliminated right away, such as overprocessing in the design, building too many prototype tires, and running tests that were not needed. We also quit starting projects that were not approved at gate 2 of the PCP process.

During this time we also spent a lot of time training everybody in our global innovation centers. Although engineers appreciated the training, it was a challenge to get functional managers and leaders to participate in training. For those that did not or would not be trained, most eventually learned by other, less obvious means employed by me. For example, during this time I held many small seminars, explaining lean principles very informally. I noticed that I did not need an elaborate PowerPoint presentation. In most cases a flipchart did a better job. Another effective training tool was the use of "coaching moments." This technique is popular in sports coaching: if you see something worth talking about, you stop the drill and explain, and then you start with the improved execution. I would take a similar approach in meetings when a problem came up that could be addressed with a lean countermeasure. I called these instances out as coaching moments, and gave a short education. Some people appreciated this kind of teaching—others resented the interruption, but I had success with it. Fortunately, our sponsor Jean-Claude supported me, and did a lot of the coaching himself.

Today I still call a timeout for coaching moments, but I can count on a leader or manager to chip in with the lean lecture—that is when you know that the culture has changed. But that was light years from our introduction of lean principles. The lesson: Keep at it, and eventually others will buy in and offer support.

With our emphasis on waste reduction (muda, muri, and mura), we began to make small changes at the highest level of Goodyear's global R&D process. We picked some low-hanging fruit and gained a better understanding of our bottlenecks. The training helped us garner more support from all levels of the organization. But to get more substantial gains, we would need to move further along the Womack Wheel—we needed to create flow.

Notes

1. James P. Womack and Daniel T. Jones, *Lean Thinking*, Free Press, New York, 2003.
2. John Shook, *Managing to Learn*, Lean Enterprise Institute, Cambridge, MA, 2008.
3. Jim Womack, *Gemba Walks*, Lean Enterprise Institute, Cambridge, MA, 2011.
4. Jim Womack, *The Context of Lean Product & Process Development*, LPPDE, Raleigh, NC, September 24, 2014.
5. Noriaki Kano, Seraku Nobuhiku, Takahashi Fumio, and Tsuji Shinichi, "Attractive Quality and Must-Be Quality," *Journal of the Japanese Society for Quality Control* (in Japanese), April 15, 1984.
6. Shigeo Shingo, *The Sayings of Shigeo Shingo*, Productivity Press, Cambridge, MA, 1987.
7. Shoji Shiba and David Walden, *Four Practical Revolutions in Management: Systems for Creating Unique Organizational Capability*, Productivity Press and Center for Quality of Management, Cambridge, MA, 2001.
8. Richard Sheridan, LPPDE 2013, Savannah, GA, September 2013.
9. Steve Heinecke, *Enable Individuals to Be Better Innovators*, Savvy Consortium, Bloomington, MN, September 2013.
10. Jim Jacobs, Host remarks at Savvy Consortium, Bloomington, MN, September 2013.
11. Joshua Kerievsky, *Sufficient Design*, Lean Software and Systems Conference, Long Beach, CA, May 2011.
12. Andrea James, "Amazon.com CEO Jeff Bezos Says Company Goals Not Changed," Seattlepi.com, April 20, 2009.
13. Michael N. Kennedy, *Product Development for the Lean Enterprise*, Oaklea Press, Richmond, VA, 2008.
14. Michael George, James Works, Kimberly Watson-Hemphill, and Clayton Christensen, *Fast Innovation*, McGraw-Hill, New York, 2005.
15. Peter Drucker. Peter Drucker on Managerial Courage, Harvard Business School, Working Knowledge for Business Leaders, June 12, 2006.

16. Allen C. Ward, *Lean Product and Process Development*, Lean Enterprise Institute, Cambridge, MA, 2007.

17. Dave Logozzo, Lean Enterpreise Institute, presentation to Goodyear, Akron, OH, February 2012.

18. Håkan Ivarsson, *50 Nyanser av Lean*, Leadership Design Group Sweden AB, 2013.

19. Eric Ries, *The Lean Startup*, Crown Business, New York, 2011.

20. Richard Sheridan, *AME Innovation Summit*, Irvine, CA, March 2014.

21. Taiichi Ohno, *Toyota Production System: Beyond Large-Scale Production*, Productivity Press, Cambridge, MA, 1988.

22. Mary Poppendieck and Tom Poppendieck, *Lean Software Development*, Addison-Wesley Professional, Boston, 2003.

23. Allen C. Ward and Durward K. Sobek II, *Lean Product and Process Development*, Lean Enterprise Institute, Cambridge, MA, 2014.

Chapter 5

Making New-Product Value Flow

With our product development value stream clearly identified and efforts underway to remove many of the wastes that had historically plagued Goodyear R&D, such as waiting and overproduction, the Herbie team was ready to turn the Womack Wheel and focus on creating flow and implementing pull. In this chapter, I will tell you about the lean tools we used to do that as well as the many lean R&D principles that must be understood to successfully wield these techniques. Also during this time, the Herbie team truly began to see the fruit of our efforts and gain momentum—and, better yet, many of our early detractors began to believe in lean principles as we did.

Break Down Large Projects into Quick Learning Cycles

Mats Magnusson, professor at the KTH Royal Institute of Technology, has a unique way to describe a product development process. He compares it to a hydroelectric processing plant: the water behind the dam is the "potential" of a company, all of its available knowledge and capabilities. Magnusson correctly concludes that all that potential energy is of no use if not applied to create energy (new products).[1] And in order to create energy, the water must efficiently flow.

The Herbie team at Goodyear R&D had established a value-stream map, learned about value and waste, and had actually removed some waste from the process. We felt ready to move along the Womack Wheel to establish flow. The bar for flow was set quite low within Goodyear. We had done a lot of good things in Goodyear R&D over the years, but flow management with predictable delivery—they are linked—was not one of them.

We had established a value stream for the product development process, but there was a catch. Our project process included the potential for a loop—an iteration or learning cycle. In fact, an individual project could have as many as 10 loops. This meant that regardless of the end-to-end value-stream time, some projects could take up to 10 times longer than others due to repeated loops.

When we showed project managers our value-stream map with the loop step, they were thoroughly confused. They wanted to see how to effectively schedule projects that comprised a variable and an often unknown number of loops. We looked for a resource to learn how to schedule projects with this much variability—which is not that unusual in R&D—but we had to dig deep to locate one. About that time a new book hit my desk. It was the Harley-Davidson story by Dantar P. Oosterwal (*The Lean Machine: How Harley-Davidson Drove Top-Line Growth and Profitability with Revolutionary Lean Product Development*).[2]

According to Oosterwal, Harley-Davidson spaces their large projects evenly, like one big new project released every year. The typical large projects last several years, so there are always two to three active big projects in any one year. The company also allows a fixed number of medium projects on a faster cadence, and they fill the remaining R&D capacity with small projects. Durward Sobek and Allen Ward indicate that Toyota uses a similar scheduling system for product development projects[3] (see *Harley-Davidson/ Toyota Schedule*).

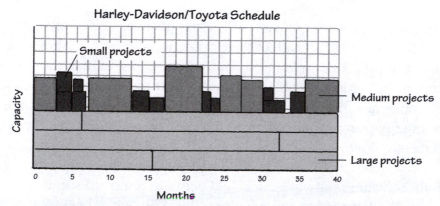

Large projects are first placed in the schedule. Medium projects are then spaced throughout the schedule, and the remainder is filled with small projects.

We once had tried the "schedule the complete project" approach, but our business does not allow us to start large projects on a preset cadence because we follow too many different OEM schedules. Sometimes we must start several big OEM projects simultaneously—not by our clock, but by theirs; I think most companies will be in a situation similar to Goodyear. We depend on external customers, and we can only determine a certain portion of our schedule by ourselves. We also have a very large difference in duration between our projects, ranging from months to years. So we developed the "Tetris method," although we did not initially call our method by that name. The name was coined recently by our metrology labs that use this method in the visual planning of their work, and refers to the classic video game, which produced a pattern similar to our capacity scheduling.

Of course, just like with the Tetris game, the pieces are easier to fit if they are the same shape/size and small. Just as the Tetris game would be trivial if there were only small, same-sized pieces—you would always find an open spot—scheduling might be easier if we could find a way to break up our larger projects into smaller pieces (see *Fitting the Tetris*).

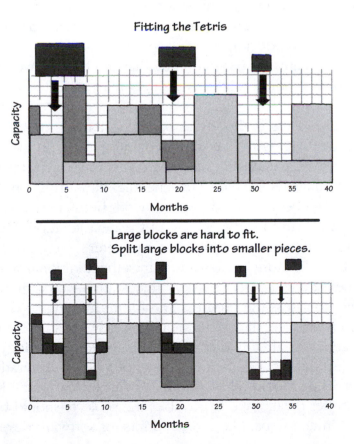

Fitting the Tetris

After additional benchmarking, I became fascinated by software development methods for scheduling, such as agile methodologies, scrum, and use of kanbans, which had begun to replace the dominant waterfall methods where one step spills into the next, with smaller project pieces laid out from start to finish on a timeline:

- *Agile:* This software development method is based on iterative and incremental development, in which requirements and solutions evolve through collaboration between self-organizing, cross-functional teams that work closely with a customer.
- *Scrum:* Teams and customers determine the highest priority objective that should be accomplished in the next 4 weeks (a sprint), and they list the tasks required to meet the objectives (sprint backlog). This is done by posting on a backlog board highly visible sticky notes, one for each task that is supposed to be completed during the given time period. When a team member finishes a task, he/she places the sticky in a "completed" section on the board and pulls the next task. The team reviews the board daily. When the sprint is completed, the team and customers reflect on how it went and plan the next sprint. The goal is a potentially shippable product after every sprint; for software development this would be a "chunk" of programming that can be reviewed with a customer. Project funding is allocated similarly by objectives/sprints.

Our waterfall process in Goodyear handled monster projects, and we thought something more like scrum could be a step in the right direction, especially since we already had a logical chunk (sprint) defined: an iteration. Short iterations are easier to schedule than a full, lengthy project, and they also are a better way to perform work because what is learned in one iteration can be used in the design of the next iteration. I also like the fact that the team regroups with the customer after every sprint and decides if the product can be launched or determines the additional work must be done in the next cycle. For more risky projects, this would give leadership an opportunity to assess the progress and future funding.

In the Goodyear case, the breakdown was easy because for many projects we had iterations already defined. Fundamental technology at Goodyear R&D and projects in other companies may not follow the iteration breakdown pattern. They should be broken into other logical, small learning cycles. If no better breakdown is possible, the projects should be broken down in time-limited steps, like scrum sprints for software development.

Lean R&D Principle: Break large projects down into small steps or learning cycles.

By incorporating smaller, faster learning cycles into project development, you learn more quickly, you can adjust frequently, and are able to assess progress with customers more often. Other advantages of this approach are

- Easier to schedule and better resource utilization (Tetris principle)
- More frequent pivot points, where the customer can request a change in direction if needed
- Many more decision points to stop a project if it does not show enough chance for success, or to launch the product if ready
- Reflection and quick learning occurs more often, and every new cycle can be designed with the learning of the previous cycle in mind
- Money and resources can be allocated in small manageable chunks and the risk can be better managed
- Mistakes are caught more quickly (almost immediately) and they are not passed on

At Goodyear: We have used development iterations for a long time, although we used to call them "submissions" or "builds." All our OEM customers ask us for several submissions in a program, and they expect us to improve the tire performance from submission to submission based on their assessment. Although the iterations are not all the same in duration and difficulty, they are easier to schedule than complete projects. Projects with high risk, like new-technology development, are funded from iteration to iteration based on progress made. We see benefits in evolving our process into the direction of agile and scrum when appropriate.

Traditional R&D Process

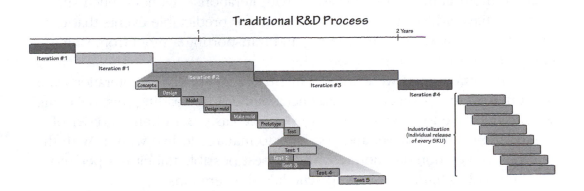

When applying the iteration concept in Goodyear (our version of scrum), we realized one problem was the difference between software development and tire development (and many other environments similar to our own): software developers like to make their sprints equal in duration (about 30 days), but our sprints needed to vary from *3 weeks to 6 months* due to varying content (e.g., some iterations need a mold, while others do not), differences in task durations (e.g., snow testing and long-wear testing), and variations caused by physical objects moving from or to suppliers and customers (e.g., shipping distances). We looked at further breaking down the iterations, but that began to take us down the same unmanageable path as before when we tried to implement a big project-management software solution (see *Chapter 2*). There was no way we would go there again!

We felt an iteration was the correct, manageable sprint for us, but there was not much we could do about the variability. We could, though, minimize variability from the R&D processes by eliminating some waste. Other components of variability—e.g., number of iterations needed, risk, difficulty, changes—are just part of a development process, and we needed to figure out a way to manage them.

Again, *Factory Physics* was a great inspiration: Wallace Hopp and Mark Spearman dedicated an entire chapter to the "corrupting influence of variability."[4] And even though our variability was an order of magnitude greater than that found in manufacturing operations, we knew we could rely on the principles described in the Hopp/Spearman tome and some that we discovered.

Because our iterations had a lot of variability, we early on had grouped them into eight categories. Some colleagues thought that we needed close to 100 different categories to group them, but we went with eight and eventually used only five. It has been about seven years now, and we have tried to become more granular and consistent with iterations—without much success. We have added "modifiers" to account for predictable events that can extend an iteration, such as ordering and transporting a mold from China compared to one made in Akron, Ohio.

An important point we learned while trying to standardize iterations was that often *close is good enough*. Engineers will cringe reading this, believing we should strive to be exact in every possible case. But often an order of magnitude is all you have, and you have to manage to live with it. With the question of iteration duration resolved as best possible (albeit not perfect), we then had to figure out how to schedule the iterations.

Iterations/Learning Cycles

We did not invent iterations nor are they often cited by lean literature; Goodyear learned the method from car developers, who requested a submission of tires every time they tested a new generation of prototype vehicles. I learned the term "iteration" from my math professor in college in Germany, who taught us an iterative method to converge an algorithm to a solution. When I used the term for the first time at Goodyear 35 years ago in a leadership presentation, one of our directors was assigned by our VP to look up the term in the dictionary.

An iteration is a logical learning cycle, and I promote the idea to break a complex development project into logical small chunks or learning cycles. The difference between our iteration and a scum sprint is that the scrum sprint is a fixed duration (1 month), but the iteration spans one logical learning cycle, for example from the design to the testing. The breakdown adds many decision points where progress can be assessed, decisions made, and money allocated. There must be learning between the iterations. For example, we would first build an iteration to compare three different tire tread patterns. After the testing, we learn which pattern works the best and then we evaluate four different rubber compounds in that design in the subsequent learning cycle.

I promote the use of the short learning cycles for all projects, including capability development or continuous improvement projects.

Pete Yap, R&D associate Tire Engineering, develops tires for commercial trucks. Pete likes the lean process because he gets all iterations run as he needs them to develop a quality tire, but he says the process is still too slow. He would like to break the process into even smaller, faster iterations. He believes the acceleration of the learning cycles will help him develop a better product.

Early Attempts at Visual Planning

Several of our leaders had visited the Delphi technical center in Luxembourg where they learned about visual planning—a popular tool in lean—and they suggested we try visual planning to schedule our iterations. We made a strong attempt—but because all work at the time was still managed with priority lists, our visual planning effort added no value to the process. My colleagues made sticky notes to schedule every iteration in every function, but they could not keep up with the changes occurring every day.

We also noticed that all the functions had an informal scheduling system in addition to the priority list. This informal schedule was there to please those managers who did not get a high enough priority through the priority system.

Even if we had stuck with this visual planning attempt, at best it would have been a lagging copy of the "official" priority list. But the Herbie team did learn a few lessons about visual planning that would prove to be beneficial:

- If the visual board only visualized an existing plan—and struggled to accurately reproduce it—there was no interest.
- All the value-stream stakeholders must see value in the visual plan.
- The planning must be very simple—it cannot require a large amount of resources.
- Do not attempt to update and be evergreen on a daily basis.
- Dependencies are hard to incorporate into the plan—they make updates too complicated.

Finding Our Bottleneck—Herbie Meets Herbie

Whenever you try to improve the flow of a process, one of the first questions you want to ask is, "Is there a bottleneck?" When the Herbie team initially asked that question, we could not get an answer because no one wanted their function or role to be identified as a bottleneck, especially since our team's sponsor was our CTO. All functional leaders claimed that they followed the priority list. Their function could not be a bottleneck— even though about several hundred iterations were queued in front of them. So we decided to get data.

Factory Physics describes a bottleneck as the step in a process with the highest utilization.[4] When the Herbie team initially looked for the bottleneck, we could not measure the utilization of some steps because we only received a small percentage of the available capacity (e.g., from mold- and tire-manufacturing plants). So we identified the critical path and counted the items in all the queues. Then we multiplied the number of items in the queue by the average process time, which gave us the waiting time of the last project in line. This allowed us to evaluate all queues with the same denominator, and we made a Pareto chart. (As I noted in *Chapter 4*, the analysis showed that every project spent about 50% of its time waiting in the queue of the prototype manufacturing operation.)

When we showed the results from the bottleneck study, our sponsor immediately asked if we had considered theory of constraints (TOC) as a potential solution; we reminded him of our team name "Herbie."

Theory of Constraints

Dr. Eliyahu M. Goldratt and Jeff Cox promoted the management approach of theory of constraints (TOC) in 1984 with the business novel *The Goal*.[5] The title refers to how constraints can limit a system or process from achieving its goal. Principles of TOC include

■ Most processes have many steps.
■ Steps are hard to synchronize or balance due to many reasons that are hard to control.
■ Usually one step in a process cannot keep pace with the other steps; this step is the bottleneck.
■ The total process cannot produce more than the bottleneck can produce (i.e., the bottleneck keeps the total process from achieving its goal).
■ To improve the process, first improve what occurs at the bottleneck.

Goldratt and Cox advise five steps to manage a bottleneck:

1. Identify the bottleneck.
2. Get as much capacity out of the bottleneck as possible.
3. Align and schedule all other connected processes to the pace of the bottleneck and make sure the bottleneck does not run out of work.
4. Keep working to improve the performance of the bottleneck to the point that it is no longer the bottleneck.
5. When the initial bottleneck has been removed, begin again and identify the new bottleneck that has taken its place in the total process.

Bottlenecks within a process can be

■ People: An inability (lack of skills) or an unwillingness to perform as required
■ Equipment: Capability or use of equipment limits ability to produce
■ Policies: Written or unwritten policies that intentionally or unintentionally establish a threshold of production below that required

Applying TOC was difficult because Goodyear's constraint was not physical in nature—plenty of potential capacity was available in the plants. Our ongoing challenge was to convince production leaders to allocate more production capacity for prototypes. Even though prototype capacity was eventually specified in our annual operating plan, some plant managers could not resist the temptation to dip into prototype capacity when they were falling short on their production numbers.

We still felt there was a piece missing in the TOC teachings, until a colleague of mine, Cigdem Gurer, suggested the drum/buffer/rope technique. This approach also is known as "TOC pull," although Cigdem and I were not aware of that nor did she call it that when we applied it at Goodyear:

- The *drum* is the physical constraint or bottleneck (and pace maker) of the process, system, or value stream.
- The *buffer* protects the drum, so that it always has work ahead of it.
- The *rope* is the work release mechanism for the process.

This did not sound like a revolutionary concept—the drum keeps the bottleneck producing at capacity, and every time a piece comes out of the drum or bottleneck a new piece enters the value stream (in this case, our product development system), thus keeping the WIP of the value stream constant with a little buffer in front of the drum. The buffer exists to ensure that the bottleneck never runs out of work—since the entire workstream is aligned to the bottleneck, any problem from the beginning of the workstream to the bottleneck could cause stoppage of output without the buffer. In our case the buffer was not as important, since we had negotiable capacity available if we needed it. The rope merely indicates the need to pull a new piece into the process (like with a rope) based on the signal from the drum, and this sounded like a great idea because it seemed to solve our problem of starting more iterations than the bottleneck was able to handle.

If the bottleneck falls behind, we throttle the start of iterations down; if it speeds up, we automatically put more work into the system to keep the bottleneck busy … as if that would ever happen. Projects could wait ahead of the process because there was nothing invested in them yet. Marketing or the customer could change or cancel them at no expense or hard feelings. Unfortunately, there was a time lag between one project coming out of the bottleneck and a project entering the system: a new project could take up to 24 weeks to reach the bottleneck. For that reason and although TOC as illustrated in *The Goal* does not suggest it, we put a buffer at every function, not just at the bottleneck (prototype manufacturing). In 2009, The Goldratt Institute would at least partially confirm the efficacy of this approach in the book *Velocity*.[6]

Another suggestion from *Velocity* that we had already validated when the book came out was to make the bottleneck our schedule point and then to keep it that way even after the bottleneck was eliminated and a different bottleneck was identified. All the Herbie team had to do was put 2 and 2 together—we had a schedule point, we had a tool to manage the WIP, and we only needed the right tool to schedule the bottleneck (see *Drum/Buffer/Rope*). We dusted off our visual planning board. But unlike our previous attempt, this time we would have to only schedule one function: prototype manufacturing.

Steve Rohweder, Regional Technical Director, says that we picked the right step to schedule: "The prototype building is close enough to the end of the iteration where problems accumulate, but it is not too late to make up time in the testing process that follows it. We picked that schedule point because it was the bottleneck when we started. Today the bottleneck moves all the time, and you need to see it or *hear* it. The stakeholders really do know when a new bottleneck forms because somebody speaks up—all you need to do is listen."

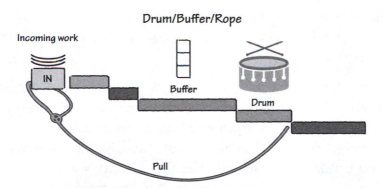

We showed the scheduling approach to our sponsor and the stakeholders, at least those who bothered to come see our plan. Except for the sponsor, nobody was impressed—we were still only playing in a sandbox, since the schedule was still done by the priority lists. The business director commented, "I cannot see how we could manage a multibillion-per-year business with sticky notes on a wall." This shaped up to be a tough battle, and as we continued playing around with the concept and trying to get buy-in, the United Steel Workers (USW) union called a strike in September 2006.

The Kaikaku We Needed

In September of 2006, all unionized Goodyear factories participated in the USW strike. The strike eventually ended with Goodyear selling its engineered products division and setting up one of the first VEBA (Voluntary Employees' Beneficiary Association) plans in the automotive industry, where the union now manages their own retiree health care funds; some Detroit car manufacturers followed the same route in 2008.

Product development was shut down during the strike because we could not get prototype tires from the plants. As the strike went into the second month, all development projects had been reviewed and most of them were cancelled or postponed. Planning decisions for product ramp-up after the strike did not include much new development work for the first few months, since the warehouses had to be filled with tires again and there would be little time for other activities, such as building prototypes.

It was around this time that Jean-Claude Kihn, general director GIC*A and our sponsor at the time, came to see me. He convinced me to charge full speed ahead with the lean process. I was surprised by his suggestion, but then he shared his three-point plan:

1. We will plan all the new work on the visual planning board—no place else.
2. We will be ready to run when the strike ends—that was my job!
3. If our lean process did not work, we could point to the difficult, strike-related aftermath.

As marketing firmed up plans for the new projects, we planned the iterations on the visual planning board (and nowhere else). We even learned to print the sticky notes directly from marketing's spreadsheet.

On January 1, 2007 after 4 months away, the USW workers were back in the plants and production resumed. The first priority was to fill inventories at the warehouses, dealers, and stores—but before we knew it, we were back to a full schedule of development work in the plants. Reluctantly, one after the other, our stakeholders showed up at the weekly planning meeting at the visual planning board—the only schedule we had (see *Goodyear's Visual Planning Board*). We asked the plants what prototype capacity was available, and we were given a total of about 300 iterations a year, based on what they had historically done for us. So we laid out the available 300 prototype-building slots, distributing them appropriately among the plants represented on the board.

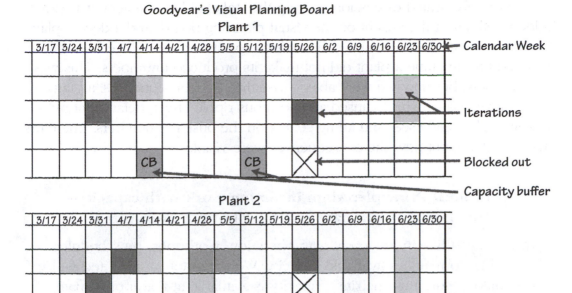

Slots are blocked out on the planning board because they indicate a shorter work week for a national holiday.

Then we went back to the business and asked what they needed. They presented us a list of projects, although it was evolving based on the strike recovery plan. Together with the project managers, we laid out what iterations were needed, and we made one sticky note per plant iteration (either prototype tires or release to production), and we ran out of capacity about half way through the list that marketing provided. We put the remaining notes into a "need capacity" category, and showed the board to our sponsor and the stakeholders. *Then we witnessed the first "aha" moment.*

We needed either more capacity or fewer programs! Who would have guessed it? Production was absolutely shocked to see how much more capacity the customer needed, and the customer was upset that insufficient capacity was made available. All blame was directed at the Herbie team for another bad idea and at R&D for running too many iterations.

So we took all the tags off the board, and we gave them to marketing. We told them the board was theirs, and they should arrange the tags as they wanted. They proceeded to rearrange the tags, focusing on higher-potential-revenue projects, but they could still only fit 50% of the tags on the board. The problem now was very visible and more obvious to the doubters: more capacity was needed for prototypes in order to give the business what the business needs. *It was amazing how quickly people understood the problem once the problem was made visible.*

After many heated discussions among the stakeholders, capacity was slowly added until all of the tags fit on the visual planning board, and a decent plan began to emerge. Unfortunately, the added capacity was short lived—it was revoked the first time a plant did not make its production numbers. This was nothing new, but now we were able to visualize the consequences: all tags were moved back, which caused an enormous ripple effect, delays that marketing could clearly see, and a huge effect on the business numbers. The damage was done, but now the consequences were visible.

Lean R&D Principle: Align incoming work with capacity— the business can have anything but not everything.

In R&D, just like in any other lean operation, work must be scheduled according to real and available capacity. Work cannot be accepted without making sure that the right capacity is available at the approximate time the work needs to be done.

R&D work requires special skills and expensive equipment that may not be available at the time needed. It is also very unpredictable.

There are many tools and techniques that allow us to schedule close to capacity:

- The requirements versus capacity and capability (RvCc) process matches requirements with capacity and capability
- Visual planning
- Many principles discussed in this chapter like work leveling, takt, pull, flexible capacity, and so on
- Phase-gate process

At Goodyear: The business pays for R&D, and they decide how much total capacity is available. All work is accepted and scheduled based on the available capacity. If additional capacity is needed, it is created by working overtime, outsourcing, and/or moving or adding resources before additional work is accepted. Many tools are used to manage this process, including stage and phase gates, RvCc, and visual planning. If capacity cannot be made available, new work is not accepted or other work is stopped, dropped, or moved.

Many R&D executives are convinced that you cannot control WIP because you would close the door to your customer and new ideas. But Don Reinertsen counters, "You cannot match marketing requests with capacity—one creative marketing person alone can come up with more ideas on a weekend than an R&D organization can handle in a year."[7] Remember, they can have anything they want—just not everything (more on this subject in *Chapter 6*).

The alignment of our requirements with capacity and capability is important for both planning and execution. To help with this alignment for the longer term, Goodyear implemented an RvCc (requirements vs. capacity and capability) process. This process manages both the allocation of the resources to the tasks in the execution phase and drives the talent management process, including recruiting and training (see *Planning Work to Available Capacity and Capability*).

Planning Work to Available Capacity and Capability

In R&D, just as in any other operation, there is a finite amount of capacity, and work (*resource requirements* = R) should not be planned beyond the capacity (*capacity* = C). In a difficult technical environment, it takes time to recruit and onboard new talent. It also takes time for people to learn, get up to speed, and be fully productive—you cannot add and reduce people on demand. We also know that not every engineer in product development can do every job—and certain tasks need specialists. That is why we cannot work and plan using only capacity, but also need to add capability (*capability* = c) in the planning process: RvCc.

At Goodyear, leaders get together on a monthly basis and look at the work requirements (R) versus capacity and capability (Cc) for their area of responsibility, and roll all areas up into a total RvCc. This is the planning process for hiring, moving people, creating more flexibility, outsourcing, and investing in capability development. Although this process cannot instantly match capacity with quickly changing requirements, it assures that over time the right resources are available to do the work when it must be started.

The good news was that the planning board and our team's work provided us with numbers to quantifiably discuss the problem and solutions with stakeholders. Eventually, the plant's AOP was adjusted to account for more prototype tires, thus allowing the plants to meet both production tickets and prototype builds.

Having the right visibility was critical to our lean initiative—to any lean initiative. With the confusing priority lists, nobody really understood what the problems were. Nobody knew what capacity was needed, consequences were invisible, and the business did not really care because they could not see the effects of the problem or do anything about it (e.g., they would not have affected plant production targets without clear data indicating why it was necessary). Suddenly, the customers had visibility, and they could actually decide what they needed at what time. It was amazing how much a little bit of visibility could do.

Lean R&D Principle: Resolve scheduling problems with visual planning.

Visual planning is not making a copy of a computer plan and then posting it on a wall or replicating it with using sticky notes. Visual planning is making scheduling problems or deviations visible so they can be resolved by an empowered and collaborative team of experts, who review issues and make changes while looking at the visual scheduling tools. Visual planning works best when all stakeholders and all functions involved look at the same information at the same time—especially if they can clearly see where the problems are. Options and consequences of decisions must be visible as well, so a decision can be made and expectations resulting from the decision can be set. All pertinent information should be visible through use of colors, icons, stickers, and so on.

At Goodyear: One step of all iterations is scheduled on a visual planning board with a pull upstream and first-in/first-out downstream from the schedule point (completion date). Although our visual planning board had a slow and painful start, it is now what the business leaders, regional executives, project managers, and functions use for product planning and decisions. Conflicts are resolved during regular stand-up meetings with all stakeholders. We could still use much better visual planning options for some other levels of the organization, but everybody is used to what we have, comfortable with it, and believes it serves its purpose. The process is more important than the boards and the sticky notes. There were many requests to computerize the visual planning board, but we decided not to do that based on what we had learned with a previous electronic-scheduling experience.

A key issue for Goodyear's lean initiative involved the collaboration of R&D and manufacturing. Our factories and innovation centers are not colocated. Within R&D, there is a function called "QTech" (Quality and Technology). This organization, which has existed in Goodyear for years under various names, represents the manufacturing organization in every new product development project. QTech engineers also communicate the weekly prototype schedule with the plants. A similar function with identical duties exists in the Toyota product development process, called "the simultaneous engineer," as described by Jim Morgan and Jeff Liker.[8] The QTech manager was part of the Herbie team.

A cross-functional team of project managers, engineers, marketing managers, and QTech engineers now started to meet every week at the visual planning board, and members became increasingly comfortable discussing problems in the open with their peers from other functions. Sometimes the regional technical director also joined them. Real collaboration started to happen—the profit of the value stream started to get priority over the interests of the functions. And we had a meaningful success.

The priority lists for the plants were abandoned. This occurred quickly after the visual planning board was up and running and done without a fallback position. The QTech manager led the effort. Everybody who had historically used that list understood that since all the stakeholders were involved (or at least invited) in setting the visual plan in the right order, there really was no more reason to duplicate that work with another list. Now a "copy" of the planning board is emailed weekly to the plants by the QTech organization, and the plants integrate the prototype work into their production schedule.

But as one problem was solved—scheduling and having the right capacity at the bottleneck—others emerged: how can we manage the additional work upstream in engineering and mold manufacturing and downstream in testing that resulted by having more iterations running through the additional capacity we had been given?

It was quickly decided to align testing with prototype-making on a first-in/first-out (FIFO) mode, and immediately the testing priority list was abandoned as well. This was a major thing for the R&D organization. Everybody hated the lists because the process was so time-consuming and stressful. Nobody was in the mood yet to celebrate, but everybody was happy. This is what the Herbie team needed based on all the principles of good change management—a little success amid the chaos of implementing big change.

Drum/Buffer/Rope Airline

A former Goodyear VP in charge of North American business knew nothing about lean, but in the kickoff meeting with our first consultant in 2005, he described his vision of a better product development as follows: "Last week I flew from Akron to Chicago, and my plane was not allowed to take off at the scheduled time because there was bad weather in Chicago." He went on to say that they waited until they got a landing slot in Chicago, and then they took off in a late-start mode and landed without delaying the plane any further once it was in flight. The VP was wondering why we could not run product development like that. Nobody in the room at that time, including myself, had any idea what the man was talking about. But, of course, now we know, and I still wonder how the VP came up with the idea.

Exploring Pull and Flow Concepts

We had established a landing slot (plant schedule for the prototype tires). We still needed to tell the planes when to take off according to the rope concept (and we certainly were not planning to stop the planes in the air, either).

From Rope to Kanban

We chose to signal the planes (the start of our iteration) using a *kanban* card. In Japanese, kanban means "sign" or "signal," and in a lean operation, it is used by a downstream process to signal to an upstream process that something needs to be supplied; it also tells what needs to be supplied and how much. Kanbans can be verbal (somebody shouts out that something is needed), electronic (an email or software notification), space (an empty space on a shelf, like in a supermarket), or physical (a card that is sent to the upstream process when something is needed).

Herbie chose to use kanban cards, which we quickly implemented. They made the schedule and work—at every level—visible. The QTech folks loved the idea, since they could keep all the upcoming work right in front of them, pinned to their workstation. Our sponsor was excited because he understood how hard and frustrating it is to manage something that you cannot see. The Herbie team could now literally *keep an eye* on how engineering and testing were coping with the addition of prototype capacity. And except for the engineers—who immediately became concerned that everyone could now see their pace and that the kanbans would be used to compare performance—we thought this would go OK.

We even had developed a somewhat sophisticated kanban release concept. We grouped the iterations into eight different buckets. Every category or bucket had a different estimated time to complete. The computer printed the kanban cards when it was about time to start work, and then we passed the cards out to the technical project leaders (TPLs) based on the TOC rope principle: for every job that comes out of the bottleneck, the next job that must be started enters the process.

But the kanban excitement was short lived. A couple of weeks after the first kanbans were passed out, Jon Bellisimo, who is now general director of GIC*A, came to my office. He brought with him a very large stack of the kanban cards that had been printed for the project managers. Jon said, "Nobody likes these!"

Maybe it was too early for the kanban cards, and we had more change-management work to do before the next attempt. When the kanbans came back, I remembered an "unwritten" lean principle: "You must try everything three times for it to work." I now recall the advice of Jim Womack, who insisted that when you implement flow you must give the system time to stabilize and that you cannot implement change faster than people can adapt to it.[9] We had the drum working now, and, although we had a setback on the rope, we were confident that we would get it to work. So while we gave things time to stabilize, the team focused on the last piece of the TOC concept, *the buffer.*

Push and Pull

Although we use a very simple form of pull (drum/buffer/rope or TOC pull) in our master process at Goodyear, I need to mention a few more general aspects of push and pull and also explain "station-to-station" pull, since this is a popular form of pull that has widespread use in lean operations, including some in product development.

In a push system, a master schedule is established and every step is scheduled individually. Many companies use large master scheduling systems, such as a materials requirements planning (MRP) system, to schedule their manufacturing production in a push manner, but they have become less popular for that usage since their introduction in the 1970s and 1980s as lean principles have taken root. At Goodyear, we told our

MRP system how many tires to produce and the system told us how much raw material to put into the mixer; scheduled all components, assembly, and curing; and managed the warehouse and sometimes the supply chain, the financials, and the procurement. That is still a great feature, and pieces of MRP systems can be adapted to work with a pull system.

In a push system, material is pushed downstream from one operation to the next. This is done in large batches, so there is always enough material to buffer for variability. The disadvantages of push are high in-process inventory and long cycle times. In addition and no small consequence, feedback is slow and quality problems are discovered hours or even days after they occur.

In a pull system, the process takes care of the variability because only one operation is scheduled (schedule point), and when it needs material it sends a signal upstream to tell the upstream process that something is needed. In a typical pull system, there is a little buffer between the stations that is called a "supermarket," which works just like the bread supply in a supermarket: as bread is pulled off the shelf it is periodically restocked to a set level. Since material is only produced when needed, all upstream steps in a pull remain in sync regardless of variability. Advantages of a pull system are low in-process inventory and, consequently, short cycle times and quick feedback. This kind of pull can be used between all steps in a process or the steps upstream of the schedule point can be combined in a FIFO (first-in/first-out) mode if variability allows that.

Imagine one operation in a push system stops or falls behind because of an equipment breakdown. In that case all operations ahead of the broken step keep producing. If this happens in a pull system, the upstream operations will stop producing once the small buffer is filled.

Push and Pull Systems

The rule in lean is "flow when you can, pull when you must." In our product development process, we have a one-to-one relationship between all the steps leading up to the bottleneck, and we can operate them in FIFO mode with good flow because they are relatively predictable operations. Because of this, we decided not to pull between those operations. We use the TOC pull from the bottleneck (prototype manufacturing) to the start of the process. Since we pull between prototype and the start of the process, we have a long time lag between those two points, which requires a capacity buffer.

We tried a station-to-station pull, but could not see the benefits, and that approach has longer cycle times than the TOC pull. We do, though, use station-to-station pulls in our labs and testing operation, and this was recently implemented at GIC*L. There are two sets of mounted tires sitting in a garage, ready to go on a car. When the test car pulls into the garage, one set of tires is mounted on the car and leaves an empty spot. The empty spot is filled in by another set of four tires that is moved from the mounting station to the garage. The gap at the mounting station is noticed, and the mounting technician mounts the next set of tires by pulling the next four tires out of the storage rack. The gap in the storage rack is replaced by four tires that are ordered in from the plant. The same system is used for all the other test machines.

Replacing the tires in the rack requires bringing tires in from the plant. When the tires are released in the test system, the order goes automatically to the plant. Since it takes a few days for the tires to arrive, a larger buffer is needed in such a storage supermarket.

Lean R&D Principle: Flow when you can, pull when you must.

A pull system is a powerful tool to align the steps upstream of the schedule point in an operation like a product development project or an iteration. The kind of pull (station-to-station or TOC) should be tailored to the operation. The most popular type of station-to-station pull aligns operations with high variability with minimum administration, but it requires buffers that increase WIP and cycle time. If the process is aligned and repeatable enough, some stations can be linked in a FIFO mode, so the buffers and cycle time can be minimized.

At Goodyear: We use a TOC pull in our master process. Three steps in the process—cavity modeling, mold design, and mold manufacturing—are aligned well enough that they can be operated in a FIFO mode. Other operations still require small buffers. We use a station-to-station pull or a two-bin kanban system in the material test labs. (A two-bin kanban system uses a buffer for two items only. If the first buffer is depleted, it is immediately replaced. The second buffer is only there if something unexpected happens.)

Buffers are good tools to manage variability and make a process predictable. They ensure that a process never lacks for work or capacity, thus enabling the overall value stream to deliver to the customer as intended. According to *Factory Physics*,[4] a buffer can be capacity, time, and/or inventory (see *Types of Buffers*), and they all have one thing in common: they cost money.

As mentioned earlier, we like to add buffers where needed. But which kind of buffer should we use? We really did not have much inventory per se, and we were not going to get any more capacity. So we were left with time. Understanding the cost of a buffer on the profitability of the value stream can help you make good decisions about what kind of buffers to apply and where to apply them, and it helps you avoid the temptation to buffer everything with time. Recently, we justified additional capacity in order to speed our timing—something like that a few years ago would have been impossible.

Despite having grouped our iterations into eight somewhat logical categories, we still had significant variability between the content and the duration of the iterations. In order to minimize startup problems when we implemented the lean process, we added a time buffer to every step of the process for three reasons: the buffer absorbs some of the variability, reduces the risk for being late (the most important reason), and makes sure no step in the process runs out of work. We actually added a very generous buffer—we wanted to make sure that we never had a case where the "process" was blamed for late deliveries.

Lean R&D Principle: Consider buffers to manage the variability in R&D processes.

Buffers are used in a lean operation to help manage variability and make the process more predictable. In their simplest application, they assure that no operation runs out of work.

There are only three types of buffers: inventory, time, and capacity. Finished-goods inventory is rarely used in a project management or product development environment, and rarely is there enough money or resources available to add capacity. Consequently, most projects are buffered with time. The addition of a time buffer automatically adds WIP (work in process or progress) to the process.

There is a cost for every buffer, and buffers must be chosen based on economic considerations. The cost of the buffers must be justified based on the gain in resource utilization and efficiency. The most popular buffer in an R&D organization is time—most executives understand the cost of capacity, but they rarely understand the cost of time. In many cases where there is a choice, the cost of time is much larger than the cost of capacity.

It is a good idea to use sufficient buffers when implementing a lean process. They add a safety net to help through startup problems and the learning curve. They must, however, be removed as soon as enough process stability is achieved.

At Goodyear: When we started our lean product development process, we added a time buffer to every step in the iteration (design, modeling, mold production, etc.) to assure the predictability of the process through the uncertainty of the startup. We could not use inventory as a buffer, since nobody would have left finished work sit around, and capacity was not available. The plan was to reduce the buffer time as we learned and improved the process. But it never came to that. As the process improved, more and more work was added and the buffer time was used to do additional work. We also started to understand the cost of time buffers, and we started using cost of delay—missing sales and profit targets associated with not launching products when the market is ready for them—to calculate the cost of time.

	Types of Buffers[10]
Inventory	When you go to the store to buy groceries, chances are that the store has several brands, price ranges, and varieties in stock. Inventory must be managed wisely, and the store needs to make sure they never miss a sale, so the most economic buffer in this business model is inventory.
Capacity	When you drive by the town's emergency department, you normally see several fire trucks and ambulances. When a fire truck is out on a mission, chances are that a second 911 call could come in and a second truck is needed. Making the 911 emergency wait for the next available truck could have disastrous consequences, so emergency departments buffer with capacity.
Time	This occurred to me recently while in São Paulo, a town with a challenging traffic situation—the city actually limits the cars on the road by the last digits of the license plate. Despite that measure, the traffic can be a real challenge, especially at rush hours and during heavy rain. If you have a plane to catch around rush hour, you better double the average time to the airport, and an additional time buffer is needed if the weather forecast calls for heavy rain.
	Time is typically the default project buffer. Since project managers rarely get extra resources, they buffer with time, and since every project manager buffers with time, the times are additive. There are two major problems with time buffers in R&D projects:
	1. The work always seems to expand to fill the time.
	2. The cost of time is rarely known, and the profitability of the value stream can be seriously affected by time buffers.

The plan was to gradually reduce the buffer as we learned and gained stability. But we had to fight to reduce the buffer, even though the process got a lot better. This is a lesson in change management: functions will not give anything back that you give them, especially not something that makes their job easier. The buffers were eventually reduced to a minimum only as more work came in and had to be done in the same time frame. In this case, the excess buffer worked in our favor because that is how we were able to pick up the additional upfront work when we doubled the capacity at the pacemaker. Sometimes you just have to be lucky (but there is no lean principle to manage that).

From Variable Demand to Leveled Operation

We had one problem that TOC could not really eliminate, and that is the seasonal nature of our business:

- Many OEMs launch their new vehicles late in the year and put new models in their showrooms in January when many car shows occur.
- We like to have new tires available for the Goodyear dealer show in January.
- Winter tires need to be on sale in October or November before the first snow falls.

The seasonal nature of the business creates large fluctuations in the demand for new products. This is one of the reasons at Goodyear R&D our functions used to be staffed for highest demand—a very inefficient solution.

Product development, like any other operation, would prefer perfectly flat demand, because that makes capacity allocation and scheduling easier. So how can we accommodate the variable demand in a lean operation and still run a relatively efficient and quick development? We could stock up on engineers in the fall and winter and give the engineers time off in the spring, but a better solution was to stagger launches and to level the work as best possible, which means that we pull ahead or delay certain programs to take better advantage of our capacity.

Sometimes, a minor project can be delayed to take advantage of open capacity later in the schedule. Most frequently projects are "moved ahead" for the same reason. Other solutions that are used from time to time to manage the temporary workload are overtime and/or outsourcing.

Moving project schedules ahead means they would finish earlier than needed, which of course violates several lean principles: it is overproduction and creates inventory. This creates muda, which has to be weighed against the muri and mura of the unbalanced situation. In a case like this, the business leaders are able to assess the tradeoffs and make the best decision for the business based on data and facts.

Lean R&D Principle: Level the work on the highest level.

We already discussed the need to improve processes on the highest level; the thinking also applies to the leveling of the work. Projects should be leveled on the highest value-stream level, and all functions aligned with that approach to assure the best use of resources.

Incoming work into an R&D organization can be extremely variable for many reasons (e.g., seasonal business cycles, emergencies, poor planning). Chances are that R&D flexibility will not be sufficient to handle all fluctuations. The business in collaboration with all the stakeholders should look at the complete portfolio and stagger the project launch dates as best possible to optimize the return to the business and balance, when possible, with affordable capacity.

Further leveling may have to occur at the functional level or temporary capacity may be used. Both those remedies should be used, but they are difficult without at least some level of staggering of the launches.

At Goodyear: We have a seasonal business. Winter tires must be launched during the fall. OEM car launches happen around the same time because they want new models ready to sell during car shows in January. Goodyear wants most renewal tire lines ready to sell before the dealer conference in January. As much as possible, the tire releases are staggered by the business based on plant capacity; this staggers the start of the development work as well. Sometimes if the business numbers demand it, short-term additional capacity is added (overtime).

Even a perfectly staggered launch schedule will not eliminate all the variability in the project development schedule. Launches need a different number of iterations, and not all the iterations have the same content and difficulty. Some iterations need tooling, others do not. Some are long, others are short. Some iterations require snow testing, which can only be done well in the northern hemisphere winter. And there are always projects that do not go as expected because, by its nature, R&D work does not always go as expected. In order to understand how we manage that variability, we must first understand the concept of "takt."

Cadence/Takt

So what is the right level of resources in a function to support all the variable iterations? The cadence or takt for a process is needed to get that answer. Let us go back to the airport, which is a great place to see cadence or takt in action.

You can usually see the line of planes coming into a busy airport, often three or more back into the sky as far as you can see. The time between those planes for safe conditions sets the cadence or takt. There are slow planes, fast planes, they all go to different gates, some need a lot of landing runway to brake, some only need a short strip—regardless—they all get the same time allocated (like one plane every five minutes). Takeoffs follow the same approach.

Early on in my lean education, I had the opportunity to visit a car assembly plant in Germany, where they taught me all about takt—the cadence at which cars come off the line. "Takt" is a German word for "meter" or "beat," and it also represents the beat or rhythm of a process, as with music. Musicians in training use a metronome to help them "keep the takt."

Takt is computed as the available time divided by customer demand. The car plant in Germany produced a car every five minutes, because that is how many orders they had for cars. I was impressed by this state-of-the-art plant and the employees in white shorts and shirts, but one thing intrigued me: some workers finished their task on the line before the line moved, and then did something else or just waited. "We buffer with capacity," I was told. "Everything in the plant is subject to the takt."

The plant built many different models on the same assembly line, and the cars had a variety of features. This caused a lot of variation in the task of the workers because some cars needed the feature and others did not. In addition, some stations were staffed by more than one worker (a lot of assembly work took place in those stations), and some stations were empty (spare capacity to catch up if needed). The plant ran smoothly despite the fact that no two workers were identical, no two tasks were the same between stations, and many different cars came off the line as expected. I thought, "If they can do it, why can we not do it in product development?"

When the Herbie team was finally able to determine what the real weekly customer demand was, we were able to introduce takt into the process. For example, in order to give the North American business what it needed, our project managers had determined they needed about 800 iterations every year. With 50 workweeks in the plants, that gave us a takt of about 16 iterations per week.

We made an *average* of 16 iteration slots available on the visual planning boards, and asked the project managers and business leaders to place the iteration tags where they needed them. Although the releases were staggered, what resulted was still a feast or famine schedule (see the left side of *Seeking Cadence*). I would not have liked to see the schedule without the staggering of the launches. Since we did not want to go back and schedule for the worst case, we needed something like the planes at the airport—approximately the same number of completed iterations every week.

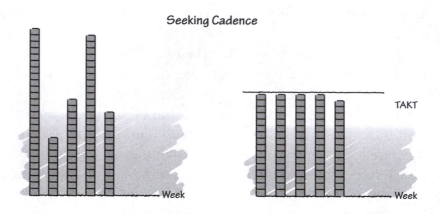

Seeking Cadence

We had to figure out how to work to a cadence of delivering 16 iterations per week every week. You might say that this needs more leveling, and that is correct. Without leveling the business or projects on the highest level, this process to schedule iterations may be impossible. But now the leveling occurs in small pieces (by iteration, not project) and is split over many projects, so the business effect to a single project is very small with a negligible effect on delivery, speed, or efficiency. We asked the project managers to move some tags ahead and move some back where possible, while respecting the limit of 16 iterations per week. We ended up with a relatively even distribution (see right side of *Seeking Cadence*). This was no easy exercise the first time around, and some feathers were ruffled or lost. But since then we have the takt line firmly established, and when new iterations are added to the visual planning board, project managers only exceed the takt line if they have secured extra capacity.

Our first attempt at scheduling involved a random mix of projects: some iterations needed a mold, others did not. Some needed special modeling, others needed special tests. These variations could create all kinds of new bottlenecks in the functions that perform the work. If we put all the iterations that need a mold in one week, we quickly create a new bottleneck in the mold plant, which cannot be solved with flexible capacity due to the need of expensive equipment. On a car assembly line, cars are not sequenced randomly nor are the special models all sequenced together. We needed to take into account different, critical work content of the iterations and match them with available functional capacity (see *Item Takt*).

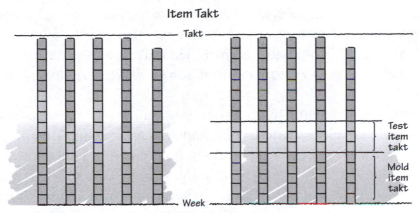

Similar content is represented by shades, for example, medium-gray tags indicate that a mold is needed for an iteration; light gray tags mean a durability test is needed.

We needed to deal with *item takt*—to manage the content variation per iteration. (Item takt in an assembly plant is based on customer demand; in R&D, we use the concept for available capacity.) The takt calculation is similar: a separate takt is established for each item (in our example, the need for a mold or a specific test). We chose to limit iterations that required a mold or test to three or five slots of capacity per week, as in the example. It would be cost prohibitive to create mold manufacturing or testing capacity to match maximum demand.

Jeff Plauny, then director Global Tire Engineering, says, "We sized everything to the bottleneck, but we also had to optimize all the resources. When you have specialists, it's still difficult to level resources. The need of the specialist is an issue because it hurts the flexibility. This is where you need item takt."

We established an item takt for each item based on available capacity. We also found that we had to limit a couple of other unique iterations because a rare talent was required in computer modeling to complete those iterations. The resulting example board (see right side of *Item Takt*) incorporated a maximum of three test items per week and a maximum of five mold items per week.

Although we limit the schedule to average customer demand and available capacity, there are cases where some of the capacity can be increased. In that case, the technical director has to negotiate the funding for the capacity with the business and request the additional capacity from the R&D organization. For example, we can work overtime in the plants and/ or outsource mold drawings and mold manufacturing. Sometimes we transfer a lot of product between plants, in which cases the resources in the plant have to be increased. It normally takes quite some time to transfer or train additional plant engineers, but in every case now the engineers are in place before the work is accepted. Today we also shuffle work between our three innovation centers to optimize R&D talent and capacity. *We do not allow project managers (any more) to schedule capacity that does not exist.*

After these improvements in the process and a few changes based on lessons learned, we felt ready to try the kanban cards again. This time we gave TPLs and the engineers some training on the use of kanban systems. We also appointed a contact person from the Herbie team to work with the engineers on their first cards, and we did gemba walks to see how the engineers liked using the cards. We also planned time to allow the change to stabilize before applying any further adjustments.

On our first gemba walk, Ricardo Gloria, senior engineer, who at the time was on a training assignment from Brazil, called us over and said, "I would like to show you what I did with the kanban cards." He had thrown all his cards in the trash basket. Today Ricardo is a certified lean product development specialist, who actively promotes lean process improvements, including our use of kanban cards. Ricardo laughs about his reaction to the first kanban cards, and explains that the cards we initially gave him were out of sync with his work. The TPLs had continued to assign work independent of the kanban cards—a problem that had to get fixed. We learned many other things in the gemba walk that we needed to fix. For example, there were still queues in some areas because engineers were not on the same level of competency. Of course, there also were "discipline" issues because people were not following the process after years of working around processes to get ahead.

Kelly King, who was a lead engineer when we implemented the kanban cards, remembers that they were viewed negatively. It was a change, something new, and people thought management had merely found something else to make them work more. In fact, there was hardly any extra work that was added. The system adjusted itself when we started doing more iterations and the buffer time was used up. In fact, the system is now so predictable that we really do not need kanban cards anymore. It is pretty obvious now when projects need to get started, and everyone knows to start them as late as possible with or without a kanban card.

Now that we understood takt, and we were able to identify the needed resources in each function that contributed to the value stream, the resource assignment was simple: *Every function should be staffed or equipped to keep up with the takt.* This is easier said than done, of course, because even after the introduction of a cadence, there is still some variability. There are still easy and difficult iterations, not every engineer has the same abilities, and there is the potential for underworked or overworked functions. But there are a few tools that can help, such as standard work and flexible resources.

Lean R&D Principle: Establish a takt or cadence and allocate resources to meet the takt.

Takt is defined as available time divided by customer demand. This levels the variable demand to a certain extent (in small increments) and allows for a relatively smooth operation. Resources should be made available to meet the requirements set by the cadence. For example, if the cadence calls for 16 iterations per week, engineering should be staffed to deliver 16 iterations per week. If there are capacity limits in some functions caused by expensive equipment, then a separate takt (item takt) should be calculated for the available capacity. For example, if the mold capacity is limited to five molds per week, then only five iterations needing molds should be scheduled each week. Plans can be made to add temporary capacity if needed and *only when the capacity is in place can it be included in the schedules.*

At Goodyear: We have established a cadence or takt in our product development process based on staggered customer demand, and iterations are planned according to that cadence. We watch the mix of the iterations and avoid bottlenecks caused by expensive equipment by limiting the iterations that need that equipment. Functions that are not limited by capital equipment try to meet fluctuations in tasks by a flexible workforce, outsourcing, and other lean and traditional tools (e.g., buffers, overtime).

Standard Work and Flexible Resources

I had earlier mentioned that when we doubled the prototype capacity in the plant—and literally doubled the amount of iterations or work we could achieve—we were concerned that we would be understaffed or under-resourced in all the other functions in the value stream. It turned out that we never had to add a single resource, despite additional requirements to further improve capability and product performance over time. We out-sourced a small part of the development work, but real gains came from improved efficiency, mostly waste elimination and standard work. In addition, we saw that we were overstaffed prior to lean, and now began to more fully and efficiently use these resources.

Goodyear teams had historically been staffed for the worst case. Now that we have lean terminology at hand, we call this a "very large capacity buffer." One reason for the overcapacity was that teams did not share resources because they were convinced that the product development process for Ford tires was different from the process used for GM or Chrysler—and the processes for the European and the Japanese OEMs were even more special.

With engineering and science processes, there is perceived to be a lot of specialization. Even without specialization, every engineer seems to work differently. It is true that our iterations vary considerably, and that some tire projects are more difficult than others (e.g., developing high-performance car tires as opposed to just adding additional sizes to a line). But frequently if you give two engineers the same task, they will require a different amount of time to accomplish the task because they use different methods and they work at different speeds.

A powerful tool to level engineering work is the use of work standards. There are many definitions for work standards (or standard work) in lean literature. For the purpose of this book, I use "the best processes and practices that engineers follow doing their work every day." Standards are not corporate policies or company behavior rules; standards are the best method to do work. Engineers often do not like standards, and they claim that following standard work interferes with creativity and innovation.

Best practices to establish good work standards include

- The people who do the work are the best qualified to establish the standards.

- People must be trained so they know the standards (and engineers also like to understand "why").
- Standards must be easy to understand, visual, and readily available.
- People should follow the standards—many companies have audits or other tools to assure adherence to the standards.
- Just like product standards, there should be a fixed and a variable portion. There are exceptions when work must be done outside the standards.
- Improving upon a standard must be possible and uncomplicated.

If something did not go as planned, management standard questions should be

1. Was the standard followed?
2. Is the standard good enough?

At Goodyear, some engineers immediately liked standard work because it made their work easier and mistakes were avoided. They also understood that standards made routine work faster, which left more time for thinking and creative work. Other engineers called standards "monkey work" because they felt like it took the thinking out of the work.

Following good standards makes work predictable and creates outcomes that are of the highest quality and consistent. The time to do the work also becomes predictable and generally shorter. The more the work is standardized, the easier it is for other people to pick it up—less specialists are needed and there is a lot more flexibility, which means it is easier to find a resource available to do the work. All of these reasons make it is easier to schedule work.

At Goodyear the global functions (including operations) are responsible for their work or process standards—this includes establishing, communicating, enforcing, maintaining, and improving the standards. This can be done by using the same tools that we described for the design standards (see *Chapter 2*).

Lean R&D Principle: Standardize development work as much as possible.

Standard work is defined as the best method to do certain tasks. The work standards improve speed and quality of the work as variation is removed from activities and everyone follows the one "best method" for doing the work. Use of standard work also makes it easier to train engineers and can expand the variety of tasks an engineer is able to perform.

Standard work is one of the elements that lets companies take good advantage of their matrix organization. Work standards are normally documented in functional operation manuals or playbooks.

Do not, though, confuse standards with corporate policies or other work rules, nor should standards be used to control work or associates. Responsibilities must exist for establishing, validating, and maintaining standards. Standards also are the basis for training and the baseline for continuous improvement. Lean scholars will say "there is no kaizen without standards"—it took me many years to understand that.

At Goodyear: The people who do the work are asked to develop and document the best way to do the work. The standards are used to train new employees. Engineers can concentrate on what they do (create new solutions or technology) since they spend less time on figuring out how to best do the tasks. Standard work makes it easier to shift engineers to where the work is and helps to eliminate bottlenecks. Today at Goodyear, engineers can be assigned to a very large variety of projects. Kaizen events or workshops are held on a regular basis to improve the work and update our process standards. Our functions maintain and improve their standards relative to the product and the work they do. Cross-functional and project standards are maintained and improved by the operations function (the Goodyear Operations Management group in R&D charged with managing highest-level, cross-functional lean improvements).

Leyla Renner, development engineer, says, "When I joined tire engineering, every group did things different, and you could not transfer from one to another without a lot of training. Now we have a consistent process, and people get trained when they hire in, and they can work anywhere. It is easy to get help, and it is so easy to go help out."

Resource flexibility creates capacity. Good examples of the use of flexible capacity are the highways leading in and out of the cities. Many cities now use flexible lanes, alternating the number of lanes that lead into town in the morning rush hour with those heading out of town for the evening rush hour. Similarly, standard work makes resources more flexible and it is easier to find an available engineer to do standard work than it is to find somebody for a specialized task.

At Goodyear, we also encourage flexibility by rewarding engineers for developing a broader set of skills. The effort definitely paid off. Engineers can now be moved much easier to where work needs to be done. Flexible resources are a key requirement to make a matrix successful.

Despite leveling of work and the use of standard work, there are still times when more capacity is needed to handle peak work requirements. The simplest method to temporarily increase capacity is the use of overtime. Another technique is to retain retired employees on a part-time or standby basis. A popular method to temporarily increase capacity used by Goodyear and many other companies is outsourcing. In a sense, this, too, is flexibility, as outsourced engineering tasks can be insourced when the work inside the company is low. We use this approach carefully, but the right amount of outsourcing added a pool of resources when needed. At Goodyear we also outsource testing services, mold-making capacity, and other services if needed.

The more standardized the work is the easier it is to outsource. I am not an expert on outsourcing of engineering work, but most agree that you should not outsource your most critical functions—you may want to focus your outsourcing on the lower end of your technical routines.

Lean R&D Principle: Create capacity with flexible resources.

One of the main purposes of the matrix organization is that it allows sharing of resources and moving resources to where the work is. This is possible if there is enough resource flexibility. This flexibility can be increased by standard work and cross-training, so engineers are capable of performing a wider range of tasks. Sometimes engineers must be encouraged, and incentives are needed to increase the versatility of the workforce. Temporary capacity can also be created by working overtime or by part-time labor. Outsourcing a variable size of work is another option. All the above tools are capacity buffers that are more efficient and more economical than time buffers.

At Goodyear: Ever since we started the matrix organization in 2006, Goodyear has pursued all the above options to develop a flexible workforce in R&D. This has allowed us to manage the peaks in the work schedule and accommodate any unexpected variability.

Cycle Time and Little's Law

"Too much work" is a common problem in most R&D organizations. But why do we have too much work in R&D?

One reason for too much work is the absence of a good process to control incoming work. Operations with too much work—work-in-process inventory (WIP)—often do not understand Little's law (see *Little's Law*).

When we started to talk about Little's law at Goodyear, a lot of people told me they did not believe in it. To me, it was like not believing in the law of gravity. I think what those folks meant was that they did not think a law as simple as Little's law could be used to show them how to resolve the biggest problem with their process: the process is slow because there is too much work in process.

Little's Law[11]

John Little's early research involved traffic control, and his law was a theorem in queuing theory. The law stated that "the average number of customers in a system (over some interval) is equal to their average arrival rate, multiplied by their average time in the system." For our purposes, we refer to Little's law with the formula below.

Cycle time = Work-in-process inventory ÷ Throughput

The following charts show cycle time and throughput as a function of WIP for a four-station process, with identical process times at each station and no variability. The charts illustrate Little's law in an ideal case.

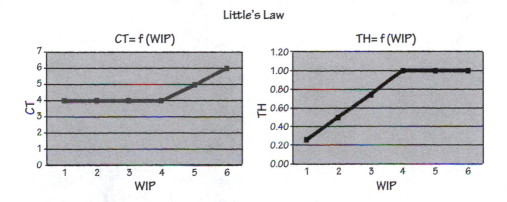

Little's Law

Little's law reveals that if we apply the law to one single person, the fastest cycle time can be achieved with a WIP of one or single-piece flow. In reality, for a multistation operation (as in the chart), throughput is not independent of WIP and goes up until a certain WIP level is reached, and then it stays constant. In the above example where the work is identical in all the stations, the optimum WIP number is identical to the number of stations. For most processes, even when different work is performed in the stations, there is an optimum level of WIP, and it is important to control the WIP at that level.

Batch processing can also be described by Little's law: the larger the batch, the higher the WIP, and the longer the cycle time. I like to run the following exercise as an example of batch processing in the context of Little's law, which helps trainees make the connection:

> One person flips a batch of 20 pennies, and moves them to a
> second station to be flipped, and then to a third station to be
> flipped. In order to maximize functional efficiency, all coins are
> flipped in one batch before they are transferred to the next sta-
> tion. After being flipped at the third station and several minutes
> having passed, all 20 pennies get transferred to the customer; the
> customer wants one penny to buy a piece of candy, and the next
> penny when it is time to buy the next candy (just like our custom-
> ers want their projects quickly and one at a time).

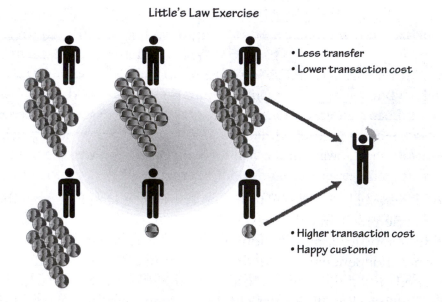

Little's Law Exercise

- Less transfer
- Lower transaction cost

- Higher transaction cost
- Happy customer

Contrarily, if the first station flips one penny, then transfers the penny to the second station, and then transfers the penny to the third station, the customer is better served: he gets the penny and is able to buy the candy after a couple of seconds.

In the simulation, we also illustrate that one-piece flow has a transfer associated with every single penny—flip and transfer to the next station, flip and transfer to the customer, and so on. There are a lot more transfers in the one-piece-flow mode (60 transfers) than the batch mode (three transfers), and the total transfer time (and cost related to transferring) will be higher for the one-piece flow. Thus, the exercise also shows trainees that there is a tradeoff with one-piece flow versus batches: cycle time (and customer satisfaction) versus transaction cost.

The exercise further shows that if only one penny moves (WIP = 1), two resources are idle. We will not reduce cycle time if we increase WIP (WIP = 3), where everybody is busy and we still have the same short cycle time as with WIP = 1.

A good application of Little's law can be seen at Disney World. There are signs posted along the waiting lines that tell people how long their wait will be. What the park did is count the people in line and divided it by the "throughput," which is the average number of people getting on the ride in one minute—that gives them the waiting time in minutes. The waiting times you hear from phone-support lines are calculated in the same way. Companies who do not understand Little's law tell you how many people are in front of you rather than give you the waiting time.

A practical consequence of Little's law is that if you want shorter cycle times—as we did at Goodyear—it is generally cheaper to reduce the WIP than to increase the throughput. The following help to reduce WIP:

- Control WIP at the start of new project or iterations (what goes into the pipeline). This is easier and more efficient than controlling it by throwing work out of the pipeline.
- Know what the capacity of the pipeline is and do not allow more work to enter the pipeline than available capacity (and adjust for the law of utilization).
- Assess and continue active projects based on their true potential (cost of delay) and not based on what has already been invested in them.

At Goodyear, WIP is one of our primary process indicators. We know that when the WIP is high, the cycle times are long, so we make sure that we have a daily WIP gauge on our operations dashboard. Since we can calculate cycle time from the WIP, it also is a good leading indicator. We do not need to wait until pieces are delivered to know the cycle time—we know it when we see the WIP.

Lean R&D Principle: Use Little's law to balance the cycle time, work in process, and throughput to desired levels.

Little's law states that cycle time is equal to work-in-process divided by throughput. This law, like the laws of physics, describes a relationship of parameters in a mathematical equation. Little's law can be used for any process—underutilized, overutilized, balanced, and leveled—and with any level of variability.

Cycle time will always be minimized by minimum WIP. Increasing throughput typically costs money (e.g., more resources), but there is normally little or no cost associated with reducing WIP. If you apply Little's law to the work of one engineer, it will reveal that the cycle of that engineer's task is lowest if the engineer only works on one project at one time. This aligns with the multitasking principle.

In a complicated, variable, multistep process, there is an optimum amount of WIP: if the WIP is too low, steps will run out of work; if it is too high, it will result in long cycle times. It may take a few experiments to determine the optimum WIP level of a complicated process.

At Goodyear: If I were to teach only one aspect of flow and speed management, I would teach people Little's law. An understanding of Little's law at Goodyear helped convince people to pay attention to WIP. Today, most functional managers have visibility for how much work is assigned to one engineer at one time. They watch a "dashboard" indicator that shows when total or individual WIP goes over the optimum level in critical areas. The understanding of Little's law also helped me convince leadership that we had to create standards to manage the incoming work.

A good example for WIP limitations are the tunnels through the Alps. Especially at the beginning of the spring vacations, there is an enormous increase in traffic toward the south. At the tunnels, they are very careful to only let as many cars into the tunnel as there can be for constant flow—flow breakdown in a tunnel can lead to catastrophic outcomes.

Jeff Plauny, who was a director of Global Tire Engineering, says his understanding of Little's law made the biggest difference in understanding the problems we had with our product development process. "People at Goodyear had to understand the effect WIP had on cycle time. This was totally counterintuitive to someone who wants to get the job done the old-fashioned way." The old-fashioned way that Jeff refers to is also called the "hydraulic or forcing" principle, which says the more you force into a system, the higher the output will be from the system.

Multitasking

When engineers thought that their leaders would assess their performance based on the number of kanban cards they had on their desk, they did not yet understand multitasking and Little's law. When we talked to the engineers, we found that they practiced a lot of multitasking, working on many different project iterations and functional projects at the same time. The reasons for that were a lack of flexibility and managers often giving the engineers several jobs so they could be more productive, which was how productivity was supposed to work. Sometimes, engineers got stuck on a job because information they needed was not available, so they could move to a different iteration and remain productive. Often they got stuck on many jobs, and it was easier to assign more work than to find the root cause of why so many jobs were interrupted.

The manager's approach encouraged multitasking because we still had many problems and inefficiencies in our processes. But there are inherent disadvantages to multitasking:

- *There is little true multitasking in engineering work:* Engineering work is not like working out while listening to music. When engineers work on several jobs at the same time, they switch tasks and perform one task at a time, which leads to a lot of stop and go.
- *Stop and go is not efficient:* It always takes time to get up to speed when a parked job is picked back up. This is similar to stop-and-go traffic. If you are waiting at a red light with cars in front of you, look how long it takes until you can get your car moving when the light turns green.
- *Stop and go opens the door to more errors:* Engineers who switch tasks often can lose focus, and it is easier to get confused.
- *Tasks take longer in the multitasking mode:* Multitasking sometimes gets confused with concurrent work. Concurrent engineering work is mostly performed by different resources that work independently at the same time. Multitasking is done by the same engineer moving from task to

task—presumably simultaneous—but with time-wasting interruptions as no two tasks occur simultaneously.

- *Multitasking hides flow problems:* If people continue to multitask, the real flow problems will never surface.

In our lean training, we have individuals play a multitasking video game. The game starts with a simple arcade game, like balancing a ball on a bar. Once the player gets comfortable, a second game starts, and the player has to switch quickly between the two games. Some people can master two games at once. Eventually, a third game starts. I have never seen anybody switch quickly enough to master all three games simultaneously.

We also help engineers understand why they cannot and should not do many jobs at the same time by showing them the financial impact of their multitasking (see *Multitasking versus Monotasking*): juggling four projects throughout the year generates revenue for all four projects at the end of the year when they each are completed at nearly the same time. Conversely, they can start the project with the highest cost of delay first—the project likely to lose the most sales and profit if not launched when the market is ready for it—and finish it in a monotasking mode in 3 months. Then that project generates revenue 9 months sooner than what would have occurred with the multitasking approach. Then the project with the second highest COD is completed and finished 6 months into the year, and so on. The fourth project is finished after 1 year, and we end up with 18 months' worth of extra revenue.

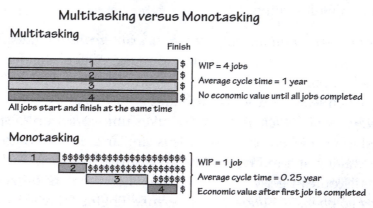

Multitasking versus Monotasking

Multitasking

Finish

1	$	WIP = 4 jobs
2	$	Average cycle time = 1 year
3	$	No economic value until all jobs completed
4	$	

All jobs start and finish at the same time

Monotasking

1	$$$$$$$$$$$$$$$$$$$$$$$$	WIP = 1 job
2	$$$$$$$$$$$$$$$$$$	Average cycle time = 0.25 year
3	$$$$$$	Economic value after first job is completed
4	$	

The four jobs/projects represent business priorities, that is, the delay of #1 is more costly than a delay of #4. The monotasking sequence of the four projects delivers cash to the business sooner.

Through training we encouraged engineers to *try* to work on one job at a time. This concept was one of the favorite subjects of our CTO Jean-Claude

Kihn. Jean-Claude would show up whenever possible at our training sessions and take over instruction. He loved this subject and would almost always end up drawing the *Multitasking versus Monotasking* graphic for the class.

Monotasking schedules are not easy to make with jobs that are highly variable, but the reasons for work stoppages should be minimized. And it is probably impossible to run a perfect monotasking work approach because adjacent processes that support engineers are not perfect and never will be. But the benefits of single-task work are so great that it is definitely worth working on, which requires improvement of the surrounding processes so that they can better support monotasking. Rather than giving an engineer several projects, it may be possible to give the engineer "filler" tasks like specification maintenance, knowledge documentation, and so on.

> **Lean R&D Principle: Avoid multitasking in engineering work, which in reality is just inefficient stop-and-go task switching.**
>
> There is virtually no multitasking in engineering work—if you try it, you really do task switching. This will create waiting time and reduce efficiency due to the constant starts and stops. This method also can lead to more mistakes. Processes should be designed and work scheduled so that engineers can, as much as possible, only work on one task at a time.
>
> *At Goodyear: We had several improvement activities to design the processes so that engineers can concentrate as much as possible on one task or one iteration at one time. Rather than assign engineers to many iterations at the same to keep them busy, we work at eliminating the root causes for the work stoppages. Tasks and skills are variable, and perfect monotasking is not always possible. But it was possible to reduce multitasking, which reduced the cycle time and improved the quality of the work, by standardizing work, increasing flexibility, and better resource planning.*

Multitasking can lead to more mistakes by having to focus on many things at the same time. Try working with three or more computer systems at the same time and watch how quickly you make a mistake. Monotasking is also a requirement for people performing very difficult tasks that have a very small margin of error. Imagine if an air traffic controller in an airport tower were guiding many incoming and outgoing planes simultaneously.

On an aircraft carrier, each crewperson has only one function during the critical operation of landing jets in order to avoid possible mistakes.

Late Start

Our push for monotasking brought up another challenge: In order to coordinate a lot of dependent tasks between a lot of different resources, we needed a *consistent* method to start the tasks. Should we start activities as early as possible? Intuitively, project managers wanted to start everything as early as possible. In fact, we used to educate engineers to get going on a project as soon as the minimum amount of information was available to begin. So they would begin, stop, and wait until there was enough information to proceed, finish the task early, and put it in the queue of the next operation.

Lean is counterintuitive. We eventually realized that all tasks should be started as *late* as possible—late start (see *Late Start*).

When I used Microsoft Project several years ago, I noticed that it had a late-start option (in addition to an earliest-possible option and a few others). I always wondered why anyone would use such a feature. Little did I know at the time that late start would become our standard for starting all activities.

This principle took more education than most lean principles—we must be out of our minds to think that we get faster and more predictable by starting as late as possible. But it works, and, with a buffer in most tasks or a shared buffer at the end, the tasks finish on time.

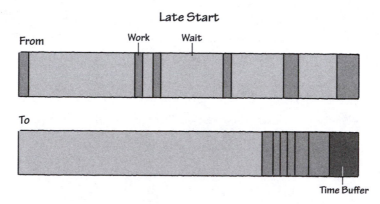

Late Start

Late start has many advantages:

- Engineers can always work with the best, most complete technical and marketing information.
- Benchmarking uses the most current products and the most current technology available.

- The chances that the work is interrupted for changes are minimized, and, as the speed of the processes is improved, the chances for changes will further be diminished.
- Late start helps with cash flow and also increases the return on investment.
- Late start leads to making decisions as late as possible, which keeps the design space and the options open as long as possible.
- Avoids the "Parkinson effect"—Parkinson's law says that work always expands to fill the space and the time provided.

There is a corollary to the late start in Toyota literature, where all important decisions should be made as late as possible to keep the options open as long as possible. Late start accommodates that principle, and

- Changes happen before anything is invested, and the cost of change is low.
- Latest technology and opportunities can be integrated.
- The risk can be reduced.
- The most information is available, making for a more informed decision.

I still remember the times when our goal was to order molds as early as possible (to get a better spot in the waiting line, I guess). Sometimes those molds were delivered early, and everybody was happy, just to find out a few weeks later that the customer had changed the size or that a problem was discovered with the tread design. This turned the early mold into a late mold, which then seriously affected the project outcome.

The late-start principle also provided a consistent point in time to issue kanban cards, one that project leaders would adhere to. This made Ricardo and other engineers happy, and he started to use the waste basket as intended: for waste.

Late start alone does not guarantee timely project completion. But the chances for a successful iteration or project are drastically increased. Looking back now at all the changes we made to the process, I think late start is one of the most effective ones. Late start has all but eliminated late changes in our programs. There may be rare changes, but they usually have good reasons, and we have buffers built in to accommodate them.

We used late start when developing a tire for a landmark edition of a popular sports car. During that project, the customer notified Goodyear that they had changed the tire size and apologized for the inconvenience. The customer also asked for the bill for the now useless mold and tires, which they were liable for based on the contract. When we told them that the mold had not been ordered yet and no tire was built, the customer was happy because it saved them a significant sum. But they also did not understand how Goodyear would possibly be able to supply the first set of test tires on time: "What do you mean, you have not started work on the project yet? What are your engineers doing then?" We told them the engineers were working on other iterations and projects until it is time to start this one, to which the customer replied, "Maybe we should do that, too."

Jon Bellissimo, general director GIC*A, says that for him late start was one of the most important improvements we made to our process. "The idea of not starting a project early, especially when you have a target date for delivery, was difficult to implement. The natural tendency is to start early. However, we have learned time and time again that starting early can lead to waste in the process. After projects start, customers modify requirements; new concepts, technology, learnings become available; and business requirements change. You lose the opportunity to adjust quickly, and you waste resources if you start earlier than needed to make on-time delivery."

I also advise people in other Goodyear divisions about late start. And even though they complain about WIP and too many customer changes that they have to accommodate, they have trouble buying into the concept.

Lean R&D Principle: Start late to finish on time.

Contrary to common thinking, all tasks in an R&D environment should be started consistently on a late-start schedule. This assures that the most complete information is available and it minimizes the changes. Late start helps with cash flow and ROI, improves efficiency, and avoids many costly late changes. It also accommodates postponing important decisions as long as possible to keep development options open.

Like many lean principles, late start is not an intuitive concept, and it may take some education to obtain buy-in.

At Goodyear: We consistently start every iteration on a late-start schedule, but we allow a small buffer at the end to mitigate unforeseen events. Although the concept was a hard sell at the beginning, we were able to quickly validate the principle by documenting cost savings, efficiency improvements, and gains in speed. Late design or project changes are a rare occurrence today. We even documented savings to external customers.

The Turning Point

The pull- and flow-related principles described in this chapter were introduced into Goodyear R&D over a period of about 6 months. It was rapid and, therefore, resulted in a lot of fun and challenges—we certainly stressed the tolerance for change of most our engineers and managers. We then let things settle in a little and gain some stability. We also decided to create a set of metrics to track our process.

R&D Lean Process Metrics

Now that we started to see flow in our operation, the Herbie team had enough knowledge to make the right recommendation for our first process metric: *on-time delivery (OTD)*. But most managers and leaders thought that the Herbie team had once again presented the least logical recommendation. Some leaders wanted development cost as a metric, others suggested engineering hours per iteration, and still others wanted to measure cycle time. Then, I asked them what is the most important metric for R&D, and everyone said, "Safety." Second most important metric? Again, unanimous chorus, "Quality."

Safety and quality were already tracked religiously within Goodyear R&D. When I asked for the third most important metric, a slight majority wanted cost, and delivery/service had fewer votes. So I asked, "What is a higher efficiency worth if we don't have a product to sell?" They kind of agreed with my logic, but I was reminded that cost is listed ahead of delivery on many company scoreboards—are most of our customers wrong?

I eventually convinced most of the group that our first lean metric should be on-time delivery, followed by cycle time: if we get faster, we get more efficient at the same time. We continued to look at cost savings, but only a collateral result because we did not then nor now want to suggest that cost savings is a primary goal of our lean initiative.

Defining "on time" was harder than agreeing to track it. The only way to get manufacturing on board was to use a window of plus/minus 1 week, which would be applied to all functions and activities. Minus 1 week meant 1 week early, which is the waste of overproduction. Plus 1 week means we missed delivery by 1 week. If we accepted that approach, we would look good even if we made few improvements. Nonetheless, we ran with those tolerances for a while, but as soon as we made enough improvement, we tried to tighten the tolerance, a day at a time. One time we had to move all delivery dates to Friday because some people were convinced that it was easier to meet a Friday delivery date than a Monday or Thursday delivery date. These delivery games continued for about 6 months as we made steady progress.

Another big issue was the delivery date itself—the TPLs constantly "renegotiated" the delivery dates with the business to get the business to share the responsibility of the missed dates. Eventually, we stopped doing that, too, and instead tracked every delivery to the day that was established in the gate meeting. This initially put a big dent into our on-time numbers, and everybody panicked. After playing games for so long, though, our new CTO Joe Zekoski fixed OTD to the day (no plus/minus) and to the original gate-meeting date. The progress we had made to OTD encouraged everybody that we were getting better and could live with a truly visible target.

On-Time Delivery and the Law of Utilization

By now you should be well aware that all work should be scheduled to available capacity—but that alone is not enough to keep projects on time. For example, you drive to work early in the morning. The expressway is largely empty and an accident happens. No problem because there is plenty of room for cars to pass the accident area. You go home during rush hour and an accident happens. Now the expressway is crowded (high utilization) and traffic grinds to a standstill as cars try to get around the accident. It is no different for projects falling behind (accidents) and maximum utilization of resources (rush hour). There is a delivery delay (you driving home from work).

Law of Utilization—Accidents Happen in R&D

5:00 am
Traffic flows
despite an
accident.

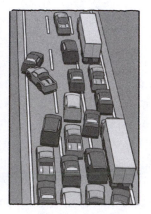

5:00 pm
Accident causes
traffic jam due
to high utilization.

You might ask, "What if there are no accidents?" Accidents happen in R&D, and you should plan for that. Things will not go as scheduled, and there can be any number of technical or scheduling issues that occur. If all capacity is filled (rush hour), there is a huge ripple effect and no way to get delayed projects caught up (after the accident is cleared).

Sometimes we fell behind in R&D, and an iteration spilled into the following week, or we had to repeat an iteration in the following week. When that happened it affected all the other work scheduled for the new week, which we tried to cover by working the weekend and overtime—which has its limits.

During this time, we noticed that if we carry over two or three jobs every week, we were still able to manage by working weekends and using overtime. But beyond three carryovers, things rapidly went downhill. There seemed to be an exponential increase of late deliveries when we got to five carryovers, and things came to a complete standstill when we got to eight or more carryovers. We were running into the law of utilization, which says that cycle time in queues increases in a nonlinear fashion (almost exponential) when utilization gets close to 100%. The law also states that the effect worsens if variability is higher.

Law of Utilization

$$CT_q = \left(\frac{c_a^2 + c_e^2}{2} \right)\left(\frac{u}{1-u} \right)t_0$$

c_a and c_e are coefficients of variability for arrival and exit times
u = utilization, expressed as a fraction: 80% utilization is 0.8
t_0 = base processing time
CT_q = queue time

Math-savvy readers will recognize that as u closes in on 1 (100% utilization), the denominator will go toward zero, which will trend the fraction toward infinity.[4]

Ed Pound, chief operations officer of Factory Physics, explains that the waiting times become increasingly dominant as the utilization increases, and because of that the above formula can be used to approximate total cycle time (see *Effect of Utilization on Cycle Time*).[12]

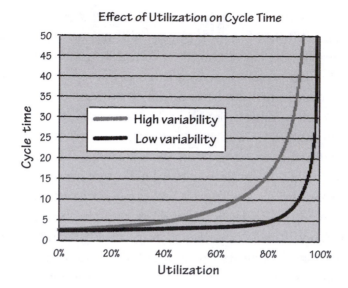

What the law of utilization means to us at Goodyear is that if we schedule R&D at 100% and something unforeseen happens during the week, requiring a repeat prototype build or test the following week, then that affects the schedule of everything in that week and a ripple effect begins. However, if we keep a space open every week so we can repeat a test, run an extra experiment, or rerun a set of prototypes, then we do not affect the remainder of the schedule and we avoid the ripple.

Although the law may be difficult to understand, the theoretical part is easy compared to explaining this to the business: "We now schedule everything at 80%" was heard as "You are cheating us out of 20% capacity." We tried to explain to them that we still operate at 100%, which we did, but we only *schedule* at 80%. We also explained that if we have no carryovers, we pull an iteration ahead to make good use of the time. No argument seemed to work, but in GIC*A we inched our way toward 80% scheduling and eventually our carryovers disappeared and the OTD increased dramatically.

We now schedule an average of 80%, and if there is a difficult program (i.e., high variability, like some difficult plant releases or an unpredictable new technology program), we add one or two "blank" tags on the board. This means that we schedule only 40% or 50% of the capacity because we have additional variability.

We used the same principle to schedule one of our materials labs. We started at 80%, but we were soon able to schedule at 95% or above because that process had much less variability. So what happens if everything goes well and the extra capacity is not needed? In that case, we "pull ahead" an iteration. This creates an open slot later in the schedule, which normally gets filled quickly.

We had an especially hard time making this case to our European business. It took more than a year, and Jean-Pierre Jeusette, general director GIC*L, the technical director during the lean conversion, remembers the hours-long discussions. Jean-Pierre pleaded with his business leaders, "We scheduled 120 iterations last month, and we delivered 40 on time. Please let me schedule 80 iterations next month and we will deliver 70 when you need them—a gain of 30 iterations!" The arguments did not work, but after a year they agreed to try it, and Jean-Pierre's team delivered what he had promised, which finally convinced them.

Steve Rohweder, regional technical director, defended the law of utilization recently in a meeting with the business, during which they wanted to pack more projects into the schedule without increasing the capacity. They asked Steve, "Why can we not overbook the schedule like the airlines overbook the planes?" Steve said, "We can do that if you volunteer to get off the schedule, and take the next open capacity."

The law of utilization is easy to validate. We tracked carryovers, and over time we discovered the magic number—the number of carryovers that would shut down the system. Those who ignored the formula got convinced by the process. In GIC*L, they called the carryovers "snowbank," like what forms in front of a snowplow. You can only push the snowbank so far before it grows and eventually you lose traction and then stall.

Lean R&D Principle: Schedule product development processes at 70%–80% utilization or lower.

All work should be scheduled according to available capacity, but that is not always sufficient because of variability and the problems and delays that variability can cause.

Cycle time will go up in a nonlinear fashion the closer utilization approaches 100%. So as a rule of thumb, development processes should not be scheduled over 70%–80%. If variability of the process is higher, utilization should be scheduled at even lower percentages. If you find little variability in your development process, begin scheduling for a higher percentage of utilization.

At Goodyear: We keep our iteration schedule point around 70% of the available capacity. If there are particularly difficult tasks or iterations on the schedule, we add an additional buffer; if all jobs on the schedule are easy, we may pull work ahead. Although this was another hard sell, we have proven the principle with real data many times. We follow the same principle when we assign people to tasks. People who really understand this principle, leave some open time in their daily schedule so they can attend to unforeseen or emergency business without affecting the rest of their schedule or working very long hours. In our materials test labs we are now able to schedule at 95% because most of the variability has been eliminated.

Even before we were performing to our current level of on-time delivery, I attended a meeting between the business leaders and the technical leaders, including our CTO. Looking at the participants of the meeting, I expected the same old, "Why can't the business get what we need?" from the business staff in attendance and, in response, a catalogue of excuses from R&D. The meeting started with our business leader telling the CTO, "I do not know how you did it, but we seem to get what we need, we get it when we need it, and it shows in our financial numbers." We had not reviewed our OTD data with the CTO, so he was caught by surprise. His answer was, "In my career, I never dreamed about a business leader telling me the business got from R&D what it needed." Even our strongest opponents knew it was time to give up resistance to our plan for achieving OTD! It was obvious that we were on our way toward our delivery goal, that our efforts were reaching the bottom line, and it was time to focus on the next goal: development speed.

Lean R&D Principle: Show real results to get leadership attention and support.

There is nothing more important in a lean initiative than to show real results. We are not talking about a few early successes that are important for good change management. We are talking about results that get noticed by the business and top management. These results are important for the support of the initiative, and normally they are the turning point for an initiative and the starting point for real change in the culture.

Although all initiatives start small, there should be a plan to obtain real results as early as possible. Success of an initiative is not measured by how many tools were implemented or by how many "green belts" were trained. *Initiatives have to show real business results to get buy-in by all levels of management and associates and to gather the support that they need to succeed. This is especially important for a lean product development initiative, which needs a significant culture change through all levels of the company to be successful.* The best results are when an initiative can be traced to the bottom line of the income statement. Often, it is enough if important goals or targets are met.

Quick results often can be obtained by "picking a low-hanging fruit" (i.e., opportunities that can yield significant results without a lot of effort). But even a low-hanging fruit must be detected, and you need to look for it as you begin to apply lean tools to the process.

At Goodyear: Our lean transformation yielded results early for on-time delivery that were immediately acknowledged by the business. The results could later be traced back to improved financial results. The results were shared by R&D leaders, both with all the associates in town-hall meetings and with the company leadership, for buy-in on all levels.

Jean-Claude Kihn, at the time our CTO and sponsor, says, "When I started my job at the innovation center in Akron, I heard a lot of complaints from the leadership, up to the chairman, that we were always terribly late with our new products. Their complaints reflected what they heard from our customers, and they urged me to fix this. I am not sure, however, whether they truly believed we could change something because when I shared the improvements a year and a half later, they were very surprised. Our chairman actually said that he had never heard or read about such an approach in R&D."

Unfortunately, many companies start their lean efforts with small initiatives that also generate very small results. These efforts may be a 5S initiative in the office, drawing a value-stream map for a subprocess, or having a random kaizen blitz. These efforts are then repeated in other areas, which exposes a lot of people to lean tools and is good training, but the efforts themselves often do not yield results that are visible or can be tracked to a business objective. Such changes are also hard to sustain because management does not see a real result that goes to the bottom line, and eventually they begin to view those efforts against the time and resources involved.

I often ask other companies: "What did you get out of this initiative?" I normally get a lot of blank stares and comments like, "It was a good exercise in teamwork" or "We now understand the process better." There is nothing more important to sustaining a lean initiative than making a right choice of where to begin, based in large part on getting visible results.

Jon Bellissimo shared his experience with the associates in GIC*A. "At the innovation center we have a quarterly informational town hall meeting with the associates. Shortly after implementing lean and practicing it, the question was asked: 'How are we sure it is working?' Being able to share data that showed real improvement since the time we started the lean process in OTD, product performance (adjustments), customer satisfaction metrics, etc., really hit home. I think that is when everyone 'got it' and jumped on board."

The Critical Path

With improved delivery times and better flow of work, we wanted to use flow to improve speed in our processes. But we can only improve the speed of a process if we take time out of *the critical path*—the path with the longest duration. We can remove waste from all our processes and improve the efficiency of those processes, but if we do not improve the speed of the activities on the critical path, improvement to the value stream may be hard to achieve.

If we focus on the critical path, the effects from cycle time reduction are more visible (more speed, better on-time delivery, higher efficiency), and they have a bigger effect on the profitability of the value stream, which is because a lot of collateral improvements come with gains in speed.

Good practices for managing the critical path include

■ Do not allow waiting or batching on the critical path.
■ Minimize processing time on the critical path because it affects cycle time.
■ Subordinate noncritical tasks to those on the critical path.
■ Run the activities independent of those on the critical path in parallel.
■ Minimize variability on the critical path.
■ Avoid high-risk activities, like experiments, on the critical path.
■ Make sure that appropriate resources are available for critical-path tasks.
■ Carefully assess requirements for buffers on the critical path—capacity buffers may be justified in place of time buffers.

I would love to make a list of critical path activities and noncritical path activities. Unfortunately, that is not possible for the R&D work at Goodyear because any activity could potentially go on the critical path.

In a typical Goodyear iteration, the critical path consists of computer modeling, mold design, mold making, prototype manufacturing, and the longest test that would need run. Other activities take less time and they can be done in parallel. For example, we put only the longest test on the critical path because all other shorter tests are run in parallel with the longer test—only the longest test affects the iteration time. Similarly, materials development takes less time than the procurement of the mold, and it can be done comfortably during the mold procurement time.

The critical path for a project can also change during the project. For example, if we already have a mold and have to redevelop a tread material, then the material-development activity suddenly is on the critical path. Similarly, if we make enough improvements to the mold-procurement process it will eventually become so fast that a parallel process, like materials development, moves to the critical path. For those reasons, we apply lean to *all the functions* that participate in the product development value stream, but continually focus on activities along the critical path.

**Lean R&D Principle: Focus on the critical
path for cycle-time reduction.**

The activities on the critical path determine the cycle time of a project
or an iteration. Waste and waiting times first should be removed from
the critical path. Any initiative to reduce cycle time should focus on
the critical path first. Activities with high risk or variability should not,
if possible, be put on the critical path. Although there are typical and
most frequent activities on the critical path, activities that are run in
parallel (not on the critical path) might end up on the critical path after
improvements are made, so those activities should not be exempt from
lean and speed improvements.

*At Goodyear: We spent a large effort defining the critical path of the
development iterations and projects, and ran all activities in parallel that
did not have to be run in sequence.*

Overlapping Activities

Of all the lean principles and tools, overlapping activities is one with the
most potential for gain in speed, and it has other benefits as well. It reduces
development time, promotes closer collaboration between the contributing
functions, manages the interaction between the activities, and improves the
quality of the development process.

A typical R&D sequence goes like this: Drawings for a mold or a tool
are made by a draftsman (done digitally or with hard copies). The drawings
go into a vault or a computer folder before they get checked and approved.
Then the drawings go into a queue in purchasing, and whenever purchasing gets to them the drawings are sent out for bids. After many days, the
quotes come back and wait in purchasing for analysis. Eventually the quotes
are studied, and an order is placed—30 weeks or more after the engineer
started the request, the mold arrives.

The same process with overlapping activities goes like this: Every
couple of years purchasing obtains quotes in an internet reverse auction
and picks a few mold vendors. The draftsman produces drawings one
day at a time. The first day, all drawings go to the vendor that are needed
for the vendor to order material and rough cut the material. The next
day enough detail is released to the vendor to start the detailed cutting.

The process repeats on a daily basis, and the mold ships a few days after the last drawing is supplied to the vendor. Compared to a typical R&D process, cycle time is reduced by 70%–80%. You may wonder where the inspection went: the mold designers check their own work, and if there was a mistake, they would find out the next day when the drawings get to the machine shop.

When we started the lean product development process at Goodyear, we carefully removed everything from the critical path that could be run in parallel. In fact, this was one of the rare occasions where I needed a computer during the lean implementation. The computer helped me to analyze all the steps in a process, the patterns that the engineers and the project managers used, and the probabilities and the frequency at which activities affected the cycle time. This effort defined the critical path; all other development activities were scheduled in parallel.

Then we looked at the critical path itself and overlapped the activities on the critical path as much as possible. We had always accepted the fact that fully completed drawings were needed before ordering molds, but we challenged that paradigm. We also realized that the plant can start building prototype tires before the mold is physically in the plant. We could not fully overlap those tasks, but we could overlap them as much as possible.

At this time, we ran into another "policy bottleneck." We had many rules in the company that forced us to do things in sequence. Most of those rules were based on past mistakes and had not been removed even though the root causes for the mistakes had long been eliminated. For example, long ago a plant had built urgent tires ahead of the anticipated arrival of the mold. But the mold was delayed so the uncured tires overaged and had to be scrapped. The consequential rule was that no plant would even look at a new spec until the mold was physically in the plant. This is a large waste of time because virtually all molds ship on time and the time they spend in transit could be used to build tires, so the tires could be cured as soon as the mold arrives. We also had to change policies and rules in the way procurement and testing operated.

I learned that rule changes are the toughest bottleneck to remove in a process, but, with a lot of persistence and support, we removed the rules one at a time.

Another lesson we learned about the parallel execution and overlapping of tasks is that they require a lot more attention during the execution. Handoffs still require attention, and now we have many handoffs where we only had one handoff prior to our lean initiative. Today, we plan and discuss all the iteration handoffs in a kickoff meeting with all the participants in the iteration or project. That way everybody knows when they can expect the information to move their contribution along. Weekly or monthly project meetings had to be replaced with daily stand-up meetings (called "huddles").

Lean R&D Principle: Overlap all tasks as much as possible.

All activities in a project or an iteration should be run in parallel as much as possible. This will significantly reduce the cycle time.

There are a lot of tasks on the critical path that you think you cannot run in parallel, but at least review those. You may be able to run them partially in parallel—start the dependent task as soon as enough information is available, rather than when all the information is available. A rule of thumb would be to release all information on a daily basis if it has the potential to move a subsequent step along. Closer and often daily attention to the schedule is required with the concurrent execution of critical tasks. Some tasks cannot be run in parallel because there are internal policy or rule restrictions—those rules should be challenged as they may be outdated or residue from functional power.

At Goodyear: We moved all tasks that do not have to be on the critical path to a parallel path. We were also able to run some critical-path tasks in partial-parallel mode that had been run sequentially before. Today, we like to release mold-making information to the mold maker on a daily basis. We also start the work on the prototype tires while the mold is in transit. Even the testing process can start before the tires are physically available. Testing can obtain special rims and procure the test vehicles while the tires are in process or in transit.

This part of parallel execution focused mainly on flow and speed. There are other advantages to parallel work in a product development process, like studying interactions and avoiding rework—concepts that will be discussed in *Chapter 6* in the broader context of concurrent engineering.

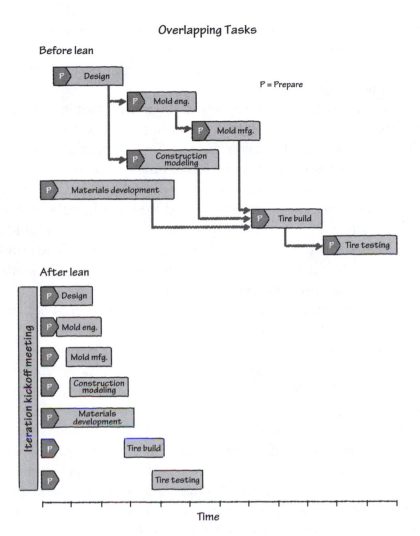

Other Lean R&D Tools That Help Flow and Speed

There are a few other tools and principles that can support flow, and they deserve a brief mention; most of them have been applied within Goodyear R&D to some degree:

■ *Horizontal project management:* This technique was discussed liberally in *Chapter 2*, but I want to mention it here again since it has a big impact on flow, speed, and quality of a project. Sports teams perform so much better when they have a coach that integrates each player's talent for the good of the team, and orchestras perform better with a conductor who gets individuals to cohesively play as a single entity. Project managers who extend beyond a single function play an important role in the strategy and the execution of the projects and have a huge influence on flow and speed.

■ *Colocation and obeya:* Placing design engineers with staff from other functions, such as testing or manufacturing, promotes collaboration, helps with flow, and eliminates wastes of movement and transportation. Unfortunately, it is not always possible, unless engineers are assigned to long projects. For that reason in Goodyear R&D we rely on iteration strategy meetings, kickoff meetings, and frequent huddles. Goodyear is experimenting with some colocation concepts, and when building new headquarters in Akron incorporated collaborative-layout features. But our effort is still far from the level of collaboration seen in some companies, especially in software development. An obeya—war room—is good for brief periods of colocation and collaboration, if actually used as an obeya. They too often end up as a permanent meeting room with leftover samples and drawings.

■ *Experiments:* Although engineers constantly do experiments on their projects, they do not like to experiment with their process. Experimenting with processes can be fun and necessary when trying to improve flow and speed. Because processes sometimes behave in a scientific and consistent manner, you can change a parameter, see what happens, and predict results of the changed process. Small experiments with the process can lead to significant improvements. I always find it very hard to "sell" leadership on running process experiments. There is fear of hurting metrics if the experiment does not succeed. Good leaders accommodate the experiments as a valid method to make improvement.

Experiments with processes also will surface problems that may have been hidden by buffers (time, resources, inventory) and force changes. A famous example from Taiichi Ohno of Toyota is that of lowering the water in a river to reveal the rocks. In the Toyota example, the water is work-in-process inventory (high WIP levels lead to long cycle times) and the rocks are the problems that go unnoticed. The high WIP level can hide all kinds of problems that prevent flow, and make it hard to see waste like overprocessing. You might think this process of lowering the water is too dangerous and leads to project delays, but it really works—and you do not have to drop the water level all at once.

- *5S:* There has not been a lot of focus on 5S—sort, straighten, shine, standardize, sustain—in lean product development, but it does have a place with intellectual work. This practice of organization and waste removal applies to physical objects, such as test tires, as well as to information and how and where it is stored, and when old information is deleted. The time to find something can be significantly reduced by keeping an organized and up-to-date filing system, which will allow engineers to do their work faster. Another example for the use of a 5S approach in the office is the organization of routine tools like e-mails. Most of these computer programs are used many times a day, and they can be organized and personalized for high efficiency.

Do not be constrained to this short list of lean tools. Find additional methods to create flow and improve speed in your processes. But note that you did not see queue management on my list. At Goodyear, we do not believe that queues should exist. We do, though, have small buffers to help with variability, but the management of those buffers is either by FIFO or they are governed by cost of delay. Many scientists and lean scholars point to the management of check-in queues at airports and in supermarkets to illustrate a lean best practice. We refuse to accept the fact that we should manage queues, instead continually learning to manage our processes without queues. We have been largely successful in doing that.

This being said, I must admit to one very long queue in Goodyear R&D— the queue of projects and iterations waiting to get into the pipeline. We keep them there as long as possible because we have nothing invested into them, and they do not get in the way of active projects. The business can change the requirements or cancel them altogether. We start those projects or iterations as late as possible, prioritized by business potential, and when they enter the process they get executed as fast and as efficiently as possible.

The Hidden Factory

In manufacturing, they say that the companies that have been successful with their lean implementation have "gained a factory," which means that they eliminated enough waste and created flow to yield a large amount of additional capacity—sometimes as much as another complete factory. The same is true for product development.

Lean Takes You from Stop Lights to Traffic Circles

I have shown a lot of traffic analogies to illustrate flow problems. Many traffic flow problems in society have been resolved by the use of traffic circles (see *Traffic Circle*). Cars normally move through traffic circles slowly but at a steady pace without stopping and starting. I encourage lean R&D practitioners to look at traffic circles for another reason: flow is a lot easier to create and maintain if the processes are simple and steady. When hustling and hurrying are at a minimum, your processes are likely to be at their optimum performance levels.

Think about all the stress and the energy spent to go through a big intersection with traffic lights. First you must stop and start—maybe several times. You must pay attention to the yellow lights, too, because some cars will stop, but others will not. Left turns are sometimes difficult, and often cars are still in the intersection when the light turns. There may even be an emergency vehicle getting in your way.

In a roundabout, all you do is look left when you enter and yield to the cars in the circle. Then you set your turn signal and exit. In a lean R&D environment, you similarly focus on a few critical elements and proceed with your work.

Try to make all of your R&D processes as simple as a roundabout, which will result in fewer process or flow issues and significantly less work stress and panic. The application of lean principles creates flow, speed, efficiency, and a much less stressful operation where engineers can spend all their time creating value.

Traffic Circle

Cars move through a traffic circle at a slow and steady pace without stopping and starting.

Capacity gained in R&D can be hard to see. In many companies, it disappears amid cost-reduction efforts or is applied to risk mitigation or quality improvements. In the worst case, it is used for wasteful activities (e.g., unnecessary testing). As your lean efforts yield results—and capacity—it is important to put the capacity gained to the right use.

When the Herbie team began our lean product development initiative, throughput was not an explicit goal. I had read about the creation of capacity in manufacturing, but was not sure if it would occur in R&D.

At Goodyear we became much more efficient. It was hard to see this initially because we had added such large time buffers, and any free capacity was used for risk reduction (e.g., running additional tests or iterations). Eventually, though, our throughput tripled without adding resources or spending more money—*we executed three times more iterations in the same time with the same number of engineers.*

So what did we do with our additional capacity?

1. It was applied to the additional work that the business requested—remember that we increased the number of iterations by 100% without adding capacity or adjusting the budget.
2. More iterations and tests were run per project to reduce the project risk—this would not have happened if there had already been risk-management standards in place. Over time, we made progress managing the project risk more appropriately and also learned to specify the right amount of testing in each case.
3. Engineers used the capacity to learn more or to make the product just a little more perfect, although achieving those ends rarely happens.
4. OEM tire-development efficiency is measured on "approvals" from the customer, and we are in a race against competitors to get approvals. Since it can be difficult to know where we stand relative to competitors, additional iterations were used to increase our chances to get the approval faster and ahead of the competitors.
5. Quite a lot of capacity was used for fundamental research and innovation, which we were not able to do before lean.
6. New value-added tools were added to the process like FMEAs and PFMEAs (see *FMEA, DFMEA, and PFMEA*). They help with the assessment of the project risk and iteration planning.
7. Resources were used for capability development and process improvements.

8. Since more time was available now before a launch, more production volume trials were run to assure a smooth launch.
9. Engineers spent more time checking the work they pass on to the next step. We now have metrics tracking this, and engineers are responsible to make sure everything is accurate before it is passed on.

Traditionally in Goodyear R&D, a lot of resources were needed on a project close to launch time. Often the resources were moved from a project that was in the earlier stages. That cut short the work that has to be done early on in a project when all the design options are still available. Today, a lot of exploring, benchmarking, modeling, predictions, calculations, and so on is done in the early stages of a project. That work (which is started on a late-start schedule) assures that an appropriate amount of options are considered and that the best options are selected to move forward. This not only improves the quality of the design, but it also reduces the project cycle time by cutting back on iterations later in the project. This concept is described by Morgan/Liker as "front loading."[8]

One note of caution on the capacity gains: The capacity increase is largest at the beginning of a lean initiative, flattens off, and less capacity may be needed one day. At Goodyear we noticed that we were increasing our development efficiency faster than our need for new products. We also needed less learning cycles or process improvements, and we learned to better manage the project risk.

FMEA, DFMEA, and PFMEA

FMEA (failure mode effects analysis) is a methodology developed by NASA in the 1960s in conjunction with space exploration. You cannot experiment when you send men to the moon and learn from the mistakes. The FMEA process looks at everything possible that could go wrong on a mission along three dimensions:

- Occurrence—how likely is the problem to happen?
- Consequences—what are the consequences if it happens?
- Detection—what are the chances to detect the problem early?

Every dimension gets a rating of 1–10, and the three ratios are multiplied to generate a composite score. Thresholds are set for action, and countermeasures must be taken.

FMEAs were embedded in quality standards like QS9000. At one time they lost their popularity when they were used in court against some automotive companies. Today, I see a resurrection of the tools in many areas even beyond project risk management. The underlying principles of the methodology are universal, and they are used in many other tools (quality matrix). For us, FMEA is a valuable exercise to manage risk and improve the robustness of designs and manufacturing processes that add value to our processes.

DFMEA *(design failure mode effects analysis)* assigns a composite score to the "design" step of a process.

PFMEA *(process failure mode effects analysis)* assigns a composite score to the manufacturing process intended to produce the new product.

Although there is pressure now to reduce any overprocessing, what happened to us was initially a good thing. We put the gained capacity to good use: more value-creating work, better quality, and more good learning. More than anything, this helped us gain stability and confidence. Of course, if I had known that this would happen, we could have planned for it a little better. I am glad about one thing: the additional capacity was not used to reduce resources and cut cost. That is a huge temptation for companies that consider R&D as a cost; at Goodyear, we reinvested the capacity even during the global recession at the end of the past decade.

The capacity we created also allowed for a more stress-free product development process. Engineers can focus on engineering rather than following up on work and managing late changes.

Leyla Renner, development engineer, who works part time to balance the needs of her family with work, says that she is more intellectually challenged now than she was before the lean initiative. Although quite busy, she feels that her time is now better spent creating value for customers.

Before lean, Rachel Graves, development engineer, used to go home frustrated. She felt she had spent most of her day spinning her wheels rather than designing tires. Too much time was spent trying to get things caught up by expediting, following up on projects, and accommodating changes. Now she says she goes home feeling that she did a day's worth of good work because she was able to focus on what adds value to her programs, and she can use her talent for what really matters to the company.

Fast Is Better than Slow

Jim Morgan says that speed is a formidable weapon in product development.[13] Peter Senge says, "The only sustainable competitive advantage is an organization's ability to learn faster than the competition."[14]

When we achieved our target for OTD, we surveyed a global cross section of Goodyear leaders. They were happy with the delivery, and confirmed that we were hitting schedules and that the process had become faster—but they said we were still not fast enough. What we did not know when we started lean was that making a development process faster often also makes it more efficient. *Today, if I was only given one thing to improve in an R&D process—after safety, quality, and delivery—I would choose speed; a lot of value can be created when you speed up your processes.*

> ***Today if I was only given one thing to improve in an R&D process—after safety, quality, and delivery—I would choose speed; a lot of value can be created when you speed up your processes.***

Lean R&D Principle: After safety, quality, and delivery, focus on improving the speed of your process.

Developing speed capability can lead to another competitive differentiator due to first-mover advantages. Speed creates agility to capitalize on opportunities and leads to a more favorable ROI and cash flow. It also creates faster learning and quicker capability development, which can become a great competitive advantage in R&D.

Application of lean principles, knowledge management, and investment into faster tools can increase the product development speed. *As you increase process speed, you also will achieve, at the same time, collateral efficiency gains.*

At Goodyear: An increase in development speed became a priority for lean after we were satisfied with safety, quality, and delivery. Before lean, Goodyear already had invested largely into knowledge management, modeling, predictive tools, CAD systems, and rapid prototyping. But these tools had a limited impact due to the slow process in which they had been applied. Increasing the capability for speed remains a priority at Goodyear today, although most additional speed gains will come from improving complicated processes like prototyping and mold making—for all our improvements to speed, collateral efficiency gains were achieved.

Jean-Pierre in GIC*L has a dream: Launch a new line of high-performance tires every other year. High-performance tires are high-value products for Goodyear. When we launch a new product, we normally get great ratings from the magazine tests and rankings in Europe—crucial in that market because a lot of buyers seek out those recommendations. As soon as Goodyear launches a new high-performance tire line, the copying among our competitors starts, says Jean-Pierre, and within 2 years many competitors have caught up and rate as well as we do in the magazine tests—that is, until Goodyear can launch the next-generation tires. Jean-Pierre thinks that we will soon be fast enough to get to the 2-year cycle and develop tires faster than the competitors can copy (i.e., we develop our next tire before they can copy and market the existing tire).

Speed has many advantages:

- *First-mover benefits:* New stuff sells. Innovation capability is critical, and development speed is a great asset to an innovative company. And, eventually, if you move fast enough, you outpace copiers.
- *Tap new technology:* Speed gives a company the agility to quickly take advantage of emerging technologies or scientific discoveries.
- *Agile capability:* Speed allows a company to quickly react to changes in the market (higher fuel prices), raw material prices, a competitive threat, or an upturn or downturn in the economy.
- *Faster learning and process improvements:* The faster you can experiment, the faster you can develop knowledge and process improvements, and, thus, the faster you develop capabilities. This higher development potential can lead to a great competitive advantage.
- *Capitalize quickly on cost savings:* If a cost-saving opportunity arises, the faster you can integrate it into your products, the faster you can enjoy the higher profits.
- *Better cash flow and faster return on investment (ROI):* When cash flow is quickened, expensive tooling is leveraged faster, which means that tooling ROI is shorter. In fact, any development investment has faster ROI. These types of gains are hard to see because, like many others, they come back to the business and are not postmarked "from product development."
- *Motivated and engaged engineers:* Engineers want to see the results of their experiments as fast as possible, not at some time in the future when they are working on a different project and they have nearly forgotten about their experiment.

To be fair, speed is not only achieved by a better flow in the development process. At Goodyear, many other factors helped us become faster:

- Using existing knowledge as the best starting point and avoiding trials
- Developing predictive tools and computer models
- Aggressive global capability development (rapid prototyping, computer modeling, etc.)
- Establishing faster logistics processes to reduce transportation and movement times

- Speeding up all subprocesses using better processes, technology, and capability:
  - Faster drawing capability using computer tools
  - Faster prototype manufacturing
  - Faster testing
  - Faster mold manufacturing
- Installment of horizontal project managers and the development of project management knowledge and capability

Stephanie Brown, lead engineer, develops truck tires. She says that they replaced a 12- to 18-month-long field test with a lab test that can be run in 3 weeks.

Another major process change that increased our speed significantly was front-loading, which leads to a much better assessment of project options and can cut down on the iterations or learning cycles that are needed. We traditionally had applied our resources to the end of the process to ensure we were ready for the launch. With an improved process, we now can apply resources or staff to earlier parts of projects, which helps our speed and, thus, drives more capacity gain. It is a beautiful cycle.

We also learned that a focus on speed in the process made the process more efficient because of things we did to achieve the speed gains, such as removing wastes (overprocessing, unnecessary iterations). So we clearly gained speed, and we also saved a significant amount of money. In order to reduce our WIP, we control what comes into the pipeline—we learned to let the good projects in and keep the not so good ones out. We also developed new capabilities—drawing tools, predictive testing, knowledge management—that make the process faster but indirectly led to efficiency gains.

Create a Kaikaku

By 2010, we had stabilized OTD in both our Akron and Luxembourg innovation centers, and we were ready to make our next loop through the Womack Wheel, starting again with the customer. Joe Zekoski, CTO, knows how important development speed is for creating value for our customers, and he believed we had stalled at improving development speed. He was right; in fact, there was a lot of resistance to further push any improvement of our development process. This was a time for another kaikaku—as Womack and Jones write in *Lean Thinking*, if you do not have a kaikaku event, you should create one![15]

For this kaikaku, Joe announced a contest: The challenge was to create a process to complete a full iteration with a new mold and all required prototyping and testing in less than a week. Since we had slightly different competencies in the three innovation centers, they hand-selected one team from each center. Young, high-potential engineers, who were not totally set in their tracks yet, were chosen to head up the teams. The teams were given 24 hours to come up with the 1-week process.

Phil Dunker, leader of the GIC*A team, picked members with a good balance of competencies, but he also picked a mix of experienced and less-experienced people. Phil wanted neither a team set in their ways nor a team that lacked experience. Phil also made sure he had members who "rock the boat," but he also wanted those who stabilized the boat so it would not capsize.

At the time Joe said, "We set a big audacious goal (1 week for an iteration) because we wanted to force teams to think outside the box. We know we could have given the teams weeks or months for this task, but we only gave them 24 hours. They had this much time to develop a process for a full-length learning cycle, including a mold, to be executed within a week—a process that takes at least 12 weeks."

The team leaders had picked their members, and the date for the contest was set. A team of senior R&D leaders evaluated the results and declared the team from the German center the winner because they had used the most innovative thinking, but that was only a small beginning to the story.

The three teams were told to meet for a week in one of the innovation centers, and combine the best parts of their three processes. They were asked to reduce their ideas to practice, and actually complete a full iteration with a mold in 2 weeks—they were given an extra week to make it more feasible.

Phil says that when they got together, they decided that it was not a good idea to pick process pieces out of context. They reasoned that the Akron center had the best modeling concept, the Luxembourg center had the best prototype concept, and the German center had the best idea to make the mold. They picked those three coherent processes and filled in the blanks around them. Then, leadership chose the Hanau center in Germany to execute the plan and run a complete iteration in 2 weeks.

The center was successful and completed the iteration. They met the improvement targets of the iteration, except for one minor item: they missed a tire-noise target by a small margin. Joe was surprised how well the contest worked. A contest like this is not something he would try regularly, he said, but it was a great way to shake things up. This was not about the contest—it was to give people the freedom to think outside the box and empower them to transition their idea to practice. And since the team proved it could work, Joe said, "I want to see what it takes to run *all iterations* in two weeks' time."

Pit Crew Tries to Accelerate Speed

In order to "see what it takes to do all learning cycles in two weeks," as Joe had commissioned, a cross-functional team was formed. Since the team could not rely on unlimited resources and the process could not disrupt any other work of the shared resources, the target for the team was changed to a 50% cycle-time reduction. The name "Pit Crew" was originally chosen for the team based on the Goodyear racing heritage and to highlight the fact that a project is in a race, just like a race car. The name was later changed to SPF (which stood for single-piece flow) because the team realized that engineers and operations had used the newly created capacity to put more projects into the pipeline and that multitasking had become our biggest problem. For me, the initiative would force us to deal with the multitasking.

Lean Pit Crew

A lean pit crew works on the critical path of a process and against the clock, just like a pit crew in a motorsports race when a car pulls into the pit. The car does not wait in line, and the tires are not changed one at a time.

First of all, a pit crew is staffed appropriately—all the resources are assembled so that the pit stop can be completed as fast as possible, but not overstaffed so that members would be in each other's way.

Pit crews have standard work. They figure out the best possible way to do their job, and they practice it hundreds of times to get each role perfected. They also work as a collaborative team where all the team members have the same goal—as fast as possible with the work perfectly leveled (they do not want one member finishing after the others).

Every job the crew performs adds value; there is no time to waste.

Joe appointed a project manager (Brandy Moorhead) to lead the team. Brandy had experience in tire design, project management, and had recently completed the lean product development certification. Brandy had the lean background and also the respect of the organization. The Pit Crew project was run in "sprint" mode in a 12-month time frame and split into three different charters or learning cycles.

Because of the work from Pit Crew, cycle time was further improved by approximately 45%. Joe's aspirational target was not quite met, but the 45% reduction is a big difference. Joe then asked the team to "institutionalize" the process—extend it to all projects in all innovation centers and to make sure the gains were sustained. Today, the operations managers in the innovation centers keep a good eye on the process and look at cycle-time metrics every month and take action if the cycle time is not on target. Many kaizen activities are still underway to further reduce the cycle time. One of them is an initiative that takes all the shorter learning cycles and finds the best way to turn them into faster *projects*.

The Pit Crew team made many big changes:

- *Creation of an iteration strategy meeting:* In this meeting, all the stakeholders, customer representatives, and engineers get together and discuss the targets of the iteration and a possible strategy to achieve them. Engineers are not left on their own to come up with the plan, which helps to keep them from being second-guessed later. This also assures the buy-in of all stakeholders.
- *Iteration kickoff meeting was added:* As if we need more meetings! At Goodyear, the learning cycles are short, and engineers run cycles for different projects, so colocation is not an option. The kickoff meeting (in the obeya, if possible) lays out the day-to-day plan, and the team members discuss what information is available at what time and what is needed at what time to run as many activities concurrently as possible. This way, information can be released on a daily basis and there are clear expectations for delivery and handoff.
- *Better planning for the resource availability:* Every team member should only have one task to worry about: the current iteration. The secret to this better planning was better visibility of where the resources were being used and what work was coming down the pipeline.
- *Eliminate time buffers that were not needed throughout the process:* We also sought to remove a lot of the time buffers that still remained in the process.

After the project was completed, Brandy commented, "These short, intense projects need a structured project management approach. If I had not started with a clear charter and held everybody to it, we would never have gotten anywhere. Functions needed to deal with the change by being involved, yet the measure for progress was cycle time, not their happiness. The change management process took much longer than a sprint project because we had to stabilize emotions within the functions."

"From an organization perspective, our sponsor realized that we had pushed the organization to the limits," added Brandy. "It was very unusual to give somebody outside the functions the authority and empowerment to make proposals for significantly changing the way their work was done."

The Goodyear focus on speed did not stop with the Pit Crew/SPF initiative. Brandy moved on, and project managers were assigned in every innovation center to specific projects to further develop speed capability. One of those teams works on the speed of the computer modeling process, which is now on the critical path. A global project called "Lean Tire Performance Assessment" is sponsored by two global directors. This team sets standards for the content of iterations and testing based on project risk. This is just to name a few of the ongoing process-improvement initiatives geared toward speed.

Teaching Flow

The absence of flow in R&D was a big problem at Goodyear, as it is in many companies. It took me some time to understand it and even longer to create it. And as a champion, I need to make my role obsolete and empower Goodyear engineers and leaders with the knowledge required to carry on further improvements, including flow. To get this information across, I tried book clubs and we brought in instructors, such as Don Reinertsen and Mark Spearman. I personally made a few hundred PowerPoint slides on flow, which I used for training, and all this helped.

In 2013, Jon Bellissimo, our general director at GIC*A, asked an important question inspired by zero-loss thinking: "What would be the theoretical fastest that we could operate?" At the heart of this question was flow. I dug through the usual publications and used a dozen formulas and graphs to try to answer Jon's question. But I was unsuccessful. I could not explain this to Jon or anybody else. Then I tried a model using Excel spreadsheets, but I had forgotten that engineers (and their leaders) will not believe results if they cannot see and understand the formulations used in a spreadsheet. The biggest problem in all my attempts was that variability plays the biggest role in everything related to R&D flow, and that is hard to calculate and model—let alone explain—because it gets approximated in many scientific approaches and is based on many assumptions.

Then I found something that works to teach product-development flow in a way that everyone walks away able to analyze a process and improve flow in the process. I developed a product-development simulation that makes the principles of flow visible, and, although many people may not understand the math behind it, they learn what happens to flow if you play with known parameters (WIP, variability, capacity, flexibility). The simulation uses only pennies or tokens, a dozen dice, a flipchart, and a spreadsheet to visualize results. Most important, though, is that this simulation walks trainees through concepts they encounter when trying to implement or improve flow, allowing them to see the concepts in action and the effects that changing parameters can each have on flow. Using multiple rounds of simulations, I incorporated the effects of

- Little's law
- Variability and flexibility
- TOC and TOC pull
- Station-to-station pull
- Constant WIP system (CONWIP or optimum system)
- Managed operation (flow overseen and adjusted as needed)

Rather than tell you how to construct my simulation in elaborate detail, I encourage you to develop your own simulations based on these same concepts and tailored to your R&D process and culture. I found the following books helpful in developing my simulation: *Factory Physics*,[4] *The Goal*,[5] *Velocity*,[6] and *The Lean Games Book*,[16] and they may help you as well.

Goodyear had always delivered safe, high-quality products. Now, thanks to our lean initiative, we could deliver them on time, fast, and efficiently. We used lean to improve *how* we create value and profitable value streams for the products we develop. But *what* products should we develop? R&D plays a key role in deciding what to work on. Can lean be applied to the creative and innovative part of the R&D process?

Notes

1. Mats Magnusson, *Lean in R&D—A Way of Combining Creativity and Efficiency?* LPPDE 2014, Copenhagen, June 2014.
2. Dantar P. Oosterwal, *The Lean Machine: How Harley-Davidson Drove Top-Line Growth and Profitability with Revolutionary Lean Product Development*, AMACOM, New York, 2010.
3. Allen C. Ward and Durward K. Sobek II, *Lean Product and Process Development*, Lean Enterprise Institute, Cambridge, MA, 2014.
4. Wallace J. Hopp and Mark L. Spearman, *Factory Physics*, Waveland Press, Long Grove, IL, 1996.
5. Eliyahu Goldratt and Jeff Cox, *The Goal*, North River Press, Great Barrington, MA, 1984.
6. Suzan Bergland, Jeff Cox, and Dee Jacob, *Velocity*, Free Press, New York, 2009.
7. Don Reinertsen, Goodyear training, Akron, OH, January 2015.
8. James M. Morgan and Jeffrey K. Liker, *The Toyota Product Development System*, Productivity Press, New York, 2006.
9. Jim Womack, *Gemba Walks*, Lean Enterprise Institute, Cambridge, MA, 2011.
10. Inventory and capacity examples modified from *Factory Physics*: Wallace J. Hopp and Mark L. Spearman, *Factory Physics*, Waveland Press, Long Grove, IL, 1996.
11. J.D.C. Little, "A Proof for the Queuing Formula: $L = \lambda W$," *Operations Research*, Massachusetts Institute of Technology, Cambridge, MA, 1961.
12. Edward Pound, *Factory Physics for Managers*, McGraw-Hill Education, New York, 2014.
13. James M. Morgan, presentation to Goodyear Innovation Center Luxembourg, June 2014.
14. Peter Senge, *The Fifth Discipline*, Doubleday/Currency, New York, 1990.
15. James P. Womack and Daniel T. Jones, *Lean Thinking*, Free Press, New York, 1996.
16. John Bicheno, *The Lean Games Book*, Picsie Books, Buckinghamshire, UK, 2009.

Chapter 6

Lean and Innovation

Up to this point, you have read a lot about Goodyear's journey with lean and how we improved our product development processes. But only occasionally did the topic of innovation come up—I have focused on how we develop better value for the customer and profitable value streams for the products we develop. Innovation is a lot about what to create and develop. Many R&D professionals and scholars—maybe you—do not think that lean can coexist with innovation and creativity, let alone synergize and flourish. In this chapter, I hope to put that misperception to rest as I show how we used lean thinking and principles to overcome these challenges at Goodyear.

Dispelling Lean Innovation Myths

There are many sophisticated definitions of innovation. To be consistent with the lean principle of simplicity, I describe innovation as "turning ideas into commercial success." Goodyear is one of many companies that knows how important it is to have both a successful lean product development program and a winning innovation culture. The two must go hand in hand.

Peter Fritz, manufacturing technology manager at 3M and former director of the Society for Concurrent Product Development (SCPD), gives the following recipe for successful product innovation:

- Seven parts hard work
- One part stealth
- One part luck
- One part support[1]

Fritz does not give a breakdown for hard work. You should expect your lean initiative to alleviate but not eliminate that innovation ingredient.

It took a while for organizations to figure out how to have lean and innovation coexist; as long as lean was confined to manufacturing and the supply chain, the compatibility of the two was secondary. But as lean moved away from the plant floor and into product development, the need for them to find synergy grew.

In *Gemba Walks*, Jim Womack states: "I have long felt that a great weakness of the lean movement is that we tend to take customer value as a given, asking how we can provide more value as we currently define it, at lower cost with higher quality and more rapid response to changing demand. This is fine as far as it goes. But what if the customer wants something fundamentally different from what our organizations are now providing?"[2]

Did lean fail innovation? Or did innovation fail to leverage the benefits of lean?

Lean developed a reputation for being counterproductive to innovation. There were some powerful industry leaders and innovation scholars who went on record about the negative effects of lean, six sigma, and lean/six sigma on a company's ability to innovate. And they were able to point to corporate examples to illustrate their argument. For example, 3M was one of the most innovative U.S. companies when James McNerney (coming from GE) took over in 2000. He promised improved profitability by following a rigorous six sigma program. But many within 3M, including Art Fry, inventor of the Post-it note, say the six sigma program stifled innovation and nearly destroyed the company.[3] McNerney left 3M in 2005, and, subsequently, the company's measure of innovation—new-products vitality index (NPVI)—steadily rose as its focus on six sigma lessened.[4]

At a conference on product development in Silicon Valley in 2013, the recently retired CTO of a highly innovative company told me, "Lean is a bunch of baloney and cannot be used for product development, except maybe knowledge management." I do not think that this CTO had any personal experience with lean, and he based the statement largely on what he had heard from colleagues at other companies.

Frank Hull, honorary visiting professor, Cass Business School, London, and board member of the Society for Concurrent Product Development, has studied more than 100 R&D organizations for best practices. He concluded that lean initiatives are similar in their laser-like focus to prior initiatives, such as six sigma, but those who apply lean risk focusing it on the denominator of cost reduction, just as many did with business process reengineering (BPR).

Eliminating waste by connecting activities in workflows is valuable for cutting costs, but may neglect the affect it can have on the creative capabilities of people and innovation. Frank concludes that this was not the case, though, within Goodyear, where the surplus gained from lean initiatives and waste reduction were reallocated to innovative kinds of work activities.[5]

Lean R&D Principle: Reinvest the gains from waste elimination.

Many people look at lean as a tool to eliminate waste from a process. In manufacturing operations and even in other functions and industries, such as administration or healthcare, that can have a large effect on direct cost reduction.

In R&D, the same can and has been done by many companies. Some companies put the R&D savings toward the bottom line and operated with a reduced staff. Conversely, other companies reinvested savings and used the gained capacity for additional value creation or capability development.

As explained earlier, since most R&D organizations have a relatively small direct effect on the total business cost, the cost savings are relatively small. It is a better idea to reinvest the cash and resources back into R&D and leverage the investment for innovation capability and increased profitability of the value streams and the business.

At Goodyear: We reinvested the savings to develop more new products for the business. Other resources gained via lean were used to develop fundamental technology and for capability development, especially innovation capability. And, of course, a small portion of savings was applied to our lean initiative and our work on the value stream, resulting in exponentially more value and profits than the investment.

Does six sigma and/or lean deserve the reputation of killing innovation? I do not think so, and here is why:

■ *Don't mix the methodologies:* Many publications and authors combine lean and six sigma—"lean/sigma"—into a single methodology, an approach that has become popular in many companies. As a master black belt in both disciplines, I know the commonalities of lean and six sigma, but I do not think the effects of lean and six sigma on innovation should be judged together or equally.

Six sigma emphasizes variability reduction. Although lean/sigma scholars have tried to explain the synergy between lean and DMAIC tools, lean too often gets associated with variability reduction in these efforts. In a development process, especially in one that pushes innovation and risk taking, there is a lot of "good variability" (unsuccessful experiments, unpredictable results). Of course there also is bad variability (tests that must be repeated, mistakes). The bad variability should be attacked by a six sigma protocol and is waste in a lean protocol. Unfortunately, sometimes it is hard to draw a line between the two. In many cases, the good variability was eliminated with the bad and that hurt the ability to innovate.

Both six sigma and lean/sigma use a relatively rigid protocol that works well with analytical and data-rich problems. But it is difficult and often awkward to force some or all R&D-related process problems into that protocol, especially problems or processes that deal with creativity.

■ *Downsizing and cost-cutting stigma:* Six sigma and lean were introduced in the business world at a time when many companies were downsizing, dramatically cutting staff as they tried to reduce high costs. Although it was tempting to use lean/sigma to support that trend, the cuts probably would have happened anyway with some other tool.

In most publications about negative effects on innovation, a range of corporate initiatives and tools get cited, from BPR to six sigma to the quality movement (TQC, ISO, QS). I have yet to find an example where lean *alone* is identified as compromising innovation. (I wonder if the "lean and mean" slogan from the downsizing era has played a role in the negative feelings about lean.)

Early in the lean deployment in product development and following the pattern in manufacturing, some companies used lean tools extensively for cost reductions; after all, lean identifies waste and waste costs money. Although the cost reductions did not necessarily kill innovation, they did not help it either. Some of these initiatives cut some meat as well as the fat, and innovation resources are often the most vulnerable. "Use lean to build strength, not to lose weight," advises Dan Markovitz.[6]

■ *Follow the money:* With the introduction of six sigma and lean/sigma, many companies established quotas for the number of trained black or green belts and the number of projects initiated, with funding tied to these targets. Unfortunately, many leaders met their quota by putting everyday functional work of cost cutting under the banners of both lean and six sigma, and they used the new funds and newly trained staff to promote their pet agendas. For example, six sigma initially received substantial leadership attention at Goodyear, and there were a lot of resources applied to the initiative at the start. Globally, we trained several hundred six sigma black belts, and we even had a VP in charge of six sigma, following the GE and Motorola pattern. For this reason, many cost-reduction exercises and a lot of regular functional work that never received any other resources or priority were run under the banner of six sigma—even though six sigma was often not the right tool to use.

Some Goodyear R&D managers were very creative and forced all kinds of functional and cost-reduction projects in the six-sigma mold. This was one of the reasons why, within Goodyear R&D, six sigma quickly got a bad reputation and did not generate a lot of good results. Eventually the program lost support but, worse, people lost their faith in the initiative, and they approached lean with the same suspicion and bad taste in their mouth.

- *The wrong lean tools used the wrong way:* Many companies used the lean tools they knew from manufacturing and tried to plug them into R&D. Many tools, such as 5S and quick changeovers, will have only nominal impact or even a negative effect in R&D, especially when they are the only lean tools being applied.

  Another popular tool in manufacturing, standard work, has to be introduced with care in R&D. Restrictive standards and the abuse of standards can affect the ability of an R&D organization to innovate. I have even seen leaders focus on standards and standard work try to increase their "control" over the organization, especially in times of crisis. In most of these initiatives, the value-creating aspect of lean took a second stage to waste elimination.

  Many R&D leaders struggle to control costs and adhere to their annual operating plan. After travel has been cut and merit raises stopped, the choices become tougher and eventually include project cutting and staff reductions. Cutting projects or funding are difficult to do in a typical R&D organization because work is mostly invisible and it is difficult to identify or control what is being worked on. In an environment like that, standard work and work visibility are welcomed tools to control R&D work and manage the budget. This management practice can lead to a lot of collateral damage.

- *Not a lot of lean history in R&D:* When companies looked at lean in R&D early in 2000, there was not a lot of experience in the industry nor were there good examples to follow. Womack will respond that not many people had read the chapter on R&D in *The Machine that Changed the*

World,[7] and I think he is right—or that many probably read it without understanding how to translate what they read to their R&D work. In the absence of a better understanding, initial lean R&D efforts focused on what worked well in manufacturing, and not noticing the potential for negative impacts from a manufacturing-centric approach in R&D.

■ *You get what you measure:* Metrics are an integral part of lean, both in production and in product development, and they are a powerful tool. But remember that you normally get what you ask for in a metric: some metrics can be counterproductive to innovation. A good example at Goodyear was our focus on on-time delivery (OTD). We had a target of 100% OTD and noticed that project managers started to avoid risk and stayed away from the more innovative concepts to meet their OTD delivery target. The Goodyear target was reduced to 90% to make a statement that it is OK to miss the OTD target if you have a good reason. Cost-reduction metrics are even more likely to drive anti-risk, anti-innovation behaviors (especially among management), inadvertently fueling a focus on short-term profitability rather than creativity.

■ *Structure bad, freedom good:* Innovators and inventors prefer an environment with the least amount of structure. They have a hard time functioning in *any* environment that promotes process discipline, standard work, and knowledge reuse. So lean tools and other improvement approaches that make work visible, track progress, or promote standardized processes cause a negative kneejerk reaction.

Lean R&D Principle: Move lean closer to value creation to increase synergy with innovation.

Many initial definitions of lean focused on waste elimination. But if you go back to the pioneers, such as Taiichi Ohno, you will see that they also talked about speed and the complete value stream. More modern definitions of lean focus on customer value first. With a focus on customer value first, it is a lot easier to find good synergy between lean and innovation in R&D processes.

At Goodyear: In R&D, we used the "Womack Wheel" as our path for the implementation. This path starts with customer value and forces a look at the complete value stream. Waste reduction comes indirectly in the third step when we were looking at flow and speed. Doing so, we found enough collateral efficiency gains without making waste-reduction our primary objective.

To incorporate the perspective of those suspicious of lean's value to R&D and innovation, I looked to Sam Landers, with whom I have spent a lot of time throughout my career. Sam retired from Goodyear right about the time we started lean product development. Sam is one of the best innovators the company has had in recent times. During his long career as a Goodyear product development engineer and team leader, he and his teams created many successful innovative products, such as the Aquatred, the first 100,000-mile tire, first fuel-economy tire, sealants to reduce flats, and the TripleTred. Sam knows tire technology, the company, and the customer like nobody else.

Sam calls himself a "serial innovator." He lived through many initiatives to improve the company and R&D, from BPR to the quality movements to six sigma and even our start with lean. Sam is an excellent thinker and still has the best interests of his former company in mind as he tried to coach me through this chapter to make sure I got the innovation piece right. Like many innovators, Sam is concerned that lean can negatively affect innovation. I followed his advice many times to avoid problems where lean and innovation collide and to help lean and innovation coexist and synergize, and present Sam's concerns and advice in this chapter.

Discovery of Lean Tools in the Innovation Creation Process

The closer lean is to value creating, the harder it is to misinterpret its effect on innovation, says Sam, and the closer lean is to waste reduction, the easier it is to misinterpret its effect on innovation.

The synergy of lean and innovation may have been known to some lean practitioners, but it certainly became ready for prime time after Eric Ries' best seller *The Lean Startup*.[8] Ries used the term lean to describe an efficient process to create customer value—not the traditional sense of waste reduction to which many are accustomed. His book was quickly followed by other articles and books, such as *The Lean Entrepreneur* by Brant Cooper and Patrick Vlaskovits.[9] Gradually, the positive attributes of lean and innovation, such as quick learning cycles and quick prototypes, were popularized.

Today lean innovation is the subject of many lean product development conferences, such as those by the Lean Product and Process Development Exchange (LPPDE) and Association for Manufacturing Excellence (AME). Many innovation experts—such as Mats Magnusson, professor at KTH, Royal Institute of Technology, and Hongyi Chen, associate professor and MSEM director of Graduate Studies at University of Minnesota Duluth—are exploring and explaining the relationship of lean and innovation.

I gradually have seen many companies, in addition to Goodyear, with a long tradition of innovation start to implement lean and develop a great synergy. For example, DJO, a medical devices company, has flourished by mixing lean and innovation under the direction of CTO Rich Gildersleeve.

At Goodyear, we concluded that if you understand the lean principles and empower people in the process to correctly apply those principles to their work, you can achieve a great synergy between lean and innovation. Lean does not create innovation nor is it a way to become innovative. But lean principles can help solve some notorious problems in the innovation creation process. I think this will increasingly become apparent in the years ahead as more research occurs in this area.

Innovation without Monetization

Innovation is often depicted as a funnel—on the large side of the funnel a lot of ideas are coming in. These ideas get filtered or reviewed at some gates positioned farther down the funnel. Some of the ideas move down the funnel and, emerging at the smaller end, get developed into profitable products. When illustrating this, there is normally a dollar sign ($) shown with the projects to signal that those ideas that made it through will help the company make money. At Goodyear, we had a funnel, too, but it was closed at the narrow end, which created a big idea bubble inside and no dollars signs at the exit.

This happened when I worked in a department in the 1980s at Goodyear (with Sam Landers) that was called "Innovative Products." About 30 engineers were colocated and asked to "innovate"—we had little oversight or interference. This group used the same services and processes as all other engineers to build prototypes, design molds, test, and so on. But we also had a little job shop where the technicians did not laugh at the engineers who showed up with a piece of carpet and said, "I want to build this into a tire." On paper we had a dedicated capacity of shared resources (testing, prototype building, etc.), but in reality it was revoked regularly when needed for a panic or a product launch.

During that time, Goodyear had many diverse divisions—aerospace, industrial products, wheel and brake—that it does not have today. These other divisions helped us find technology, connections, and spinoffs. I used the technology for producing crash-proof gas tanks to make tires and built other prototypes in an engineered products plant where we made tank tracks. Sam used the blimp hangar workshop to build a machine to study tire noise. Now that we do not have these industries any more, we need to work with other companies to "recreate" that diversity.

After 3 years, the Innovative Products engineers had generated hundreds of ideas, built hundreds of prototypes, and gave countless presentations and demonstrations, but all that seemed to happen was the number of projects and ideas grew bigger inside the department. *Nothing* was developed into a marketable product. There were many reasons for that:

- We enjoyed creating stuff and always found something new to create so that we did not have to finish anything.
- We had excess resources; using them all was more important than how we used them.
- Nobody challenged us to take something to market (marketing protected their domain).
- There was a very strong NIH (not invented here) in the company, even within the Innovative Products department.
- People did not want to give their idea to somebody else or even let anybody contribute for fear of losing the credit for their work.
- There were many "pet projects" that were not worth pursuing, but we worked on them anyway.
- We had no linkage to marketing, sales, manufacturing, or any other stakeholder—certainly not to a customer.

Eventually leadership appointed an "implementer" as the director of the department, with a clear assignment to pick the best ideas and market them. Some of the successful products that came out of that department were run-flat tires, the Aquatred, Unicircles, flat-tire sealants, and foam-filled tires, but some only matured for the market 10 or 15 years after they were first imagined.

When the department was eliminated to reduce cost, engineers were reassigned to regular functions. A lot of the good ideas were abandoned in the process, but some innovators tenaciously continued their work in the regular functions and their ideas made it into the market. Some of the transferred people resurrected their ideas many years later when both the company and the market were ready for them.

I personally learned many lessons during my time in Innovative Products and most are reflected in this chapter: There *is* a way to manage boundless creativity and produce profitable products out of it, and the principles of lean product development can help. There are right-brained, divergent thinkers, and they are indeed creative. They have a new idea every day and drive the less right-brained people nuts. The right-brained thinkers had one thing in common—they were only good at generating ideas; do not ask them to manage a project, not even their own idea, because they will abandon it for another idea tomorrow. We also had left-brained, convergent thinkers (fortunately not a lot of them). They would analyze everything to death just to conclude that more analysis was needed.

There also is a rare breed of people who are right-brained enough to think abstract and see connections. They are also able to focus on one idea at a time and manage their own work.

You need a good balance of talent in an innovation-creation organization. You need people who rock the boat, but you also need those who stabilize it and prevent it from turning over. And if you can find a person who can do both, that is best of all. Sam Landers, who knew that he was primarily a right-brained innovator, always made sure he had a left-brained person working with him because he needed somebody to focus on the details, write specs, make tires, interpret test results, and so on.

Isolating the best innovators alone will not lead to many successful products in the market. The skills we have today at Goodyear to manage projects, assess ideas quickly, collaborate through the value stream, and efficiently get products to market would have been invaluable at that time. Every time a shining idea would have come through, it would have been assigned to a project manager and a competent team who would have turned it into a commercial success.

The one who initiates an idea is rarely the only one to translate it to commercial practice. An innovator must understand that to be truly successful they must share the credit and let others get involved and even take ownership to make them successful in the market. And likewise, a good innovator can pick up somebody else's idea and build on it to make it successful.

A team of inventors working together has a higher chance for success than a few individuals tinkering independently. Team synergy is especially important in the creative phase of a project: Inventors feed off each others' ideas and evaluate each others' thinking. If complementary skills can be leveraged, the team is even more productive. This behavior must be supported by a performance-appraisal system that encourages collaboration over competition.

When I worked in this innovative environment earlier in my career, there was one facet that I truly missed: I wished my project had been picked up by an experienced project manager. Young innovators, like me at that time, usually do not have the contacts, the knowledge of company personalities, awareness of corporate dangers, and the project management skills that are needed to move from innovative idea to innovative product.

It Takes More than One Process

Which statement is true?

- 60% of new product development *projects* succeed.
- 99.7% of new product *ideas* fail.[10]

The answer is both. The first number applies to the launch of products, while the second number applies to the development of new ideas.

Consider the R&D gate process within Goodyear, particularly the Success Assured gate 2 of our PCP. There is a lot of creativity and technology development work ahead of the Success Assured gate:

- Innovation creation process (ICP)
- Business model innovation (BMI)
- Free exploration of ideas
- Technology creation process (TCP)

Success assured is the stage where we split our product development process into two parts—a frontend phase called "kentou" (Japanese for study, examination, investigation, and good fighting) and a backend called "execution." Innovation occurs within both phases, and lean and learning have a prominent role in both.

The goal of the *execution* phase is to develop a profitable product for a launch, whereas the goal of the *kentou* phase is to develop new ideas and technology that can be incorporated into a product. Both phases need to be efficient, fast, and aligned, but there are also significant differences in risk taking, predictable outcomes, and focus (see *Two Halves of Product Development Process*).

Two Halves of Product Development Process

Because of the varying requirements of kentou versus execution, there really is no *one* overall process that will work across the diverse requirements of both phases. At Goodyear we learned this through trial and error and are now moving along the right path.

So, let us consider the *project* and *idea* statistics again:

- 60% of *projects* in the execution phase are successful. At Goodyear that percentage is almost 100% now since we have not missed a launch since we implemented the lean processes and applied the lean principles described in this book, and most of our projects now are profitable.
- 0.3% of the *ideas* that get considered or developed in the kentou phase are successful. We work very hard at this at Goodyear, and our percentage might be a touch higher (although it is difficult to assess this measure across the entire company). In any case, a low number in this category may suggest that at least a lot of new ideas are tried.

Years ago my friend Sam would have emphatically stated, "Lean will not work in R&D because you have different requirements in the two phases." My response to that is: "This is why we need different processes for the two different phases."

I believe that a good lean product development process can raise the project success rate of any company to close to 100% and the idea success score by an order of magnitude.

The relative amount of effort and resources a company dedicates to these two phases depends on the business, the technology, the maturity of the products, and the organization. At Goodyear, we spend about 30% of our effort in the kentou phase. The execution phase takes about 70% of the time and the resources because we launch an average of 1,500 new SKUs (stock-keeping units) every year, and we need that level of resources and time to make our business successful.

Highly innovative companies with mature products or commodities (this is not an oxymoron) are so focused on execution that they do not need a matrix organization and, instead, integrate and colocate R&D into the business unit. This is the case within Goodyear with our racing, aircraft, and earthmover divisions. Contrarily, businesses with few technically difficult product lines and a small number of customers may, essentially, make a different product for every customer, and, thus, their products are highly customized (e.g., medical devices, defense contractors, customized equipment, aerospace). These companies are heavy on the kentou side of the R&D process, and they often run a functional organization with functional project managers.

Execution Phase

The best idea is useless unless you can bring it to market successfully—the job of the execution phase.

The execution phase develops profitable products for market launch and has to be as fast and as efficient as possible, which Goodyear primarily achieved through application of lean principles. This process also needs perfect alignment—there cannot be a handoff in the traditional sense, where the project is completed and handed off to the next function in the value stream. As I have noted before in this book, prior to lean, manufacturing used to wait and see; any early involvement was considered waste because the product was not even fully developed yet. It was like, "You guys (R&D) release this thing so we can change it." When the new product was finally handed to manufacturing, they redeveloped it to fit the manufacturing process, which took months to accomplish. Then product development had to get involved again and redesign pieces to get back to the original requirements. Today, manufacturing is involved in a new project from Day One, and the manufacturing/plant development portion takes only a couple of weeks—there is no handoff, and the plants hit the ground running when their time comes to industrialize the tire.

In the execution phase, the objective is to have everything that gets started finish on time as planned and deliver a profitable value stream. There should be only a limited number of projects in the execution phase at the same time, which makes the risk of missing the launch date relatively low.

When I was explaining this to Sam, he asked whether engineers and project managers could work on projects in both phases at the same time. He indicated that he personally had difficulty quickly switching mental gears in this way and was concerned that the mindset he needed in one project might inappropriately be carried over into another, that is, analyzing test results in execution and exploring new tire concept in kentou. We do encourage execution/kentou flexibility among engineers, but rarely do people work on projects in both phases *at the same time* because both phases require a different mindset.

Kentou Phase

The kentou phase develops knowledge and technology around promising ideas or concepts that eventually find their way into new products. Kentou deals with high uncertainty and a lot of variability, and the outcomes are not very predictable. In most cases, the deliverable of the kentou phase is knowledge that reduces the risk of the idea to the level where it can be integrated into a product in the PCP.

The kentou phase needs speed, efficiency, and alignment—just like the execution phase—to be effective, and many lean tools have been validated to increase speed in this phase as well, such as flow, late start, flexible resources, schedule at less than 100% capacity, and waste elimination. Other requirements of the kentou phase are not as easy to explain because they involve creation of innovation, especially disruptive innovations. And because of that the use of lean must be judicious. For instance, Sam asked how we will mitigate the negative effects of standard processes and other lean tools in the kentou phase. Fortunately, we learned a lot about effects on innovation from past improvement experiences and our lean experiences with the execution phase.

Opinions on how to innovate are as numerous as the stars, but I like to refer back to Steven Jobs' secrets to being innovative:

- *Do what you love.*
- *Put a dent in the universe.*
- *Creativity is connecting things.*
- *Say no to 1,000 things.*
- *Create "insanely great" experiences.*
- *Master the message.*
- *Sell dreams, not products.*[11]

Jobs' thoughts on innovation are more inspirational than actionable (we had a hard time figuring out how to dent the universe), so I asked Jim Euchner, Goodyear vice president of Global Innovations, and Paul Zaffiro, an innovation expert at P&G, for their opinions of what is important in an industrial kentou phase. They identified four simple and actionable criteria:

- Generate a product that the customer actually wants.
- Be as fast as possible to assure first-mover advantages.
- Enable innovation by developing capability, creating the space to innovate, developing the processes, and allocating resources appropriately.
- Develop a group of talented and motivated innovators.

Lean principles can support those four innovation requirements, but it requires what Sam would call heresy—*structure, discipline*, and the *right process*. Like many innovators, Sam thinks that creativity and innovation function best with maximum freedom, and maximum freedom cannot be structured and organized. Innovators are self-directed and talented in finding options that a structured process may miss, he argues. I believe that maximum freedom and an effective lean knowledge-building structure can coexist in the kentou phase. And we have plenty of proof at Goodyear that an innovative product department with no structure and no process is not the answer either.

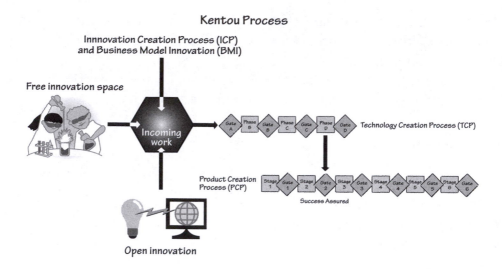

New ideas can come from many sources, both internal and external. Internal sources can be as simple as a suggestion box or free innovation space, which gives company innovators the freedom to explore and create. An important source of ideas within Goodyear is ICP and BMI, which start with the customer and lead to technologies developed to specifically address customer needs. We have increasingly looked for idea input from the outside, and we refer to this as "open innovation"—input from suppliers, outside research contractors, partners, universities, and so on.

At Goodyear, there can be a discretionary level of funding to explore ideas from all sources, including letting a Goodyear innovator tinker with ideas for some periods of time. But when an idea looks promising and significant amounts of R&D funding must be invested, the ideas and the concepts must go through gate A of the TCP. Incoming ideas are not judged the same way in the TCP as they are in the PCP. There is more focus on opportunities than return on investment or profitability.

Because variability and uncertainty is so much higher in the kentou phase, the rigor of the process must be less than is found in the well-defined and efficient PCP. We have not perfected the process of kentou within Goodyear, but we do have a recognizable process so that we can learn from what we do and lock in our learning, allowing us to improve. Without a process, too much knowledge created in kentou would be lost and wasted. In the kentou phase, it is sometimes important to know what not to do in addition to knowing what to do with ICP and TCP.

At Goodyear we found that lean principles can be used to improve the kentou phase. They help most to

- Create capacity and resources for innovation
- Manage innovation talent and serial innovators
- Add room for failure
- Standardize innovation
- Manage incoming work
- Manage the innovation process
- Avoid lean innovation killers

Lean principles are most effective when used *after* the fuzzier ideation piece (the right side of *Kentou Process* graphic). Sometimes less lean is better in order to not push an agenda that could affect creativity. Sam knows the "fuzzy frontend"[12] very well and he knows how fragile it is. Because of this, you need to make sure that when you apply lean concepts in kentou that they create real synergy with innovation without adverse effects.

Create Capacity and Resources for Innovation

If there is one item that all scholars, lean experts, and innovation experts agree upon, it is that lean in R&D can create capacity and resources for kentou and innovation, if a company, like Goodyear, decides to use them for that purpose. For many years at Goodyear, all the R&D capacity had been consumed by launching products, firefighting, and fixing problems that we should not have had in the first place. Lean product development returned capacity to us to innovate and develop longer-range technology.

Sam notes that creating capacity is only part of the challenge—correctly using it is much more difficult—and that too often capacity created is capacity cut during subsequent cost-reduction initiatives. In addition, there have been times when the R&D resources allocated to the kentou phase were not used for real innovation, and it was not for lack of projects. If you allocate money, you can be assured the money will be spent, but how? It took time for us to recognize how money was spent and figure out why it was spent that way.

This again seems to be a universal problem, and there are various schools of thought on how to apply new resources for innovation and what form of organization is the most appropriate to do this: colocated innovation teams with or without their own tools and resources, innovators integrated in the functions, think tanks or "rapid action teams," and even outsourced innovation. Between Goodyear and other companies, I have seen all of the above at work alone or in combination. I do not think that there is a "one size fits all" approach, but there are some best practices to consider:

- *Give them tools:* Regardless of the approach, innovators may need certain tools, including rapid prototyping and benchmarking capabilities. At our Luxembourg center, a new flexible manufacturing cell was added to provide new global prototype capabilities for innovations. In the past, resources and knowledge from nontire-related divisions of Goodyear (aerospace, industrial products) were used extensively when those entities existed. At Goodyear, we need to rely on outside sources now for that capability.

- *Leverage tools and best practices:* Although the R&D processes are different, some expertise and tools can be shared between the kentou and execution phase, such as market research, design systems and processes, materials labs, mold technology, testing, and prototyping. Any efficiencies gained by the use of the tools must be available to all phases of the development process.

- *Sharing increases capacity:* Leveraging and sharing of all global resources—like mold manufacturing, prototype building, testing—adds capacity. At Goodyear we used to dedicate part of that capacity to innovation to assure that the capacity was not consumed for firefighting and launch emergencies; this led to inefficiencies in the use of the resources. Today the capacity is available for whoever needs it, regardless of the phase. Engineers working in the kentou phase enjoy the same predictable delivery and speed for their services as the folks working in the execution phase. Funds are allocated through all the stages as needed.

- *Build a bridge from kentou to execution:* Alignment and early involvement of all stakeholders through the kentou process fosters collaboration and early stakeholder involvement for the execution requirements to follow, which makes the transfer of the new technology into the TCP easier.

- *Put like minds together:* Colocation of innovation teams has advantages and disadvantages. Innovators like to challenge each other, but colocation also can lead to isolation. It may not be possible to colocate all R&D teams as in Goodyear, but it may be possible and advantageous to just colocate the innovations teams.

- *Appropriately fund innovation:* All phases of the kentou should be funded appropriately. Funding should be allocated prudently and in small chunks.

■ *Must have a process and standards:* Learning and capturing the learning is difficult without a recognizable process and at least some standards to document best practices and learning.

Fund the Innovation Space

Innovation talent or serial innovators need a funded "space" where they can thrive. Funding affords a virtual component of intellectual freedom and some physical space in the form of an organization, resources, and an environment free of barriers.

Companies that excel at innovation, such as 3M and Google, allot discretionary money for free-space innovation, sometimes as much as 15%–20% of the total R&D budget. A recent visit to the 3M innovation center in St Paul, MN, convinced me that they get big returns for that money: reinventing mature products, creating new ones, and leveraging their technology across many products.

I, too, believe it is worth investing in the free space to give the *right* individuals—the serial innovators—the opportunity to explore and play around with ideas. This can be ideas that they come up with on their own or it can be evaluating or enhancing ideas that come from suppliers or from open innovation. This innovation space does not need to be "messy and chaotic," as many advocate. Complete freedom and "messiness" may not work for everybody; different inventors like different environments.

The funding of free space for innovation should be done with minimum administration. Sam says that if project cost-accounting is too rigorous or controlling, there will not be enough free space left for new ideas to sprout. He also says that funding that appears "random" should be avoided, as should excessive funding. A slightly underfunded environment drives more prudent thinking. If an innovator truly believes in their idea, they will try to find a way to get the funding they need.

Sam says that whom you give the discretionary money to is more important than the amount or any intentions attached to it. He says innovators do not work 8 hours a day on their ideas, but instead "they take their ideas home and think about them all weekend." The dollar amount provided to the innovator is much less relevant than the signal it sends to the innovator—you and your work are important and appreciated and we give you what you need.

Goodyear used to have several programs to seed innovation money: A discretionary funding program allocated money directly to an innovator or team (the best approach to innovation that I have experienced). Our Innovative Products department in the 1980s was a less successful funding mechanism—and knowing what we know now, I believe that approach could work well. (When the department was discontinued in the 1980s, key innovators like Sam were placed into other functions, and he and a few others continued to thrive, whereas most left the creative space and went back to regular engineering jobs.) Currently at Goodyear we experiment with various funding approaches again, based on our needs and a lot of learning from the past.

Manage Innovation Talent and Serial Innovators

Processes do not create innovation, people called innovators do.

What does the innovator have to do with lean? The innovator creates value for the customer! What could be more important? So you clearly want innovators and they must be developed and managed like any other talent in the company. This can be done by providing an environment that nurtures innovators and allows them to grow and flourish. Growing innovators—a dual-ladder career approach with upward movement without management responsibilities—is still quite rare and embryonic within Goodyear. It can be found in companies such as Google and 3M, where their approach helps to develop individuals like Sam and allows them to become serial innovators.

Innovation talent represents a tiny investment, but like most things in R&D it has a huge shadow; not managing innovation talent correctly is a huge loss. A distorted pareto rule applies to innovators: most of a company's innovation is created by a small percentage of people—much less than 1% of the scientists or engineers in a company, and sometimes only one or two individuals in the company. Greg Stevens and James Burley find that in the early stages of an innovation project, *one key individual* often plays a critical role in a project's outcome.[13] And based on my experiences, it is frequently the same innovator for many projects. That also was the case at Goodyear where my friend Sam was involved to some degree in most company innovations that occurred during in his career.

Sam says it is important to understand that the specifics of significant new ideas can never be anticipated within an annual operating plan (AOP), but are instead born out of independent, self-directed thinking and actions. As long as enough good ideas turn into products, few executives will ask where the ideas originated. But if leadership realizes there is a shortage of new ideas (and new products), then a metric is created to encourage more ideas and patents. But this scenario does not necessarily improve the innovation capability, but it will result in more patents.

Leaders cannot force real innovation, adds Sam. It only happens by supporting the innovators and creating the right environment. When I asked Sam to describe what made him such a good innovator, he says, "Why not look at yourself?" I worked with Sam on innovations, and I have 60 patents and trade secrets (patentable idea that the company decided not to publish as a patent) and invented/commercialized my share of new products. I did not recognize *myself* as an innovator. So how are you supposed to recognize your innovators in order to foster them?

Who are these rare, valuable people, the innovators? They will not jump out at you. You do not recognize them as innovators because they do much of their initial creative work in a stealth mode because their ideas are not yet on a sanctioned project list. They fly under the radar as long as possible, out of fear that if detected they will be shot down and forced to stop working on their idea. Good managers know when to look the other way, and allow a proven innovator some room to fly and develop their ideas, knowing that they will eventually have to come out in the open to get official funding.

Innovators are not the misfits or hard-to-place people, as is often the perception. At Goodyear, I sometimes had the impression that some colleagues in the innovation department were there because they did not fit in anywhere else. And although they love to create, innovators are not necessarily chaotic, right-brained people, who should have been an artist rather than an engineer.

What does this serial innovator look like, this man or woman who has a hand in so many of your company's innovations? Here are a few general characteristics and some specific traits found when they operate in a lean environment:

- *Balanced brain:* They are ambidextrous thinkers; they can be holistic, right-brain-oriented but they are left-brained enough to perform engineering work. They also can quickly switch between divergent and convergent thinking.
- *Questioning:* They question everything, including what they know, in order to learn and understand, and they learn quickly.
- *Scientists:* Technical innovators are first-class scientists, although they could cut corners in the scientific methods. Both technical depth and breadth are needed to innovate these days.
- *Company knowledge:* They know the company well—the people, culture, tolerance for risk, capabilities, and strengths and weaknesses. They also know the products of their company well, and they know the

products of competitors. They also know how not to trigger the corporate immune system.

- *Customer knowledge:* They know the customer and can empathize with them. They are good observers and often notice what nobody has seen before, allowing them to see connections between technologies, customer needs, opportunities, and so on.
- *Individualistic:* Self-starters, resourceful, and independent, they like to use the roads less traveled and collect many ideas in their heads. They also are very good at objectively evaluating their own ideas, dropping the bad ones for better ones.
- *Sharing:* They like to share and collaborate. If flying under the radar, it is not because they do not like to share—it is to avoid early, uninformed judgments, criticisms, and obstacles. To the contrary, they love to informally discuss ideas with trusted colleagues, who can build on or enhance their ideas and challenge their thinking.
- *Freedom seeking:* They need empowerment, which can be a problem in companies that lack tolerance for empowerment.

Louis Pasteur once said, "Chance only favors the mind which is prepared." Serial innovators need time to learn about the company, the customer, the technology—by the time they have acquired the knowledge, most have enough seniority to be trusted with the empowerment and freedom they need. Self-motivated, empowered innovators do not need much supervision, but the occasional gemba walk or informal updates are good ideas. This also shows respect for the work they do, especially in an environment that does not have a career plan for innovators. Innovator deliverables also are assessed using a different, longer period of time, and should examine large-spectrum issues, such as creating customer value, and not a percentage of successful ideas.

There also can be problems with innovators. If you let some of them do what outsiders consider "play," some will do nothing but play and outsiders will fret about that. Sometimes you must "kill the innovator" and commercialize the product. Sam was able to do this on his own. He balanced his right-brained tendencies by partnering with left-brained colleagues, folks who could pick up the ideas and do the work that Sam knew that he was not so good at.

Once you recognize your innovators, manage and make the best use of them (see *Serializing Serial Innovators*).

Serializing Serial Innovators

Sam endorses the following methods in getting the most out of innovators:

- *Empower*—Innovators are self-starters and self-motivated. Their mind is on their ideas every minute of the day. They should be trusted, so long as they have a track record of eventually delivering. Many leaders have a hard time with this trust and want to always see what people are doing and need to supervise them in some manner, such as daily or weekly activity reports. Less is better in terms of constant project updates and financial justification. But remember that empowerment is an earned status.
- *Show respect*—A good way to show respect to an innovator is a regular gemba walk for a show and tell. Appreciative inquiry works well, and a good innovator likes a challenging discussion about technology and customer needs. Trust and respect go well together.
- *Full process involvement*—Engage innovators in all phases of new product development: ideation, gate decisions, and even in the execution phase. Encourage innovators to collaborate with all value-stream stakeholders, both in R&D and outside R&D, to assure successful commercialization.
- *Give them space*—Create (and fund) an appropriate innovation environment. This can range from open innovation space to a more structured and integrated environment. Small teams or individuals function well in that environment. To some degree, there should be a process to capture the learning and improve.

Innovation Teams

Marty Wartenberg is an innovation consultant, former R&D executive, and an instructor at the University of California, Irvine Extension. At the AME Innovation Summit, he told how he seeded money for innovation. He got the biggest returns when he seeded money to a team or a project manager as opposed to individual innovators.[13]

I increasingly see that practice in industry today, and it is especially popular in the software industry. Inspired by the lean startup thinking, some companies establish small, permanent teams called "rapid development teams" or something similar. They often colocate the teams.

The following are common characteristics of innovation teams:

- Staffed with very creative individuals, including a variety of complementary talent, which gives the team the critical mass to take ideas quickly to a stage where they can get implemented or where they can get picked up by the existing development processes.
- Self-directed or -managed by a project manager, who also knows how to foster synergy between the members.
- Equipped with capabilities and tools that are required by the nature of their work, such as the right computers, modeling tools, quick prototyping capability, and 3D printing.
- Manage their work in "sprints" (quick learning cycles with well-defined deliverables and funding).
- Too small to be self-sufficient, the teams must involve all other parts of the organization early and collaborate to successfully implement their ideas or projects.

Some companies call their teams a "think tank." I do not like that idea because, based on my experiences, just "thinking" up ideas and then "selling" them is a difficult and frustrating endeavor. Ideas are a lot easier to sell and obtain funding for when a certain amount of homework has been done and maybe crude prototypes are available as well. Innovation teams should be empowered to do something with their ideas, beyond think of them. These teams represent a relatively small investment, and they should be given the freedom and the empowerment to think outside of the box, but they also must responsibly use the resources they receive.

Sam was a team leader on a more traditional R&D team and enjoyed the team approach. He would discuss every idea that came up and empower the innovator to further develop the idea if it looked promising. Sam says that the team members picked up his lack of enthusiasm as a signal to come up with more convincing data or redevelop their ideas. Team leaders can have a large influence on the team members, not only by coaching and mentoring, but in a light-handed way through the leader's reactions and behaviors.

Add Room for Failure

Part of the innovation space is room for failure. Innovators operate in an environment of high uncertainty and variability and they consider many ideas and run many experiments, most of which will be unsuccessful. This is part of creating knowledge and cannot be considered waste.

Just as we add buffers for variability with flow in product development, buffers also are appropriate to cover for innovation failures, which are part of every learning process. Buffers for failure may include a portion of the budget dedicated to "write-offs." You may have to call it "learning" or "knowledge development" in the budget to get away with it, which is often true—there can be some knowledge generated by a failed experiment (provided the knowledge is captured and shared).

Failures should be celebrated and rewarded just like the success of a good idea. Chris Helsel, former director Global Technology Projects, says that it is important to recognize failed experiments, otherwise people will continue to work on ideas not worth pursuing and hope for success. Another important factor in the room for failure is making clear to everyone the consequences for failed experiments or ideas. It must be seen as OK to try something worthwhile but risky, and then talk about it even if it was not successful.

Just as an innovator must admit failure, you need to be able to accept an innovator's negative self-assessment as a positive in the personal performance review: "I tried many things in the last six months, but nothing worked." Recognize that the innovator learned something, narrowed down the field of possibilities, and hopefully documented the learning. But then also follow up, "Did you fail fast enough?" and "Are you still working on it?" These cover the two "must dos" regarding space to fail: Make sure you have a good learning system so that you only fail once. If you fail, try to do it fast. For example, experiments should be constructed so that the decisive yes/no answers are assessed right at the beginning.

Fear of failure certainly leads to a tendency for engineers to avoid risk. This is especially true if risk-taking could lead to missing metrics or personal goals. So you might create incentives for risk-taking, make shining examples out of those who take risks, and even add "risk-taking" to people's performance standards. Sam says it may be more appropriate to set the right standards for risk-taking and encourage the right behaviors through personal performance-management systems.

Although innovation creation has a higher risk than projects in the execution phase, there is no reason why that risk should not be managed appropriately. For example, Sam managed risk by always using a fallback position, like a more conservative design, when he developed a high-risk concept, especially when time was limited. The fallback position may look like waste to a lot of people, but I would like to call it good risk management.

Standardize Innovation

Sam will tell me that broaching the topic of standards with innovation is leading readers into dangerous territory. How can you standardize creativity? But having a recognizable process with minimal standards is necessary to establish an environment for learning and making sure that the learning is properly captured and reused. We have had many examples from our Goodyear innovation history where we should have had a process and standards, and, without them, have lost valuable innovation knowledge.

Today at Goodyear we have developed a recognizable ICP and the roles and responsibilities established to improve those processes as we learn. Do we overburden it with lean standards and stifle creativity. No. But without structure and a process—one that continues to evolve rapidly—it would be impossible to develop this important capability.

Manage Incoming Work

Managing incoming work is unique to product development—manufacturing and other operations do not have that problem, and we cannot look at them for best practices or proven principles. At the same time, the correct management of incoming work and working on the right things is most likely the biggest effect that an R&D organization can have on the profitability of the business. This also is one of the most challenging responsibilities of an R&D organization and one that is not always executed well.

When I give presentations or teach workshops at conferences, I like to ask participants; "What is the biggest problem in your R&D organization?" "Too much work" is by far the most frequent answer. When I ask for more details, it becomes clear that the root cause for "too much work" is an uncontrollable amount of projects, nonproject work and technical activities in the system, and an expectation that all must be done regardless of available resources.

Early in our lean journey, an engineer from the Materials Science department came to see me and asked whether I could help him. He said that the average time for one of his projects was 3–5 years. I asked him for a list of projects, and I counted 42. The engineer said that he could finish about 12 projects every year: cycle time = 3.5 years.

So why did this engineer and so many other ones have so much WIP?

- *Always having the right answer:* Within the Goodyear Innovative Products department, we were supposed to have an answer when marketing or management asked for something regardless of what they asked for. Unfortunately, they never asked for the disruptive concepts we were working on.
- *Never say "no":* In the case of the engineer with the 42 projects, the work was about approving new suppliers. Every time a potential supplier called the purchasing organization with a "new" and (promised to be) better raw material, purchasing forwarded a request to the materials organization to work on a technical approval for the material. In most companies, it is inappropriate to turn down a request for work. A director asks an engineer for something (other than money), and the automatic answer is "yes." Rarely does the director understand the details associated with the "yes" answer, and what engineer would challenge the director about the new work that the director has requested?
- *Pet projects:* Many people on all levels have their pet projects that seem to never die or end, regardless of the lack of progress. These pet projects range from an engineer trying to satisfy a curiosity or prove a point, to an endless attempt to make good on a long-forgotten promise.
- *No data:* Many new projects enter the R&D process with not a lot of data, which makes it difficult to make good decisions. Nonetheless, engineers will prefer to start projects just in case data become available later.
- *Lack of a process:* Even when there are data, there is often no process by which to evaluate it and make a decision. This also contributes to a lack of learning. Since there is no process, even if a decision is made, there is no going back and checking if the right decision is made. A good

process makes consistent decisions and goes back to see whether the decision was correct. If not, the process is changed to improve the decision for next time.

■ *Risk aversion:* No one wants to make the mistake of missing a potentially great project or greenlighting a potential misjudgment, so everything is accepted. This is especially true in a culture where careers are built by never making a mistake.

■ *Work equals value:* Being inundated with work gives people the feeling of being needed, which provides a sense of job security. We have experienced many times that people would not release work early, even if it was done. Engineers like to be busy, and hording work is not uncommon.

■ *Fun:* It is fun to explore new things. Unfortunately, the experiments sometimes do more to satisfy the curiosity of an engineer rather than to generate new knowledge or a new innovation.

In many companies, engineers find their own work and they flood themselves. In companies that have a good process for managing incoming work that should rarely happen. *When I hired into the company, I was swamped with work within a few months … and have been swamped until I learned about lean.*

Stuffing an R&D organization with too many projects can have severe consequences:

■ The work in the R&D organization progresses very slowly as Little's law predicts. We have seen how important speed is.

■ Resources are excessively distributed among projects, both good and bad, and so potentially great projects find no resources.

Why is it so difficult to make a decision? Sooner or later we must make a decision and separate the good projects from the time-wasters. But these decisions, like no other, can be the difference between being a profitable company or not. And worse, despite the importance of this, leaders, managers, and engineers often do not know *how* to make the decision.

Most people think that companies have secret methods held by leadership to guide an organization to new ideas and innovations. In reality, leaders typically make a decision only after the project has been worked on for quite some time and there is enough data—obvious data—to make the right decision. And if not enough good data is available to the leader, you know what will happen: more time and work are invested. Some people claim to have superior intuition and can smell the good opportunities, but that process lacks a scientific base and contributes to the misperception that the leader always will have the answer.

Sam thinks there is something to the fact that certain people seem to be able to "smell" the opportunities. He says people do not have a sixth sense, they just have more and better knowledge and experience, and they can make the right connections in their head based on what they know. So given that, the decision of what to work on should be easy when there is

- A lot of information available, including financial data
- An obvious need
- A strategic reason
- An obvious opportunity

We had concluded that engineers spend about 75%–80% of their time doing engineering work, but that engineering work comes in from many sources: It can be project work, such as developing a new tire or collaborating on the launch of a new product, or it could be investigating new technology. But it could also be work on behalf of a plant, a supplier, or from another internal source. It could even be functional work assigned by a manager or director, or it could be developing a new capability or improving processes.

Most companies have at least an appropriate gating process for new product work, but they rarely have a process for all other work that does not go through the new product gating process. First focus on the work not directly related with the creation of a new product, which we found to be quite significant at Goodyear. Here are two good examples of that kind of work from my company:

- *Small requests:* Engineers always get phone calls from the plants to tune designs and/or modify specs or materials. Those requests normally are aimed at increasing the plant efficiency and sometimes the quality of the process. Engineers would work on all requests. When we added up all the time for that work, we noticed that we only charged back a mere fraction of the work to the plants. When we started to charge back for *all* the work that the engineers did for the plants, manufacturing started to "filter" their requests. The plants now send only the ones that create appropriate value, which frees the engineer's time to work other projects.

■ *Material-source approvals:* Another example of incoming work are requests to approve a new material source. Our material organization was swamped with these requests because purchasing passed every request from a vendor on to R&D. Purchasing and R&D got together and looked at the approved vendor list, and we found that we had many more approvals than we would ever need to run our business (how about that for a lean opportunity), so we made a strategic decision on how many suppliers are really needed in each material category and identified the criteria to select the vendors. Now, every request for a source approval is evaluated by a cross-functional team against those criteria, and only the few that add value are pursued. This initiative reduced the source approval work in the Material Science department by more than 50% without affecting value-added work.

Good criteria to assess incoming work are not always easy to come by, so in the absence of good criteria, there is a method that always works: the WIP-limit method. (You saw an example of that method in *Chapter 4*, where it was applied to our product development process.) This method establishes the total number of projects in the organization or maximum projects per person and keeps that number constant. This means that a new project can only come in if one finishes, gets stopped, or is parked. This method forces the organization to evaluate new work versus existing work, and the organization can learn very quickly from the decisions that are made and establish a good process. We also learned that this method provides the visibility that is needed to have the right discussion with the person or the function requesting the work. It is rarely politically correct to say "no." This visibility helps to justify the "no" answer. What I have often found is that the requestor removes another request from the hopper or cancels the current request.

Lean R&D Principle: Manage incoming work.

In a lean R&D organization, there must be a process to manage incoming work that needs significant resources (except maybe for the free innovation space). Decisions about good projects, ideas, and work versus not-so-good projects must be made as early as possible, and it may have to be revisited if more information becomes available. Failure to manage incoming work not only creates waste, but it also plugs up the R&D pipeline so that there are no resources to work on the truly great ideas. Capacity cannot be created to match an unlimited flow of possible work—a process to manage incoming work could be one of the first and most important lean initiatives a company can start in R&D.

There are many tools available to manage incoming work—a gating process and quick assessment cycles are two of them. If the right data and information is available, the decision is easy—the problem is that is rarely the case in R&D. It is hard to make a good decision with a small amount of information, but not making *a decision* with the information available creates many problems down the road. The decision may not get easier as time passes, but the consequences will weigh heavier on the process as time passes.

This problem is not limited to the kentou phase—it happens everywhere in an R&D organization. Processes must be established that help to make consistent decisions about incoming work and that improve the decision-making over time and capture the learning. This also requires good visibility of all current WIP and work coming down the pipe.

At Goodyear: Except for some discretionary exploratory work, ICP, TCP, and PCP are used to assess projects that need major resources. Since the objectives of both processes are different, the assessment of incoming work also is specific to each process. We also established a process to assess service and work that was not related to new products coming into the functions from the plants (spec maintenance), purchasing (approve more suppliers), management (ideas from leaders or colleagues), and many other sources. Today all incoming work (above a given threshold) is assessed according to merit and available capacity, and sometimes quick assessment experiments are run. At Goodyear, we also have started to manage incoming work to develop new capabilities.

Managing incoming work is not only a problem in the kentou phase—although it has the highest consequences in that phase—but it applies to any work that comes into any phase of the R&D process. Although the subject of this chapter is mostly the kentou phase, I need to discuss both phases in the context of incoming work.

Manage Work Entering the Product Creation Process

New project work enters the PCP in stage 1 of the gated process. If new technology from the TCP becomes available, it enters the process through gate 2 (Success Assured).

To manage the work coming into the execution phase, start from the top. There should be some kind of a direction in the company on *what* product development should focus on: the products, the market segments, the technology. R&D must take its cues from there. Of course, that corporate strategy must get adjusted on a regular basis because markets and consumers change. At Goodyear we use product roadmaps that establish the new product portfolio for many years in the future. These roadmaps are based on the corporate strategy. Often decisions in the execution phase are more about product suitability, capabilities to supply a tire for an OEM, and the best timing for a launch. The new product roadmaps also define what support work is required (manufacturing capacity, manufacturing capability, distribution requirements, etc.).

At Goodyear, new-product decisions are formally made at the gate reviews with the leaders accountable for the business, but most recommendations are prepared by a team of responsible experts, including the regional technical director and the respective directors of the functions involved (marketing, manufacturing, and distribution) and their respective staffs.

The cross-functional team looks at the portfolio of projects because every decision on one project affects many other projects. For example, if a new product comes in, an existing product has to come out of the line, completely or at least partially. The new product may have to be manufactured in a certain plant that requires transfer of other products. Every decision also includes the cost of R&D and any other potential incremental cost. Most of the time products and the complete portfolio are assessed based on NPV (net present value): cash coming in minus the cash going out, as if both the existing and new project would happen today.

Due to the interaction of all the projects in the portfolio, the complete portfolio NPV is the deciding factor. The interaction also makes it difficult to estimate an accurate "profit from new products." Since at Goodyear it is virtually impossible to calculate that number, Goodyear has targets for new *content* in the portfolio, such as 30% of sales from products less than 3 years old. These targets were established by years of experience and learning. This is similar to the vitality index used by 3M, although the absolute value varies by business and company.

Jeff McElfresh, a former Consumer Business Operations manager who helped develop the PCP and the lean product development process at Goodyear, explains that the decisions about new products (what is added/removed to the portfolio or the roadmap and the best timing) is done by a very simple calculation: the total portfolio NPV with the proposed new product—factoring in all development costs, new tooling, advertising, launch, and other costs for the new product—has to be higher than the total NPV of the portfolio with the product that would get replaced. That calculation can also be used to determine the best time of a launch, or the lean COD calculation can be used for launch timing.

At Goodyear, we were always good at figuring out what products to add to the line, but removing existing products was a challenge: the original investment of the existing product has been paid off, the financials look good, and some dealers may still like the old product. Failure to remove old product, however, creates unnecessary complexity and waste. What made the difference at Goodyear was the target of new product in the portfolio, a lot of discipline, and saying "no."

Cost of Delay (COD)

If a flight is delayed, the airline may have to rebook and/or provide overnight accommodations for a lot of connecting passengers who subsequently miss their flights—there is a cost for every minute that the plane arrives late. There also is a cost for every day that a project launches late. Not having a new product when the market is ready for it results in lost sales. Profit also is lost if old products must be sold at a lower price to attract buyers because the new product is not available yet (*see Chapter 1*).

Staggering launches, leveling decisions, needing additional resources, and other timing decisions must be based on their effect on the profitability of the value stream and be calculated using good financial data, particularly regarding the COD: that is, COD versus the cost of added resources or other countermeasures.

COD is certainly not the only financial consideration that business leaders and project managers need to look at (NPV is another), but it should be on the list (see *Goodyear COD Calculation*). If your company is anything like ours, you may have a challenge in getting your financial organization and all other stakeholders to buy into this concept and agree with the data used for the calculation. People with experience in "profit estimating" know this is not a terribly accurate science. As Don Reinertsen says, "A less than perfect COD still beats the best intuition."[15]

There is a margin of error to every COD calculation and it can be significant. In my experience, when COD is used to justify decisions (e.g., spend extra resources to move a project with a high COD ahead), the cost of the resources is usually a mere fraction of the COD and easily falls within the margin of error. For that reason, I do not advocate ultimate precision in the calculation of the COD.

Lean R&D Principle: Consider cost of delay (COD) when scheduling projects and allocating time and capacity.

Cost of delay (COD) is the loss in project value if a project is late or the additional value that could be made if a project was moved up in a schedule (i.e., beating competitors to market). The simplest method is to express the project value in potential profit.

Most projects are buffered with time because companies find it difficult to put a price or cost on time. If companies do put a price or a cost on time, they are often surprised how high the cost of delay is compared to countermeasures to avoid the loss of time, like adding more resources. The cost of project time can be assessed by computing a COD, and COD should be used in any project decision where time is a factor (delay, pull ahead, priorities, etc.).

The COD should not be viewed as another parameter that R&D invented. It must be something the business calculates and uses to make key decisions.

At Goodyear: We developed a standard method to calculate cost of delay and provided training on how to use it. Last year at Goodyear a decision was made to move a large project up by 6 months based on a COD calculation. The whole team had to travel to the plant to help get all the prototype tires built, but the extra development cost was justified based on the high COD.

COD for continuous events are easier to calculate than for "discontinuous" events or events with strategic consequences. For example, missing a winter-tire launch makes you wait a year for the next opportunity. Missing an OEM submission can exclude you from the program, forfeiting all R&D effort invested. In these cases, the consequences are often clear enough without ultimate accuracy in the COD calculation.

Goodyear COD Calculation

$$\frac{\text{Project financial benefit value}}{\text{Project benefit opportunity days}} + \text{Any daily fees or penalties (if applicable)} = \text{Daily cost of delay}$$

This general formula may be easier to understand when the financial benefit value is potential profits. In that case, you divide the total potential profit by the number of days and add daily fees or penalties.

Manage Work Coming into Technology Creation Process

First, let us again consider from where incoming work arrives at Goodyear's TCP and PCP. There are generally three sources (see *Kentou Process* earlier in this chapter):

- *ICP and BMI:* ICP and BMI create alignment with the business so that Goodyear only develops what the customer and the business need (market-back innovation). This process defines what Goodyear will need globally in the market over the next 5–6 years (needs and concepts), but does not necessarily produce specific ideas and solutions—those are generated and funded later in TCP.

  Romain Hansen, the current director Global Technology Projects, says that originally the ICP was used to brainstorm ideas for the TCP. "Today we use the process to figure out with all the global stakeholders new opportunities to work on, then we generate the ideas and develop the technology." Good examples of this are development of the air maintenance system and the nonpneumatic tire. The air maintenance system is based on the alerts that customers with tire pressure monitoring systems get when tire pressure drops below a minimum setting. We discovered that customers became annoyed at having to go to the pump every time this happened, so we created the concept for a tire that automatically maintains proper air pressure. Whether this concept turns into a commercial success remains to be seen—the project is now in the TCP, where technology will be created that a customer will be expected to value and pay accordingly.

■ *Free innovation space*: Research has shown that the biggest innovations over the last 50 years came mostly out of R&D. It generally was a scientist who saw a customer need and solved it with a technical solution or who connected a new technology to an opportunity in the market. These breakthrough innovations rarely come from a market research program or directly from customers. Most inventions never had a clear path from idea to commercial success.

It is important to provide discovery opportunities for the inventors, the serial innovators. This can be done by giving them opportunities to observe and to explore. There are many names used for this phase of the innovation process, one of the most common is "skunk works," which supposedly dates back to Lockheed Martin's work on rockets in the 1940s and was associated with the Li'l Abner cartoon.

■ *Open innovation*: Receiving ideas from customers was common, but other outside sources are relatively new to many companies, including Goodyear. There is an abundance of resources out there with an enormous potential that should be tapped. Google claims that today they receive most of their new ideas from outside sources.

These days most innovation happens on a relatively high level of science and technology, so the more knowledgeable the idea source is, the higher the chances are that the idea can go somewhere. In this context, good outside sources for open innovation are

– *Customers*: Your customers, especially OEMs, are probably your best source—you may not get ideas that you can implement immediately, but you can get good input on future needs.

– *Suppliers:* Goodyear successfully developed several innovative products based on input from a supplier, which sometimes resulted in an exclusive supply for that company. For example, the "Silent Armor" concept was based on a carbon fiber material developed in cooperation with a supplier.

– *Research partners:* Surendra Chawla, senior director External Science & Technology, explains that Goodyear first pursued a broader range of open innovation, including the use of some innovation service providers and software packages. This approach was not effective because it was too broad and too general. Due to the high technical nature of innovation today, Goodyear had to look at more specialized sources around the world. Chawla says, "We are collaborating with private and publically funded research institutions, including organizations like SBIR [Small Business Innovation Research] to focus ideas on our specific needs." Goodyear's efforts have led to ideas being found for the use of silica from the ash of rice husks (technology discovered in India). Goodyear also collaborates with Qingdao University of Science and Technology in China to determine if trans-polyisoprene (TPI), which the university developed, can be used in tires. Sam cautions that external innovation may tend to prevent companies from generating their own capability.

Assess Incoming Work into TCP

All concepts, needs, ideas, and suggestions must eventually show up at the front door of the TCP, if significant amounts of money or resources are needed to further their development. Some ideas come in from innovators funded through the innovation space and may already be partially developed, and so these ideas could be ready to have a project manager and team assigned to them. Other ideas are embryonic and more work is required to establish their potential. Some input may just be a customer problem that may need to stay in the ICP for a little more clarification and exploration. Regardless of the kind of input, experience has shown the following:

- There rarely is a shortage of input.
- You can rarely match the flood of ideas with capacity.
- There are gems in the flood of ideas, but they are hard to find.
- Companies tend to err on the side of working on everything that looks promising for fear of missing a gem.
- Companies hopelessly overload themselves with work (WIP).
- Many projects last a long time.
- It is not enough to assess ideas coming in—they must be reassessed many more times when in the first stages of the process.

If you plot innovations from the last 30 years on a grid of project value versus uncertainty or risk, most ideas fall in the low-uncertainty/low-value category. Innovation experts call these ideas "incremental" innovation. This is the area of innovation where familiar scientific, logical thinking can still be used. Incremental innovation still largely relies on known technology and existing customers. This also is the area of largest benefits from lean, where true customer value can be established—the area where customers can tell you how products should be modified or what they consider real value. But this also is where your competition will play, where it can be hard to secure meaningful patents, and where it is hard to get a jump on the competition.

Only about 5% of ideas venture into the high-uncertainty/high-value area, which innovation experts call "disruptive innovation." This is where you can get a jump on the competition. Mats Magnusson says that the incremental innovation looks more like a strategy game, such as chess, while the disruptive innovation is closer to a game of roulette.[16]

Disruptive innovations generate the largest profit, but for most companies that area of innovation is the least explored. Customers do not ask for products in that area, current technology mostly does not apply, the customer base may change, and it really takes a crystal ball to access and explore ideas in that area. Nonetheless, if I had my choice, I would ask the serial innovators to concentrate as much as possible on the disruptive part of the grid.

Sam says that incremental innovation can and should always be pursued to at least stay even with competitors. Disruptive innovation is not an extrapolation, so it cannot be anticipated. There is a very high degree of uncertainty and potential risk because it is a virgin path. The upside opportunity of high-value/high-uncertainty is potentially significantly greater because it generates a jump in customer value, it is much less likely competitors also are pursuing it, and it will be hard for competitors to catch up or copy.

Many lean principles can be applied to the incremental part, but for disruptive innovation, Sam says that less lean is sometimes better than a lot of lean. Ries' *The Lean Startup*[8] and other startup literature have shown us that lean has a place in the disruptive innovation, and I will try to show examples from my experience at Goodyear.

Ideas, concepts, problems, and solutions that arise from around the entire innovation grid will show up at the front door of Goodyear's TCP, eventually seeking funding, so they can move through the TCP. Disruptive ideas can come in well defined, and incremental ideas can still have uncertainty—the assessment process must manage that uncertainty. The assessments discussed in the following are not limited to a onetime assessment of work coming into the TCP, but the same thinking applies to subsequent reevaluation of ideas in the early stages of the process.

Before getting into the lean principles that can help us find solutions to this selection process, remember how things used to be at Goodyear. Before lean product development, there were not a lot of resources left to do fundamental research or develop new ideas. There were pockets, of course, where that development happened, but there were certainly not a lot of visible results. As soon as resources became available, and a director position with staff was created, there was a flurry of new ideas and projects were initiated. When Chris Helsel took on the responsibility for that organization a few years later, he was faced with huge WIP—he had inherited an organization that still did not have a process to manage the front door or the early phases of the process.

The other problem that Chris was facing was the lack of visibility. Several people worked independently on the same project, some in one innovation center and others in another center. Other folks thought it was too early to talk about their projects, and some people were upset that somebody would question their work, their capability, and their integrity. Chris says that at one time the leadership got so frustrated with the situation that they considered just canceling everything and making every project come in through the front door again. It did not come to that. Together with those working in this process, a governing process was established for TCP (phase-gate process), and key lean principles were used to manage the incoming work and the reassessments.

Projects underway in the free innovation space are not exempt from showing up at the TCP front door. I believe there cannot be unlimited time and resources for ideas in any of the exploration phases. At one time or another, we need to invite the inventors or innovators to present their ideas at the front door. Rob Deanna, manager Technology Planning, who oversees that process, says that from time to time he asks the inventors to take 2 weeks to get their stuff together and present their ideas to the gatekeepers. Rob says that most inventors or innovators hate this part of the process—they would rather keep tinkering or find a better opportunity.

This point of innovation reflection reminds me when I had to "write up" my thesis in college: it was a lot more fun to continue running experiments. And based on the innovator's presentation, the decision at the gate can be to assign a project manager and fund the development through the TCP, let the innovator continue with their work and keep the funding the way it is, or freeze the work. The key is that after somebody worked on an idea for a while, it has to come out of stealth and be visible.

The first criterion that all ideas are evaluated against is its *fit with Goodyear's overall strategy*. For example, the idea must have something to do with the businesses that Goodyear currently pursues or plans to pursue in the future. Of course, if an idea does not fit, that must not be the end. The idea could still be patented with the intent to sell the patent or somebody else could be licensed to pursue the idea.

Another key criterion is the establishment of *knowledge gaps*. Some of the proposals that come through the front door may come from an innovator who already used the funding in the free space to establish feasibility. Proposals from other sources (ICP, open innovation) often are general observations or nothing more than the identification of a problem. In that case, it is a lot more work to establish the knowledge gaps. It is important to know the knowledge gaps before a decision is made on investing time and money.

In some cases, especially with ideas coming from the ICP, the BMI process, or from the outside, there may be more of a problem identified than a solution or there is not quite enough definition yet. In that case, focused ideation sessions are organized. There are many ideation tools that can be used and plenty of literature on them. A lot of people promote fresh, virgin thinking in brainstorming, but it takes quite some knowledge and expertise to make meaningful contributions in that environment. Brainstorming experts say that it is better to take outrageous ideas and make them feasible than to take conservative ideas and build them up.

If there is enough good information about an idea, especially one that falls into the incremental innovation category, the TCP can be followed. But when the crystal ball comes in play, it becomes a little more difficult. When we talked about work coming into the execution phase, I mentioned that there is not a lot of secret wisdom available in companies to make the right decisions with the minimum information. That is the same for the kentou phase, but lean startup thinking can help, especially where much less information is available than in the execution phase.

Regardless of the process you use to sort the good from the bad, there are a few key issues to address:

◼ The closer you get to the disruptive area, the less information is available.
◼ The less information that is available, the harder it is to make the right decision. Hindsight will reveal what should have been the right decision later, and that scares people.
◼ The chances to pick the *right* idea are proportional to the volume of ideas that are tried.

- The volume of ideas that are accepted will quickly clog up the system, and high WIP means long cycle times and that will negatively impact speed, and speed matters.

Learning must take place, and, regardless of the process used, the process must get better over time. This also will help innovators or inventors assess their own ideas in advance and set clear expectations. There are four situations that have to be managed:

1. There is a poor idea and we decide not to pursue it.
2. There is a good idea and we decide to pursue it.
3. There is a poor idea and we decide to pursue it.
4. There is a good idea and we decide not to pursue it.

You probably do not have problem managing the first and second situations. But how should you handle the third and fourth? What is worse, discarding the good or pursuing the bad?

Most lean and innovation scholars will agree that pursuing a bad idea is worse than discarding a good idea because if you do not have a process to discard the bad, your system will plug up with excess WIP so fast that you never find room to work on a good idea. At Goodyear, we validated this many times over the years. Maybe that is why one of Steven Job's innovation secrets is, "Say no to 1,000 ideas."[11]

So how can we tell the bad ideas from the good ones, especially if there is very little information available, we do not have a crystal ball, and we do not want to rely on intuition and sheer luck? Is there a lean tool for this? Yes. You will not find it in traditional lean literature, but there are definitely hints in the literature that covers lean startups and entrepreneurism. I believe that even Womack would agree that traditional lean has kind of failed this situation. Many R&D hardliners, on the other hand, will not even think about allocating money for that kind of work—playing the lottery may have a better return.

Those who know the game of soccer will agree that the more shots that you take on goal, the higher your chances are to score. You are likely to score more runs if you put more men on base in baseball. Your chances of winning the lottery are higher if you buy more tickets. But what if you could instead buy some insights into the winning numbers to hedge your bet? For example, what would you invest to learn if the winning number ends with an even or an odd number—that would dramatically increase your chances of winning. If you start working on a new idea, you generate more and more insights—you gain knowledge and you reduce uncertainty, and the investment increases your chances to make the right decision.

Some lean innovation scholars illustrate this method with lean startups, especially fashion companies. Fashion companies like Zara throw many concepts on the market every season and test the consumer acceptance, then they quickly produce what sells. They also carefully assess the value of a lost sale versus having leftover merchandise at the end of the selling season. There is a healthy markup on fashion garments, and you must be able to sell as many as possible when the season peaks. They may have leftovers at the season end sale and have to sell those close or below cost during the sale, but they certainly made money when they had demand and held plenty of stock during the high selling phase.

Every smart bread baker makes the same calculation: buns only cost pennies to make, but fresh buns can sell at $1 or more when they are piping hot. Do bakers want to be out of stock by mid-morning and miss additional sales, or should they have leftovers to give to the food bank at the end of the day? Of course, the calculation would be different for the baker or the fashion company if there was a high holding cost or if the investment in the inventory was high or would go up over time—then it would be more comparable to evaluating ideas.

For us at Goodyear, the situation is different than that of the garment maker or baker: tire makers run out of winter-tire inventory by December (when those products sell the best) because weather is unpredictable, tires are expensive to produce, it costs money to hold them in inventory, and last-season's tires are not worth as much the following winter.

An example that is closer to R&D work like that of Goodyear and many companies can be found at hospitals, especially rehab centers. Forget for a moment "managed care"—let us focus on the principles.

A rehab organization has incoming work (patients). Of course, the rehab clinic accepts every patient who comes in (unless they run out of beds or therapists). Most patients come in with doctors' orders, and nobody knows whether the therapy is right and works until it is tried. With every day of therapy, the rehab organization invests more into the patient and the rehab costs accumulate for whoever pays the bills.

A good therapist knows how to start the therapy to quickly assess what will work the best, and the therapist assesses progress regularly. He or she changes the therapy as needed, and the therapist stops the treatment when there is evidence that the therapy will not meet the goals. A good therapist also tries to get the patient discharged as quickly as possible, either because the patient has recovered or because the therapy does not work.

We should look at ideas the same way a rehab center:

- Takes on a lot of new ideas, as many as we have capacity for.
- Discards the bad ones with the minimum investment of resources and time.
- Identifies the good ones quickly and put them on the right path to development.
- Reassesses the good ones on a regular basis.

The more time we take to make decisions on ideas, the worse the economics become. We also pay an enormous secondary price for the inventory because high WIP shuts the door to other good ideas. Some people call this process "fast fail"—I do not like that name because we want to succeed in this process, not fail.

We must also look at ideas the way the therapist looks at incoming patients. We have to plan the investigation or experiments around the quickest go/no-go decisions, focusing on the minimum information needed for a decision and getting that information with the least investment in the shortest amount of time.

Many companies have started their lean implementation with exactly these quick learning steps on assessing new ideas because they realized that the benefits that lean can bring them in speeding up the learning cycles can have large benefits on their innovation and their profitability. This is especially true when quick consumer testing is required. Information about lean startups is fueling this movement.

Some lean scholars assert that even if an idea does not work, you still generate valuable knowledge when you work on it. This must be carefully interpreted: if you work on a bad idea, you will not generate a lot of useful knowledge, regardless of how long you keep generating knowledge. You should, though, learn to not invest into that same mistake again.

Romain Hansen, director Global Technology Projects, adds that often leaders shave some funding from *all* their WIP to balance the budget. He advises to the contrary: if you have to reduce your work, it is better to find the least promising projects and freeze them, and keep the other projects fully funded.

One big difference between the therapy example and product development is that we do not "discharge" ideas. In fact, experience at Goodyear and other companies has taught us that there is something out there that is called the "innovation chasm."[17] Innovations often need several start attempts to take off. For that reason, ideas should not be discarded but they should be frozen. Freezing them also is less traumatic to the innovator, and getting buy-in from stakeholders or teams is more likely for a freeze. Freezing an idea also allows it to emerge another day. For example, tire pressure sensors have been around since the early 1980s, and their benefits for alerting the driver of an unsafe tire pressure were known for a long time. The concept only became commercially viable after they became mandatory by law in 2000 (TREAD Act). When you freeze ideas, you close the project with the intent to enable somebody else to reopen it one day.

If an idea that has been in the system gets frozen, we cannot angst over what has already been invested into the idea—that investment has no current value and must be written off—the sooner the better if we know the idea is not going to yield a profitable outcome. At Goodyear, I have seen leaders fund bad projects far too long and then decide to launch them, *hoping* for a return on the investment and justification of the R&D expense.

Here are a few suggestions for making quick assessments or for derisking ideas:

- *Use technology*, such as computer modeling, 3D printing, and quick prototyping. There are companies specialized in these techniques that can serve as contractors or consultants.
- *Use quick learning cycles or sprints.* Along with modeling and simulations, this is my preferred method.
- *Move on as fast as possible.* Make a decision with the minimum information possible. Some people call this "minimum maturity model."
- *Speed up* what you are already doing by using lean principles. Some companies that adopt lean in product development start in that area.
- *Plan experiments* for the quickest go/no-go decision—often you only need a few data points for that. Use scientific methods and do not hesitate to do designed experiments or use Tagushi methodologies.
- *Look at lean startup* ideas. There is a lot literature out there already with great examples that may give you ideas how to do something similar in your company. Sometimes you have to be just as creative in obtaining knowledge as you were when generating the idea.
- *Outsource the service.* Outsourcing a capability that you currently do not have should at least be a temporary option.

Some traditional tools that can be used in this process are the A3 methodology, the business-model canvas, and tools like OSLO, USPO, 7 levels of change, QFD, and TRIZ.

Although we discussed these concepts in the context of letting ideas into the TCP, the same concepts apply when projects get assessed at other milestones, including subsequent TCP gates, especially gates B and C.

Some companies that I visited recently compared their new-idea assessment process to the TV show "Shark Tank," where innovators have 5 minutes to get investment money from investors. Except for the fact that it is a short process, I do not like that approach for R&D. Before the gate review, ideas should have been assessed by an empowered team or individual (serial innovator) and vetted by elders, experts, and maybe stakeholders. Gatekeepers should make sure processes were followed and criteria were considered. Gatekeepers should only get involved when there are too many ideas being passed or not enough. They also should be involved when revisiting criteria, the process, and the training of engineers.

I once visited a small company, and I was told that all the important technical decisions were run by the "three amigos." These folks were company elders and met regularly for coffee or lunch, and they were willing to take on any case or question—it does not have to be complicated. Another great advantage you can get from the elders is their ability to negotiate if buy-in from others is required. Elders have a reputation and certain amount of trust, and they are great promoters for technical concepts.

Sam says that serial innovators question everything, including their own knowledge and ideas. They would rather create room to start something new than pursue an idea of which they are not 100% convinced. But, he notes, serial innovators also should be trusted with their assessments based on their experience and their knowledge.

Romain is a gatekeeper, and he notices when a team or an innovator tries to sell an idea of which even they are not convinced. He encourages the innovator or the team of experts to make the right decision before they bring an idea to a gate because they have a lot more information and knowledge to make the decision than the gatekeepers or leaders. Romain is not so concerned about an individual idea or project, as much as he is concerned about the portfolio of all projects. He wants the engineers or teams to also carefully assess the project's fit in the portfolio.

There are a lot of stories out there about famous bad assessments of new ideas, which prove that not everybody gets this right all the time: IBM's dislike of Jobs' first personal computer or the professor that gave Fred Smith, founder of FedEx, a "C" in college when he presented the business case for FedEx (the idea was not feasible). It is not easy to always get it right all the time with all our paradigms. You will make a mistake and look bad in hindsight. Do not worry, you are in good company. Richard Branson says, "Opportunities are like buses—there's always another one coming."[18] This may be correct, but what if your competition is on the earlier bus!

Lean R&D Principle: Bet wisely to win with disruptive innovation.

Disruptive innovation is a small percentage of innovations, but do not ignore it. The more you try to allow disruptive innovations to emerge, the higher your chances for success. But the key is to know when to *stop* (drop ideas). Enabling disruptive innovation must not be costly—a lot of the research on that level is done on the computer today, not in the lab.

Experience has shown that most disruptive innovation originates in R&D: a scientist or an innovator sees a technical opportunity and connects it with a customer need (or vice versa). Companies not only need to create a space where empowered innovators can thrive, but they also need a process so that they can improve as they learn.

Although chances are maximized by looking at a lot of ideas, they must be assessed quickly, so that the good ones can enter an efficient development process and the bad ones are frozen.

Many lean principles—reinvesting capacity, talent management, and concepts popular with lean-startup thinking—apply to this part of the R&D innovation process.

At Goodyear: Over time, we had many of the components in place to promote disruptive innovation—discretionary funding, an Innovative Products department, our share of talented innovators. Having learned from all of them, we currently have an ICP, BMI, and TCP; some degree of free innovation space; and many ideas coming from a multitude of internal or external sources. We use lean principles and tools, such as quick learning cycles, to evaluate ideas as fast as possible, so we can freeze the bad ones and manage the good ones through our processes. But most importantly, we have a process in place from which we can learn and improve as we learn.

Let us briefly look at the "human" side of this process. Inventors do not like it if their idea gets rejected or frozen, and their feelings intensify the longer they work on an idea. Inventors will be especially upset if they think that these decisions are made randomly and not the outcome of a consistent process in which the innovators have had input. To help address this, some advocate the use of an escalation process that gives an idea a second look. Mats Magnusson likes the idea of an "ombudsman,"[19] somebody assigned to look after the interests of the inventor. Of course if assessments are made consistently and according to a good process, the expectations are known to the inventors ahead of time.

All ideas, information, and decisions eventually get innovations through the famous front door and the first few assessments of the TCP. But the later parts of the TCP also can benefit from lean, specifically the development of the technology that turns ideas into profitable products.

Manage the Innovation Process

Selecting the right ideas is one thing—efficiently developing them into profitable customer value is another.

I like to group the lean principles that can help with this process into four categories:

- Deliver value—observation at the gemba
- Manage the design space well
- Set-based experimentation
- Concurrent thinking

Observe the Customer

Delivering value is centric to lean, and this concept must be applied to innovation, including disruptive innovation, as well. Some of the greatest new products—cars, airplanes, TV, telephone, paper diapers, synthetic laundry detergents, sticky notes, iPhones, tablets—were created when an engineer solved a problem for consumers by connecting a new technology with an opportunity that he or she observed in the market. Brant Cooper writes in

The Lean Entrepreneur that customers do not ask for disruptive innovation.[9] Henry Ford used to say, "If I had asked the people what they wanted, they would have told me faster horses."

Of course there are many other tools to find out what the customer needs, wants, and likes, such as customer surveys, focus groups, and marketing studies. At Goodyear, we also can ask dealers and the staff in the Goodyear stores about the customer. I personally rate this lower than the direct observation of customers.

As an engineer, Sam participated in many focus group marketing events, watching from the adjacent room through the backside of the mirrors. Sam recalls an Aquatred event. The Aquatred is a tire that looks like two smaller tires put together, which leaves a deep groove in the center to channel water away. In this event, in which 12 potential concepts were being explored, a man who looked like an executive got up and put his hand on the channel of the Aquatred prototype and said, "I only buy tires from one of your competitors, but if you ever make a tire like that, I will buy it." That was the deciding moment that led to the design of one of Goodyear's most successful products.

Customers may not ask for disruptive innovation, but they know it when they see it. As Sam's example illustrates, it is critical that you test an innovation with real customers. That is best done with samples and prototypes. The lean startup literature has many interesting examples. Access to retail channels, especially company-owned outlets (to assure confidentiality), come in handy for that purpose. As Sam's example demonstrates, engineers and innovators should leverage any and every opportunity with customers to gain key knowledge about what they value.

Manage the Design Space

How can we take that great idea that is now progressing through the TCP and close the knowledge gaps as efficiently as possible to maximize customer value. What lean principles can help? Just like we have seen when considering new ideas, simple probability thinking tells us that the more options we try within a project, the higher the chances for success. The odds can be improved by the knowledge that we have about the technology, the product, the market, and by the diversity of options we consider. We like to call all the possible options the "design space."

As obvious as this sounds, experience has shown that this kind of probability thinking is not done well or often enough in R&D. Engineers like to quickly jump to solutions and get their experiments going rather than thoroughly thinking about *all* possible alternatives. We also have to remember that technical problems rarely have one single solution. This is an argument for diversity because often solutions can be found that enhance each other. The first question an R&D leader should have for the innovator, the team leader, or the team running an experiment is, "What options have you considered?"

When reviewing options, it is not only the volume of options but also the quality of the options. A good way to find good options is to start with thorough benchmarking. This of course includes "mono-zukuri," the teardown of competitor products or reverse engineering as we call it at Goodyear. The benchmarking should also include adjacent technologies and especially any new technologies that are starting to become popular. The creators of new technology around the world do not know about your project or needs, and they will not call you, so you must find them. Good examples of early technology discovery were the use of stereolithography (precursor for 3D printing) and cold metal spray in tire development in mid-1980s. Chris Helsel, former director Global Technology Projects, insisted that in every iteration there had to be one option from an adjacent area that had never been considered. Typically iterations would experiment with new designs, materials, equipment, and maybe manufacturing technology. But Chris asked engineers to consider a new option for sales, marketing, distribution, and warehousing. "Innovation often can be found in the cracks between functions," says Chris.

When Jim Morgan was a product development director at Ford, he introduced standards to make sure that every kentou experiment had at least the following options included: three internal designs, three external designs, and three competitor-inspired solutions.[20] In addition to Jim's suggestions, I think there also should be a mix of conservative, creative, and outrageous options.

This phase where the most options are available and considered must be fully exploited in product development. Since most of the value is created in the early stages of the development process, this phase of the project must be adequately exploited and staffed.

As I noted several times, at Goodyear projects have been traditionally staffed heaviest at the end of the development process, close to the launch to solve all the last-minute problems that are popping up close to the launch. We see another lean paradox here: lean thinking suggests you allocate resources early in the process ("frontloading") to take advantage of the opportunities for value creation rather than at the end to address panics.

Lean R&D Principle: Explore as many diverse options early in the design space.

The most customer value is generated by considering and exploiting as many diverse options in the design space as possible and as early in the development cycle as possible. At the beginning of a project, the design space is wide open and it will narrow down as decisions are made. When doing this remember that many technical problems have more than one solution.

Good input for what to pursue comes from benchmarking (monuzukuri, reverse engineering) and a very broad survey of available technologies. All stakeholders and all functions involved in the value stream—manufacturing, marketing, sales, distribution, and so on—need a voice in this to bring in concepts beyond technical solutions. Other good tools to use for this phase are computer predictions, quick experiments, and all forms of knowledge reuse.

Leaders must make sure the front part of the project is adequately explored and staffed, which helps to avoid the resource-consuming panics prior to product launch.

Lastly, in addition to the knowledge, new capabilities may even need to be developed along with the product.

At Goodyear: We like to "frontload" our new development programs. We try to start every new project with an extensive reverse engineering program and specify an extensive modeling effort to explore the design space. One of the development directors insists that every program has at least one nontechnical option. We also make an effort to look at a spectrum of ideas, from conservative to outrageous options.

Here is another example that Sam shared with me: When developing the first Assurance TripleTred tire, the team needed really new ideas and fresh thinking about ultimate all-season traction. Sam picked the right people to generate ideas and educated them about the problem, the technology, the competition, and the company plans. Then he sent this group out to collect as many ideas as possible—they had to generate their own ideas and collect ideas from other people. (On another project, Sam had organized a scavenger hunt to collect ideas and relevant new technology.)

Sam asked the team to sort the ideas by criteria: logic first then feasibility, which meant they had to be reduced to practice in a decent time. Then the ideas were posted, and everybody had to put dots on the cards: a red dot "never seen before" and/or a blue dot "this will work." Then they picked the ideas with two dots, which meant novel and feasible. Then two teams were formed, they picked ideas from the board, and combined several of them into two coherent product scenarios: one short-term and one long-term.

The teams presented their product scenarios to a jury of marketing and technical directors, and the best short-term and long-term concepts were picked. These product scenarios were just an input stimulus for the actual product development team, who took the best bits and pieces of each and formed three coherent product concepts that they were going to actually pursue. Those concepts were then modeled on the computer and quick, minimum viable prototypes were built and tested, which led to a few winning ideas. The best set was then combined with similar sets, including very innovative and more conservative approaches to evaluate five different molds and several materials and constructions. The Assurance tire line is still (years later) one of Goodyear's most popular tires.

Keep All Options Open as Long as Possible

Keeping options in the large design space open as long as possible makes designs more robust and allows the best value to be generated. Before revealing the lean process behind this, though, let me explain how I was taught at Goodyear 30 years ago.

I was told that the first thing to do is to design your long-lead-time items and get them in queue, so they can be made. Based on this instruction, I made sure we quickly designed the mold first. By the time we got the mold many months later, we realized that we should have designed it differently based on what we learned while the mold was being designed and made. Unfortunately, we were locked in, and it cost a fortune to change it or to make a new mold (which we would not get in time anyway), so we started cutting and machining the existing mold at great expense and with little effect. By the end of the project, the consequences of early decisions seemed to accumulate and a lot of costly and difficult changes were needed. Fortunately, my management was willing to assign more people and money to help out, so we did not miss the launch by too much.

Any new project starts with a wide-open design space. As irreversible decisions are made regarding a project, the design space shrinks and the options decline rapidly. At the same time, the cost of change increases (my example of the molds). Changes cost more later in the program and take much longer, and so the cost of cycle time grows fast and projects become delayed. Sam says we must carefully orchestrate the convergence to assure that the design space does not shrink too fast.

As we work on a project, we generate new knowledge to close a knowledge gap. The new knowledge is created fast at the beginning of the project and then tapers off. The longer we can wait with an important decision, the more knowledge is available to make the decision.

We want to keep the design space open as long as possible (a lean principle), so we have the time to consider as many options as possible, thus increasing the chances to deliver good value. At the same time, we take advantage of the late-start advantages discussed in *Chapter 5*, like the use of the latest market information and the latest technology. We also make sure that the maximum number of changes by the customer or the marketing organization can be accumulated before the decision is made. This all hinges on another lean principle that fast is better than slow. We are counting on quick tool, equipment, and prototype cycle times to execute fast after the start. Decisions as late as possible also imply that the most information is available, which means that the project risk is reduced (see "Traditional versus Lean Design Space").

A Toyota executive was quoted as saying, "Management's job is to prevent decisions from being made too early," and I agree. But just to be clear

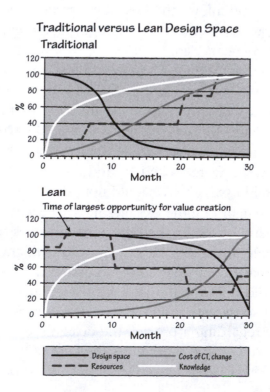

Lean R&D Principle: Keep all design options open as long as possible to maximize the value creation.

Keeping design options open as long as possible is done by making option-limiting decisions as late as possible (like late start), but also relies upon many other lean, R&D, and project management principles. This requires fast and efficient execution.

A new project normally starts with a wide-open design space and a maximum number of options. As decisions are made, design space and options shrink—as irreversible decisions are made, designs are locked and changes become time-consuming and expensive. The work required to close a knowledge gap occurs rapidly at the beginning of the project and tapers off. Making decisions late also assures that most changes requested by the customer can be accommodated, latest market intelligence and technology is incorporated, and risk reduced.

At Goodyear: We try to make all project decisions just in time and we try to avoid early decisions as much as possible. There are many scars from the times when tooling was ordered as early as possible. Project schedules are made working backward from the launch date. It helps that our development is predictable and fast. Since we not only make decisions as late as possible but also start our learning cycles as late as possible, we have all but eliminated late changes in our programs.

regarding late start, I did not say "start *too* late." I said start "as late as possible," with a reasonable buffer at the end (if possible, a shared capacity buffer).

Concurrent Engineering

Concurrent engineering became popular in the 1990s and is considered by most people to be a method to reduce cycle time, but it does much more than that. There are significant interactions between the different functions that must be understood, and they are best identified in a concurrent process. This is the case for both the kentou and the execution phase, although the benefits may be greater in the kentou phase.

For example, at Goodyear, imagine we are working with a brand new material that became available from a supplier. Let us assume the new material is used in the tread rubber of a tire. Our first learning cycle determined that the new material will provide a breakthrough in wet traction, but we also learned that the tread pattern (profile) requires a significant modification to accommodate the new material. This modification will reduce the wear resistance and our treadwear warranties will be affected. (Marketing hates that!) The first time the new material was mixed in the plant it was determined that the mix time went up significantly, which would raise the cost of the product. (Marketing hates that, too.) But it looks like we will eventually be able to reduce the mixing time.

If we would develop this product like we used to—engineering does their piece and then it goes to manufacturing—it would take forever because by the time manufacturing is done, design will have to start over. Marketing would be happy about the better traction but would raise alarms later when they realized that the cost is too high, the mileage warranties cannot be met, and the product starts another redesign cycle. Eventually the product is in its first cost-reduction cycle before it is even completely designed.

But if all functions are engaged in the first learning cycle—concurrently—marketing may say that they can absorb a little higher cost but that the wear warranty must be maintained, and production will know that whatever they do to the mixing, the stiffness of the rubber must be maintained to minimize the tread design changes. Now all stakeholders will collaborate on the next learning cycles and together move the ball in the right direction. Everyone learns together at the same time, and the right decisions can be made for best customer value.

Concurrent execution with all stakeholders involved allows everyone to constantly weigh the performance and the features versus the cost of the product. This puts the focus on the optimum cost from the beginning and not the minimum cost, which is often the focus of postdesign, cost-reduction initiatives. Because of this, cost-reduction programs after the product has launched can focus on new materials and technology rather than product redesigns.

Sam used concurrent engineering on many projects all the way back to the 1990s at Goodyear, and, he says, when working in parallel it is important that everyone respect each other and openly communicate his or her "best guesses" and interests at any point in time. Everyone must also accept that in the early stages things will change (and that annoys some people) as the team learns and gains new insights. In the early stages, people must be allowed to change their minds based on new information. As time passes, the information will stabilize and the team will converge on the optimum solution. Regular, open, face-to-face, communication meetings (open to all) and flexibility are key to employing this strategy.

Lean R&D Principle: Pursue concurrent work as much as possible in all phases, especially in the kentou phase.

There is a lot of interaction between the contributions of the different functions, especially in the kentou phase, which must be understood and addressed as it becomes visible. Concurrent development makes this possible, and it also makes the development much faster (overlapping principle) and more robust.

If one function in the value stream finishes their work before passing it to the next function, then the following function often has to send the work back for changes. This loop can be avoided if all functions are involved in all the learning cycles and all learn at the same time.

Concurrent work avoids a lot of late changes that cost money, avoids many problems during or after the product launch, and leads to more robust designs.

At Goodyear: All stakeholders and all functions are involved from Day One in every project. Significant effort is made to make sure all stakeholders accept responsibility for the project as early as possible. Learning cycles are planned by a collaborative team, including the customer or the customer advocate, and the same team reflects on the results of the cycle. By using concurrent engineering with other lean principles, like late start, we have reduced late changes to the bare minimum. I am not sure that changes can or should be completely eliminated (they sometimes add value), but they must be managed.

Most new products at Goodyear still rely largely on existing manufacturing equipment and processes, and a new tire often needs modifications to the manufacturing process not a completely new process. So what would happen if a completely new manufacturing process would be required? This was the case recently at Goodyear, and the new manufacturing process was developed concurrently with the product. This method—concurrent development of the product and the manufacturing process and equipment—is becoming increasingly popular in the industry, and a lot of experiences about the process have been published under the name of 3P (production preparation process). This approach does include a risk that the equipment and the process must change a bit when changes are made to the product, but the advantages of concurrent development outweigh the disadvantages.

The concurrent process with all stakeholders participating in all phases of the process also is popular in the construction industry. Most often that process is referred to as ILPD (integrated lean project delivery). ILPD uses many lean principles, including the "test before design" concept. These concurrent processes save time and improve the quality of product, but they do require a different approach to work with contractors and suppliers because the design evolves during the process; traditional contracts based on a bidding process are no longer feasible.

Set-Based Experiments versus Iterations

As you may have learned in school, the iterative development process has been the process of choice for scientists for a long time. It is based on small experiments that you learn from and you improve, from iteration to iteration. There are several advantages to this process for product development:

- You cut a big project in small chunks or learning cycles. The small chunks are much easier to manage and you learn faster. The learning from one iteration can be used in the following iteration.
- You can set a cadence for the project. The cadence helps with delivery and variability.
- You create a pivot or decision point after every iteration. You can redirect your project. You can decide if it is better to launch or if it is worth making another iteration. You also can decide if you need to go in a totally different direction.
- At the end of every iteration, there is a good opportunity to get feedback from the customer or to show prototypes to the customer. This is the preferred method to work with an OEM customer, where on a regular cadence the customer requests samples or prototypes. Automotive companies like to ask for samples or submissions every time they go to a new iteration of their prototype vehicles.

There also are disadvantages to iterations:

- When you do iterations, you typically pick a start point. It is a single point in the "space of endless possibilities." In most cases, the start point is the current product. Sometimes you pick a competitor product that you want to explore. This drastically limits the options for the performance of the product as better solutions may not be discovered.

- Targets are normally based on a reasonable improvement over your current product. These targets are based on what the team feels can be achieved. In many cases, this means automatically targeting small improvements.
- Only interactions that occur in one iteration are captured. Interactions between sequential iterations often remain undetected.

Iterations are not only the preferred scientific method, but it is also the most popular method in industrial research. Actually, the software industry "rediscovered" a version of the iterative process with "agile" software development. Iterations can be enhanced with set-based thinking.

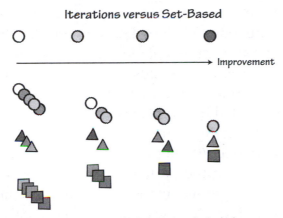

The top row represents the iterative method, which starts with one option that is transformed into a better product. The bottom rows represent set-based experiments, where repetitive trials lead to sets of better solutions.

In a set-based concurrent experiment, you start with a very broad set of options. For example, you use your current product but also several of your competitor products as a starting point, together with many options for new materials, a much wider design range, and several new manufacturing processes. Options are eliminated based of predictive tools, modeling, and experiments, which leads to a smaller set. This method also lets you study interactions between the different options, which often happen and are harder to see in sequential iterations, just as we have seen in the absence of concurrency. New options can be added as the work progresses. At the end, one or more promising options emerge. The chances that the best options are among this set are higher than with the point-to-point iteration. The set-based method starts with a lot of options, which automatically accommodates the lean principle, cited earlier in this chapter, of exploring as many diverse options as possible.

When Toyota developed the Prius vehicle, the time to launch was reduced and they assigned three sets of development options to three technical centers concurrently to make sure enough diverse options were considered in the short timeframe.[21] In this example, Toyota leveraged the talent and capabilities of the different centers to develop coherent packages to target specific groups of buyers.

Sam says that when he started development of a new tire, he began with 50 tread design sketches, 20 hand-carved designs (that is a process where the tread profile is cut into a smooth tire with a hot knife), and ordered five molds, which he evaluated together with many options in construction, materials, and other variables in more sets.

Last year a program at Goodyear was moved up by 6 months because a favorable market situation developed. The team quickly redesigned the development plan to include a large set-based experiment with 24 sets of prototype tires (different molds, tread materials, constructions, etc.) instead of the usual four at a time. In order to make this possible, the complete team traveled to the plant and everybody pitched in. The experiment put a large strain on the plant, but the team was successful in delivering the project 6 months earlier than planned, thus achieving a significant increase in the profitability of the product. There was additional cost for the experiments, but it was minor compared to the gains for the business. Marc Nowacki, the project manager for this effort, says that on his next project he will plan a set-based approach from the beginning.

Set-based concurrent engineering has advantages over the iterative method:

- It starts with a much wider design space. The chances to find a solution are proportional to the size of the exploited design space and the diversity of the experiments that are undertaken.
- It allows for the concurrent and coherent execution of the experiments, hence, you can study interactions between elements more accurately, just as occurs with concurrent engineering.
- There is rarely one solution to a problem—the set-based approach increases the chances for finding multiple solutions.
- Depending on how much can be predicted or modeled, a set-based experiment can reduce project time.
- The set-based approach is more beneficial in the kentou phase than in the execution phase.

Disadvantages of a set-based approach include

- Set-based experiments are often tedious and very demanding on resources.
- A set-based experiment explores more options, and sometimes knowledge is generated that is not needed, at least not at that time and for that idea. Although advocates of the set-based approach hail this as a good thing, R&D managers are not likely to spend resources to develop knowledge to put on a shelf.

Set-based approaches are most popular when computer modeling tools or other predictive tools, including tradeoff curves, are available because it reduces or eliminates the need for costly experiments. Set-based experiments give engineers another method to use when conducting experiments. For some engineers and companies, the method may be new and offer advantages. Others may have used it, and called it by a different name. As with most other principles cited in this book, there is no one method that fits all situations. The design of the experiments is an important part of R&D, and set-based design provides another option.

Quick Learning Cycles, Scrum, and Sprints

At Goodyear, we call our learning cycles "iterations." There is a difference in the content of the learning cycles in the execution phase and the kentou phase: The learning cycles in the execution phase have a more clearly defined content (engineering, mold, prototypes, testing); a target and numerical goal can be set and the timing is predictable. The cycles in the kentou phase are fuzzier, with more diverse content (lab studies, supplier visits, study drawings, designed experiments), and the timing is unpredictable.

Because of the high uncertainty in the kentou phase, it is important to break the work into small chunks or learning cycles. The quick cycles allow frequent pivot points to change direction or to freeze or stop a project. One of the most important benefits of the quick learning cycles is that it allows leaders to allocate money one learning cycle at a time. That is the best way to make sure that high uncertainty projects do not get out of control and hang around for too long. The other big benefit of the quick learning cycles is the ability to check back with the customer or the customer's advocate frequently.

Quick learning cycles are especially effective if fully functional or minimum viable prototypes are available to support any test or marketing data.

Prototypes refer to physical objects as well as processes, services, computer models, and renderings.

The same lean tools that were used to speed up the cycles in the execution phase can be used to shorten the cycles in the kentou phase. Despite the different content and predictability, there are common principles between the cycles in both phases:

- Have a goal or deliverable and a limited time for every cycle. The shorter the cycle, the easier it should be to come up with a goal. If the cycles cannot be scheduled around goals or deliverables, they should still be limited by time. The goals are set with all stakeholders involved.
- There is a decision point and a reflection after every cycle. Customers, stakeholders, and team members should be involved in the assessment and the plans for the next cycle.
- Lean principles should be applied whenever possible to make the cycles efficient and effective.
- Cycles must be planned out systematically, relying on good standards and methodology. For example, starting with the most important go/no-go decision in the kentou phase.

Sometimes iterations or learning cycles can use additional methodologies popular with agile/scrum:

- An empowered team of experts sets the goals for the learning cycle together with all stakeholders. The team also self-organizes to get the work done. For this purpose, it does not matter too much what function the members belong to. As long as members contribute specific expertise when needed, the work can be assigned to any team member who is capable of doing the work. For example, a designer can do the work of a test engineer. A mold-design specialist can make tire-construction drawings.
- The teams can be self-directed or under the supervision of a project manager. If the teams are self-organizing, project managers often supervise many teams.
- The variable content of the cycles favors a tool that is very popular in the agile/scrum world: the "scrum board."

Scrum boards are rapidly gaining popularity in R&D organizations. They are nothing more than white space with a tag or sticky note for every task that needs to be completed in a learning cycle. The tags are arranged by their status. The benefit of the scrum board is the visual display of who delivers what during the cycle and the status of the task. It is a tool to plan, to work out conflicts, to track progress, and to communicate. It also serves as a commitment from the person who writes and posts a tag that he or she will do the work as spelled out on the tag.

The design and location of the board and the information displayed are up to the team. Some people have scrum boards in a work area, whereas other teams keep them in a team room; I have even seen companies where a person brings the board to meetings. The scrum board could be done on a computer with a project management software application (if the team is not colocated), but it's better for communication and conflict resolution if it's physical and in the open.

Scrum Board

Time period: Feb. 10 to March 10	Goal: Assess technical feasibility of new air-maintenance idea		
Name or function	To do	In progress	Done
Engineer 1/ Function 1			
Engineer 2/ Function 2			
Engineer 3/ Function 3			

Sam likes the fact that all stakeholders are involved in setting the goals. He says that when he designed the Aquatred, there was never a fixed goal for the project. But after every iteration, Sam's team showed the test results to marketing, and then they all together came up with goals for the next iteration. They were focused on finding the highest achievable value for the customer, not forcing their innovation to hit a preset goal.

The first learning cycles should be designed carefully in this derisking process. In the article "Piloting the Rocket," the authors point out that the first few "plays," as they call them, determine the outcome.[13] Logical breakdowns can be according to importance—such as the most important question to which you need an answer—based on finding the cheapest, fastest, and most relevant information. You may want to do an FMEA or use another tool to determine where your biggest uncertainties are and attack them first.

In the absence of any better criteria, the breakdown should be by time alone and the time intervals should be short.

You also need to know when you are done with the quick learning cycles. And if you are done, you move on. Jim Euchner, vice president Global Innovations, says, "I keep telling my engineers, you do not have to be perfect. You need to learn what you set out to learn, then move on." This is good advice for engineers because engineers love perfection, and time is often filled with perfecting a prototype or concept or just waiting for an inspiration. In this phase of a project *good is good enough*! Anything more than what you need from a learning cycle is overprocessing, and that is waste. There is nothing more effective to avoid overprocessing than to set a time limit.

This concept of the "minimum maturity model" is illustrated in *The Big Bang Theory* episode, "The Scavenger Vortex," where the characters participate in a scavenger hunt. They get one clue by putting together a jigsaw puzzle. Most teams get the clue after assembling about one-third of the puzzle. But the highly left-brained Sheldon looks for absolute guarantee of the clue (a perfect solution), and he completes the whole puzzle hoping for more clues rather than just the one that is needed, driving his partner nuts, who got the solution long before and now finds herself delayed by half an hour.[22]

If making quick prototypes, keep the minimum viable in mind as well. As Tim Brown points out in "Design Thinking," you will get more feedback if your prototypes look rough than if they look perfect.[23]

Since the learning cycles are quick, you may want to split the team and have several groups work independently for a short time, like in a competition. This is not waste (overprocessing) because the intent is to cover a larger design space and have the different groups attack the problem from different angles or look at different options. Then after a short time, you get the teams together and let them share their results and learn from each other. This approach, like building on others' ideas in brainstorming (cross-fertilizing), often gives you a much better starting point for the next set of cycles, and it is a fun exercise that sometimes leads to surprisingly good results.

One good practice with Goodyear's OEMs tire programs is that the OEMs require many submissions of prototypes and that we get feedback after every submission. Every effort should be made to get customer feedback after every cycle. Here again, the computer folks are ahead—they often embed the customer with the team at regular intervals.

Important tools and capabilities that can be used for rapid learning cycles include 3D printing, rapid prototyping, and computer modeling, which can be accessed internally or via contractors. When I worked in Innovative

Products at Goodyear in the 1980s, we had a "pattern shop" at a local subsidiary factory that we developed for that purpose.

Speed is a powerful weapon in the execution phase of product development, and it is equally and occasionally more important in the kentou phase. The more potential a new idea or technology has, the more important it is to be fast. You should not only worry about the competition, but do keep the cost of delay in mind. Sam says that whenever you have a great idea or work on a good concept, there is a high probability that someone in a competitor company also has had the idea. They (the competitor) likely have been exposed to the same insightful information at the same time. The race is on. Do not assume that you are the only one in the race, and do not wait for the next bus.

Of course there is always the question of how many scrum cycles you should run. Sam suggests you freeze concept work projects if no progress is made in two consecutive cycles, but I think it is hard to establish a general rule for this. It may be better to tie this decision to learning than to results.

Lean Innovation Management Skills

In this book, we have now gone from a process that took forever to meet a large goal set by marketing or leadership (maybe) to a quick and effective process that advocates lots of small cycles with quick feedback where a goal is set for every cycle by a cross-functional, collaborative team—and there are a lot of additional options in between. There are advantages and disadvantages in every method discussed in this chapter. Therefore, project managers must assess the needs of the project, make the right decision, and remain flexible to change that decision any time a change in direction is needed. None of the methods assures success—there will always be ideas that do not work. But the right choice of the process can speed up innovation creation and increase the efficiency.

The management of programs, especially fuzzy ones, requires lean project management skills that engineers and project managers must learn to master. One thing is for sure, there is no "one size fits all," and the more tools they have in their toolbox the more effective they can be. This is why I do not promote project templates, such as those often used in computer software.

First of all, set-based, diverse *thinking* and concurrent execution is always required regardless of the experiments. And you *must* always explore the design space as much as possible, which is most important at the beginning of a program or for more fundamental research. Close to the launch of the product, the design space is normally narrowed down by the decisions that already have been made.

Second, you must keep the design space *open* as long as possible. Expensive and option-limiting decisions like tooling purchases should be made as late as possible.

Third, you should make the best experimental design and plan that fits the situation and gets the most learning in the most efficient manner. The project plan should be made by the empowered project team. The empowered team should start by laying out an effective derisking strategy: FMEA tells you where your uncertainties are, and you need to decide what knowledge is needed. Focus on the most critical uncertainties first, to understand the true risk, and formulate a mitigation design strategy to move forward.

Fourth, use quick cycles whenever possible with a lot of feedback, including customer feedback, and learning. Strive for the fastest learning possible so that unseen or overlooked risks can be found as soon as possible—minimum viable is often good enough.

Fifth and final, have the goals evolve as the cycles are completed. The empowered team, the stakeholders, and the customer should be involved in those decisions. The team may find a higher-value product scenario than the one originally envisioned or an insurmountable barrier may be uncovered. Use the frequent pivot points for a good decision point to launch the product. Assess the market opportunities versus the current performance of the product. And remember that most often good is good enough.

Avoid Lean Innovation Killers

So with so much good that lean can do for innovation, why is Sam even concerned about its application to innovation processes. It is somewhat simple, he argues. If some of the lean tools and other tools are used incorrectly or if the wrong tools are used, none of the lean approaches will stick and none of the lean benefits emerge. Some of the following killers have been discussed in previous chapters, but a bit more detail on some, such as standards, may help you avoid them:

- Not making good use of standards
- Limited tolerance for good variability and empowerment
- Counterproductive metrics and goals
- Risk aversion, poor risk management, and fear of failure
- Project goals established too early with insufficient information or engagement
- "One size fits all" gating and project management processes
- Cutting corners, believing it will increase speed

Not Making Good Use of Standards

Standards are a good thing in lean, but the inappropriate use of the standards hurts innovation. Some companies make product standards rigid as if there was nothing outside those standards that could possibly work or should ever be tried. That does not leave a lot of space to try something new. Standards should have a fixed and a flexible part. The fixed part is based on quality and safety standards of the company that is not negotiable. Other parts of the standards have to be flexible and allow experiments that push the envelope or allow experiments outside the standards. If the experiments are successful, the standards can be updated.

There is no reason why innovators should not follow best practices that make work easy and efficient, as long as those standards do not prevent them from doing what is needed to create new ideas and innovative products. Creativity should be applied to new products, not challenging or bypassing best practices. Sam, the serial innovator, actually likes good product standards! He says he tries to focus his innovative changes in a small area that has the greatest potential effect on the benefit, and keep everything else a verified standard. "I had enough experiments to run—it was as good to know what I did not have to worry about. Following design standards also reduced the risk of my projects. It was still high enough with all the new things we were trying."

But Sam also is cautious about standards. They are sometimes an excuse for not thinking. They only represent the current best practice not the ultimate best practice. The quest is to continually seek and incrementally move toward the ultimate best practice. For Sam, the temptation for risk-adverse people is to hold too tightly to established standards.

For some people, following standards is like documenting learning or writing expense reports—standardized work is lumped in with the chores of work or the "not so fun" parts of work. There is a fine line there. Work standards cannot increase the nonfun/chores part of work—they must reduce it! If not, chances are that they should be revisited. If people do not see and appreciate the values in what they are doing, they will be reluctant to do it.

Limited Tolerance for Good Variability

There is good variability in a good innovation process, and it must be embraced and managed. Due to the increased variability—from higher uncertainty, complexity, and complications that arise—the amount of good variability is higher in the kentou phase than the execution phase. Variability management has always been difficult in R&D and maybe that is why it normally does not get a lot of attention.

> *We discourage the setting of rigid goals or targets at the beginning of a new project with high uncertainty, despite trying to know how much work is involved and how long it is going to take.*

With the use of project management tools, like project management software, there is a temptation to use "standard" project management templates. With the use of those templates comes the urge to standardize the number and content of iterations and the work durations. This may work to some extent in the execution phase, where the work becomes relatively predictable, but it is virtually impossible at the beginning of the kentou phase. We discourage the setting of rigid goals or targets at the beginning of a new project with high uncertainty, despite trying to know how much work is involved and how long it is going to take. At Goodyear, we tried for years to standardize the number of iterations needed in the execution phase, and we really never succeeded—let alone trying to define that for the kentou phase. A better way to manage the need and content of iterations is to set the right standards for project risk management.

Rather than trying to standardize kentou work processes to reduce variability, have a reflection after every iteration, learning cycle, or sprint, and assess possible improvements. Over time, you will see patterns where the process can be improved and maybe even the variability reduced.

Lack of Tolerance and Empowerment

It not only takes tolerance for failure in the management of the kentou phase of an innovation creation process, but it also takes tolerance for diverse behaviors and empowerment. There are serial innovators, geeks, and expert inventors who sometimes exhibit behaviors different from the expectations outlined by HR standards and the company's performance management system. There may be frowning and complaints from the coworkers, too. Remember that there are not a lot of innovators, and looking the other way sometimes benefits your organization. Creative individuals may not be on the succession plans for future corporate leadership, either, especially if you have adopted a dual-ladder advancement system. A long-term focus on the value delivered by serial innovators is more important than trying to correct their day-to-day behaviors. The idea is to value and utilize people for their strengths and accept their faults.

It is hard to control the work in the kentou phase, regardless of the individuals involved, and trust and empowerment of individuals and teams must exist. I noticed that leaders and managers often have a hard time switching to a more empowered management style, which I will cover with a leadership discussion in *Chapter 7.*

Counterproductive Metrics and Targets

Metrics are an important part of a lean product development process, but they also can backfire on innovation. At Goodyear in the execution phase we had a metric of OTD of 100%. We noticed immediately that project managers avoided risk to make sure they met the delivery target. We eventually reduced the target to 90% to restore the entrepreneurial spirit and it worked. Today we run around 95% OTD in the execution phase, and we get the products that we need. You get what you measure!

A good example for a business target that facilitates innovation is the Goodyear target for new products in our portfolio. Many companies have targets for profits from new products. At Goodyear we could not measure or manage that well enough, so we just have a target for new content in the portfolio similar to the 3M product vitality index.

Brant Cooper says that the biggest innovation killers are "ROI" (return on investment) and "when can I get it."[24] In the early phases of a project, the focus should be more on the opportunity than ROI or other financial considerations. The main reason for that is that the financial information available at the beginning of a new project is scarce and inaccurate at best. Financial targets should not drive projects in the kentou phase, but even in the kentou phase, some progress should be demonstrated after every learning cycle. But if no progress is expected *yet*, then the inventor should be left alone.

"When can I get it" may always occur with impatient management, but ROI should not be part of the first criteria upon which an idea or project is judged. If you are sure you want to stop a disruptive innovation project, all you have to do is ask the innovator for detailed financial and milestone data. Some companies generate the data on behalf of the innovator, but the result is likely the same. Some companies even have tight standards that make the detailed financial and timeline information mandatory for projects to move forward or be stopped—adhering strictly to such a standard early in the kentou phase may get them the data but not the innovation.

Other goals and targets drive engineers too tightly toward predetermined results. Engineers always like goals, targets, or specs, and since most managers and leaders in an R&D organization are engineers, they like them too. I have seen software engineers spend more than 6 months coming up with an almost perfect spec for a very large computer program. The spec was obsolete after 1 month of programming and the project was canceled. It is really hard to come up with good project goals and targets at the beginning of the kentou phase, although there must be a general idea based on technology, marketing considerations, financial expectations, and a line of sight to the company business strategy.

Goals and targets are criteria to let projects pass in the gating process. As you have seen, at Goodyear we use a different gating process and different criteria for the kentou phase than we use for the execution phase. All the gating processes have evolved to where the empowered teams suggest the right decisions at the gate meeting, and gate keepers worry more about resource availability (including funding), changes in the corporate strategy, market conditions, and the availability of enough good ideas and projects.

Our current kentou gating approach differs remarkably from the way it used to be at Goodyear. We had too much WIP when we started the gating processes. Consistent with the original stage-gate teaching, the gates were used to "kill" projects when precise targets were not achieved at the gate. Fortunately at Goodyear, we found better methods to control WIP. Unfortunately, I see many other companies use the gate process to control their initial WIP, and since it works so well, they maintain the process. The gating process resembles more a process where competent engineers present brilliant ideas and get a thumbs-up or -down, determined more for the quality than the content of their presentation. Only a few of the gate keepers—if any at all—have the background and the information to make those decisions in the first place, and the innovation will deteriorate very fast in such a process.

Lean R&D Principle: Avoid innovation killers.

Some lean tools can be easily abused, and the perceived gains from such applications could kill a valuable initiative for your company. Prominent innovation killers include

- Not making good use of standards
- Limited tolerance for good variability
- Lack of tolerance and empowerment
- Counterproductive metrics and targets
- Risk aversion, poor risk management, and fear of failure
- Project goals established too early with insufficient information
- "One size fits all" gating and management processes
- Cutting corners believing it will increase innovation speed

With all these, less is often better than more. This is especially true in the more creative and exploratory part of the kentou phase. As much as lean tries to simplify processes, reduce complexity, and look for global solutions, the "one size fits all" use of lean can be counterproductive in some places. As we have seen, the objectives of the kentou phase are different from the goals of the execution phase, and standards and processes may have to be adjusted. Carefully assess the use of lean tools and measures in the kentou phase for a possible negative impact on creativity and innovation.

At Goodyear: We do have design and process standards, but engineers can experiment outside the standards to seek improvements if they perform the required testing and validation. Thus, freeing innovators to explore, while also making them accountable for their exploration. We understand that there has to be standards for risk management, which includes the management of the good variability. The Goodyear metrics had to be adjusted to allow engineers and managers to take an appropriate amount of risk. I see many behaviors that could be seen as counterproductive to innovation (cutting corners) disappear as the culture matures and people realize those practices are not working any more.

Cutting Corners Does Not Increase Speed

Development speed is a key competitive advantage in an R&D process. But sometimes project managers try to achieve higher speed by running less experiments or learning cycles or by only exploring a small part of the possible options. Other times, they give up on a project after a negative, maybe poorly executed, experiment. This happens a lot when they are pressed for time, when the project is far behind schedule, and when they are in danger of missing a key milestone. This method of speeding up projects seriously affects the quality of the innovation work and compromises the customer value being created.

In my discussions with Sam in finishing this chapter, he concluded, "I wish we could turn the clock back to the 1980s and apply what we learned about lean to our Innovative Products department. The department might still be in existence, and it would have created a hundred successful innovations by now." Thanks, Sam.

More Innovation than Ever Before

At Goodyear, we have received more innovation and product awards (see *Goodyear Innovation Awards*), since we started the lean process than ever before. The awards are not just a result of our lean efforts, although lean principles have contributed here and there, but most likely because we started the innovation creation process and the technology creation process after lean had freed up enough resources to do so. I also think that we learned from mistakes made early on, and corrected them, not allowing lean thinking to negatively affect the innovation potential, as it has in some companies.

Today we have achieved a good synergy between lean and innovation, but we have only begun to move lean principles into the kentou phase. Our history with lean in other areas of R&D has helped prevent us from considering certain measures that could be detrimental to innovation. I also am glad to admit that our leadership had the right idea in trying lean with innovation, and that they did not waiver on innovation amid corporate setbacks and the economic crisis. We have truly used lean to eliminate waste and use that capacity to create value for the customer, as Frank Hull noted.[6]

Goodyear Innovation Awards

Below is a partial list of major innovation awards recently received by The Goodyear Tire & Rubber Co.

Year	Award	Organization
2010	• Goodyear and the National Aeronautics and Space Administration in recognition of the design of an airless tire	44th annual R&D 100 Awards
2011	• Top 100 Global Innovator	Thomson Reuters
	• Tire Manufacturing Innovation of the Year for retread multipiece cushion technology	*Tire Technology International*
	• Automotive Sector 2011—Innovation Technology Category	*AutoData Publishing* (Brazil)
	• Goodyear UltraGrip Ice+ tire received Tire Technology of the Year award	Tire Technology Expo in Cologne, Germany
2012	• Air Maintenance Technology awards	*Popular Mechanics* and *Time*
	• Top 100 Global Innovator	Thomson Reuters
	• Prix de l'Innovation de la Fedil award for Goodyear's Interlaced Strip technology	Prix de l'Innovation de la Fedil
	• Goodyear Assurance Tripletred All-Season and ComforTred Touring receive Best Buy recommendations	*Consumer Digest*
	• Air Maintenance Technology named one of "10 most promising future technologies"	*Car & Driver*
2013	• Top 100 Global Innovator	Thomson Reuters
	• Air Maintenance Technology receives Luxembourg Green Innovation Award	Luxembourg Green Business Awards
	• Goodyear Assurance TripleMax named 2013 Tire of the Year	*Motor Trend* (China)
	• Goodyear S200 awarded Best Commercial Tire of 2013	*Commercial Motor World Magazine* (China)
2014	• Top 100 Global Innovator	Thomson Reuters
	• Jim Euchner earns 2014 Technology Innovation Management Research Award	International Association for Management of Technology
	• Goodyear EfficentGrip SUV awarded 2014 Best SUV Tire of the Year	*China SUV Weekly* and *Chinasuv.cn (China)*

At the 2015 Geneva Auto show, Goodyear introduced two new tire innovations (see *Recent Goodyear Innovations*). The first is a tire that generates electricity when it deforms. As the deformation is needed to provide cushioning and steering, the deformation also generates heat, which is lost. Some of that energy can be recovered and used to charge the battery. The second innovation is a concept tire that has three internal chambers that can be inflated to different pressures, enabling the tire to adapt to operating conditions as needed (soft for cushioning, hard for cornering).

These tires currently are minimum viable prototypes. They were used at the car show to gauge the response of consumers. This is just another example of Goodyear's innovation potential and one more validation point for the delivery of lean-driven innovation.

Recent Goodyear Innovations

Notes

1. Peter Fritz, *Annual Conference of the Society for Concurrent Product Development*, St. Paul, MN, June 2014.
2. Jim Womack, *Gemba Walks, Expanded 2nd Edition*, Lean Enterprise Institute, Cambridge, MA, 2013.
3. "At 3M, A Struggle Between Efficiency And Creativity," *BusinessWeek*, June 10, 2007.
4. *3M Innovation Story: Uncommon Connections, Innovative Solutions*, 3M, 2011.
5. Frank Hull, "Promoting Concurrency to Achieve Strategic Objectives," *Concurrency Newsletter*, Issue 2014, No. 2, Volume 19.
6. Dan Markovitz, *A Factory of One*, Lean Island 2015, Reykjavik, March 2015.

7. Daniel Roos, James P. Womack, and Daniel T. Jones, *The Machine That Changed the World*, Harper Perennial, New York, 1991.
8. Eric Ries, *The Lean Startup*, Crown Business, New York, 2011.
9. Brant Cooper and Patrick Vlaskovits, *The Lean Entrepreneur*, Wiley, Hoboken, NJ, 2013.
10. Greg A. Stevens and James Burley, "3,000 Raw Ideas = 1 Commercial Success!" *Research-Technology Management,* May/June 1997.
11. Carmine Gallo, *The Innovation Secrets of Steve Jobs*, McGraw-Hill, New York, 2011.
12. Preston Smith and Donald G. Reinertsen, *Developing Products in Half the Time*, Wiley, Hoboken, NJ, 1997.
13. Greg A. Stevens and James Burley, "Piloting the Rocket of Radical Innovation," *Research Technology Management*, March–April 2003.
14. Marty Wartenberg, *Making Innovation Work for You!* AME Innovation Summit, Irvine, CA, March 2014.
15. Donald G. Reinertsen, training presentation at Goodyear, Akron, OH, January 2013.
16. Mats Magnusson, *Lean in R&D*, LPPDE 2014, Copenhagen, June 2014.
17. Geoffrey A. Moore, *Crossing the Chasm: Marketing and Selling Disruptive Products to Mainstream Customers*, HarperBusiness, New York, 2006.
18. Richard Branson, @richardbranson, November 2012.
19. Mats Magnusson, *Lean for Innovation*, LPPDE 2014, Copenhagen, June 2014.
20. James M. Morgan, LPPDE 2014, Copenhagen, June 2014.
21. James M. Morgan and Jeffrey K. Liker, *The Toyota Product Development System*, Productivity Press, New York, 2006.
22. "The Scavenger Vortex," *The Big Bang Theory*, Series 7 Episode 3, October 4, 2013.
23. Tim Brown, "Design Thinking", *Harvard Business Review*, June 2008.
24. Brant Cooper, *Lean Intrapreneurs: Lean Startup for the Enterprise*, AME Innovation Summit, Irvine, CA, March 2014.

Chapter 7

Operating the Lean Product Development Factory

Goodyear successfully implemented lean in R&D, and if that were the whole story, it would not be a complete continuous-improvement story— transformations are not finished with the implementation. In this chapter, I describe our evolution to a lean R&D operation, one with alignment of day-to-day operations to corporate strategy, and how we manage the process and people to sustain and continuously improve. It took Toyota many decades before it looked back and codified the "Toyota way," describing the management beliefs that guide the global automaker. This chapter is a look at the nascent "Goodyear way." We have a long way to go and much yet to learn, but I hope that one day many will look to Goodyear for lean inspiration and principles, as so many have looked to Toyota. Even today, though, we have one huge success factor in common with Toyota, without which lean sustainability would not be possible—leadership, especially that of Chairman, CEO, and President Richard Kramer, has consistently held our focus on lean and the objectives it allows our company to achieve. There has not been a new flavor of improvement to emerge in Goodyear for more than a decade, and I credit Goodyear leadership for allowing our lean R&D to begin, grow, and flourish.

From Lean Initiative to Lean Function

About 4 years after we had started lean product development, I had my hands full. We had hired an administrator who managed the visual planning boards, printed the kanban cards, and updated the homemade database, while I tried to juggle managing the fledgling lean operation with some other major projects. A lot fell between the cracks. Some of the former Herbie team members tried to pitch in.

During this time, we were on the last step of our initial spin around the Womack Wheel. We were supposed to be "working to perfection," but I could not keep up with the daily operational chores. We had undertaken as many kaizens on the first go-around as was possible, all of which led to improvement (as well as more work for me). I remember wondering *when and how* we would reach perfection or *if* the Womack Wheel would end in a different fashion. Soon thereafter we reached a critical point with our lean initiative—lean product development was either going to continue with leadership support and resources of its own or it would suffer the fate of other recent Goodyear initiatives. The new process had spawned some power struggles and an organizational vacuum. In the last months of the Herbie team, arguments were constant between those who worked hard to help the initiative and those who were perceived to not be carrying their weight or blocking the initiative.

In this power vacuum, some functional managers still used lean to promote themselves, but most managers and leaders visibly supported the program and had adapted to the change. Even among supporters, some still regularly asked why we were doing this lean stuff. And we still had those who were willing to convert as long as they got their way, and those who stubbornly waited for lean to go away before they retired.

Meanwhile, our sponsor had shifted his attention to other initiatives. He felt that lean product development could support itself. I personally became totally stalled! No matter what I was trying, somebody with enough power interfered. It was as if we had done as much change as the organization could tolerate. I read a lot about this phenomenon, but the opinions are divided. Change management experts say, "Keep going, do not let up." Jim Womack says to give it some time to stabilize. In retrospect I agree with Jim—except that Jim did not say that after the stabilization we would have to jumpstart the engine to get things going again.

In Goodyear's case, Joe Zekoski, at the time VP Global Product Development, jumpstarted lean product development with the Pit Crew initiative (discussed in *Chapter 5*) and by establishing the Goodyear Operations Management (GOM) team. GOM was a cross-functional team of leaders chartered to come up with the organizational structure to institutionalize the lean product development process. After new processes were developed, we had to get all the activities properly aligned to get the full benefits. We had to create something permanent and sustainable to release approximately 1,500 new SKUs every year, which involved some 4,000 learning cycles. The SKUs needed to be delivered efficiently, on time, and according to global standards. A key question for the GOM team was, "Who owns this process?" Everyone pointed to me.

The GOM team met every other week for about 9 months—brainstorming, discussing, maturing, and making lots of suggestions but not getting a lot implemented. I personally have never seen so many RACI (responsibility, accountability, consulted, informed) charts in my life as those created by the GOM team in an effort to define and agree on responsibilities.

I was part of the GOM team, and it was a difficult time for me, because this was the end of *my* lean project: I had to let go and collaborate on a new way to operate an R&D organization.

Then in 2012, based on recommendations from the GOM team, Joe announced the appointment of a global director for lean product development operations ("operations"). There was an operations manager in each of the three innovation centers, and there also were staff positions to continue development of the lean process. The PMO was moved into the operations function. We had several global workshops with all people involved to come up with the details of the organization and the processes.

The creation of an operations group as a function was a very important step in further developing and sustaining the lean product development initiative: we finally knew who owned the process, and who was responsible for operating, standardizing, and improving the process and developing new capabilities.

Goodyear R&D had established a new function, and we had to learn a new discipline: R&D operations. There was a lot of resistance, and it was hard to explain to the functions that they now had to report to an operations function, just as the project managers report to a function called project management. Yet this was done so that knowledge gets generated on how to best operate an R&D lean operation and to assure that functions improve their processes. The operations function also had to design the interfaces, develop and manage the RvCc (requirements vs. capacity and capability) process, and develop the cross-functional work standards (kind of "diagonally" across the matrix). These were all R&D operations aspects that we would have never even considered—let alone managed—prior to lean.

Today the Goodyear operations function has its second global director, and there is no longer any doubt that it was the right decision to establish that function. The integration with the PMO organization also was the right idea. The PMO organization has included the lean processes in their playbook. The operations group keeps having global kaizen events (we still call them workshops) to develop and improve the organization and the process. I think we not only have the right organization in place now, but also the right process and mindset to grow into what is needed to continue operating an effective lean product development organization.

The operations team has a short, global, weekly, cross-functional meeting to review metrics and identify problems. Problems are addressed, new knowledge is shared, and new capability is developed.

Get the Process Right and Results Will Follow

There have been many management schools about how to achieve results in corporations, such as MBO (management by objectives) and MBM (managing by means). Management schools also have gone through cycles of total control versus hands-off, result-focused leadership.

I have observed different management philosophies at Goodyear. When I hired in, management was based on command and control. Later, there was a trend to hire leaders with a proven track record—give them an objective, time, and resources to achieve the objectives. Some of the leaders achieved some or all of the objectives some of the time. I observed high leader turnover (both those who made the numbers and those who did not) during that time, and every time a new leader came in, it looked like we started over, as if we had learned little in the previous generation.

Even though R&D has been shaped by different management styles rather than improvement philosophies over the years, knowledge creation and developing quality products always prevailed. But even with that, we had inefficient processes and did not make as much progress as we should have. More recently, one principle—get the process right and results will follow—has been validated many times in our R&D organization. Today, I see a situation that is much more stable. Leaders develop processes and people, there is less turnover, there are better results, and the processes continue when leaders change.

Goodyear Chairman, President, and CEO Rich Kramer has promoted this idea throughout the last 10 years in different leadership positions: "Efficient, repeatable processes increase the accuracy of both forecasting and results, and reduce errors and variation. I also think of processes like the current in a river. If the current is right, you'll get to your destination without having to paddle as hard. Plus, time can then be spent on ways to improve the journey."

Lean R&D Principle: Get the process right and the results will follow.

The lean approach promotes creating stable processes, learning, and continuous improvement, which ultimately will lead to the desired results. With this approach, if desired results are not achieved, the root cause is determined and the process is improved until the results are achieved. The lean approach—which can be integrated with most existing management or leadership philosophies—locks in the improvements with standards and sustains the gains through management and leadership cycles. The lean approach works well in R&D, but it will take time and effort to implement and a lot more patience than other approaches, yet if offers greater likelihood to achieve sustainable results.

At Goodyear: We have seen many leadership approaches over the years as leadership changes occurred, but in the past decade have reached a period of stabilization. We would always pride ourselves on our good products, but also admitted that our processes were slow and unpredictable. Today we still have excellent products, and now our focus on processes has started to show consistency and the right results.

In Goodyear R&D, we now have the process right and are seeing the results. The Goodyear operations group, like most other functions, spends much more time improving the journey now. The functions in R&D that contribute directly to the product have discovered that they had to change their processes to support the lean operation, the businesses, and the company. They follow the lean principles discussed in this book.

Even support and service functions that are not directly involved in the development of products—such as human resources and finance—must adapt to the lean thinking and processes to support product development.

Nothing could be further from R&D than accounting, so let us look at that example.

Lean Support—Accounting for Value

At Goodyear, the business finance organization provides all new-product financials, and R&D finance prepares the annual operating plans and tracks the monthly charges to the budget. For more than 50 years, R&D finance spent a lot of its time and energy figuring out how to split up the R&D charges and create a fair chargeback to the business or the project teams. The allocation of fixed cost alone kept many accountants busy. There also was a decades-long fight by the business leaders to get as little of the allocation as possible—less allocation helps individual functions or business leaders make their financials look good.

R&D finance was fueling an internally competitive environment, where a lot of money and time was wasted chasing internal goals as opposed to giving priority to company goals or reducing the R&D spending. In R&D, for example, Goodyear would only use expensive dedicated trucks to transport individual sets of test tires because there was no accounting system to share the cost between project managers; managers would not pick up a tab for peer projects.

Unless the allocation exercise leads to an improved process (which it did not), the exercise really does not add value or help the company. Like everybody in R&D, the finance organization should think about value first and ask questions like, "What is the value created for every dollar spent in R&D?" or "How can we help the R&D organization add more value for their customer?" Other traditional finance services can be minimized using the same criteria. Are all the numbers that the finance organization provides useful? What value do they add? Of course, when they ask the customer, the answer is, "We need everything from accounting." That is especially true if there is no explicit charge for the service. The answer would be different if the customer was asked, "What services are you willing to pay for?"

Providing some financial data is still important: leadership needs data to manage the budget, some data are required by the businesses, and numbers are necessary for corporate accounting and regulatory financial reporting. After these fundamentals, though, R&D accountants or finance experts have to change from distributing charges to helping the organization create value.

This happened at Goodyear when we focused on speed, and our CTO commissioned a white paper on the value of speed, that is, what quantifiable financial benefits can the company achieve by having a faster product development process. The Goodyear financial R&D organization spent time on helping define and calculate COD and helped provide the training to all associates who need to understand the concept. Finance will also play a big role in educating the engineers who must understand the effect of their engineering decisions on the profitability of the value stream. The financial organization also spent quite some time on helping assess project risk.

Similar thinking must be applied to other support functions, like human resources, purchasing, and IT. They all must learn principle-based lean and feel empowered to develop the capabilities needed to provide the right level of focus on how they impact the business and what service is needed to help the organization create value, make money, and grow.

Responsibility for Quality

A key question in any lean transformation is, "Who is responsible for quality?" The answer is simple: *everybody.*

When we started our lean initiative at Goodyear, we were under a mandate that there could not be a drop in the quality of our design work. I can say today that the new process further improved our already high-quality standards.

Before our lean transformation, we had different processes for generating tire specifications for our innovation centers in Akron and Luxembourg (GIC*A and GIC*L). In Akron, every engineer was responsible for the accuracy of their specifications for test tires, and they used checklists to avoid mistakes. Of course the system also has a poka-yoke built in, so that as many mistakes as possible could be avoided. In Luxembourg, there was a "spec control" group that inspected all specifications that were issued. In neither case was any mistake passed on to the plant, but in Luxembourg the spec control group was a major bottleneck. They caught the inaccuracies and sent the specs back to the engineers for correction. It turned out that the engineers knew that someone would check their specs, so they paid less attention.

In manufacturing, everybody is responsible for the quality of their work, and everybody is responsible to pull the andon cord and stop the line if they cannot deliver perfect quality or if they discover something that is not right. Never, ever should known bad quality be passed down the manufacturing line. The same is true for an R&D organization. Every engineer must be responsible for the quality of their work. All work that is not perfect must be corrected by the function that created it, or, if not caught there, rejected by the function that follows in the value stream. Either way, the reject must be investigated, a root cause identified, and proper countermeasures implemented. Tools like andon systems, poka-yoke, and checklists work just as well in an R&D organization as they do in a manufacturing organization.

Recently, we experienced the first andon pull in product development. One of our new products was in the production release phase when the plant reported a high incidence of a cosmetic condition. Although at the time it looked like the launch of the product was in question, the team decided to stop the release and send all molds out for correction. The business was concerned about the launch and making its targets, but nobody questioned the decision of the empowered team. At the end of the day, the team had enough buffer, and everybody pulled together to make the launch on time and without the cosmetic condition.

Lean has done more for the quality of our R&D process than just introduce some better processes. For me, one of the most important factors was that it allowed us to create time, ensuring we do things right before a launch. We have time now to do additional testing if needed, even if we have to add an additional learning cycle. Manufacturing is involved early in the development, and a lot of the possible manufacturing issues have been checked out long before it is time to industrialize the product. Even during the industrialization, there is buffer time to run more preproduction runs if needed.

Many other lean tools that are known to help improve quality were validated: engineers focus on one job at a time, applying jidoka in computer tools, quicker error detection due to faster cycles and the elimination of queues, and many more.

Lean R&D Principle: Use lean tools for better design quality.

The increase in quality in a lean manufacturing operation has been well documented. Tools like the andon system, not passing on defects, small-batch processing with fast feedback, poka-yoke, jidoka, and people engagement are effective at improving quality. The same is true in R&D, where the following lean quality impacts were validated:

- Eliminated the passing of inaccurate information between functions and, thus, the risk for mistakes
- Empowered engineers to "pull the andon cord" in product development and stop projects if needed
- Raised awareness that all are responsible for customer value and quality through collaboration across the value stream
- Prevented mistakes with poka-yoke
- Eliminated engineer stop and go and heightened engineer focus of project quality
- Quickened feedback due to faster cycle times and single-piece flow
- Reduced the number of changes and chances to make mistakes with late start and late decisions
- Resolved handover issues immediately when discovered via concurrent development activities
- Improved the validity of the tools and eliminated errors with the addition of jidoka to modeling tools

Lastly, what helps the most is that everybody has time to do it right. The buffers before launch allow time to address any last-minute challenges that could occur before the launch.

At Goodyear: We always had good quality of design, but it was accomplished by the use of a lot of resources and a lot of time. Inspections were prominent, and many things were done over. Today the lean tools and the better processes deliver better quality of design in a much more effective process by implementing all the improvements listed above.

The End of the Herbie Story—Managing Purpose, Process, and People

This is the end of my "Herbie" story—the story of how we *created* a lean product development system at Goodyear. But this is not the end of the book and certainly not the end of lean at Goodyear R&D. Now it is time to address how Goodyear operates and will *sustain* what we built. The more we sustain and improve our processes, the more opportunities we discover.

The remainder of this chapter shows how Goodyear manages the many lean aspects that may or may not fall under the responsibility of a lean operations group. We need to remember here that R&D is one piece of the value stream, and it must align with other stakeholders and the corporation. It is these aspects—like hoshin kanri, talent management, and supplier management—that are vital to managing and sustaining lean, but are also distributed throughout a company. I like to group them into categories of purpose, process, and people.

Lean Purpose

The purpose of product development is to help create profitable value streams and reusable knowledge. So what is the purpose of the *company*? Where do we find that? Like most companies, Goodyear's mission is to provide sustainable value to the customer and profitable growth to the company and stakeholders.

Hoshin Kanri

A Goodyear strategic roadmap was established in 2011, and it was updated for the first time in June 2014 (see *Goodyear Strategy Roadmap*). For the first time in my career, a Goodyear strategy had lasted more than 3 years—the work in June was an update, not a change. I personally was not used to seeing a coherent strategy at Goodyear; there used to be the occasional announcement by the chairman, but it was hard to distinguish what was meant for associates and what was meant for Wall Street.

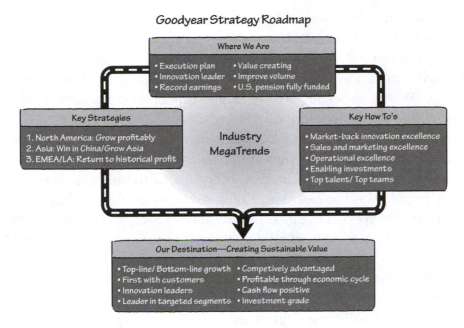

In 2010, Chairman Kramer pulled a team together that was chartered to come up with the strategy roadmap, and he explains the importance of the roadmap:

> In 2010, coming out of both the company's turnaround and the global recession, we needed to clearly articulate our strategy for the long term. Developing our Strategy Roadmap was a unifying moment for our company because it didn't just result in words on a page, it defined our destination. It gave us a "North Star" to guide our decisions and actions in building a business that would deliver sustainable value. Both the original Strategy Roadmap and the update (2014) reflect: SBU (strategic business unit)-specific mile-posts ("Key Strategies"); long-term goals ("Our Destination"), and how we would achieve both ("Key How Tos"). In March 2011, the Strategy Roadmap was unveiled to associates in a global town hall meeting and to the financial community at our Investor Day. SBU presidents were responsible for engaging their region leaders to communicate the Roadmap to their associates, with support from global communications.

Goodyear had a hard time initially to communicate this strategy through all levels of the company. I am not surprised because, based on our history, people were numb to this kind of message. But in this case, the same message went to the associates, the stock analysts, and the shareholders. Why should it be different? The Goodyear associates have the same stake and interest in the company as other stakeholders and shareholders. That is why Chairman Kramer says: "Consistency of message leads to trust and confidence. When associates hear the same things we are telling Wall Street, they know that we are committed to our strategy and direction."

I noticed that for a long time our chairman repeated the same message about the strategy in every communication, and he still refers to them in most communications today: He says, "The rule of thumb in advertising is that most people need to hear something seven times before they acknowledge it. That rule applies to all communication: repetition is critical. It's also a very effective way to remind all audiences that there is a constancy of purpose and direction guided by our strategy."

Another consistent message that Chairman Kramer has used in many communications with associates, shareholders, and stakeholders is, "This strategy works." If it did not work, I am sure the appropriate changes would be made the same way the strategy was established: with those involved and then clearly communicated to all the levels of the organization.

By now, most associates in the company know the strategy and have aligned to it. What helped with the alignment was that every part of the organization wrote their strategy to support the corporate strategy. Based on the corporate strategy, all businesses created roadmaps. Roadmaps are timetables for the major new product introductions, for example, they show when the next global HP passenger tire will be launched and how long it will stay in the market. Then there is a capacity roadmap that makes sure that the manufacturing capacity is available to produce the tires on the roadmap. A capability roadmap shows what manufacturing capability must be available at what time to make sure that we can produce at the right level of quality and performance. There also is a major materials and sourcing map. Capital planning follows the roadmaps, and makes sure that the budgets are in place and the expansions line up with the need for product. R&D takes its cues off those roadmaps and aligns all development work with maps, to assure that all the new product is ready when the map calls for it and that the needed capabilities are developed.

The mission of Goodyear R&D also aligns with the corporate strategy: R&D *efficiently* delivers continuous flow of *consumer-relevant, innovative* products and processes that align with business strategy and drive profitable growth. This is the first time I have seen an externally (customer) focused R&D mission. I was accustomed to missions that make R&D a better organization.

After the creation of the corporate strategy, Jean-Claude Kihn, then CTO, created six workstreams in R&D to support the global strategy and the product roadmaps:

- *Product performance leadership* establishes high customer value and profitable products.
- *Business model innovation* develops both innovation capability and innovative products.
- *Product material cost* assures the right product at the right cost.
- *Manufacturing capacity* assures that the right capacity is in place to efficiently produce.
- *Manufacturing capability* develops the manufacturing means to enable high quality and high-value products.
- *Global R&D capability* assures the efficient development of the tools that are needed for the best product development engine in the industry.

All these work streams have a direct line of sight to our corporate destination. They focus on being first with customers and becoming the innovation leader in the industry by relying on the key "How Tos," such as operational excellence (lean) and top talent/top teams to achieve their goals.

Lean practitioners will recognize this as hoshin kanri or policy or strategy deployment. Yet even at that, you may say this looks awfully simple for a global organization of Goodyear's size. There has to be more to this. But there really is not. Remember the lean R&D principle about simplicity.

The right strategy is set at the top and communicated through all the levels of the organization so that everybody aligns with the strategy and moves in the right direction. To stay with the image posed by Chairman Kramer about the canoe in the river: now that we have the right flow, we must have everybody paddle in the same direction and in unison.

In R&D during our lean initiative, we had the same consistent message from Jean-Claude, our lean sponsor. We had a lot of setbacks and tons of criticism and resistance during our lean implementation, but Jean-Claude never wavered. He defended the initiative with the same arguments every time he was challenged, always referring back to a lean principle that applies regardless of whether we were successful on our implementation on the first try.

During his gemba walks, Jean-Claude also liked to ask associates how their work fits with the R&D strategy and the corporate strategy. A few years back, he would get answers like, "I design a mold" or "I am working on a specification." Today the more frequent answers are "I am part of the team that develops a great, new, high-performance tire line," or "I am proud to make driving safer."

Lean R&D Principle: Set the right strategy for the company and cascade it down to align all parts of the organization.

When you start a journey or run a company, you must know where you are going, and you need a compass or a map to get there. The "True North" points you in the right direction, and a good set of maps gives all employees of the company assurances that they are marching in the same direction toward the same destination.

The direction, though, has to be set by the top leadership with stakeholders involved. It has to be clearly formulated and communicated through the whole organization. Different parts of the organization have to align their strategy and actions to the corporate strategy. A good strategy is consistent over enough time so that results can be achieved. Changes to the strategy should be made the same way the strategy is established—with stakeholder involvement.

In lean, this process of strategy deployment is often referred to as "hoshin kanri." Like many Japanese terms associated with lean, a lot of people think that this is something new. But many companies, like Goodyear, have been following this approach for years, not knowing of Toyota methods or terms.

At Goodyear: Chairman, President, and CEO Rich Kramer commissioned a cross-functional team in 2010 to propose a strategic roadmap. The roadmap included long-term goals and business-specific mileposts, and the means of achieving both. In March 2011, our strategy roadmap was unveiled to associates in a global town hall meeting and to the financial community. SBU presidents were responsible for engaging their region leaders to communicate the roadmap to their associates, with support from global communications. All business units developed their individual strategies to support the corporate strategy. All functions aligned their strategy to support the business and the corporate strategy. The strategy roadmap was first updated in 2014. There were no special tools or campaigns needed to implement this process at Goodyear.

Developing Customer Value and Capability

Goodyear's longtime functional leaders would say, "We have developed capability for 50 years. What's new about that?" I disagree. We did develop good functional capability and tools all those years. But before we started lean at Goodyear, we did not have much *cross-functional* capability that focused on the customer. Cross-functional capability is equally important as functional capability. A lot of the development of the R&D cross-functional capability is now falling under the responsibility of R&D operations.

An example of cross-functional capability is the PMO playbook. These are the project-management standards that summarize all the Goodyear knowledge on the subject of cross-functional project management. Other important capabilities we have recently developed at Goodyear are the lean product development processes.

Chairman Kramer summarizes his thoughts on delivering product and capability as follows, "*We live in a world of 'and.'* At Goodyear, we must deliver results *and* build capabilities. Not one or the other, but both. We have to continue to lead the tire industry with products and services that win in our targeted markets *and* help our customers build their businesses. At the same time, we have to build the capabilities and skills that will be necessary in the future to sustain our value creation to meet constantly changing consumer needs. This ambidexterity is a skill necessary for all successful business leaders."

Before and after the transformation to a matrix organization at Goodyear, we did very well with the development of tools and technical capability. The functions are still responsible for that effort—some of the tools are developed by a rather large team that reports to a function. Examples are computer modeling or predictive tools. A separate work stream was created to coordinate the global R&D knowledge and tool development. In this context, the functions have a harder time identifying the need for what capability is needed because functional leaders are not as intimately involved in the projects. For that reason, the functional leaders must rely on different tools and practices like gemba walks, design reviews, and huddles to identify the opportunities.

Lean R&D Principle: Develop products *and* capability.

People in R&D understand the development of innovative products well. Sometimes they also recognize the need for capability development within their functional organization (technical expertise, knowledge, tools, etc.). But they had to learn to develop the capability to collaborate across functions to develop profitable value streams.

Within a matrix organization, functions have a harder time identifying the need for cross-functional capability development and only reluctantly assume the responsibility for it. R&D matrix organizations may ignore developing the "horizontal" capability and many aspects that support it (e.g., people development, creativity, collaboration, knowledge development). In a lean R&D environment, all associates have to understand that capability development is their responsibility and not the job of the CIS organization.

Process capability can pay rich dividends for the company—more so than just cost savings. Capability development in R&D can have a large effect on the profitability of the value streams because of the large R&D shadows. This must be emphasized in training so that all levels of the organization understand it. It should also be reflected in personal performance systems. Some of the capacity gained through a lean initiative could be used for capability development.

At Goodyear: The operations function is responsible for developing the capability to manage projects across functions. We have a global coordinator for global functional capability and tool-development initiatives. Renewed effort is placed on the development of technical expertise and various aspects of talent development. Many functions assign project managers to major capability-development projects and execute the capability development efficiently using good project management standards. People at Goodyear start to understand that they must do their jobs and improve their jobs, and managers know that part of their responsibility is developing people.

Pawan Handa, director of Strategic Integration, is responsible for the coordination of the global technical capability development. Pawan says that functions used to develop their own capabilities, with a focus that was good for the function. "Today we take a strategic, cross-functional, and global approach for capability development, and spend our resources on initiatives that improve our overall efficiency and effectiveness," he says.

Chairman Kramer explains the reasons to invest in the development of lean or operational excellence capability: First, operational excellence is within our control. We can continuously improve our operational efficiency regardless of what is happening in the marketplace. Second, the "size of the prize" makes it clear that operational excellence delivers real and significant financial benefits.

Under the leadership of the operations function at Goodyear, we spent a lot of time and effort on the development of lean capability, including the capability to deliver in full and on time and the development of agility and speed to support the business by having the right product at the right time. Other examples are the capability to consistently deliver profitable value streams and investment in innovation capability.

Where does all the capacity come from to develop the additional capability? In R&D, the capacity was created when we eliminated waste from out development processes.

Global Goodyear

Don Reinertsen told a Goodyear audience that more value is created by overall alignment than with local excellence.[1]

Maybe at Goodyear we are spoiled: we have a truly global R&D organization, and most other functions in the company (e.g., operations, HR, finance) are global as well. And we have been at it long enough to work out the bugs. From a lean standpoint, there are big advantages to a global organization: everybody uses the best methods to do their work, and we only have to maintain one set of design standards and one set of operating standards. If improvements are made, they automatically cascade down and all affected global entities can take advantage of the improvement.

Global Innovation Centers

Our global organization was not easy to create. In the 1990s, we merged the two technical centers (we called them technical centers back then) in North America: the Kelly-brand center in Maryland and the Goodyear-brand center in Akron. Both development centers had operated independently and developed vastly different standards and processes, and it took more than 10 years to learn and align all engineers on one process, even though the Kelly engineers had relocated to Akron. After that lesson, when the innovation center in Hanau, Germany, joined the R&D organization (through acquisition), the center was not relocated but aligned around a global organization and global processes.

For the lean product development implementation, we piloted our lean product development process in our Akron innovation center (GIC*A) and then rolled it out in our innovation center in Luxembourg (GIC*L). The Luxembourg center is larger and they develop more tires for OEMs than Akron. The alignment was not easy because they always thought that they needed different processes because their customer base was different (European vs. American OEM accounts). It also took GIC*L longer to get the lean change going because they did not have a disruptive event (strike) like we had in Akron. R&D is intertwined in different ways with the rest of an organization, and we eventually realized that we could not change the development organization alone in GIC*L—we had to change the organization of the complete value stream. For that reason, we started the change in Bruxelles with the European business unit.

Today we have the same lean principles implemented in all three innovation centers. I will not claim that the details of our one R&D process are precisely the same. Some of our leaders had insisted originally that everything be exactly the same, including the color-coding of the kanban cards. This is another case where good is good enough, and you should accommodate differences caused by the demands of local customers. There also are remnants of prior processes and organizations with which the centers are comfortable. Changing all those just for the sake of being "exactly" the same is waste.

Recently, I talked to a lean champion from another company. This company has several development centers in the United States, and each is rather independent. Every center had a lean champion, and, although the champions collaborated well, they had a terrible time aligning all the centers on one set of best practices. As a result of this lack of alignment, they left a lot of efficiency on the table. Soon after I talked to this champion, the company largely disbanded the lean product development initiative.

The more satellites you have, the more work it will be. And because of the difficulty, integration of acquisitions often gets put off. The longer they are put off, the more difficult it gets. If this is your company and challenge, I have one tip: at Goodyear we integrated our most recent acquisition by aligning processes with our existing processes and involving the engineers, but we did not relocate staff—it worked better than our prior integration where we relocated the employees without aligning the processes.

Joe Zekoski, CTO, thinks that Goodyear had a relatively easy time creating a global organization because *all* Goodyear R&D leaders worked in management or leadership positions for a domestic as well as a foreign innovation center. They experienced firsthand the cultures, needs, preferences, and challenges of a global organization.

Today at Goodyear we also try to leverage R&D resources globally as much as possible, but we also recognize that local parts of the organization will need to deal with local customers, including OEMs, large dealers, fleets, and so on. Our global functions strive to use engineers in all three innovation centers based on availability and talent. And we can do this because the processes are mostly standardized. Global leverage in R&D can help with the following:

- Global processes assure maximum gain from standards and best practices.
- Global processes allow global leveraging of resources and knowledge.
- Less management and general administration is needed, leading to a more responsive, flatter organization.
- It establishes a much more effective base for continuous improvement.
- Global platforms or global products become possible, which helps with efficiency and quality.

Global Product Platforms

The automotive industry has taught us the value of global platforms (VW, Ford), with companies putting down roots from East to West and from West to East. Global product platforms take a page out of the global process playbook. I have stressed several times in this book that processes should be managed on the highest level, ideally global. If you have only one global process, you only have to maintain one process, and any improvement can be leveraged globally. The same is true for a product platform or family: if you have only one product that you can leverage globally, you only have to develop and maintain one family of product.

We also know from the automotive industry that global cars really do not look and perform exactly the same in every part of the world. But companies still get tremendous leverage in both cost and quality from their global platforms. The same benefits apply to tires and other global products. There are examples in the auto industry where the challenges of developing a global platform have been substantial. The same is true for Goodyear, but it is a challenge that is quite worth addressing.

The questions that need to be asked when considering global platforms are certainly different from industry to industry, but there are a few general practices that can help achieve success:

- Align on global standards.
- Understand what must be unique in each region or country, and what can be standardized.
- Understand regulatory issues and other compliance issues country to country.
- Clearly define the manufacturing capabilities you have around the world, including age-related traits of facilities.
- Understand regional performance and marketing requirements.

Based on my experience, global platforms sometimes have more organizational and policy restrictions than technical challenges. Many companies are managed by regional business units that are responsible for their own P&Ls. Often leaders of these units also are compensated and promoted based on the performance of the unit. Many companies have difficulty leveraging global production capacity because the business units have not learned to give priority to the performance of the company over the performance of the local business unit. If these organization issues cannot be adequately addressed, a compromised global product is often the result and products are everything but globally competitive.

Goodyear started its global platform development in the innovation centers, but we quickly realized that this effort first needs alignment of the global businesses.

One Goodyear

Goodyear is trying to leverage capabilities and capacities globally as much as possible and the same is true of our intent to leverage lean. "Reinventing the fundamentals of our business—supply chain, sales, product development, manufacturing, and so on—from region to region and business to business is inefficient," says Chairman Kramer. "Our customers won't pay for inefficiency, and today's advancements in communication and technology leave no reason or room to duplicate or reinvent. Driving toward standard work and processes will eliminate wasted time, effort, and resources. It will also enable us to be more efficient from a global perspective, as best practices can be easily shared in all regions if they are applied in 'One Goodyear Way.' While this can be a competitive advantage, it is quickly becoming 'table stakes' in today's ultra-competitive world. When we do that, it also lets us focus on serving the customer and the consumer where we can add real value."

We apply the same standards to our lean capability and try to leverage this capability globally as much as possible. Goodyear has embarked on lean in many other divisions, especially in manufacturing and in the supply chain. I am not going to detail those efforts, but like with most lean initiatives, there were a few false starts. In Goodyear R&D, the implementation of lean preceded the implementation in manufacturing. Maybe that was a good thing: R&D did not feel tempted or pressured to invite somebody from manufacturing to spearhead the R&D lean implementation in R&D, and, thus, we did not feel compelled, as do many companies, to plug in tools that worked well in manufacturing into the R&D environment.

I am convinced, though, that the lean principles that we developed and validated for R&D could be plugged into other parts of Goodyear, an R&D organization in another company, or even in many service organizations (many are more like a product development division than manufacturing). With all Goodyear divisions embracing lean to at least some extent, the challenge now is to share and leverage the lean knowledge developed in the different organizations across the company, to collaborate on aligning divisions (as our standards are globally aligned in R&D), and filling the gaps between divisions.

Lean Process

It is hard to manage what you cannot see and what you do not know. And so if lean works well for visible objects and processes, it reasons that if you make invisible development work (and the problems embedded within them) visible, lean also will work in those settings.

A lot of companies say they have a hard time implementing lean in a product development process because they cannot see the work. So look around you: Do you have prototypes? Do you have labs? Do you have testing? The work in those functions is certainly visible. I did not know this when we started our lean initiative, but this is where I would start if I had to do this over. (I perceived, like many others, that most of R&D is invisible and difficult to illuminate and improve with lean.) There can be significant gains and a lot of learning by deploying lean to even the few visible processes, in addition to a lot of confidence that can be gained.

Start with What You Can See

The invisible nature of product development work is even truer today than it was many years ago because of computerization. I still remember when mold designers drew molds with paper and pencils, and you could see the progress they were making. Today that visible work has been replaced with computer drawings stored in a folder on a network.

Few lean scholars, though, mention that most product development processes have a fair amount of "visible work." For example, most companies that manufacture products make prototypes that are tested and visible. Other development processes require dies, fixtures, or jigs; these, too, are visible. Work is visible in most labs—samples can be used to track flow through the lab. The same validated principles that are used in manufacturing can be applied to the making or handling of "visible" work in R&D. Here are a few examples of how this was done at Goodyear:

- *5S*: I recall a number of "expansion projects" in the test labs at Goodyear that needed new floor space. Historically, we would budget for new floor space in a new building, but in recent years we have been able to *create* the necessary floor space for new equipment by doing a 5S initiative in an already existing area. Emmanuel Robinet, manager Product Evaluation, told me that before the last expansion in the test facility at the innovation center in Luxembourg, they created the space by scrapping more than *10 tons* of useless stuff that occupied valuable floor space.

- *Quick changeovers:* In our labs and our prototype factories, we change over molds, building drums, test wheels, machine setups, and so on. Quick changeovers can significantly reduce the testing or prototype manufacturing time and increase the capacity. A new prototype tire machine installed in GIC*L has quick changeover capability.
- *Lean scheduling:* The cycle times in our mold-making plants are normally quite long. Any request to reduce the mold-making cycle time was formerly answered with a request for new and very expensive machinery and additional resources. We wanted to see for ourselves, so we took a gemba walk in one of our mold-manufacturing plants. It turned out that the slowest step in the tool-production process had more machines than it needed and that the next slowest step was not restricted by resources but instead restricted by policies and internal work rules. In fact, we determined that the cycle time could be reduced by at least 50% without additional investment or manpower if the rules were changed. You cannot believe what you see sometimes just by looking.
- *Inventory management:* We used to have a global inventory of more than 150,000 test tires. Applying lean principles like flow and pull helped us eliminate dedicated warehouses globally, saved us a lot of money every year, and reduced cycle time per iteration by 6 weeks. We also learned how to manage a very difficult project with a cross-functional team, and we set a precedent: in a lean initiative we do not eliminate people and that we are better off after the change.
- *Visual kanbans:* Difficult lean concepts—flow and pull—and their effect are made visible in R&D by kanban systems. For example, in the materials labs, we use a two-bin kanban system between pulling raw materials, weighing the materials, and mixing them in a rubber mixer.

Developing a lean flow system around visible material is easier than developing it for "invisible" work. Since a lot of the product development processes have some form of visible materials in their process, look at those first. The key is that a lot of the processes involving visible materials also are on the critical path. The removal of the waste from these processes—done easily because they are visible—will result in savings in development cost. But more important than the savings in the R&D cost are the gains in cycle time (speed and its impact on COD) and the collateral gains in quality. Most important, however, is the experience, knowledge, and the confidence that can be gained in the implementation of the lean principles.

Lean R&D Principle: Start lean R&D with work that is visible and work to make other work visible.

Most R&D organizations have some physical objects and areas where work is visible (e.g., tools, prototypes, testing, labs). They are a good place to start a lean initiative. The work in those areas is not only visible, but also relatively close to manufacturing, and validated tools can be used. This is a good training ground for lean learners, and the results help sell the initiative in areas of invisible work. Initial successes are relatively easy to generate, which is important for good change management.

But after having learned to improve the processes that deal with visible, physical objects, the challenge is then to make invisible R&D work visible, so it is easier to observe and apply lean principles. If you walk through a product development operation, you will see many facets of invisible R&D work (engineering work, specifications, drawings, calculations, modeling, knowledge). This invisible work must, too, be somehow connected to lean principles. Popular tools to make invisible development work visible are

- Visual planning
- Process maps (including value-stream maps)
- Kanban cards
- Scrum boards
- Relay batons
- A phase-gate process

Flow is significantly easier to manage if R&D work is visible: queues, excess WIP, bottlenecks, and capacity issues can be observed and managed similar to the way they are managed in a manufacturing environment.

At Goodyear: By applying lean to visible R&D work, we achieved large cost and time savings and a lot of learning that gave us momentum for the rest of our lean initiative. One example of this was changing the process for handling test tires from build-and-warehouse to a direct-ship process. By implementing a lean process in the plants to produce prototype tires, we were able to improve cycle time by 50%. One of our first autonomous lean implementations happened in the testing organization in Luxembourg, where the manager, with the support of his lean experts, built a first-class lean operation with a station-to station-pull. The operation improved efficiency, cycle time, and inventory.

Some of our more impressive, value-creating results have come by making invisible R&D work visible, and using lean principles to improve flow and speed. For example, kanban cards have proved to be a good system to make work visible. Engineers pin the cards at their desk, and it becomes obvious when an engineer gets overloaded. Functional managers like to paste cards to whiteboards in their offices to manage the distribution of the work in their division. The cards also make the flow of the work visible and make planning in the functions easier. One function uses highly visible relay batons that engineers display at their desks to signal that they are working on a task that is on the critical path, indicating that they should not be given additional work at this time.

Make Visible What You Cannot See to Detect Process Problems

In a lean R&D operation, one reason why you want to make the invisible work visible is to be able to see deviations from the normal or the standard situation. You want to be able to recognize problems you encounter with your existing processes or the processes you are trying to develop.

"If you want to make things visible, you ask the people," says Guenter Wartusch, operations manager. What Guenter meant by this is that he would ask the engineers to write down the answer to, "How many projects are currently active?" Initially, no one wrote anything down because they did not know the answer, or, at the least, they were convinced that they did not know the answer. "Everybody has to first realize that we do not know what we cannot see."

In order to know, you must first look, and you need visibility into what you cannot see. Guenter explains the need for visibility like this: If you fly a plane and you have great visibility, you can use that visibility to perform a landing. But there are still some things that you cannot see when flying, for example, you need to see how fast you are going. You cannot see the rudder and the flaps directly, and you need to see how they are set. That is why you need a dashboard where you can see those things. When the weather is not so good, you must have visibility in the cockpit for many more things, like altitude, distance to the runway, and so on. In R&D, we sometimes need tools to see, but often all we have to do is look.

Yogi Berra said, "You can observe a lot by just watching," and I recommend to start R&D visibility by learning to observe. Virtually every book about the Toyota manufacturing process (Toyota Production System) talks about direct observation in the work area, the gemba. I was always impressed how much time they say a lean plant manager spends on the plant floor—certainly a lot more than a Goodyear plant manager spent on the floor when I joined the company more than 30 years ago. So why is it so important to spend time on the plant floor? The answer is simple: that is where you can *see* something! What you really want to see is what does not work as intended, like a process that is not functioning well, process breakdowns, and problems like work stoppages or oil leaking from a machine.

Because of this "go to the gemba" approach, Japanese companies teach employees to become good observers. They and other good companies strive toward making visible what cannot be seen on a plantfloor so that deviations can be quickly detected and fixed. I once observed a TPS expert explain to a Goodyear employee why every machine in the plant must be so clean that it shines. "How can you see when your machine leaks oil when the whole machine is covered with oil?" the TPS expert asked. R&D work and deviations from the standard may be harder to see, but you will definitely not see anything if you do not look.

One of the best examples of the value of visibility I learned from my grandmother on our family farm in Europe. She used to have all the family cash in her pocket, which was safe where I grew up. She always saw what money she had (and what she did not have), and she would never buy anything for which she did not have the money.

At Goodyear in R&D we had many cases where simple visibility has made a big difference. Every month, our CTO receives a red/green report that shows the on-time delivery of all global new products. This has helped us achieve and maintain our on-time delivery target and is in dramatic contrast to 2005 when our CTO had trouble even finding proof that we had an on-time delivery problem.

In our Akron test laboratory, all tests planned/completed for a given day are displayed on a planning wall, letting everybody know if they are ahead or behind. Our materials test laboratory shows what equipment is down and how long it has been down. Any capacity conflict on the visual planning board in the operations management center (OMC) is highlighted by a tag

Lean R&D Principle: Make problems or deviations highly visible to improve the likelihood of fixing them.

If work is visible, it is easy to see a deviation from a standard. In R&D as in manufacturing, there are many things that can be seen on the work floor just by going there and looking. But in R&D not *everything* that is needed for good management is directly visible, and it must be made visible by gauges, trend charts, alarm lights, measurements, and so on. Some people even say that you must make problems stick out or look ugly to increase the chances of it getting fixed. In a strong functional culture, managers did not always want other functions to see their problems, and in a culture where only achieving the numbers mattered, nobody wanted to see or even publicly display problems.

In a lean culture, it is OK to have a problem or be in the red, as long as you do not stay in the red for a long period of time. Making problems visible, however, implies that somebody is interested at looking at them and doing something about them. This includes empowering associates to fix problems in an area for which they are responsible. Making problems visible and not doing anything about them quickly sends the wrong message.

Making work and problems visible does not, by itself, solve the problems. People must be willing to address and solve the problems. If a visual does not address problems or does not change the way people do their work, it is not needed.

At Goodyear: Today in R&D we use many tools to make work and problems visible, such as resource conflicts, delivery issues, downtime, etc. Many functions created tools specific to their operation. It took some time for people to get comfortable with openly showing problems. People used to be very defensive and creatively disguise the "red." People only became comfortable with showing "red" after they experienced that there were no negative consequences for doing so. People also had to understand, through experience, that when they show a problem or a deviation, it will often be their responsibility to address the problem—there is no automatic allocation of resources to the red, and the red is not a signal for a CIS team to show up and fix the problem.

turned 45°, so that in the huddle with the technical director the team can quickly see it and resolve the conflict.

There are not a lot of rules or processes around the subject of how to make problems visible in R&D, and sometimes you just need to get creative: simple dash lines or tick marks on a piece of paper (like a tick for every day the machine has been down) are often enough to get the message across. You do not need a computer, either.

Chris Helsel, former director of Global Technology Projects, wanted to make sure that during a critical phase of a technology development project, the primary investigator could dedicate all his/her time to one single project during the sprint. Chris did not want the engineer getting interrupted for trivial jobs. Every primary investigator, when working on the critical path of a project, was issued a red relay baton to symbolize that the engineer is in a race and has to get the baton to the next runner as fast as possible. The red batons are visually displayed at the engineer's desk, and people think twice before they interrupt the relay runner.

Today in R&D we use kanban cards to make invisible work visible. Most Goodyear engineers pin the cards to their desk, and it is obvious what the engineer is working on. Unfortunately, the cards do not turn yellow and red at the end of the cycle, but they do have dates printed on them. Many functional managers have a whiteboard in their office with a kanban card for every major job on which their engineers are working. This gives them great visibility for the WIP that every engineer is assigned to as well as the resource availability, delays, and many other issues.

Another advantage of the kanban cards, the late start, and the pull that we use is that we see all work that comes down the pipeline. We know weeks ahead when a kanban for an iteration will be released to a function. This avoids surprises—the functional leaders know what new work comes up on what day. That allows for good resource planning and assures that the right resources are available when it is time to start the work. Testing knows when a test request will come in for a special vehicle that they must lease or purchase. They know if equipment resources get constrained and they can reroute tires to another lab.

Seeing the work, especially seeing the upcoming work, helps resolve a lot of problems before they become real problems. This visibility also helps with resource requirements versus capacity capability planning (RvCc).

At Goodyear, we know that if the WIP in a function goes over the optimum level, then we create queues and we increase cycle time. That is why many functions (including operations) use a WIP gauge like a speedometer in a car. We also know how important cycle time is. For that reason, we make WIP visible, and operations make adjustments if needed. When we started the lean implementations and we had long queues, we had a computer application that showed the queues "live" and alerted management as soon as a queue exceeded the buffer limit. Fortunately, this system became irrelevant in our process (we do have sporadic queues in certain areas and rely on more specific tools), but I would definitely recommend a queue visibility system during the start of a lean R&D initiative.

Another big advantage of visible work is that work and resource hording can be avoided. I still remember when engineers notoriously kept work on their plate in case the company was playing musical chairs—nobody wanted to be the person or the department without work when a reorganization was looming.

In Goodyear we did not always celebrate the red as we do today. Some time ago, managers would only share the good news and celebrate the green. In fact, sharing bad news would never have occurred to them—although they did handle big problems in one-on-one sessions with their superiors. They were too afraid that "having problems" would reflect badly on their performance and advancement.

A word of caution: Some companies like to visually highlight bad performance, which is different than highlighting a problem. At Goodyear, they used to hand out a stuffed red rooster to the leader of the business unit with the poorest performance. I am glad we discontinued that practice. Visibility of a problem points out an opportunity to make a process improvement—in no case should it be used as a form of motivation that embarrasses an individual or a team.

Visual Planning

Planning has never been popular at Goodyear. Before we started lean, planning used to be an exercise in futility. After all, why waste your time planning if nothing is executed according to the plan. At Goodyear, the unpredictable priority lists controlled everything.

With lean, we made a 180° turn on planning. Visual planning is simple, logical, and makes sense, and everything happens according to the plan or it is discussed among stakeholders. I wish I could say that visual planning was the only tool that made the difference, but I cannot; it was, though, certainly the tool of choice that helped us create flow and achieve our on-time delivery performance. What makes visual planning work is that the visual part facilitates the collaboration among all stakeholders, who then resolve the visible conflicts.

Recently, I visited a company that makes products for an OEM, and their whole business runs off visual plans. Compared to Goodyear product development, this company has very low variability and they do not use a pull process like we do. They make visual plans of all their projects and all their sub-processes. They huddle every day in front of their plans, and they identify and reconcile problems and interferences. You might argue that this could be done just as well on a computer, but I disagree. The interferences could be identified on the computer, but it would be extremely difficult to resolve all the conflicts daily by e-mail and by looking at the computer schedules.

In Goodyear, we have very high variability in our projects, but we found that visually scheduling the completion date of a single step with a pull upstream and FIFO downstream is enough for everybody to get the picture, and it sufficiently aligns the variable work between the contributing functions.

We have a half hour huddle every week in front of our planning board (see *Goodyear Visual Planning*): one week the meeting consists of the business, project managers, and the regional technical director; the alternative week, the meeting is held with functional leaders. The focus of the meetings is on problems, conflicts, and anything that needs a cross-functional decision. With the board in front of them, stakeholders see the consequences when they move things around, and the folks who suffer the effects of the move are right there to speak up. Frank Hull, who studied best practices in product development for more than 30 years, said when he visited Goodyear, "I pray that you never computerize this planning system."

Jon Bellissimo, general director GIC*A, says that the dialogue with the business and the stakeholders makes this process work. Jon says, "No one function is able to solve most of those problems. They can only be solved when everyone is in there together. The good thing is you see the whole picture, you see the consequences, and you are assured you have the best plan going forward with the information that you have available there."

Ricardo Gloria Oliveira, project manager, likes the cadence of our schedule and the fact that he exactly knows when his work will be delivered. The visual schedule is extremely important. Ricardo says he uses it every day and that it resolves 95% of his conflicts with his peers—they accommodate him because he accommodates them. Ricardo feels that all TPLs follow the process now because they realize that following the process assures the best results for the company; earlier when starting this type of scheduling, the tendency was for some TPLs to "beat the system" and move their projects ahead, but that does not happen anymore.

Goodyear Visual Planning

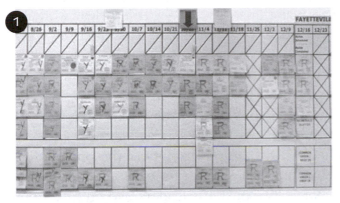

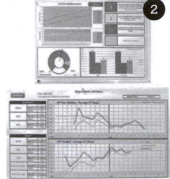

1. Visual planning of the pacemaker for iterations in one of our plants: Status is noted on the tags. "Y" means the iteration was completed on time. A red "N" would be used if it had been late.
2. The dashboards show WIP and cycle time. The text discusses the root causes and corrective actions. These charts are discussed weekly with the global operations team.
3. Tags are turned sideways on the schedule to show a problem. In this case, a project manager wants an iteration slot but there is no capacity. This alerts the participants in the weekly business meeting with the technical director that this issue must be resolved.
4. This board shows planned versus actual iterations and releases for every function. Use of colored dots signals a late delivery, and corrective action is discussed in a weekly standup meeting.

When we started the visual planning system, we created a "tilt" meeting to escalate problems that had to have leadership involvement. We only needed a few of these meetings when we started. After that the TPLs understood that there was a pattern in the decisions of the tilt meetings, and the decisions became predictable. We have not had a tilt meeting in a long time because the TPLs work out the conflicts among themselves or in the weekly huddle.

Recently, the business identified a major opportunity to gain market share by moving up the product launch of a major new product. Mike Wilps, operations manager GIC*A, says, "The expectation from the business was that with their declaration of need, the project would be pulled ahead with minor consequences. Reviewing the visual planning boards showed that the time-frame was not workable based on other key commitments already earmarked for the time slots needed. There were a lot of exchanges and meetings back and forth about how to pull this major line forward—with no clear workable strategy. The holistic view of the full scope of workload was missing."

Mike continues that it was suggested to have the next discussion at the visual planning boards to analyze the situation. This was unconventional and grudgingly accepted, but all agreed to try, including the business leaders. Conflicts were reviewed, and decisions were made about what can be moved and what other key projects needed to stay as planned. Cost of additional capacity was weighed against the profitability of the project. Key decisions and strategies were worked out in front of the visual planning boards and its array of sticky notes. The business leaders had an "eye open-ing" moment when they realized how this visibility allowed them to see the issues, resolve the conflicts, and reach a consensus in a collaborative and agreeable manner. Ultimately, the board was rearranged and the critical products were successfully pulled forward with an anticipated gain in mar-ket share and profitability.

Keep in mind this happened 5 years after the then business director decided that you cannot run a multibillion dollar business with sticky notes (see *Chapter 5*). We had used sophisticated computer programs for this kind of planning in the past, and we still have those programs. But today our business leaders prefer the OMC and the visual planning wall.

I am still surprised how well that visual planning process works, and here is why I think it works:

- All empowered stakeholders look at the same picture at the same time. They look into each other's eyes, ask questions, and they learn to trust each other.
- Conflicts are on the table, and they get resolved in the meetings. There is no compromise, if the compromise would affect the profitability.
- Participants can see, to a large extent, the impact and consequences of all decisions; the interferences with other projects are visible.
- You can distrust computers, but it is hard to distrust notes written on a piece of paper.
- Somehow in a standup meeting people are more focused on the essen-tials. Physically standing must somehow convey the message that time is limited.

The process forces discipline because it makes all deviations visible. When we started lean, I remember a discussion that I had with one of my many bosses at that time. We were wondering how we would ever get the discipline from the people within Goodyear to make *any* lean planning work. The Goodyear project managers had spent years developing sophisticated methods to work around the system, and we had concluded that our company could compete for the top spot if companies were ranked by their lack of discipline. Today that has completely changed, and the same people are still in place.

Some companies say that visual planning is difficult when offsite participants are involved in the scheduling. We experienced the same problem at Goodyear because we schedule the iterations for the Latin American business in the innovation center in Akron. We have a person in Akron who represents the Latin American business. For me, the simplest solution is to involve offsite participants by using common, internet-ready cameras. The cameras capture high-definition images. This makes the planning tags readable at the offsite location, which controls the camera via the internet and turns it on when they have a question about the schedule.

Metrics

Metrics are an important part of an improvement system. The word "metrics" is used for something that is measured on a regular basis and visually displayed to show a trend or an irregular situation. Examples include cycle time and percentage of on-time delivery. Metrics and visibility overlap as they are used to highlight problems and deviations.

"If you cannot measure it, you cannot improve it" is a phrase often erroneously linked to Peter Drucker.[2] Regardless of its origin, I believe it to be true for lean initiatives. It is important to track what needs to be improved or sustained, and review the trend with all the stakeholders and the process owners to make sure the improvement yields the right results. Joe Zekoski, CTO says, "It is amazing how quickly things change after you use metrics—nobody wants their function outside the metric."

I always thought that metrics were just common sense, and the implementation of metrics would be a slam dunk—but I was totally wrong. At Goodyear, as at other companies, there was resistance to the introduction of metrics, and it took many iterations to get them right. There were many reasons:

■ Both engineers and managers thought the metrics would be used for their performance evaluation and advancement.

- "Phony" or "massaged" metrics had been used in the past to promote certain agendas, and this metric residue plagued us at the beginning of the lean initiative.
- The owners of the metrics seemed to have a certain power.
- Metrics have typically been used to drive efficiency and that is not popular with engineers.
- People were afraid to create visibility of a problem, which metrics do.
- Engineers know how hard it is to measure certain things accurately, and they often have seen statistically inaccurate metrics being used to support already made decisions.

It took about 2 years for the fear of lean metrics in Goodyear to dissipate. People now trust that the metrics are accurate, and leadership only uses metrics to drive process improvements. We also are reticent to seek perfection with metrics; for example, we reduced our on-time delivery target from 100% to 90% to encourage more risk-taking. We also recognize that it is OK to be in the red once in a while—it just is not OK to remain in the red for a long time.

Companies have used metrics for a long time, although they may not always have been called metrics. There are metrics about the financial performance of the company, the performance of individual functions, the scores of engagement surveys, and even the performance of individuals. Many people ask if we really need all these metrics. The two purposes for metrics in a company should be to comply with laws and regulations and/or improve something.

There are many books on lean metrics, and most offer sound suggestions for establishing meaningful metrics that can help a company improve. To that base of knowledge, I will share a few experiences and lessons learned.

Before you introduce a metric, establish a baseline. The metric often shows a trend over time, and you quickly lose sight of where you started. In order to establish a baseline, you may have to go back and look for data which is not always possible to find. In that case, just collect enough data on the current situation before you implement the countermeasures.

Metrics must have a line of sight to a corporate goal. Hoshin kanri mandates that goals cascade down from the corporate goals to the business goals and the functional goals. If that is the case, it will be easier to establish the line of sight. For example, at Goodyear R&D, on-time delivery is correlated with having a profitable value stream, which leads to company profits.

Metrics should be causal and actionable. They must lead to a root cause and action to correct the undesired trend.

Metrics must be specific enough that clear actions for improvement can be decided based on the data. If "business profitability" is a metric in R&D, and the business loses money—will R&D know what to do to meet that metric? Probably not! But if R&D has a metric that says it will improve business profitability by maintaining a product portfolio that includes a minimum of 30% new product (i.e., less than 3 years old), then R&D knows what to do when the new product percentage falls below 20%.

A clear responsibility must be established with every metric, ideally with the responsibility for a metric assigned to a person or team that has the capability and authority to influence what is measured. An R&D executive at a company showed me that he was responsible for 14 metrics, but there were only two metrics that the executive was able to directly influence (he contributed to some extent to the other 12). For example, R&D has an influence on company profitability, but cannot be made responsible to meet a certain profit target. Making a person responsible for a metric that the person only has limited influence on can be counterproductive.

You may just as well measure something relevant rather than something trivial. I have, over time, seen Goodyear track use of printers, use of computer memory, and the cost of office supplies. I do not deny that these items cost money, but not as much as it costs to keep metrics on them. At the same time that Goodyear was tracking trivial metrics, large sums of money were wasted on expedited transportation, unnecessary testing, and molds and prototypes that went unused.

Metrics must drive the right behavior. We used to track test-tire backlog, and higher was better. High backlog assured high-machine utilization, which was the goal of the test division. This created long queues in testing and very long cycle times. When the backlog was low, testing asked for more tests and engineers complied by writing test requests and sending tires. Today the testing organization measures cycle time and on-time delivery. Their machine utilization is still high because they use a pull system to bring the tires in and a visual planning system to minimize machine idle time.

Metrics can be leading indicators, which is necessary when you want to signal that there is a problem early in a process, so that corrective action can be taken immediately before the cycle is finished. For example, we can measure cycle time by stopping the clock when a job is finished. We also can count the jobs in the queue or in process (WIP), which will let us calculate the cycle time before the jobs are finished. Shane Yount gives the example of the thermometer and the thermostat. A thermometer can measure when the temperature is wrong (lag indicator). A thermostat adjusts immediately and assures that the temperature remains correct (leading or self-adjusting indicator).[3]

Early indicators or milestone indicators can be of a great value as well because they still often allow a course correction. For example, if we miss sales targets for a new product in the first few months, we can still adjust advertisements, price, or distribution. Modern computer tools, including social media, can be used to get that quick feedback from a wide range of customers or consumers.

Metrics must be simple so that they are easy to understand, easy to interpret, and easy to gather. I like metrics where every engineer or manager updates a chart on the wall manually before every daily huddle. At one of the daily R&D huddles at Goodyear, every functional leader puts a red or green mark on a calendar to signal if the team met the goals for safety, quality (work returned), and on-time delivery. In the laboratory, they add a tick mark for every day a piece of equipment is down. People trust simple metrics a lot more than the complicated or computer-generated ones.

Metrics are not just about common dimensions like time, cost, quality, and speed. Remember that the goal of an organization is not only to deliver value, but also to create knowledge and develop capability. You should develop some appropriate metrics around those deliverables as well.

There are some key challenges with metrics that you must understand:

■ *Every action has a reaction, and every metric has a counter metric.* If we improve something, something else could get worse. For example, we learned that while we improved on-time delivery, project managers were less likely to take appropriate risks, which hurt innovation. So, it may be prudent to create a metric for on-time delivery in conjunction with a metric to assure appropriate risk-taking. At Goodyear, we now use "balanced" scorecards, which means we put all the metrics that affect each other on a single scorecard, so all the aspects of a value stream are managed. This way the interplay of one metric on another can easily be seen. Goodyear's corporate balanced scorecard includes metrics like safety, quality, OTD, unit sales, total delivered cost, market share, working capital, operating cash flow, product vitality, associate satisfaction index, and retention rates.

■ *Be careful how many metrics you introduce at one time.* Single-piece flow may be the approach to follow here, too, or at most one metric and one counter metric. I have seen people introduce 10 or more metrics at the same time, and then wonder why they did not work. As you have seen already, the metric itself may not be difficult, but accepting, taking appropriate action, and managing all the metrics becomes the challenge, and these challenges seem to double with every additional metric.

■ *Creating a metric and posting it somewhere where nobody sees it is a waste.* A metric should drive action and to do that effectively it must be seen by the right people at the right time. Having metrics displayed at a huddle and where they can easily be seen on gemba walks is a good practice. Emailing a metric is OK, but I prefer when all stakeholders look at the metric together, react together, and take action together then and there.

■ *A bad result for a metric is rarely the fault of a single person, and it is rarely the fault of a person at all.* In most cases, a bad metric is the result of a bad process or the absence of a process. Management and leadership need to learn to ask the right questions, so people do not take metrics personal and become defensive.

Characteristics and Examples of Good Metrics

Good metrics should

- Provide a line of sight to a corporate goal
- Fulfill a legal obligation or lead to improvements
- Be accurate and transparent
- Be causal and actionable
- Link responsibility to an individual or organization who are able and empowered to improve it
- Be relevant/significant (not trivial)
- Have buy-in
- Move in the right direction (drive the right behavior)
- Be a leading indicator or early warning if possible
- Be simple—as simple as possible!
- Drive collaboration—nobody should take the metric personally
- Separate the common cause from the unusual or special cause
- Be visually displayed and show the goal and the direction of "better"

Some popular metrics and measurement techniques in a lean process include

- Safety records, including near misses
- Design process quality indicators, such as first time through, mistakes on a deliverable
- Delivery, on-time and in full
- Speed, cycle time
- Efficiency/cost, such as completed work/resource
- New knowledge created, patents obtained

A useful tool to assess the metric of flow performance for an R&D process is a cumulative flow diagram (CFD).[4] On the CFD, you plot the cumulative work that comes in and gets completed on a daily or weekly basis (see *Cumulative Flow Diagram*). For example, in day 1, you use the amount of incoming work. In day 2, you add the work from day 2 to day 1. In day 3, you add the work from day 3 to the total of days 1 and 2, and so on. You also plot the completed work in the same fashion. This generates two curves—the vertical distance between two points on the curve is WIP, and the horizontal difference between the two curves is cycle time. When the two lines converge it means that you are completing more work than you take in. When they diverge, you are not catching up and the WIP grows.

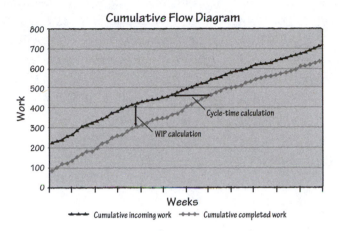

CFDs can be easily made by using spreadsheets, but I prefer that they be drawn by hand, like in a daily huddle. The people responsible for the work just add the new data points to the curve. After a slow start, CFDs now have become one of the most popular lean tools at Goodyear R&D.

Lean R&D Principle: Drive improvements with the right metrics.

Some problems are visible, and when they are solved, it is visible that the problem went away. More often measurements, trends, and a more formal process are required to establish that there is a problem. Metrics are data or facts that make conditions (and problems) visible and, ideally, lead to reliable action. Metrics will allow you to identify trends and identify abnormal conditions.

Measuring something is not enough. Somebody must look at the measurement and take action or empower somebody to take action. After the action is taken, the metric should reveal if the countermeasures were effective.

Some metrics are required for financial reporting, to confirm compliance with laws and regulations, and other such audit-like purposes. The only other metrics that are needed are those that drive improvement of processes, and people should understand that they are only used for that purpose (not to reward or punish individuals). A few key metrics that are used correctly and drive the right improvements are better than a lot of metrics that have little or no impact.

> *At Goodyear: We use metrics to drive the development of capability and continuous improvement. Goodyear uses safety and quality metrics on all levels of the company. All functions use metrics to track performance, need for improvement, and effectiveness of improvements. There also are project metrics—like number of learning cycles needed, on-time delivery, cycle time, and efficiency. In our material test labs, every test and every piece of equipment keeps a running metric for on-time delivery, cycle time, and throughput, and every significant deviation from the standard is discussed in the huddles. The business uses a balanced scorecard because most metrics adversely affect other metrics.*

Collaterals

We have seen several times in this book that improvements in one area can cause an adverse condition in another area. For example, if lean principles are not well understood or applied, there can be a loss of innovation and creativity. Fortunately, a lot of the collateral damages are consequences of change, and most eventually disappear or they must be managed. Having good visibility of the adverse effects can help minimize, mitigate, or eliminate the adverse effects.

There also are significant collateral *gains* with a lean implementation:

■ *Fewer tests and prototypes:* The most common collateral gain in a lean R&D transformation is a drop in requests and orders for tests and prototypes. In a typical development process with long waiting times, people are used to fighting for every single schedule slot, so they plan for the worst case and ask for everything possible because there is virtually no chance to get a second shot if needed. This leads to a substantial overprocessing, and a lot of tests are run and prototypes are built that will never be used. Before lean, only 30% of all prototype tires that were built were used. Today that number has been reversed—we use more than 70% of the tires.

■ *Discipline:* At Goodyear, we have seen a large improvement in process discipline. Dave Hrusovsky, director Global Process Quality & Auditing, who worked for Goodyear for more than 35 years, says, "The discipline came with the [lean] process! The process enabled collaboration, which generated the trust and the discipline." I have to admit, we did nothing extra to create the discipline, but I do remember the lack of discipline before we did lean: everybody worked against everybody else to get work done; from a process standpoint, everything that was not explicitly forbidden was attempted. Today, an individual or two may still think it is better to work around the process, but most people understand that if all follow a good process, all will get what they need and the company profits.

■ *Employee satisfaction*: Many people maintain that employee satisfaction, such as that measured in an engagement survey, goes up after the lean implementation. At Goodyear, the scores in the engagement survey also improved, but I primarily credit our HR organization and functions for the improvements they made for the improvement in the scores. There was initial dissatisfaction when we implemented lean, and our leaders were expecting a drop in satisfaction. But after we had reached a good level of stability, a lot of the concerns disappeared. People admitted that there was more work after lean but also a lot less frustration. Engineers also appreciate that they do not have to worry about complicated processes and procedures any more that have no direct bearing on their work and that they can focus on what they like best: creating great products that add value for the customer. After we implemented our matrix organization, engineers lost the sense of belonging to a functional team. Now, instead, they have a passion for delivering the best value to the customer.

■ *Efficiency:* A big collateral gain comes with the focus on speed, as noted in *Chapter 5*. You may recall that when you focus on improving the speed of the processes, you gain efficiency at the same time.

■ *Collaboration:* The level of collaboration within Goodyear today is unprecedented. Joe Zekoski says that what impressed him the most in the 35 years he has spent with the company is the improvement in the cross-functional collaboration. Jon Bellissimo, general director GIC*A, is part of the team of North American business leaders. Jon says that he is an integral part of that team and participates in any discussion and decision, including financial, marketing, and HR. "This team is so seamless, you do not even see the competency lines anymore," says Jon. Similar collaboration can be seen on all levels of the value stream.

■ *Requests for more work:* The most unexpected collateral I have seen so far is when engineers or technicians ask for more work. We hoped this would occur, but never really expected it. As we discussed before, engineers always find a little more to add to a job and are reluctant to turn in work before the due date. They also like to wait for more preferred jobs rather than take any job. Ralf Mruk, chief engineer in one of the test labs in Luxembourg, says his technicians or engineers frequently ask for new projects or more test work.

Managing Variability

Variability in R&D must be embraced and managed because it contributes to the value we create. Having talked about good and bad variability in *Chapter 6*, it is now time to discuss how to manage variability in an R&D process to improve the process and to make sure you do not eliminate the good variability with the bad.

Some variability is an obvious waste, and it should be minimized or eliminated. Examples are variability in routine testing, prototype building, or inaccurate tooling. Undesirable variability also can come from poor processing, discarding knowledge, and not following a standard process. For the following discussion, assume that these kinds of variability are at least under control if not eliminated. I will focus on "good variability," which is inherent to a good R&D process and needs to be managed rather than eliminated.

Where is the source of good variability?

■ Difference in jobs—small jobs, large projects, difficult tasks, different phases of the same project
■ Difference in what is known about projects—technology versus routine execution
■ Unpredictability of experiments
■ Difference between engineers—some engineers work faster than others due to experience, capability, and specialization
■ Availability of specialized or rare resources
■ Risk that is taken to achieve large benefits—needing more iterations and causing rework loops and mistakes
■ Irregular arrival times, seasonal business, and work flow that cannot be leveled

This list may not be complete, but it should be enough for you to consider the potential sources of variability in your company. We cannot eliminate this variability because the variability is inherent to R&D and linked to discovery in R&D. But if we do not manage the variability, we allow for a slow and inefficient process. This means we lose a lot of speed, predictability, and money.

You may notice that a lot of the principles presented here have been explained in the chapter on flow. This is another collateral gain—good flow also helps to manage variability. Because I am a big fan of "pareto" thinking, here, too, I will list my recommendations (in order from the most important to the least important) for managing variability. Note, I do not have a lot of data for R&D variability, so my list is based mostly on observations rather than measurements:

1. *Manage incoming work:* Without controlling the incoming work, you will have so much waste mixed in with value-adding work that tools lose effectiveness.
2. *Break the work down into small increments:* Use quick learning cycles or sprints with many decisions and pivot points.
3. *Manage knowledge generation and reuse:* Consistent reuse of knowledge eliminates experiments and makes the process more predictable.
4. *Use a standard process and standard work wherever possible:* A consistent execution of every block of work or learning cycle makes work predictable. Make good project plans and execute according to good project management principles and standards.
5. *Level the work where possible:* Work leveling reduces peaks and valleys in the schedule. Work can be leveled by the business by staggering launches.
6. *Implement a cadence and assign resources to meet the cadence:* This is a consistent practice in manufacturing, and it works just as well in R&D.
7. *Use a good pull process and FIFO:* The upstream pull adjusts for a lot of the variability by self-aligning the tasks. Downstream activities should follow a first-in, first-out schedule.
8. *Watch the utilization and use buffers:* Make schedules and assign work based on available capacity (generally 70%–80% of total capacity) to avoid ripple effects and allow for other appropriate buffers as needed.
9. *Use flexible capacity:* Flexible resources and standard work accommodate peaks in the schedule without waiting. Engineers with a large skillset are more flexible and can handle a larger variety of tasks.
10. *Start late:* Consistent late start can reduce or almost eliminate changes and assures one standard method to start work.
11. *Ensure a good risk-management process:* A good risk-management process and standards lead to a more consistent process by avoiding overprocessing.

12. *Collaborate:* Having everybody involved and collaborating makes execution a lot more consistent. Colocation can do great things for good variability, too.

13. *Daily, visible actions:* Daily huddles and visibility of what is important adds a natural cadence, and it also helps to immediately address anything unusual that can significantly reduce the variability.

At Goodyear, we have implemented all the above, and we still have our share of good variability, but I think that is due to the fact that today we do a lot more high-uncertainty, high-potential work than we did before. Today, at Goodyear, the biggest improvement will come from the creation of an appropriate risk-management process, which should eliminate a lot of unnecessary iterations and testing.

Recently, I was made aware of a problem in our European innovation center that looked like variability out of control, with large queues growing in one function. As had often happened in the past with such a problem, the variability came from a breakdown in the process, not from a new or hidden source. With variability, just as with any other process problem, the first question must *always* be: Was the process followed?

Lean R&D Principle: Manage variability.

In a product development process, there is a lot of "bad" variability that affects delivery, cycle time, cost, and predictability. Good six sigma thinking and waste elimination tools can be used to eliminate some of that bad variability.

A lot of variability is a natural effect in R&D, especially in a process that encourages innovation. It is the result of taking risk and trying something new. This "good" variability must be embraced and managed. A lot of lean tools like pull, late start, and use of buffers can be used to manage good variability. Failure to manage the good variability causes waste, slows processes, adds costs, and limits innovation.

At Goodyear: We largely manage our variability with the same tools we use to manage flow and speed. Other important additions were the management of project risk and the assessment of every iteration or learning cycle. Other tools, like standardizing the duration and content of iterations, were not very successful.

No Problem Is Big Problem[5]

With good visibility of things outside of a standard comes the need to do something about them. Early in our lean journey, many consultants knocked on our door and offered to teach us how to make A3s. At the time, however, I felt we had more important things to do. That changed when we got to the last step on the Womack Wheel—the "work to perfection" step. This is when I realized we were missing something, but I was not quite sure what that something was. Peter Fitz says 10% of success is luck,[6] and I and Goodyear got lucky when John Shook's book *Managing to Learn*[7] was published.

I quickly ordered a copy of *Managing to Learn*, knowing that it was written by Shook. I read it, shared it with our lean sponsor (and CTO), and we soon decided we'd found what we needed. I finally understood what problem solving was about, and how we could use the managing to learn (MTL) or A3 process as a roadmap for the problem solving and our continuous improvement/kaizen process.

Shook is the chairman and president of the Lean Enterprise Institute (LEI), and we brought LEI in to teach A3 classes at Goodyear. We educated Goodyear trainers, and today MTL training is one of our more popular training programs and the use of what we call A3s, the A3 process, and the A3 way of thinking has taken off. Shook has personally presented to Goodyear's R&D leadership team, after which everyone was convinced that many other Toyota management principles that Shook addressed made a lot of sense as well. Principles in *Managing to Learn* also complement a popular management training program that Goodyear has been using for some time: the manager as coach.

Find Problems

A3s are about problem solving, so let us start with a discussion of problems.

At Goodyear, we did not like to use the word "problem." I was told by my first manager that the word "problems" was not in the Goodyear vocabulary. We called them "opportunities," and my first boss told me: "Do not bring me problems, bring me solutions." But the disconnect for me (and throughout Goodyear) was that he asked for solutions right away, saying that it is important to have a solution before one of his superiors would find out and ask him if he had a solution. But when I presented my solution to my boss, we went into long arguments because my solution rarely matched his paradigms. Eventually, I was told what to do—which I knew would not work, but I had to at least try it. As I got smarter to the Goodyear ways, I also added my own solution in my plans to address the problem. My boss back then rarely followed up because he dealt with so many new problems every day, that he could not possibly remember all the instructions he gave me.

If we solved a problem—and we solved a lot of them one way or another—the next reaction of the managers was: "We cannot tell anybody this because this would not look good for our function if our peers and leaders found out this happened." There was very little sharing of our good ideas that could have prevented a similar problem elsewhere. Remember, we are a global organization, and many sites around the world are doing similar activities.

The first big problem that I solved was a problem with tires in one of our former plants. I actually went to the plant, not to go see or find the root cause, but to certify the solution. While I was at the plant, certifying the mixing and preparation of the rubber, I became suspicious of something that I observed in the mixing area, and I sent a rubber sample to the lab, which confirmed my suspicion. The root cause for our problem was not the rubber formulation that I was asked to implement, but it was that the weight of some ingredients was off and the operators could not see it. My countermeasures included a thorough cleaning and 5S in the mixing area to increase the visibility of the weight scales and a calibration of the material delivery system. Going to the gemba (although I did not call it that at the time) was critical to fixing the problem. But sharing the root-cause of the problem would have been embarrassing for the plant at that time, even though I am sure that other plants could have benefitted.

Back then when we implemented a solution, we rarely went back to check if the solution was effective. Often we did not even implement a solution, we implemented a "workaround." We had targets to meet and needed to keep moving toward the targets, which were normally met despite the problem—but the root cause was not fixed, the solution was rarely documented, and, as a result, we learned nothing—the problem came back and everybody was wondering why it was not fixed in the first place.

This Goodyear culture toward problems was widespread in the industry at a time where "managing by objectives" was popular. Objectives were normally met, but the processes and the capability were secondary. Whenever the objectives were not met, there were consequences for the person responsible for the objectives. Whenever there was a problem, management was looking for a person responsible for the problem. This, of course, spurred a lot of denial, confusion, and defensive people.

In a lean environment, if there is a problem, we like to ask: "What is wrong with the process?" People normally try to do a good job. If they are not able to do a good job, it is very likely that they lack training or that there is a problem with the process.

At Toyota, they say that problems are "treasures."[8] Problems are opportunities to identify something that needs improvement, which then leads to a better process. At Toyota and many other companies, they have a systematic approach to *finding* and *solving* problems.

So how do we find those problems or treasures? Ideally, we create a process to assure that the problems find us! That can happen through visibility, good metrics, and a regular practice where the right people look at the metrics or the process (e.g., design reviews, huddles, gemba walks). Another good tool to identify problems are reflections; every activity (e.g., iteration, project, launch, workshop, training session) should end with a short reflection.

Fix Problems

Now that we found the problems, or at least know how to find the problems, here are the key steps in a good problem-solving process: these suggestions are based on my experience and have been validated by several years of using them at Goodyear; they have been taught for years in our lean product development classes.

If you are familiar with lean tools, you will say this is similar to the MTL/A3 process,[7] and you are right. Maybe this is why this process was such a very easy sell inside Goodyear.

1. The responsibility for solving the problem should be assigned to an individual or an empowered team. The "owner" of the problem or the manager of the function with the expertise could make the assignment; the "owner" of the problem could also be the sponsor. I find this formal assignment important because I have seen too often where several people or functions started working on the same problem, and then fighting about who had the best solution. If there is a team assigned, the team should have cross-functional representation. If an individual is assigned, that individual may have to assure cross-functional perspectives in solving of the problem.

2. Problems are best solved by the people who know the process and work in the process. The people working on the problem should also know the technology and have an interest in the improvement because they have to live with the process after the improvement.

3. The person or team dealing with the problem must understand the background and the context of the problem. Why is it important to solve this problem? Is there a line of sight to a corporate goal? Sometimes this step may take some education or research.

4. Solving a problem starts with understanding and verifying what is happening now. It is not good enough to assume what is happening. Even the people who know the process well should take the time to go see and collect facts and data to assure that all involved *really* know what is happening.

5. Write down what the problem really is. For me, this is the biggest challenge in problem solving—people think they know what the problem is, but in reality they do not. Charles Kettering said: "A problem well stated is a problem half solved." Albert Einstein said: "If I had one hour to solve a problem, I would spend 55 min to think about it and five minutes to solve it." Very often people have a solution in mind before they understand the problem, and I have seen managers and leaders take a problem-solving opportunity to implement a personal agenda rather than a real solution that addresses a root cause.

6. Set (SMART) goals that are specific, measurable, achievable, realistic, and timely. Goals should be spelled out and documented. You must later check back to see if they were really achieved. If you would rather set an aspirational goal than a smart goal, that is OK provided there is a check-back built in. All stakeholders should participate in the goal-setting.

7. Weeds come back unless the roots are pulled. The same is true for problems. There are many reasons why a problem exists, that is why it is important to keep asking "why" many times until you find the root cause. There may be cases where there is more than one root cause, and there may be cases when there was actually more than one problem. Go back to step #4 and identify the problem(s).

8. I encourage the person or the team engaged in the problem solving to come up with many countermeasures. Lean advocates do not like to use the word "solution" in the context of problem solving (and neither do I), as it implies that there is only one solution. I like to see many

countermeasures with a clear line of sight back to the root cause, the problem, and what is happening today.

9. The countermeasures must be evaluated or assessed for value, feasibility, and maybe cost or other criteria that are important to customers and stakeholders. The countermeasures also should be discussed with the stakeholders. They have a responsibility in implementing countermeasures and sustaining the improvement. Maybe some countermeasures get eliminated from the list because of insufficient value, too difficult to implement, lack of capital that is required to implement, or even lack of interest of the stakeholders.

10. I like to see a very simple project plan that details the steps, resources, and timelines for the implementation of the countermeasures. I also want to see how the individual or the team are planning to check whether the countermeasures are effective (typically called the "followup" section of an A3).

11. After the countermeasures are implemented, the team or the engineer has to go back and see whether they were effective in meeting the goals and solving the problem. If not, they should adjust the countermeasures and check again, or ensure the countermeasures were correctly applied in the first place. This is nothing other than good practice of PDCA.

12. After the problem is solved, a control plan must be established to assure the countermeasures remain implemented. This control plan should also spell out who (what function or other part of the organization) is responsible to sustain the change. The plan also includes updating standards and work instructions and, if possible, mistake-proofing the process.

13. Learning must be documented. Why did the problem exist, and what did we learn solving it? Can it ever happen again? Many companies document their R&D learning by updating standards and design tools.

14. Share the learning (and the A3, if that is what you use). Sharing is not dumping an A3 in a SharePoint site and hoping that those who could use it find it. Sharing means to identify other places where the same problem could come up (or maybe already exists) and then notify those parties of the countermeasure implementation. (Toyota calls this process "yokoten.") Ideally, feedback from those areas should be gathered and considered.

There are other popular problem-solving tools you might use instead of the MTL/A3 process: for example, eight-disciplines problem solving (8D) used by some OEMs, the Red X Strategy® developed by Shainin LLC, and the DMAIC process (define, analyze, measure, improve, and control). Use any of these or others as long as the steps above are followed. Many tools, like DMAIC, can be integrated into the A3 process.

At Goodyear, we use the MTL/A3 as the basic process, but we make sure that all the above steps are included in what we call the "Goodyear A3" or simply the A3 process. Even though we were well suited to use the process, we had the usual challenges when we introduced the A3 process: I saw A3s that were just a summary of a PowerPoint presentation, with all 30 of the slides reduced in size to all fit on the A3 page. I saw A3s that followed only pieces of the above process. In one of several attempts to make the A3 stick at Goodyear, one of our directors had a workshop with his staff, and they identified the major problems in the division. The director wanted to try the A3 process, and he asked every one of his direct reports to make an A3. The next day everybody showed up with a completed A3. You can imagine that this effort soon fizzled.

Despite the original challenges, which I understand happen everywhere when a version of the A3 process is begun, today the A3 has found widespread application in Goodyear. First of all, we teach the process in our lean product development certification, and we coach the students while they apply the process to solve real problems. Many engineers use A3s today for their regular R&D work.

Along the way, some new A3 uses were created: an A3 is used in tire engineering to formulate a hypothesis before every iteration. Then the experiment is run, and the results are documented on the A3. If the hypothesis is confirmed by the test results, there will be action items to make sure the models, predictions, design standards, and risk-management standards are updated to assure that similar learning cycles will not be repeated. If the results are different from the hypothesis, learning has occurred. That learning is documented and included in the models because our goal is still to accurately model our designs. This reflection on the need of an iteration or learning cycle will help set standards when iterations or learning cycles add value and when they do not, and it is the foundation to good risk management.

Remember that the A3 does not need a lot of paperwork. You can write and should write the A3 on a single piece of paper (called an "A3" because that was the original size of the paper used for A3s) or on a whiteboard in your meeting, workshop, or design review. You can keep the chart or paper and bring it to the next event.

Lean R&D Principle: Support a good continuous improvement system with a good, standard problem-solving process.

An organization must spend time solving problems to improve processes. The people who should do the problem solving are not "professional problem solvers," but they are the people who do the work.

There are many ways to do problem-solving work, some better than others. The best ways for your company must be determined, standardized, and improved along the way, and people must be trained on the use of the standards. Tailoring the problem-solving process to your organization will make it better than any method you could force feed on the organization. But whatever method you use or to which you evolve, do not miss any of the problem-solving steps.

An important aspect when looking at problems in R&D is that most problems will require (often many) cross-functional countermeasures due to the nature of R&D work.

At Goodyear: We use our problem-solving process in conjunction with concepts from John Shook's Managing to Learn[7] *as our standard problem-solving process. In the spirit of "one Goodyear," we also added a few options for DMAIC integration to align with the manufacturing organization, where DMAIC plays a bigger role than in R&D. We often refer to our problem-solving process as the "A3 process."*

I often get e-mails from people who want a copy of our "A3 form." People like to fill out forms, but that is not what the A3 is about. I encourage people to handwrite A3s and use *any* form or format that suits their problem. Instead of providing a form, we use a free form, but we prompt the problem solvers to include the important steps and information.

Goodyear A3 Information and Steps

All of the A3s used within Goodyear's R&D department should include the following information or steps:

- *Title:* Project or problem
- *Name:* Author or owner
- *Date and version:* When the A3 was completed or revised
- *Background:* Business case for why the A3 is needed
- *Current situation:* What is happening today
- *Problem statement:* Problem identified as a gap between the current situation and the desired situation (what should or could be happening) that reflect the gap
- *Goals:* Detailed goals, which are verified later in the PDCA
- *Analysis:* Root causes of the problem
- *Countermeasures:* Countermeasures linked to the root causes, and evaluated based on many criteria, including their ability to permanently work
- *Plan and implementation:* How and when the countermeasures will be implemented
- *PDCA:* How the project or problem will be checked to ensure the countermeasures have stuck and are effective (if goals are not met, adjustments must be made)
- *Control plan:* How countermeasures are made permanent
- *Learning:* Describes how learning is documented
- *Sharing:* How learning is shared with others in the global organization who may benefit from it

---

Since Goodyear has been using the A3 process—and I have been using it and coaching others how to use it—I have learned the following insights, coaching best practices, and mistakes to avoid:

A3 insights	• Processes do not solve problems, people do, so teach people a standard process like the A3 and coach them through the process. • Spend the most time *upfront* on an A3. This is sometimes difficult because both problem solvers and their management are impatient and like quick solutions. • Following the A3 process significantly improves the likelihood that a project will get finished, the solution sticks, and/or a problem does not reoccur. • Individuals new to A3s should have a coach the first few times through the process. • The author of the A3 must take responsibility for solving the problem—which means the A3 must address all 14 problem-solving steps. • Managers and leaders must hold authors of A3s accountable for finishing the work. At Goodyear I still see many A3s where the author gets promoted or moves on or just stops the work after the first countermeasure is implemented. • At Goodyear we validated that the A3/Managing to Learn is also excellent for people development.
A3 coaching tips	• The A3 is a great tool for leaders to coach their associates in real time beyond just the problem on the A3. Use the coaching process to assess the potential and capabilities of an individual. • Unless you are the process expert, focus on the A3 process, not the content. • Only ask questions when initially reviewing an A3. Do not tell the author of the A3 what to do or offer a solution. Coach in small steps, never getting too far ahead. • It takes patience to coach or sponsor an A3 author. You may not get a solution as fast as you would like it or the solution you expect. • Read A3s. Do not let people present them to you. When you read the A3 and cannot understand it, then ask questions. • It should be easy and quick to read and follow-up on a sound A3: I typically need 10 min to review an A3 and schedule 5 min for questions. • If the A3 author cannot grasp the situation or formulate a problem statement, lay out a "cookie trail" to help them along. Again, use questions not statements to guide them. • *Do not* compromise on the process; you always want to see a full PDCA cycle.

	• Look for a line of sight throughout the A3. Problems must link to root causes, which link to countermeasures, which are supported with plans, which incorporate a PDCA cycle. • In addition to the A3 coach, we often assign a "peer coach" at Goodyear. This gives a person the opportunity to discuss ideas about content and receive back questions that help them to clarify the current situation and the problem.
A3 mistakes to avoid	• Jumping to a solution. • Wrong problem or unclear problem. • Incomplete root-cause analysis. • Insufficient good countermeasures. • Incomplete PDCA—countermeasure did not fix the problem. • A3 stopped before all the steps are completed.

When leaders or managers do gemba walks or participate in huddles, the natural reaction should be to ask for an A3 when they discover a problem. Leaders and managers, of course, should know how to do an A3, how to coach an A3, and how to sponsor an A3. I have seen some A3s used in connection with major business problems. Unfortunately, I still see most of the A3s used on the lower levels of the organization, and they are rarely assigned by a senior manager or leader. Managers and directors still seem to be challenged to come up with the patience that is needed for the first steps of the process. Often the managers and directors still like to discuss the problems themselves, starting with the "remedial plan" or the corrective action. That is why in GIC*L they started their A3 training with managers and leaders.

The author of an A3 is not always a popular individual. Sometimes the problem solvers step on other people's territory. Often they need the help or cooperation from another function to implement the countermeasure or they just need collaboration to make the countermeasure successful. Up to the point of formulating countermeasures, the author is gathering information and facts, and being an unbiased contributor. Once the author has laid out good countermeasures, shared them with the sponsor and stakeholders, and gained the confidence of the affected leaders, the author can earn authority to propose and implement countermeasures, too. This is especially true if the engineer becomes an expert on the subject, as often happens.

During the author transition from observer to authority, the sponsor plays an important role. The sponsor not only knows that the problem is being worked on, but the sponsor knows *how* the individual is planning to solve the problem. The sponsor sometimes has to help by talking to some of the cross-functional leaders affected by the A3 and helping the A3 author secure authority. As the A3 methodology becomes more widespread and more people become used to it, such turf issues become less frequent.

Lean People

Billy Taylor, a Goodyear Manufacturing director who led the first Goodyear plant through the Shingo assessment process, is an expert on people engagement. Billy says, "Do not underestimate the people impact in a lean initiative, [especially in sustaining it]." Reflecting back on our lean implementation and the challenges that went with it, I have to admit that most of my challenges were about people. This section is a reflection on how a new lean organization requires a different approach by engineers and different leadership behaviors, and how we at Goodyear learned from Toyota and other companies and gained our own experience on how people work and how they should be managed in this new environment.

We do a lot of things different now since we operate in a matrix and have a fast lean product development process, but these changes did not necessitate new people. That would have been impossible. In fact, the people had a heavy hand in the creation of the new process, from the engineers to the leaders. Most have been well trained to understand why things are done differently, and they should by now know what the best practices are. The same people who helped implement the change must be counted on to sustain the change.

Most people come to work with the intent to do the best possible job, and for most people doing good work is a reward unto itself. It is up to management and leadership to create the appropriate work environment, treat the people with respect, and help them to fully develop their potential, whoever they are (engineers, project managers, empowered teams, leadership, champions, suppliers).

Engineers

I have seen people react to lean the same way they would react to any other major change—they do not like it because they do not like to be changed. When we really got rolling with a matrix organization and lean, we made a lot of changes at the same time, and it was hard to pin down specifically the many initial concerns from the engineers. Tim Lovell, now manager Tire Engineering, went through the change in several different positions. Tim says, "It is amazing how quickly the initial concerns disappeared when we reached stability, especially the issues related to working in a matrix."

Today engineers do a lot more value-added work in a given time period than before the change to lean product development. Engineers had to learn new processes and behaviors, and there is lot more focus on delivering by a certain deadline. Some people say this creates extra stress, but most people say that the more work is justified because the processes are easier and they see results every day from all the work they do.

Kelly King was a lead engineer during the change. She says, "Before, when you missed a deadline, it wasn't a big deal: most of the time you didn't even know when your work was due. Now there is a lot more accountability. Today engineers are doing more iterations but with less stress because they do not get pulled in so many directions with changing priorities." When the kanban cards initially were put in, they were viewed negatively. People thought management had found something else to make engineers work more. In fact, the system is so predictable now that we do not need kanban cards anymore. It is pretty obvious now when projects or iterations need to get started, and everyone knows to start them as late as possible.

Leyla Renner, senior development engineer, says, "The transition to the matrix was difficult—all of a sudden you were in a big group and you rarely saw the chief… There was nobody to talk to any more, and you had to talk to your peers and ask their opinion."

Tom Laurich, lead engineer, says functional managers meet one on one with the engineers on a regular basis and they do gemba walks—you get to see your chief/manager again. He adds, "It is very important for people to do gemba walks in a matrix organization. When managers do gemba walks, they just check to make sure the process is running and people have the tools and knowledge they need. It's a great thing when the manager comes out and asks people how they are doing. It shows that each person's work is important to the manager."

Engineers are now more than ever consulted or invited to participate in improvement activities. Some see this as a welcome opportunity to get involved in changes that concern them. Others feel this is yet another distraction from doing real work. Some people participate right away in kaizen events, some people need time to warm up, and some people come to the events and never say a word, hiding behind their laptop doing their regular work. I assume that it will take a lot more time to develop the same passion for the process that the associates have developed for the product and the delivering of customer value.

In the GIC*L testing organization, every associate (engineers, technicians, mechanics) has an A3 for how to improve their work. Emmanuel Robinet, the manager, reviews the A3s personally while on gemba walks or in one-on-ones, and he makes sure that the improvements developed by one associate are shared among all the associates.

Rules that used to enforce personal safety and proper behaviors are replaced with training and awareness. Truly empowered engineers should not need such behavioral rules, just as they do not need excessive work rules, which can interfere with their work and creativity. Instead of excessive rules, today Goodyear relies more on training, such as e-learning, to teach people why certain behaviors (safety, ethics, workplace etiquette, spending, legal requirements, etc.) are important.

With empowerment comes responsibility. This is the responsibility to propose a concept, a countermeasure, or an idea, and develop it into a product or implement a new process. With the responsibility comes the "earning" of the authority. Some engineers are experts in technical subjects and earned the authority to consult on major technical decisions. Engineers also need to earn the authority to propose process and capability development changes, ideally in the context of an A3.

Engineers in a lean process also have to learn to become better observers and get in the habit of collecting their own information, facts, and feedback from customers and stakeholders. Gone are the days when the engineers got the product spec and delivered the product a few years later. Engineers also must

- Learn to observe processes and question the way things are done.
- Go and see how customers use products or processes and the problems customers have.
- Study how products are manufactured, distributed, and sold.
- Develop a deep understanding of the complete value stream—understanding their role in the development of the product and how their decisions affect manufacturability, cost, and complexity of the product.
- Get their hands on the product as much as possible, even though their work is still performed mostly in offices and on computers. There is a saying at Toyota: "Never trust an engineer who does not have to wash their hands before lunch."
- Learn to balance personal preferences with customer satisfaction.

Managers should be supporting these characteristics by exhibiting the right behaviors and with good coaching. Managers and leaders are often assessed on employee satisfaction, and sometimes they take the easy way out to make employees happy by compromising between what is best for the customer and what is best for the engineers. For example, in one function the implementation of the lean product development process coincided with our internal yearly feedback survey; the survey results reflected the initial discomfort with the change. Based on the survey results, several functional leaders would not support the initiative, even a few years into the implementation.

Here are a few ideas that help get the most out of people in a lean R&D environment, provided the concepts are understood by engineers and managers:

- *Engage people in the improvement:* Allow engineers to be involved with the change and all the decisions that affect them. Many lean experts summarize this form of people management as "respect for people." Billy Taylor says that people like to be valued, and that starts with listening. The important part is to give the people a chance to voice their opinion even if you cannot implement every idea that comes up. Billy says, "I tell you" is entitlement, and "you tell me" is empowerment. The distinction is one of doing work in a way that is recommended or instructed versus being trusted to have the knowledge to come to the right work process on your own.

- *People development is more than training:* Management and leadership have to play a leading role in people development by coaching, mentoring, and consistently setting the right example. HR must get involved to set the right standards. At Goodyear what has helped most was to engage all levels of the matrix in the people development process or talent management. Today project managers, functional mangers, and HR talent managers work together on the development of the people, the succession planning, the discussion of the needs for the organization, recruiting, and transfers.

- *Pay attention to onboarding:* At Goodyear, we used to be able to onboard new engineers in certain areas that required less technical expertise or responsibility, but that is no longer possible. Today younger, inexperienced engineers are paired with experienced engineers, and they are coached/mentored by their chiefs or managers. With the pairing, the inexperienced engineers have access to all the knowledge of the function and can practice the skills in the right environment. The project managers also have a technical background and are able to direct and coach less-experienced engineers.

When I hired into the company, which at the time was a strong functional organization, I had as many teachers as there were people in the department. They were willing and eager to share their knowledge and discuss technical problems. After a couple of years, I was able to make significant contributions and earn patents, put new tires into production, and develop new knowledge. After some time as a right-brained person, I was happy to get transferred and learn other things. Some of my subsequent transfers were involuntary because the departments were eliminated, and I felt like I was not always able to learn enough to make a significant contribution.

Many companies see high value in people with broad experience because these people have good flexibility, and flexibility increases capacity. Having diverse experiences often is among the criteria for advancement. Many companies encourage and incentivize frequent moves, and some engineers like frequent transfers. The disadvantage of the frequent transfers is that the engineers never spend enough time in one area to learn enough to make a meaningful contribution.

Some engineers like to be specialists or experts. They are comfortable with being an expert in a narrow field and seeing the results of their significant and specific contribution to the company. Many invest a decade or more into developing that expertise, and they do not want to waste that investment. Many companies think that this technical experience is very important and they reward the expertise and the technical contribution to the company.

So what is the best for your company? The deep technical, vertical experience I talent or the more versatile, less-deep experience T talent—or both? Many companies promote the T talent for flexibility and leadership development; others say that the company deserves a contribution and that an engineer must first excel in a technical job before the engineer is moved around to gain a more diverse knowledge. That is often called π talent to symbolize a thicker vertical leg on the T. At Goodyear, like in other technical companies, we realize that all engineers (future leaders or not) should be given the opportunity to make significant technical contributions, which is good for the engineer and good for the company. Some companies, such as Ford, even require a certain technical maturity before any advancement.

Matrix organizations must manage their very deep technical talent differently than a purely functional organization. To do this, a matrix organization often uses a dual-ladder career path: one path for management careers and one path for the careers of technical experts. At Goodyear there are now even succession plans for technical experts.

The dual ladder often focuses only on technical expertise of the big functions, like tire engineering or material science, but there is a lot of additional expertise that must be managed in companies. There are the serial innovators, the champions, the finance geniuses, the computer nerds, and so on. Finding a peer-ranking group for those folks or putting them all into the same peer group are insufficient solutions. Not managing this talent is a huge waste for companies.

Identifying leadership talent early and developing it is important. At Goodyear, we have a development program where high potentials are identified early. In addition to them pursuing their regular work, they are placed into an accelerated leadership development program where they participate in training and work on global cross-functional teams where they tackle high-level, cross-functional problems. This program provides a great learning and development opportunity, but also gives leadership the interaction they need to assess and challenge future leaders.

Project Managers (aka "Chief Engineers" at Toyota)

When we started the current role of the project manager at Goodyear in 2006, I read a lot about the Toyota chief engineer, and I had concerns that this would never work at Goodyear. I did not think that the Goodyear project managers could be the "supermen" that the Toyota chief engineers were portrayed to be. I also was concerned about the differences in the business. Our project managers have to manage many projects at the same time, not just one like the Toyota chief engineers.

Over the last 8 years, I have seen the roles of the project managers at Goodyear evolve. Today I think that the Goodyear project managers represent the customer with passion and also carefully articulate the needs of the company in their decisions. They have learned to manage many different projects, and most project managers adapted well to the new process. At Goodyear the responsibility of project managers does not end at the launch of the product. The project managers and some of the team members stay with the project until the tire has been in production for at least 1 year.

Traits of good Goodyear project managers are

- *Technical and business skills:* The project manager should be a very good engineer, who understands the technology, the customer, the product, the company, and the people, and who has the respect of peers, managers, leaders, and engineers.
  - *Passion for product and customer:* They are proud of their products, and they represent the interests of the customer with great enthusiasm and encourage their team to rally behind the product and the customer. Project manager Matt List says he is not only managing projects, but that he delivers the best value for the customer. The display of that passion rubs off on the entire team. Project managers are expected to deliver the best customer value at the optimum cost—not products at the lowest cost. Too many companies and even whole industries have tried to save themselves to prosperity—such as cutting out costly features that are attractive to customers—and that is always a failed approach and one that Goodyear project managers avoid.
  - *Business savvy:* Good project managers also know the company and the business. They know how technical decisions influence every part of the business equation, profit = volume (price−cost), and drive toward the right business decisions.
- *Project management expertise:* They are able to build great teams and deliver results. Project managers must learn to manage a cross-functional team of many disciplines and a diversity of skills.
- *Manage people:* Project managers must manage people, often those who do not report to them. They need good people management and influence skills and need to develop and use a lot of the people management tools.
- *Good planners:* Project managers make good project plans and set good milestone goals by engaging the members of their teams. Often the projects need a highly customized plan. This is especially important for projects that enter the kentou phase. Project plans often require tactical thinking, but project managers should not be afraid to think their plans through from a strategic standpoint and include some higher objectives like capability and knowledge development.
- *Coach and mentor:* Project managers should have a responsibility in helping develop engineers by coaching and mentoring. After all, they spend more time with the engineers than the functional managers, who are formally responsible for their development. At the beginning of our lean

initiative, project managers tried hard to secure the best and most experienced engineers for their team because that was the easiest way to assure a successful project. They quickly understood that other project managers were doing the same thing and that everybody had to settle for a balance of experienced and newer engineers on their teams. Tim Lovell says today the most important thing for a project manager is to build a well-balanced team after a good dialogue with the functional managers. When Tim was a project manager, he was included by the functional managers in the performance management of the engineers, both in developing talent and succession planning. That way he felt a real responsibility in developing the less-experienced members on his teams.

■ *Drive collaboration:* Project managers used to be facilitators, trying to maintain harmony on their teams and accommodate all the desires of the team members and stakeholders, often at the expense of the project timing or the performance of the product. The project managers have figured out that conflict and collaboration creates more value than cooperation and accommodating people and opinions. Today Goodyear leadership understands that compromises lead to poor value for the customer. Project managers are encouraged to put the conflict on the table and engage the team to resolve it, with the goal of developing the best value for the customer. Team members must understand that and be willing to collaborate toward the same goals.

■ *Open communication:* The times of the "good news only" project status reports and update meetings are over. Communication now happens in huddles and team gatherings and is mostly about conflicts and problems. Communication is critical if problems come up that affect the project outcome or the timing. We still see the occasional overreacting to get attention and resources, but most communication today is honest and open.

■ *Crisis management:* Project managers should be willing to "pull the project andon cord." For example, just as in manufacturing, empowered contributors to the value stream can stop a project today if problems come up. I have not seen this situation a lot, but when it comes up it requires courage and delicate communication to get buy-in from all the stakeholders.

■ *Courageous leadership:* Project managers need courage to challenge the status quo on project and the available knowledge. They should not be afraid to set aspirational targets and challenge team members, stakeholders, and leaders. They should also challenge every attempt to trade customer value for cost.

- *Risk managers:* Project managers manage project risk at Goodyear. Risk management has evolved from an "avoid mistakes at all cost" approach to a managed approach where the project risk is assessed and the means are aligned with the risk.
- *Lean managers:* Project managers at Goodyear had to evolve to more efficient forms of project management, such as the use of A3s and huddles, which replaced project reviews and status reports. Assigning responsibility to empowered engineers is much more efficient than daily follow-ups and prioritizing. Project managers also learned that catching problems early makes it a lot easier to solve them than waiting until they become big problems.

At Goodyear, project managers can rely on a large book of knowledge for their positions that was developed by the PMO. Project managers also can count on coaching from the PMO. They must contribute to this base of knowledge as well. In the early days of the matrix organization, the PMO coaches had to advertise their availability for coaching project managers. That has changed: the PMO coaches are today in high demand since project managers see value in their coaching and mentoring.

Teams of Empowered Experts

It would be wrong to assume that managers or leaders have the background, knowledge, and information needed to make every decision. Leaders should make sure that the right people work on the right innovation and trust them to do the right work and correctly assess the value to the customers and the company. A senior leader can still be accountable for the investment of resources, profitability of the project, and details of what goes on and ask the right questions of innovators. But management should not take the responsibility away from the team to propose the right decisions.

This subject reminds me of my days coaching soccer: there are no time outs in soccer, and there is only so much you can do by shouting instructions from the sidelines. Good soccer coaches learn to empower their players, so they can make the right decisions without instructions from a coach. Trust me, it even works with 10-year-olds.

New products and processes are extremely complex and require expertise from many disciplines—no single person could accomplish this task any longer. Empowered experts have to collaborate on a multidiscipline team to create the best value. Dwight Eisenhower said: "All war plans are obsolete when the first battle starts." The same is true with project schedules, and empowered teams must adapt to changes quickly.

At Goodyear, we have had empowered *experts* as long as I can remember. Some technical experts had earned the authority, and they were consulted by their functions for difficult technical problems and decisions. Today we empower all team members to contribute their expertise and collaborate with their colleagues to develop the best value for the customer and the most profitable value stream for the company. I am convinced that an empowered team of experts has the biggest effect on the profitability of the value streams and the development of the best capability. There are a few conditions, though, for this to happen:

- Just like project managers, team members must understand the business and the influence of their decisions on the profitability of the value stream.
- Teams also should have a line of sight from their work and their expert decisions to the corporate goals.
- The team members must be aligned and willing to sacrifice any functional or personal agenda to the greater good of customer value and company profitability.
- In the case of a conflict, everybody has to refocus on the product and the support of the customer.
- Team members must be willing to take responsibility for the solutions they propose and learn from their mistakes. There must be a no-fear, no-blame environment built on mutual trust and respect on all levels.

The same is true for teams that develop capability and work on continuous improvement—they are the experts on the process and recommend the best decisions for change.

I still remember the times at Goodyear when functions were not willing to share key functional information about cost, financial considerations, and prices with the rest of the organization. That information was considered a privilege to the function that had to make the decisions, and those functions did not want anybody to second-guess their decisions. That has changed today because now a lot of that information must be available to the team members as they try to make the right value-stream decisions. For example, the manufacturing engineer on the team must provide accurate information relating to the added complexity a new design may cause a plant. In addition to having the information available, the team members also need to understand how to use the information. Designers must understand the impact of a technical decision on the acceptance by the customer, the manufacturability, distribution, and so on. The manufacturing engineers on the team must understand design limitations, which require a lot of learning on the part of all the team members. This, of course, requires a new kind of training and coaching.

At Goodyear, team members initially needed time to learn to trust each other and respect each other's expertise. They also needed to learn to challenge each other with the necessary respect for their competencies. The other thing that the team members had to learn is to support the team decision regardless of their personal preference and the eventual outcome.

Although the team is responsible to propose the best solution, the accountability for the profitability or the process performance may reside with a different person. Leaders are still accountable for the balance sheet and the long-term company goals. Leaders also have to assure the alignment of the decisions with goals and changes in the corporate strategy. I have rarely seen a good recommendation from a team of responsible experts get rejected unless there was a reason unrelated to R&D for it, like a severe financial crisis in the company. Of course, there are discussions that need to take place in design reviews or gate meetings that should challenge the team, but they should not question their expertise and integrity.

Team members cannot be afraid to ask managers or leaders for support, resources, coaching, and sharing of experiences. Helping is management's job, and so asking for help cannot be seen as a weakness.

Lean R&D Principle: Win with teams of empowered experts.

An empowered, collaborative team of experts has a high chance to develop a profitable value stream, new capabilities, and new knowledge and continuously improve.

The team members are experts—they know the technology, the customer, the company, and the processes better than most managers or leaders. The team of experts should be empowered and trusted with finding the best solutions and proposing the best decisions or courses of action. The accountability may reside with a leader who may have to weigh other factors in the decision, like the financial or economic situation of the company.

The team collaborates to create the best value for the customer, knowledge, and the highest profit for the company. Functional or personal considerations are secondary. The team members should be trained to understand the impact of all team decisions on the profitability of the value stream. The team members must all support the decision, disregarding personal or functional preferences—regardless of the outcome.

At Goodyear: For many years, we talked about empowerment, but in the end managers and leaders felt that they had to step in and make the decisions. Over time, the focus on customer value and a faster lean process to create it drove the creation of a new organization and facilitated a change in the culture and behaviors. Empowered teams of experts took root under many organizational forms: design teams, business teams, CIS teams, and rapid improvement teams. Leadership had a big effect by setting the right example. As long as leaders held project reviews to micro-manage projects, teams brought the problems to those meetings. As project meetings were replaced with a weekly 30-minute standup meeting, there was no time left for micro-management and more responsibility was pushed down to the levels where it belongs. Sometimes empowered teams need empowered managers and leaders.

At Goodyear, the biggest challenge was to get teams to collaborate. We had teams for a long time, but there were a lot of arguments and often team members fought with each other when functional goals and personal preferences came in conflict with each other. Even though customer value was often maintained through the compromises, the compromise approach often led to extra costs, features, and complexity. At Goodyear, for example, the business teams were good about adding new tires to the line, but they could never agree on which tires to remove from the line, resulting in keeping too many obsolete codes.

Team leaders used to prefer compromise because the alternative would have been to overrule team members or escalate the decision. Often the escalation pitted functional leaders against each other, and the escalation was seen as a weakness of the project manager. This compromising team behavior is well known in the industry. There is a saying, "A camel is a race horse designed by a team." There are many references in lean literature about Toyota executives saying that "great conflict makes great cars." I like to incorporate games and role-playing into our lean training to visualize tendencies of team members to give priority to personal interests over the interest of the team and the customer. These games make it obvious that sometimes the limiting factor to customer value is not technology but lack of collaboration.

Goodyear Chairman Kramer likes to use an example from the European region to show how the new collaborative lean product development process helped Goodyear win a very competitive race in an important market. New legislation in Europe requires tire companies to label tires for wet traction, fuel economy, and noise, similar to how appliances are labeled in the United States for energy consumption. Being the first tire company with the right balance and mix of the appropriate ratings provided a competitive advantage to tire companies, and he credited the superior product development process and collaboration for winning that product race in Europe.

Chairman Kramer notes, though, "The process was excellent and representative of the progress we have made. However, the 'superior product development process' is just one element of the collaborative business processes model. To be effective, all business processes in a corporation—from demand creation to product supply—must be in sync or optimized. Great companies align their business processes seamlessly."

A step up from an empowered team is a self-directed team. I have seen self-directed teams at work in some companies, especially in software development, as with scrum teams. Most of these self-directed teams are permanent teams or the team members have been together for a certain period of time. I have also worked with self-directed teams at Goodyear in plants and in product development. Self-directed teams can be effective, especially if they perform standard work and the goals are clear.

In successful teams, I observe a clear distribution of the administrative responsibilities, like obtaining resources and communicating conflicts, which are the typical responsibilities of a team leader. If the deliverables of a self-managed team fall behind or there is too much conflict between team members, a senior leader interferes and brings the team back on track.

I believe that product development organizations can and should evolve toward at least some level of self-directed, permanent or semi-permanent teams in areas where this is the most efficient organizational form to do the work, such as in the more routine work in an execution phase and in the quick learning cycles for the development of new technology and capabilities.

Ideally teams should be colocated. That works quite well with permanent or long-term teams. Some companies even put wheels on people's desks to make collocation easier. There is a lot of controversy about locating team members *too close* together. But I have heard many times that when team members were allowed to design their own accommodations, they chose a close proximity.

If teams cannot be colocated, as is the case at Goodyear with most teams, alternate solutions are an "obeya" room where samples, drawings, and plans can be kept to be used in the frequent get-togethers. Other alternatives are the iteration kickoff meetings that are popular in Goodyear and daily huddles that are becoming popular everywhere.

3E People Management

At Goodyear we have begun to summarize good, lean people management as

- Engagement
- Education
- Empowerment

Lean publications often promote engagement and empowerment, but few put the need for education between the two. It takes quite a cultural shift from engagement to empowerment, and that shift must be facilitated by training on all levels, including leadership.

Lean Management and Leadership

Effective leaders work for the people they lead, ideally in a "servant" leader style.

The lean R&D environment poses challenges for the leaders at Goodyear, and we continue to work on

- The need to adapt to the new environment of lean product development
- Techniques, behaviors, and practices to effectively manage people in the lean environment
- Our primer to help leaders develop skills and a process that is right for each operation
- Possible methods for learning, practice, and self development

At Goodyear, I enjoyed good leadership support during the lean transformation. Now after the transformation, leadership is learning to adapt to the new organization and the new processes in order to continue to drive the change in culture. Not only engineers had to change, learn new tools, and change their behaviors, leaders need to do the same thing.

Some change experts claim that the leadership that got the organization to this point may not be the right leadership to lead the new organization. I do not fully share that assessment because of reasons of engagement and sustainability, and that really was not an option for Goodyear. But I am convinced that all leadership and management, regardless of whether they supported the change or not, must learn and develop new skills to move forward.

The basic principles of leadership and people management and development are as valid and applicable in a lean and matrix environment as any other. In fact, they may be heightened. But leadership education and support has proved to be a very challenging part of our lean implementation.

Engineers were trained and coached through the transformation, but that approach did not work well with the managers and leaders. I have tried to get leaders and managers to attend training with their staff to set an example, but that was only partially successful. I tried separate classes for managers and leaders, which worked better, but still only led to partial attendance. I even proposed a survey by experts from the outside to point out gaps and help address them—this approach was never approved. I think these efforts failed because it was mostly classroom training and lacked the hands-on opportunities for practice and self-development.

I noticed that our "horizontal" organization adapted more quickly to the new lean process. This is the organization that manages the projects across the functions. The organization is headed up by the regional technical directors and the project managers who report to them. They have their cross-functional huddles in front of the visual planning board, and, over time, they figured out how to manage that process very well. From there, all the other events and processes they use to manage their work evolved. Our innovation center in Luxembourg took the lead on this and piloted the process. Steve Rohweder helped develop the process in Luxembourg, and when Steve transferred back to Akron as a regional technical director he took the process in Akron to the next level for consumer tires, and the other tire lines eventually followed.

As the project organization developed a lean process quickly, the functional organization struggled to find their way. I always heard the complaint that functional mangers did not see their people any more since most of their people were assigned to project teams that were managed by project managers. Functions tried to hold the traditional project meetings, but they realized now they were duplicating the work of the project managers, and it was not their responsibility anyway. Functional mangers were used to people coming to them when they had problems with their projects, but now those individuals went to their project managers.

I had some success with taking a group of our leaders out to other companies that were willing to share and show the group what a good process and good leadership looks like. Those companies were not always R&D organizations (I could not find any in the area), but I was able to make my point. Although I could not get good attendance at those gemba walks, I noticed that some of the participants immediately started to use what they saw, quickly developed skills by practicing, and started to transform their organizations. I informally got together with some of the adaptive leaders, and we decided on the following approach that favors observing, learning by doing, and self-development:

- Continue visiting other companies to see a good system at work.
- Create a "primer"—point leaders in the right direction and give them enough structure that they can develop the right system for their organization and learn while they do it.
- Give leaders the opportunities to practice and self-develop.
- Provide coaching to assist them in their learning and self-development.
- Provide formal training to share experiences and cover those items that cannot be addressed by coaching.

- Develop a system based on things that work for us and have the folks who helped develop it share with the rest of the organization and help develop the rest of the organization.

At our innovation center in Hanau, Germany, they came up with a good visual that can be used as a primer. They call it the *Magic Triangle*, but, unfortunately there is no magic spell that goes with it—as usual it will still take a lot of hard work, patience, and coaching to get this embedded in the culture.

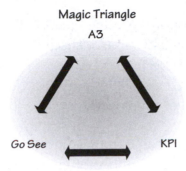

Magic Triangle
A3
Go See   KPI

- *KPIs (key performance indicators)* are the visuals or metrics required to see what is needed to run the operation, the function, the project, the lab, the test garage, and so on. It can include red/green lights that change color when a threshold is exceeded. There can be simple tick marks on a piece of paper or a more sophisticated dashboard of gauges as in an airplane or a car.
- *Go-see* events or pulse events can include gemba walks, huddles, one-on-one meetings, and design reviews. I also have tried sharing events, and I see them at many companies. I am sure there is a wealth of other great "go-see" opportunities out there.
- *The A3* or a similar process is the last leg of the process, and it is used to address the problems discovered in the other two legs and to drive the development of the required capability. I use the term A3 only because that is what we use at Goodyear. You are welcome to replace A3 with other terms, such as "systematic problem-solving," capability development, or CI process.

Lean leadership experts like David Mann go as far as defining huddles and gemba walks as standard work for leaders.[9] This means they must be done on a regular cadence, ideally on a regular schedule. (Mann uses a similar triangle—visual controls, accountability, and leaders standard work—that is similar to the magic triangle, and I am convinced it will work just as well as other possible primers.)

At Goodyear, we encourage managers and leaders to start a system of visual performance indicators and look at them in regular short huddles, conduct periodic gemba walks in their area of responsibility, and participate in regular design reviews. Any problem that comes up during these events should start an A3. Besides showing respect for people, a general theme should address the following:

- Are we effectively supporting value creation for the customers?
- Is our process working as well as it should?
- Where can the process be improved?
- Are we developing the capabilities and knowledge that we need?
- What is on the minds of employees?

All three elements of the magic triangle are important for leadership success, but because of the importance of *go see*, let us examine it in more detail.

Huddles

Huddles became a necessary management tool to manage work that is executed fast and efficiently by empowered teams. The word "huddle" comes from American football where the players get together before a play. They gather in a close formation to make sure the opposing team cannot hear their discussion or pick up clues. During the huddles, the clock keeps running, so huddles have to be short and effective. At Goodyear, we have done very well with our project huddles, chaired by the regional directors in the operation management center at the visual plan for the iterations. Functional huddles are less popular and no longer deal with projects, but now address the work that is done in the functions to support the projects (people, capabilities, knowledge).

A good huddle starts with associates and the lowest-level of functional managers discussing safety, attendance, quality issues, and the day's delivery requirements. Then the first-level managers meet with their leaders and go through a similar agenda. The last huddle is with the highest leader in the operating chain and follows a similar agenda. Huddles are on a consistent schedule (e.g., daily, every other day, weekly) and are a standup gathering that lasts no more than 15 min.

Special focus must be placed on the quick resolution of problems that come up. Problems are easier to solve if they get addressed right away before they become large enough to disrupt the operation. In a lean operation where there are daily deliverables and where the adjacent functions rely on accurate and on-time information, huddles catch problems quickly and keep the line moving. In R&D, huddles are also a good event to pull the development andon cord if a problem surfaces.

Managers and leaders will have to concentrate on what problems require their attention and when their help is needed. They will have to trust and be content knowing that all projects that are not addressed in huddles are moving along and that problems are being addressed without getting them involved in the details.

The global Goodyear Material Science organization conducts huddles on a weekly cadence, starting in the labs and offices and ending with the director huddle every Friday. Michael Rachita, manager Global Metrology, started regular huddles in his organization and says, "Although huddles can be problem-solving sessions, they are first and foremost best used as a place to highlight where the trouble spots are within a team's area of weekly responsibility."

Design Reviews

In a lean product development environment, a functional design review should focus on whether the function has the capabilities, knowledge, expertise, talent, and processes to efficiently deliver value for the customer. It may be a good idea to invite customers and stakeholders to the review to get the input from the end-to-end value stream, using a collaborative approach to address and solve problems.

In the design reviews, people should not only show results, but they should also show *how* the results were obtained and how the work was performed. That provides insights for leaders to assure the tools, knowledge, and capabilities of their organization are available and working. Design reviews should not be personal—they can only be about the product, the process, the capabilities, and the tools. For example, they should never attempt to determine whether an engineer did a good job or made mistakes.

At Goodyear, we may not have perfected our design reviews yet, but we are on the right path. We start the functional reviews in front of the visual planning board with functional leaders and representatives. The team can visually see the problems that occurred during the iterations and understand the background. The team notices if the issue was a one-time occurrence or if it is a recurring or even is a systemic issue. The functions take the problems back to the experts responsible for doing the work and use an organized process (usually the A3 process if the problem warrants that approach) to find the root cause and implement countermeasures.

Design reviews also allow functional managers and leaders to assess the capabilities of their engineers and the talent that the organization has and needs. It also allows them to see how their associates are able to collaborate with members of other organizations.

Gemba Walks

If managers and leaders are not located on the work floor, they should show up on the work floor often to stay current on what is going on and show respect for the people. In the lean, matrix environment, gemba walks, huddles, and design reviews are some of the few occasions where leaders and managers can connect and get to know all the engineers.

When we started gemba walks, engineers were shaking in their boots when it was announced that the director or the VP was coming by. This fear was reinforced by the fact that work in the engineering area is invisible and that questions are likely to be asked, and people were afraid they would give the wrong answers. Over time, the fear dissipated as leaders, directors, and staff become more used to the gemba walks.

Gemba walks allow managers and leaders to

■ Observe and see what is going on in their area of responsibility.
■ Interact and show respect for the people who work for them.
■ See, assess, and appreciate metrics or other information/facts that are needed to manage the operation.
■ Be seen by the engineers and lead by example.
■ Get first-hand, observable, and unfiltered information. The fact that all mangers/leaders go to the floor will change the accuracy of the information that gets reported through the hierarchical chain.
■ Observe and address breakdowns in the processes and problems that come up.
■ Assure that the processes work as best as they can.
■ Prove that the role of leadership and management is to help and to support the organization.

- Develop and demonstrate an interest in the process and the development of process capability.

Gemba walks are not a

- Form of micromanagement, where a leader tries to catch what other management levels have overlooked
- Gauges of people's performance or a means to find who did something right or wrong
- Audit, investigation, or witch hunt

Gemba walks are an opportunity for leaders and managers to go see, but they are also an opportunity to be seen. Billy Taylor says, "Leadership is like parenting: presence is more important than presents."

Whenever a problem comes up in a huddle or gemba walk, there must be a standard reaction: what is wrong with the process that this problem could happen? The reaction is not, "Who did this?" or "Whose fault is it?" There should not be questions like, "Why did the person directly responsible for this area not know about this and address it?"

One difficult situation that may show up in initial gemba walks is that issues get discovered by a VP that are unknown by managers. That must be expected because often the engineers do not share all concerns with their manager. Those issues are likely to go away over time, especially if all levels of management get into the habit of showing up on the floor.

When you start gemba walks, it may be a good idea to announce them— once they become more natural, they can happen unannounced.

R&D Gemba Walk Best Practices

1. Remind yourself that "respect for people" means "Hard on the process, easy on the people." It assumes that most people try to do a good job whenever they can. If there is a breakdown, it is generally the fault of a bad process or tool, not a bad person. And remember: ask questions, do not give answers. Leave the position power at the door—you want to understand, not judge, blame, or fix.

2. Introduce yourself if needed and explain why you are there.

3. Follow the 3Ps:
   - Purpose/product—How does the work done in the area visited link to Goodyear objectives, growth, and so on?
   - Process—Do we have the right process? Does it work as expected?
   - People—Do we have the right talent? Are they able to perform at their potential?

4. Look for problems. Start with visibility gained from project huddles, using KPIs and visibility to identify problems:
   - Safety—Stress that employee wellbeing always comes first.
   - Quality—Look at quality KPIs and make sure people know how to deliver quality and have the capabilities to deliver.
   - Delivery—Identify what will be delivered today, this week, and if it will be on time and why or why not.
   - Efficiency/speed—Look at KPIs for speed and ask questions if needed.

5. Ask questions to clarify or to learn, but do not to judge. Obtain first-hand, unfiltered information. Offer help and assistance.

6. When problems are identified, ask for an A3—and remember that you should sponsor some A3s and that you must occasionally coach an A3.

7. Follow up on A3s that are in process. Make notes on what you need to follow up on.

8. Thank participants.

A popular tool used by most Goodyear managers and leaders are one-on-one meetings. They are usually short meetings of leaders with their direct reports, but leaders also will meet with levels below direct reports. The behaviors and outcomes of the one-on-one meetings are similar to those of gemba walks. At Goodyear, many managers were afraid that the skip-level meetings would become complaint sessions, but they learned that in an environment of less fear and more trust those meetings are very constructive as empowered employees often make their leaders look good when talking to directors or VPs.

After a major problem surfaces in a huddle, a design review, gemba walk, or at another event, the natural reaction should be to ask for an A3. The person responsible for the area may decide to do the A3 or assign the A3 to an appropriate engineer. Remember, it is not the responsibility of the leader to solve the problem, but the leaders should empower the right people to get the problem addressed.

Leaders and managers need to learn to manage problems by using the A3 or a similar systematic problem-solving process. In order to do that, it is not enough to send all engineers to A3 training. A manager or leader must know the A3 process inside and out in order to coach/mentor the associates in the process and to use the process for the development of the people. I personally think that managers and leaders should always be a step ahead of their staff on the mastering of problem-management skills.

Respect

One of the most important management and leadership behaviors is respect for people. One of the best ways to do that is to engage people in improving the way they work.

For example, at our innovation center in Luxembourg, Emmanuel Robinet, manager Product Evaluation Luxembourg, trained his testing organization in lean and has all associates engaged in developing capability and improving the operation on a regular basis. Emmanuel says, "Engaging the staff in the CIS activities builds trust and shows respect for their knowledge."

Respect is also about asking the right questions, not giving the right answers. Recently I coached a cross-functional team in value-stream mapping after they walked a process in a plant. After a day of go see, the team had made a map, but was still divided on whether they really understood the process. I tried to coach them with questions. A senior leader in the meeting listened for a while and became impatient. Either the leader was frustrated with the slow progress or did not like the direction the team was taking. The leader, who also did not understand the process, eventually laid out his solution—inconsistent with the findings of the team—and asked the team what was wrong with the solution that he presented. We all know what will happen in a situation like that. The team will reluctantly and partially implement the leader's solution, which will likely not work or be hard to sustain if it does work.

I prefer an approach where a team is empowered by their leader to find the root cause and propose countermeasures with which the leader is comfortable. The leader then supports the team as the team implements and sustains the countermeasures. The empowered team is not free to do whatever they want to do, but they are empowered to propose the countermeasures and they are responsible for their suggestions and their successful implementation. Changes done in this manner may take a little longer and require patience on the part of the leader. But these changes are easier to sustain, and the team is motivated to check back and make the required adjustments, ensure controls are in place to sustain the change, and share the new process with all parts of the organization (they are proud to share it because it is theirs).

Showing respect to people and empowering them to take responsibility are at the foundation of what Jeffrey Liker and Gary Convis call "leading as if you have no authority."[10] Of course this management approach is often contrary to what most managers and leaders have learned and what earned them their current position in the company. Behaviors like this have to be supported by good training and opportunities for self-development and practice. We teach influence management in lean product development certification and lean leadership development, but I still have not found a good method yet for practicing and coaching. It also is critical to have consistent support from HR and the inclusion of coaching behaviors in regular performance reviews.

Many leaders know that their job is to develop products and capability regardless of whether they work on the horizontal or vertical part of the matrix. Unfortunately, many of them think capability development is about tools and technology and they forget that the most important part of capability development is *people development*. Or they think that people development is the responsibility of HR and the training department.

In the lean operation, leaders and managers are largely responsible for the development of their people by good coaching, mentoring, and setting the proper example. What could be more respectful than helping someone reach their full potential.

Lastly, a respectful leader walks the talk. Billy Taylor says, "You cannot teach what you don't know, and you cannot lead where you don't go. People do not hear what you say, they hear what you do."

Accountability

Leaders must hold people accountable.

Associates have responsibilities in a lean environment to which they must be held accountable, especially for delivering the results they committed to deliver. This is usually done well when it comes to project or functional deliveries, especially if those commitments are part of personal performance management. But when it comes to cross-functional activities aimed at process improvements or capability development, I have not always seen the same standards applied or levels of success.

I have seen many leaders assign cross-functional process projects and A3s to associates, but the deliverables fade away: the associates got promoted, moved to another area, or they simply became busy with other things and never finished the A3 or the project. Unfinished work or work that is not sustained is a large waste for the company and the organization. Finishing work includes PDCA, reflection/learning, and sharing. Sponsors of A3s must insist that all steps of the A3 are completed. If the person assigned to an A3 is moving on before finishing the A3, the sponsor must assign the continuation of the A3 to a qualified person after proper knowledge transfer.

Accountability and acknowledgment go hand in hand: it is necessary and important to recognize people who do a good job. This can be done by many means, from celebrations to personal recognitions. Here again, the fact that you do the recognition is often more important than a reward or monetary gift. CTO Joe Zekoski says, "When leaders see people do something right, they must recognize and thank them—that has amazing power!"

Leader Standard Work

If you think engineers are hard to get to do standard work—do not even think about trying it with leaders. How can leaders make time available for go see, huddles, gemba walks, showing respect, holding people accountable—all this additional work? The answer is simple: This is not additional work. This is the work that leaders must do!

Leaders should drop something less important, but we all know this is easier said than done! The first thing to drop would be attention to the kind of work that used to be their responsibility, but no longer is. At Goodyear, functional leaders used to manage projects, which in the matrix organization is not their responsibility any more. The empowered teams and individuals also need a lot less supervision and follow-up, which frees up time, and leaders should get all the information they need from others in the huddles, gemba walks, and design reviews. Besides these events, a good lean organization does not need a lot of additional meetings. Another good tip is to schedule personal time at less than 100%, and keep a buffer for emergencies and variability.

At Goodyear when we started the gated process, we had a terrible time getting the right people to come to huddles and gate meetings. At Goodyear, everybody manages their own calendars, and most leaders have to choose between many different meetings every hour of the day, and not every leader chooses the same meeting. Gate meetings were put on the same day every week, but that still did not completely fix the problem because managers still got called to a more important meeting at the same time with their boss. There was rarely a quorum at the gate meetings to make a decision. Cross-functional meetings need cross-functional participation; if key people miss the meeting, they waste the time of all the other participants.

Good companies coordinate cross-functional schedules from the top down and set times for all the important meetings—which are very short and only focus on the biggest problems. People who travel should try to call in for those key meetings, and nobody should interfere with the meeting. I have seen top leaders in major companies excuse themselves at conferences to dial into their huddles or design reviews while they were traveling. Sending an *empowered* substitute to meetings is another option.

Even top leaders know that their reports must attend certain meetings, and they must respect that and not schedule their own meeting during that time. What is more important for the company, the gate meeting or the leader's convenience?

Part of a standard agenda for leaders should be the attendance of certain cross-functional meetings, huddles, design reviews (as noted by Mann)—all scheduled on fixed days and times. Also part of standard work is time for gemba walks, coaching, mentoring, succession planning, or other forms of people development.

At Goodyear, we have started a leadership development program for lean product development. The program is patterned after the lean development certification (Lean 401). There will be signoff at the completion of the class milestones because, if that is not done, other priorities are likely to interfere and the training will not be completed. The formal leadership training is comprised of

- Lean principles for product development
- The *Managing to Learn*/A3 process
- Lean leadership
- Influence management
- What good looks like (visit other companies)
- Practicing and coaching

Humble Servant

A servant leader is also a humble leader who knows that humility and continuous improvement go together. How could you possibly motivate people to pursue capability development and improvements if you are convinced that you are already as good as you can possibly be.

Gemba walks, one-on-one meetings, coaching sessions, etc. cannot be about the leader—they must be about the people the leader serves. This also implies that in those discussions and meetings the leader asks questions and listens.

Champions

So far we talked about all the key people in a lean product development transformation: the sponsor, leadership, engineers, and consultants, but we have not talked about the position that I know the best: the champion. I played that role at Goodyear for nearly a decade. The champion can be the sensei, as was my case, but I also had many teachers.

A champion is a position for which people from inside the company rarely volunteer and, if they do, they have no idea what they are getting themselves into. There probably is not a job description, and most likely no career path either. Company insiders often "slide" into that role as a little initiative gets bigger and there is nobody else there to lead it. Engineers are usually not well trained and not well prepared to take on a role as a champion. It takes quite some time for a person to develop the skills of a champion, and in my case it was done by learning from mistakes and self-development. I read a lot of books and attended conferences and seminars, but a lot of what was taught only became clear to me when I started doing it.

I do not advise hiring a champion from outside unless it is to teach and coach an inside champion or change leaders. I think transformations work better when they are done from within. I have seen many initiatives led by outside champions fail, and there is a reason why many lean experts have a long list of employers on their resume. I have experienced several scenarios with outside experts in various Goodyear divisions. Some were successful and others were not—it was not always the fault of the outside expert if they were unsuccessful. People may initially listen to an outsider more than to an insider (the prophet in his own town syndrome), but in the long run knowing the technology, people, the company, the development process, and the culture favors the inside change agent, especially if the inside champion has the respect of peers and leaders.

Many personal characteristics, professional traits, and company factors can help a lean product development champion succeed in their role.

Support

The most important thing for a champion is the support of leadership, which comes in many forms. If you are asked to champion an initiative, make absolutely sure there is unwavering support from a leader who can make things happen. Senior members of the leadership team should be able to convince a potential champion of that support, without offering incentives. If the initiative is important to them, they should show that importance.

Support also can be found in a good sponsor, but champions cannot count on the sponsor to open doors or gain support and buy in. Like authority, the champion must earn that. It does, though, help to have a strong sponsor with close ties to leadership, as was my case at Goodyear with Jean-Claude Kihn.

Most champions also need *lean* support—this was certainly true for me. Go and see what other companies are doing and whom they use as lean experts. Retain a few consultants as coaches or advisors. Bring in experts to assess and advise during the implementation. This helped me a lot, especially with validation and buy-in, and I continue to do it.

My search for sensei has helped me to gradually establish a strong network of lean individuals who offered both supportive and contradictory opinions—both extremely beneficial. This network has grown, both internally and externally, progressively helping me to establish my own knowledge manual of standard work for a lean champion. Nobody handed me a set of instructions or a playbook. It is important to have people on every level and with many different skills to bounce ideas off. Today I can rely on my network of many professionals and champions from other companies and experts in universities.

Skills

The champion needs to have the lean, technical, and job skills to understand all aspects of the lean initiative as well as change management skills to engage others in the initiative. All of the lean management and leadership traits I described need to be exhibited by the champion. Some of the most important ones are to engage people in the process and to lead without authority. Influence can be a good tool if it is learned and applied correctly.

Attaining and exhibiting lean knowledge, technical skills, and leadership skills help a champion gain the respect of peers, engineers, managers, and leaders in the company. Respect is critically important, without which your initiative is doomed. Many people underestimate the technical competency that must be held by a champion. Engineers and managers need to be convinced in technical discussions that the process changes will work for the work they do. If people do not understand the content (like what lean is about), it is more important who says it than what is said! I believed it helped greatly that I was an engineer trusted by engineers.

Trainer and Educator

You will almost certainly underestimate the amount of training, coaching, and education that will be required in getting a lean initiative up and running. And most of that training and coaching load will land in the lap of the champion—chances are that there is nobody else to do it.

While a champion can assemble an array of tools, media, books, demos, and so on to help associates learn about and apply lean, the champion really needs to be an educator, teacher, and coach at heart and bring these ideas to others—in a classroom setting and in one-on-one discussions every day. Any opportunity to educate should be welcomed, and the champion's day is filled with such instances.

Courage, Perseverance, and Patience

A change as big as a lean product development implementation takes courage and a vast amount of time, energy, and patience. An assignment like this

cannot be viewed as a quick stepping stone on the way to a leadership position. It is a long haul, filled with frustration and rejection. Being able to deal
with these obstacles is another important "feature" of a good lean champion
and change agent.

Dealing with resistance was one of my biggest challenges. There was a
lot of open and hidden resistance, and strong influence often was used to
curb our initiative. Unfortunately, the resistance was mostly hidden and I
had no idea it existed until it was too late. If I saw open resistance, I sought
out the individuals and tried to address the issue with a good dialogue, at
the very least learning from the encounter.

Things often do not work the first time, maybe not even the second time,
but the champion keeps trying, looking for an opportunity to make a difference every day. Recognize the right time to do something and jump on the
rare opportunities that present themselves. I was often accused of "throwing stuff against the wall to see what sticks." A lot stuck because I threw so
much. I called it "experimenting."

I believe that successes must be advertised and celebrated in any change
process, and we did that. But it was not my success. Empowering people
means you let them talk about the success and give them the credit—they
must feel in the end that they did it by themselves. Champions also need to
deal with failures (occasionally celebrate them), and with all the struggles we
had at Goodyear, I got pretty good at that as well.

To some of my colleagues, certainly those who wish the lean stuff had
never started, my tireless lean march became a source of irritation. Gene
Miller, R&D associate and a long-time six sigma champion, told me to
expect to lose a lot of friends in the transformation. I hope I did not lose as
many friends as Gene anticipated.

***Once an initiative takes hold it better be successful. Failed
initiatives are hard to restart.***

Lastly, and most importantly, champions must get the initiative right at the
beginning. That sounds like a lot of pressure, and it is. There may be false
starts and that is OK, but once an initiative takes hold it better be successful. Failed initiatives are hard to restart. People would rather take half the
improvement than tolerate a completely new change.

With the right mindset, expectations, and knowledge, managing a new
initiative in a large company—the role of the champion—can be as much

fun as developing a new, innovative product. The biggest rewards are a sense of accomplishment and a lot of good learning.

Lean Suppliers

Goodyear is a great supplier to North American car companies, providing them tires for as long as cars have required tires. (Goodyear supplied tires to Henry Ford to race the Model T.) In the 1980s, Goodyear became a supplier to most Asia-based car manufacturers, and Goodyear went through a long evolution of being a supplier from lowest bidder to a development partner. When I developed OEM tires for domestic, Japanese, and European car manufacturers, we were always challenged by the OEM to push our technology in the direction that the OEMs needed. I often did presentations on technical subjects to the OEMs, organized supplier demos, and provided tradeoff curves that described the technical requirements they requested.

A similar evolution has happened with suppliers to Goodyear: from raw materials to tools to engineering services. In product development, we have the most contact with raw material suppliers through the material science function and engineering services. I recently conducted a lean training session for the supplier development group in global procurement, and I was quite surprised how similar their goals of contributing to a profitable value stream were to those of Goodyear R&D.

Any development of a raw material that can be done by a supplier does not have to be done internally. There are many reasons to outsource certain engineering services. Of course, it is a difficult strategic decision identifying the engineering services to outsource, which can create flexible capacity and increase development speed. For many reasons and given the highly competitive nature of our business, Goodyear probably does not outsource as much product development as other companies because we pay close attention to holding tight our capability and knowledge. But one good example is the long-standing partnership Goodyear has had with Sandia National Laboratories, where many of our computer modeling tools were developed. Among many other services, we engaged a lot of lean experts, especially those who can help us with product development and lean training. These lean partnerships have paid off, but they were not established in a completive bidding contest.

Another important supplier partnership for a lean R&D organization must be aimed at reducing cycle time. Some time ago, every experimental tooling purchase (and we have a lot of them) went through a bidding process, including the company-owned mold plants. Today, our own plant works the experimental tooling into the production schedule based on a day-by-day release of design information to allow for maximum concurrency. If we need outside mold-manufacturing resources, we use a similar process. Procurement picks long-term global vendors by a reverse internet auction, and new development jobs can be assigned without administrative burden and we can develop the fastest process jointly with the supplier.

After Taking Care of the Business, It Is OK to Be Selfish

You know by now that your lean R&D effort must be focused first on customer value and the complete value stream, leveraging the shadow that R&D has on the business and helping the business and the company improve the financial results. This usually means that gains in capacity are wielded to improve R&D capabilities so that the company can get appropriate return from the investment into R&D—with a caveat.

After using lean principles to get the best return for the business and the company, there comes a time when R&D leaders can and should use new lean capabilities to work on the process efficiency in R&D for the benefit of R&D. R&D may not be that much of a cost to the business, but there is no reason why R&D should pay money for waste. But before looking at any efficiency improvement, it is good to remember that there are certain nonnegotiable items in R&D:

- Safety and quality cannot be compromised.
- No step backward can be taken on service and delivery to the business.
- There cannot be a negative effect on innovation, creativity, or any other expected deliverable of the process.
- There cannot be any negative long-term effects on the R&D process.
- There cannot be a reduction in the creation of reusable knowledge.

How would you start an efficiency initiative in R&D? You could go through the Womack Wheel as you would do for any other initiative. The customer now is the R&D organization, and the customer wants higher efficiency and less waste. Next you look at the complete R&D value stream, but with an eye on waste and cost. You may not need a new value-stream map, but you may need new data. Chances are that your R&D finance organization has cost data that you may be able to use. You may need to sort through and categorize the data that finance offers into useable "buckets" for lean improvements, such as costs by project broken down into components (e.g., labor, testing, prototypes, IT) and distributed charges (e.g., buildings, utilities, overhead, services).

If you find low-hanging fruit, something that you can quickly correct, then just do it. Low-hanging fruits that we found at Goodyear were the warehouses for experimental tires. Chances are that there is a limited amount of low-hanging fruit. Then you look for the highest cost items and start to ask critical questions. Critical questions are popular in lean, and they are often used to assess projects in the kentou phase. Try the following critical questions to uncover problems with R&D efficiency:

- What would the business or customers say if you sent them R&D charges as an itemized bill? They may ask: "Why are we paying for this? This adds no value to us? Why are those charges so high?" Expecting questions like that would be a hint to take a closer look at the charges.
- Can you justify with facts and data why R&D costs are so high?
- Can you justify the use of all the tools that are used? What if the business or the customer would ask you, "Why so many molds, prototypes, and so on? Why are they so expensive?"
- What precisely was done during the engineering hours that were charged?
- Why were there so many rework loops or overprocessing?
- Did this work make the function, the engineer, or the customer happy?
- Is this the best way to do this job? Does somebody know a better way?
- Was there early delivery of expensive items, including engineering work?
- How many experiments were run where we learned nothing or very little?

I understand that this is unusual thinking for most R&D organizations, but consider this lean approach. You then will be ready to have these actual and productive conversations with the business and your customers.

If an opportunity is identified, projects should be started by using the A3 process. It is a great idea to go through the A3s with all the people responsible for the work, maybe even stakeholders or customers.

Some areas of inefficiency that we have found within Goodyear include

- Excessive prototypes, tools, and models
- Work that did not support a decision or lead to new knowledge
- Generation of knowledge that already existed
- Work based on an obsolete standard
- Expedited shipments or other unusual expenses
- Work, prototypes, and tools finished early and waiting
- Overtime

- Excessive cycle times
- Inadequate tools
- Engineers overqualified for work
- Excessive costs for services or tools
- Lack of attention to risk criteria
- Failure to stop projects that go nowhere

There are so many opportunities in most R&D organizations for efficiency gains that an investment in the resources to do that would certainly yield a return that warrants the effort and will improve the work of those within R&D and make other changes even more impactful. But, above all, remember that applying lean to R&D efficiency is not nearly as beneficial as improving the value stream and applying lean to the R&D shadows.

Lean R&D Principle: Apply lean to the R&D shadows.

For most organizations, R&D is not a high cost to the business: typically 1% to 4% and up to 7% for high-tech and start-up companies. As such, focusing lean on reducing R&D costs does not yield a lot of direct savings for the business, and it can be counterproductive. On the other hand, R&D has a large *indirect* effect on the profitability of the business.

Review the equation: *profit = volume (price − cost)*. With that in mind, know that R&D can influence the product cost by as much as 70% and lean principles can also be used to design cost-efficient products. As you learned in this book, lean principles can also be used to influence the price and the volume of a new product. Applying lean principles to the indirect effects of R&D can help increase the profitability of the value streams producing those goods. This gain in profitability is typically an order of magnitude higher than the savings due to reduced R&D cost.

At Goodyear: We now deliver almost all new products to the business at the appropriate time and according to quality and performance targets, which assures maximum volume. We achieved a significant gain in capacity and capability, which is used to develop better-performing and more innovative products that can be sold for the right price. Lean helped achieve many improvements in product cost. For example, due to the much shorter cycle times, more cost-efficient processes and materials can be developed and released much faster, which allows us to take advantage of the cost savings as early as possible.

Lean Expectations and Endurance

A good champion or change leader should go into a lean transformation with the right mindset and the right expectations. It is also a good idea to make sure that the sponsor and stakeholders have the right expectations. When setting expectations for a lean initiative in R&D, indicate that the initiative will

- When done right, generate large benefits far beyond R&D
- Not require a lot of expenses, but will need a small amount of resources
- Take time to accomplish because a significant change in the company culture is required to sustain the initiative
- Require leaders to be patient until the results become obvious
- Result in change that is relatively disruptive and affects virtually how the whole organization will work
- Like every major change, take a lot of energy and will occasionally generate a lot of frustration
- Never end

Ovidiu (Ovi) Contras, lean coach, Bombardier, is a lean champion in R&D. He says lean manufacturing transformations are difficult, and lean product development transformations are even more difficult. He notes that in big development programs, the challenges are multiplied by many factors: difficulty seeing the product (everything resides in IT systems), and, hence, keeping all the numerous stakeholders on the same page, as well as multiple conflicting requirements and knowledge gaps that are not easy to grasp and that negatively impact quality, cost, and development time. It is no surprise to Contras that the lean product development field is less understood than lean manufacturing and that examples of successful transformations are rare.

Guenter Wartusch adds, "Results are not immediate—sometimes it takes years to get results, and it takes a lot of patience to wait that out. Most management wants results fast and the results often *only* deal with reduced cost."

Rich Gildersleeve, CTO DJO Global, says the driving paradigm at DJO is continual improvement. "With our early successes in lean manufacturing more than 15 years ago it seemed obvious that many of these theories could be applied to product development and allow dramatic improvement in the quantity and quality of our new product releases. Early in our journey we drove out waste in many product development processes, from actions as simple as holding a kaizen to reduce engineering change order lead times to more complex exercises such as value-stream mapping our entire development process. We have implemented, and continue to explore, dozens of methods to improve product development output."

Gildersleeve goes on to note that a large amount of process improvements were implemented at DJO Global, but roughly half failed to meet their expectations. "Accepting these failures and not letting them inhibit our desire to continually improve is one of our core strengths. For example, we have had dramatic success with A3 methodologies for problem solving, project management, and knowledge capture, yet less-than-stellar results using A3 processes for capturing customer needs and documenting vendor capabilities."

Another important lesson from DJO Global lean product development efforts is that "the idea of failing fast and often for success applies not only to product development, but to the development of our R&D processes as well," adds Gildersleeve. "When a process fails, we ask what was the root cause of that failure so that we may determine if the process should be tweaked and retried or thrown in the trash bin so that we may move on to more important work."

Lastly, Gildersleeve points to the pleasure of the ongoing lean process: "At DJO R&D, continual improvement, largely driven with lean thinking, is a way of life. It has been a joy working with many talented people both within and outside of DJO to develop more effective design processes. Just as we receive a lot of satisfaction from delivering great products that help our customers in their activities of daily living, it is extremely rewarding to uncover and implement new R&D processes that allow us to get there faster and with higher quality."

Lean R&D Principle: Hang in there—a lean R&D initiative will take time, effort, and never ends.

You may find a low-hanging fruit quickly, but, as a general rule, a lean R&D implementation takes time, energy, and patience. The people part certainly takes time because it requires a significant change in the culture.

Many companies go into this venture with the wrong expectations. Although there should be some quick results, the culture change takes time and patience and it may take years to get sustainable results. You, like me, may encounter many false starts and poisoned wells. Even after an initiative gets on the right track, it still takes a lot of adjustments, reenergizing, and remotivating to keep it moving in the right direction. It also takes a lot of time to spread the initiative to the whole R&D organization. Probably the longest time is spent finding and educating people in all parts of the organization to help with the transformation. (Joe Zekoski, CTO, used to call those people "apostles.")

Another fact that must be understood is that improvement never ends. Toyota is still at it. Companies cannot stop the development of new capabilities and the improvement of the existing capabilities.

I have seen many companies run out of patience or steam and give up on the initiative too early for a variety of reasons: lack of visible results, budget cuts, make room for a different initiative, change in leadership. That is especially unfortunate because after an initial small investment, these initiatives do not cost a lot of money (if you do it right).

Rather than stopping an initiative, I suggest to pivot, try something else, find a different pilot, a different sponsor, a new champion. Sometimes it does help to try a lot of things in different areas—something may stick.

The long process of a lean initiative is especially difficult when it spans several generations of managers or leaders. Managers or leaders like to put their stamp on an organization and that is often done with a new initiative rather than supporting an existing one.

At Goodyear: We had what I call quick results, but it still took 3 years to get them. I was often blamed for "throwing stuff against the wall to see what sticks." My answer was always, "But at least I throw a lot." We made many turns, some U-turns, and did not always end up where we had initially planned, but we always made improvements.

> *The Goodyear lean initiative has continued unchanged through several leadership generations on all levels (but with only one champion). I personally had no idea what I was getting into, and I am still amazed at how much work it was. It was well worth it, especially since our initiative at Goodyear was not very expensive.*

If you want to lose weight, it may be enough if you diet for a while, but chances are that you will regain the weight eventually unless you change eating habits and maybe your lifestyle. The habits and the lifestyle of a company is its culture. Sustaining a lean initiative requires a major change in the culture. You can only sustain a lean initiative if you prepare the future leaders to lead it.

"Leaders get the culture they exhibit and that they tolerate," says Jim Morgan.[11] This again puts the emphasis on leadership for changing the culture and sustaining the cultural change. Sustaining change is not easy, as evidenced by the percentages of recidivism (criminal behavior, personal habits, dieting, etc.).

As I wrote in the beginning of this book, lean product development does not have the greatest track record when it comes to sustainability. Although there is a lot published about sustaining lean in manufacturing, the reasons for the poor sustainability in R&D are not as well known.

I believe that lean product development initiatives fizzle or stop because of the following factors:

- *Change in leadership:* Many new leaders start a new initiative to put their stamp on the organization. They do not necessarily abandon other initiatives, but immature initiatives disappear quickly if people now support what the new leader likes.
- *No patience:* Many organizations run out of patience because a lean initiative can take a lot of time. Many lean initiatives stretch over more than one management generation, often because management and leadership rotations occur frequently.
- *Short-term expectations:* Expectations run counter to reality in that lean initiatives in product development are a long-term investment. These initiatives will not satisfy Wall Street, which may be looking for personnel reductions and by reinvesting the early gains beyond R&D.
- *Lingering external help:* Consultants and sensei can do a great job helping a company get started on their lean journey, but they must

eventually obsolete themselves and do everything possible to help the company stand on its own feet. Companies do not like to retain the same consultant for 5 years or more—nor should they—and many initiatives fizzle when the consultant leaves.

■ *Lack of visible results:* If you need an audit to see the results of a lean initiative, chances are that you do not have a lot of visible results. Without visible results, it is very difficult to sustain an initiative. A good sponsor with a lot of patience can stretch the initiative for a while, but eventually significant results must be present to get management and leadership to believe in the effort.

■ *Early success:* Winning an award or major recognition can be a dangerous thing. After the recognition, managers get promoted and engineers think they are done. In the industry just like in politics, people like to declare victory fast, celebrate, and move on.

■ *Poor institutionalization:* When a lean initiative is carried by a sensei or even a sponsor, management often does not want to interfere. Things are, after all, going reasonably well. But this is the time when real organizational changes are needed, and the initiative must be institutionalized into the company's standards and systems.

Nobody has a bigger responsibility in sustaining lean than the leadership of a company. In many companies when a supporting leader or sponsor moves on, the lean initiative takes a hit and often disappears. I also have seen quick turnover of champions; good champions are often cherry-picked by other companies with the help of professional networking and career-building services. Many times I have seen great initiatives that stopped in their tracks when the champion left to start a successful transformation at another company. I have been on the lean initiative at Goodyear twice as long as any other job I have held within Goodyear. I tried to obsolete myself many times—maybe this book will help. Most leadership positions in R&D changed during the initiative.

What convinced me that lean product development was here to stay at Goodyear is that the business leaders started to schedule their important meetings in front of the visual planning board in the OMC. Sustaining the lean initiative at Goodyear came after a lot of hard work, and these factors abetted our effort:

■ *Everyone involved:* The more everybody is involved and helping shape the new process, the easier it is to sustain it.

■ *Succession plan:* Companies make great succession plans, emergency response plans, and disaster recovery pans, but few plans address personnel for lean initiatives. I would like to encourage companies to make plans to sustain change or to recover from an organizational setback. Virtually every personnel move of a sponsor or champion catches a company by surprise, and the organizational succession plan may not favor the sustaining of important initiatives like lean product development. Our lean sponsor changed, and we did not miss a beat.

■ *Next-generation lean leaders:* Champions and sponsors must obsolete themselves, but at the right time. They also have to make sure enough people are trained and that some "apostles" are available. If champions want to move on, maybe they have to find their own successor.

■ *Embedded lean initiative:* The process must be institutionalized at the right time. Institutionalized is a difficult word, and I learned it from Joe Zekoski when he became CTO at Goodyear. Joe actually did institutionalize lean product development when he created an operations group in Goodyear R&D. Part of the institutionalization also is standard work. Institutionalization cannot be limited to the maintenance of the process. It must also include the plan for growth (which, by the way, is normally cut short), the development of the right people, and a good succession plan. Sustaining is not enough—improvement must continue.

■ *Ongoing training:* Training was crucial in the early phases of our lean initiative, and its importance has not diminished. Training of new associates should happen through onboarding, but also new leaders and managers must be onboarded properly and introduced to lean. Everybody in the organization, especially leaders and management, must be trained. I found that managers and leaders are much better supporters of lean product development if they know at least the basic principles of lean product development. At Goodyear, we also created regular lean events to provide continuous education and sharing for all levels of the organization. They include global "lean learning" events and local "lean luncheons."

■ *Manage the managers:* I found that middle management plays a key role in sustaining a lean initiative in R&D. They must make the lean initiatives happen in their area of responsibility. Some middle managers will have moved into senior positions later in the lean transformation and they must be counted on to support the initiative at the top. Any training invested in them will have a great payoff.

■ *Do not jump on the next program with new name*: Many continuous improvement initiatives are similar in content, but they are marketed under different names. New names emerge every day. Many people at Goodyear are waiting for the next initiative, and there are many new names from which to pick. Focus on the principles—not a new name.

Operating and continuously improving a lean product development environment takes a lot of work from a lot of people. I wish I could tell you that it is simple, but it is not. I will tell you, though, it is rewarding, and you can find joy along the way.

Notes

1. Donald G. Reinertsen, seminar at Goodyear, Akron, OH, January 2013.
2. Paul Zak, *Measurement Myopia*, Drucker Institute, July 4, 2013.
3. Shane Yount, *Organizing Metrics—Driving Sustainable Business Processes*, APICS International Conference & Expo, October 2012.
4. Donald G. Reinertsen, *The Principles of Product Development Flow*, Celeritas Publishing, Redondo Beach, CA, 2012.
5. John Shook, presentation at Goodyear, Akron, OH, March 2012.
6. Peter Fritz, Annual Conference of the Society for Concurrent Product Development, St. Paul, MN, June 2014.
7. John Shook, *Managing to Learn*, Lean Enterprise Institute, Cambridge, MA, 2008.
8. Pascal Dennis, *The Remedy*, Wiley, Hoboken, NJ, July 2010.
9. David Mann, *Creating a Lean Culture, Third Edition*, Productivity Press, New York, 2014.
10. Jeffrey K. Liker and Gary Convis, *The Toyota Way to Lean Leadership*, McGraw-Hill, New York, 2011.
11. James M. Morgan, presentation at Goodyear, Akron, OH, June 2014.

Chapter 8

Lean Never Ends

In the Introduction, I promised a happy ending to Goodyear's lean product development story. Indeed, our lean initiative has contributed to the company's current success and along the way we

- *Learned a lot about principle-based lean product development, sorting through myriad potential principles and finding, validating, and clinging to those that proved effective.*
- *Institutionalized the lean R&D process, which is no small feat in a global company of 69,000 employees, causing a sustainable difference in our culture.*
- *Became a significantly different and better R&D organization—aligned globally around our lean principles—and we continue to leverage our knowledge about lean to help the business achieve better results.*

But for success to continue with lean product development, we must continue to work at it, exploring new principles and improving those that have served us so well. Ours is a never-ending story.

Lean Courage

I hope that I have convinced you that lean should have a prominent place in product development. Lean principles are especially beneficial when leveraged by R&D on the profitability of the value stream. You also learned that you can apply lean to eliminate waste from your R&D process, which can lead to significant savings in R&D. You might even find that you can reduce your R&D budget and save your company money. Imagine that.

In telling you how lean worked for Goodyear, I also hope that I convinced you that this approach has not always worked at other companies, especially when used as a cost-cutting tool in times of financial hardship. That is because R&D is normally only a relatively small charge to the business and because the emphasis on cost cutting hurts companies' abilities to innovate and their R&D performance in other areas. This did not occur at Goodyear, but it easily could have without the watchful eye of our champion (me), sponsors, and leadership. Applying and leveraging lean principles generates benefits to the business and the company that go far beyond R&D cost savings.

Good companies consider R&D an investment and they ask for dividends. Good companies even keep R&D funded through a downturn to assure new products are ready to sell when things recover. Chairman, CEO, and President Rich Kramer did this at Goodyear. If you consider R&D an investment, eliminate waste from your R&D and invest the gained capacity for R&D capability development. Lean's ability to greatly influence the profitability of value streams—setting the tracks for product value, availability at the right time, and the right cost—will continue to deliver large dividends. Keep feeding your lean R&D engine to develop products and capability.

You may use the gained capacity to develop more new products or you may invest some of the capacity gained by your lean efforts to create unique technical knowledge, which is a great investment into competiveness. I also have seen companies use the capacity to improve the quality of their products—Goodyear products were already at high levels of quality. It did, though, help us create more and better value for the customer, such as by enhancing our capability to innovate. Using lean to develop faster and more agile innovation and product development processes will give you significant competitive advantages.

At Goodyear, we were involved in many improvement efforts over the last 30 years, from business process reengineering to TQC and six sigma. Some of these initiatives certainly helped our business, especially in manufacturing, but none has had the lasting impact on R&D that we have seen from lean. I am convinced that the same lean R&D principles we used can be applied in any company, in any R&D organization, and in many other business and institutions (e.g., banks, hospitals, administration). If you are in another industry or another function, remember that the lean principles are universal. Look at the Goodyear story as an example how to implement them—it may give you a hint how you can do it in your organization.

Every good investor knows that they should not put all their eggs in one basket and that a diversified portfolio protects the investor from fluctuations in the market. Similarly, a diversified capability portfolio protects a company from the fluctuations in the market and the industry. Not all investments are equally good, so you need to find the best ones for your R&D portfolio? And, like the investment tagline, past performance does not guarantee future performance—you must weigh the risk versus the returns when developing R&D capability.

Your best advisers for what capability to develop are your customers—external (for creating value) and internal (for creating profitable value streams). Do not underestimate what your company leaders can offer, either. Chances are that somebody in your company understands the business and the culture. How can you find out? Just ask. Ask what has to happen to create better value and make a value stream more profitable. You do not need a survey—the answers will be surprisingly consistent.

When you understand from your customers and stakeholders where new capability or improvements are needed, you have completed the first step in the Womack Wheel, your roadmap for capability development. From there, get the process right, which means that you need to find out if you even have a process. You do not need a perfect process to start, as long as you can keep improving it right from the start. In order to do that, learn the lean R&D principles. Use the lean R&D principles to find solutions, countermeasures, processes, or whatever you need to develop lean capability. Use them just as you use the principles of math and physics to develop technical products or financial or marketing principles to develop capability in those disciplines. I believe they are like gravity—they will not fail to deliver.

Throughout the book, I have presented the lean R&D principles, putting them in the context of our story to explain and illustrate our progress and how they were used to facilitate that progress. They appear in concert with Goodyear's progression with lean (see *Lean R&D Principles*), a journey that your lean initiative may mimic. But the principles do not appear in order of importance. I have favorites that, I believe, have been most important for us, but your list of favorites and importance will likely vary from my own. It is the same situation as when you use mathematics, physics, or chemistry principles in your design—there is no hierarchy! You learn to use them by education and practice.

And while you are at it, something new will catch your attention. Use your knowledge of the principles to assess if it is really something new or if it is something repackaged and sold under a different name.

Lean will not be the end of continuous improvement in R&D—it was a kaikaku, and many kaizens must follow, but there will be the next big thing, the next kaikaku. If that comes around, focus on the principles and start your change from the inside out.

Get Started

So what will you do tomorrow after you read this book?

Nobody handed us a recipe, and I do not have one for you either because it depends! It depends on where you are on your lean journey. If you have not done anything yet, start with education and training and then go ask your customers—internal or external—what their biggest problem is (lean training will help you to do even that small step more effectively). Do not ask about the biggest problem with R&D, but ask about the biggest problem "period"—that problem could appear to be well beyond the responsibility of R&D, but you'll be surprised how many of those problems can be traced back to R&D's influence on the value stream (e.g., procurement, manufacturing, sales).

One thing that I firmly believe is that your order for addressing the problems must adhere to the following improvement progression: safety, quality, delivery, speed, and efficiency. Then start turning your own Womack Wheel to improve these measures.

I recently learned about a recommendation by Jim Womack and John Shook of the Lean Enterprise Institute (LEI) for how to go about starting a lean initiative. Their instruction would have been helpful when we started our lean initiative, but, then again, it probably would have met the same level of resistance that we encountered with the Womack Wheel. If you are like I was then, with little real or practical knowledge of lean, then consider at least the first three steps of the five-step approach suggested by Womack and Shook:

1. Find a change agent.
2. Find a sensei (knowledge).
3. Seize or create the crisis.
4. Map the value streams.
5. Get started on creating better value streams.[1]

If you started down the lean road, but are having trouble generating results, reflect and adjust your approach to get back on the right track. Reapply the lean R&D principles.

If you are farther down the road, and you know you are on the right path but momentarily stuck—you should expect that—again review the principles. What worked? What worked best? What principles did you skip? The principles can help you assess your lean capabilities and find gaps in your processes.

Lastly, if you are well down the lean road, on the right path, and getting the right results, please share your story. This will help build the lean R&D knowledge base.

During his keynote speech at the LPPDE-North America 2014, Jim Womack said, "In the application of lean in R&D, the best is yet to come."[2] Once again, I agree with Jim. I hope that I was able to contribute a little bit to that with this book.

Good luck.

Lean R&D Principles

The following are the lean R&D principles in the order of appearance through the book:

Chapter 1

- Learn the universal lean principles and expertly apply them to your process.

Chapter 2

- Learn to manage your knowledge well.
- Develop product standards and use them to lock in knowledge.
- Define your processes and responsibilities, so you can improve them as you learn.

Chapter 3

- Carefully manage change to make change easier and more effective.
- Be cautious with computers—computerizing a bad process creates an expensive bad process.
- Develop project management standards and competencies.
- Combine risk management with project management.
- Improve processes from the inside out.

- Train, train, train—and then train again.
- Find a sponsor to support the change.
- Make process improvements on the highest level and align functions end to end for highest benefits.
- Make things simple (again!).
- Focus on the baton, not the runner.

Chapter 4

- Take waste out of your operation and replace it with value-added work.
- Never stop eliminating waste.
- Expect most lean product development problems to need multiple countermeasures.

Chapter 5

- Break large projects down into small steps or learning cycles.
- Align incoming work with capacity—the business can have anything but not everything.
- Resolve scheduling problems with visual planning.
- Flow when you can, pull when you must.
- Consider buffers to manage the variability in R&D processes.
- Level the work on the highest level.
- Establish a takt or cadence and allocate resources to meet the takt.
- Standardize development work as much as possible.
- Create capacity with flexible resources.
- Use Little's law to balance the cycle time, work in process, and throughput to desired levels.
- Avoid multitasking in engineering work, which in reality is just inefficient stop-and-go task switching.
- Start late to finish on time.
- Schedule product development processes at 70%–80% utilization or lower.
- Show real results to get leadership attention and support.
- Focus on the critical path for cycle-time reduction.
- Overlap all tasks as much as possible.
- After safety, quality, and delivery, focus on improving the speed of your process.

Chapter 6

- Reinvest the gains from waste elimination.
- Move lean closer to value creation to increase synergy with innovation.
- Manage incoming work.
- Consider cost of delay (COD) when scheduling projects and allocating time and capacity.
- Bet wisely to win with disruptive innovation.
- Explore as many diverse options early in the design space.
- Keep all design options open as long as possible to maximize the value creation.
- Pursue concurrent work as much as possible in all phases, especially in the kentou phase.
- Avoid innovation killers.

Chapter 7

- Get the process right, and the results will follow.
- Use lean tools for better design quality.
- Set the right strategy for the company and cascade it down to align all parts of the organization.
- Develop products and capability.
- Start lean R&D with work that is visible and work to make other work visible.
- Make problems or deviations highly visible to improve the likelihood of fixing them.
- Drive improvements with the right metrics.
- Manage variability.
- Support a good continuous-improvement system with a good, standard problem-solving process.
- Win with teams of empowered experts.
- Apply lean to the R&D shadows.

Notes

1. Jim Womack and John Shook, *Lean Management and the Role of Lean Leadership*, Lean Enterprise Institute, October 2006.
2. Jim Womack, *The Context of Lean Product & Process Development*, LPPDE-North America 2014, Durham, NC, September 2014.

Index